Advance praise for *House of Diggs*

"An impressive and important book about an overlooked figure in the fight for civil rights. Marion Orr tells the story of Charles C. Diggs Jr. with deep insight, diligent research, and crisp writing."
—**Jonathan Eig,** Pulitzer Prize–winning author of *King: A Life*

"Marion Orr brings us deep into Congressman Charles Diggs's world, brilliantly capturing the fullness and complexity of a legendary political icon who fought segregationists at home and abroad in the pursuit of a more equal and just world. Diggs—gifted, brave, and yet deeply flawed—was far more than a consequential civil rights activist and legislator during the tumultuous 1950s, '60s, and '70s. He was also a self-promoter who spent lavishly and irresponsibly, costing him his reputation and legacy. This page-turning biography is riveting and timely!"
—**Kate Clifford Larson,** author of *Walk with Me:*
A Biography of Fannie Lou Hamer

"This wonderfully readable biography rewrites the history of Black urban politics and civil rights through one of its most compelling and flawed characters."
—**Thomas J. Sugrue,** author of *Sweet Land of Liberty:*
The Forgotten Struggle for Civil Rights in the North

"A skillfully rendered, scrupulously researched, and highly readable portrait of an important civil rights leader long overdue for recognition."
—**James McGrath Morris,** author of the *New York Times* bestseller
Eye on the Struggle: Ethel Payne, the First Lady of the Black Press

"An unmatched and wonderfully complex exploration of Charles Diggs Jr. Marion Orr has probed, explored, and added a great deal to our understanding of many different areas of politics."
—**Dianne Pinderhughes,** coauthor of *Contested Transformation:*
Race, Gender, and Political Leadership in 21st Century America

"The best full-scale assessment of Diggs's remarkable career that I know of. *House of Diggs* provocatively and compellingly demonstrates Marion Orr's claim that no other Black member of Congress can match the tangible impact of Diggs's life and work."
—**Waldo E. Martin Jr.,** author of *No Coward Soldiers:*
Black Cultural Politics in Postwar America

House of Diggs

JUSTICE, POWER, AND POLITICS

Heather Ann Thompson and
Rhonda Y. Williams, editors

Editorial Advisory Board

Dan Berger
Peniel E. Joseph
Daryl Maeda
Barbara Ransby
Vicki L. Ruiz
Marc Stein

The Justice, Power, and Politics series publishes new works in history that explore the myriad struggles for justice, battles for power, and shifts in politics that have shaped the United States over time. Through the lenses of justice, power, and politics, the series seeks to broaden scholarly debates about America's past as well as to inform public discussions about its future.

A complete list of books published in Justice, Power, and Politics is available at https://uncpress.org/series/justice-power-politics.

House of Diggs

THE RISE AND FALL
OF AMERICA'S
MOST CONSEQUENTIAL
BLACK CONGRESSMAN,
CHARLES C. DIGGS JR.

Marion Orr

The University of North Carolina Press
Chapel Hill

© 2025 Marion Orr
All rights reserved

Designed by April Leidig
Set in Kepler by Copperline Book Services, Inc.

Manufactured in the United States of America

Cover art: Charles C. Diggs Jr. in South Africa, August 1971.
Courtesy Library of Congress.

Library of Congress Cataloging-in-Publication Data
Names: Orr, Marion, 1962– author
Title: House of Diggs : the rise and fall of America's most consequential Black congressman, Charles C. Diggs Jr / Marion Orr.
Other titles: Justice, power, and politics
Description: Chapel Hill : The University of North Carolina Press, [2025] | Series: Justice, power, and politics | Includes bibliographical references and index.
Identifiers: LCCN 2025013266 | ISBN 9781469689319 cloth alk. paper | ISBN 9781469689326 pbk alk. paper | ISBN 9781469686677 epub | ISBN 9781469689333 pdf
Subjects: LCSH: Diggs, Charles C., Jr | African American legislators—United States—Biography | African American politicians—Michigan—Biography | LCGFT: Biographies
Classification: LCC E840.8.D48 O77 2025 | DDC 328.092 $a B—dc23/eng/20250602
LC record available at https://lccn.loc.gov/2025013266

For product safety concerns under the European Union's General Product Safety Regulation (EU GPSR), please contact gpsr@mare-nostrum.co.uk or write to the University of North Carolina Press and Mare Nostrum Group B.V., Mauritskade 21D, 1091 GC Amsterdam, The Netherlands.

To my wife, Ramona L. Burton and our daughter, Willia.

For their love and for helping to make every day a joy!

Contents

Prologue ix

Abbreviations xv

Introduction. Charles C. Diggs Jr. and the Politics of Strategic Moderation 1

1. From the Delta to Detroit 14

2. Growing Up in Black Detroit 21

3. Lieutenant Diggs in the Jim Crow South 29

4. A Reluctant Politician 37

5. Political Ambitions: A Close Run for City Council 44

6. I Could Beat This Guy 51

7. The Battle for Control of the House 57

8. Aboard the Diggs's Special:
   The Arrival of a New Black Congressman 64

9. Returning to the Delta 70

10. On the Scene:
    Diggs at the Trial of Emmett Till's Murderers 78

11. Desegregating Commercial Air Travel 91

12. Fighting Discrimination in the US Military:
    On-Base and Off-Base 101

13. Brothers in the Struggle:
    Diggs and Martin Luther King Jr. 111

14. The Founding of the Congressional Black Caucus 141

15. The 1972 National Black Political Convention 153

16. Restoring Home Rule in Washington, DC 167

17. Learning about and Discovering Africa 177

18. Awakening America:
    Diggs and the Africa Subcommittee 186

19. Mr. Africa 197

20. The Fall of the House of Diggs 209

21. The Chairman's Portrait and the
    Indictment of Congressman Diggs 220

22. The Trial 230

23. Diggs Meets Newt 239

Conclusion. After Congress 248

Epilogue 257

Acknowledgments 261

Notes 267

Bibliography 313

Index 327

Image gallery begins on page 125

Prologue

ON JULY 31, 1979, Congressman Charles Coles Diggs Jr., one of the nation's foremost voices in the struggle for civil rights and perhaps the most consequential Black federal legislator ever to serve in the United States Congress, was among the first to enter the House chamber. The stocky and somber looking fifty-six-year-old Diggs, wearing a patterned tie and light blue suit and carrying a briefcase, took a seat alone in the front row, near the middle of the chamber. Diggs opened his briefcase and pulled out a yellow legal pad. With his briefcase on his lap, he sat alone.

The House chamber was familiar to Diggs. He had arrived in Washington, DC, twenty-four years earlier, in 1955, at the age of thirty-two. Since then, it had been his life's mission to fight for social justice and civil rights, using his bully pulpit as a congressman to forge coalitions and alliances in the often-fractured civil rights movement, while working inside the halls of Congress and leveraging his experience and expertise to push for substantive change. Over the course of his career, he sat alongside the mother of Emmett Till at the trial of her son's murderers; he advised Martin Luther King Jr.; he pressed for civil rights legislation; and he spearheaded the congressional response to apartheid, among a host of other issues. Those efforts had helped change America, and after nearly twenty-five years in Congress, Diggs should have been at the peak of his career as a public servant.

As other members filed in, Democrats took their seats to the presiding officer's right, the Republicans took their seats to the officer's left. Colleagues nodded at Diggs as they walked by. Charley, as everyone called him, was known by all except a few of the new members.[1] An only child, Diggs was born in Detroit. His parents had moved there during the Great Migration. They soon established the House of Diggs Funeral Home that, beginning in the 1940s and through the 1960s, dominated Black Detroit's funeral market.

Diggs grew up in comfortable circumstances, and the House of Diggs's success made the family a part of Detroit's Black elite. Junior, as his parents continued to call him, became a licensed mortician and helped his parents manage the business. Diggs's father, Charles Sr., parlayed his business success into electoral politics, winning election in 1936 as the first Black Democrat to the Michigan State Senate and setting an example of service to his son. Due to the father, the Diggs name became an institution in Detroit. Due to the son, the Diggs name became nearly as well-known in Washington's political circles as the Kennedys in Boston. And it was now about to become notorious and sweep the Diggs name, if not into obscurity, at least to the margins of history.

ON THIS HOT JULY DAY, Diggs sat alone in the front row of the House chamber, waiting. Two staff attorneys for the Committee on Standards of Official Conduct, known as the Ethics Committee, sat at a table behind Diggs. All the members knew this was not going to be a typical debate on the House floor. It had been nearly sixty years since members of the US House of Representatives had convened to censure, or issue a formal statement of disapproval of, a member. In the House, censure is the body's most severe punishment of a member, short of expulsion.

More House members took their seats, and as the chamber filled near capacity, Speaker Thomas P. "Tip" O'Neill slammed the gavel and recognized Representative Charles E. Bennett, chair of the Ethics Committee. Bennett came forward and stood before a podium in front of the chamber, just a few feet from Diggs. Congressman Louis Stokes, a member of the Congressional Black Caucus and a close ally of Diggs's, took a seat behind Diggs's left shoulder. Congressman Bennett explained that the members had convened to discuss a resolution submitted by the Ethics Committee to censure Diggs for violating House rules.

In October 1978, a federal jury in Washington, DC, had convicted Diggs on twenty-nine felony counts for padding his congressional payroll and accepting kickbacks from his staff to pay his personal bills and creditors. Yet despite his conviction, in November 1978, Diggs's district overwhelmingly reelected him. A few weeks later, Diggs was sentenced to three years imprisonment.

Diggs's indiscretion had drawn more national attention than his decades of work in Congress. Diggs, however, steadfastly maintained his innocence and remained free while he appealed his sentence. House rules allowed a convicted member to vote on the House floor if they were reelected after their conviction, and Diggs planned to exercise his full rights as a duly elected member of Congress. Then politics intervened. Due primarily to the efforts of freshman Republican Newt Gingrich of Georgia, Democratic House leaders removed Diggs from his committee chairmanships and stripped him of his hard-earned congressional power.

Diggs eventually admitted to the Ethics Committee that he had violated House payroll rules; he agreed to repay the government and to accept censure.

Now Diggs sat, alone and outwardly emotionless, with his briefcase in his lap, occasionally taking notes. He was ready to accept his punishment.

The debate was brief. For thirty-five minutes, Democratic and Republican members of the Ethics Committee explained why expulsion would be inappropriate. On only three occasions, all three during the Civil War, had the House ever imposed the penalty of expulsion. The vote to censure was 414–0, with four members, including Diggs, voting present. A *Washington Post* reporter observed that Diggs's punishment "was administered quickly and gently."[2]

A few minutes later, Speaker O'Neill, a Massachusetts Democrat and towering physical figure with his trademark unruly thatch of white hair, slammed his gavel. The chamber grew silent. The censure resolution required the Speaker to read the resolution and Diggs to stand in front of his colleagues during the reading. Speaker O'Neill, in his deep voice and strong Boston ascent, said, "Will the gentleman from Michigan kindly appear in the well?"[3]

Diggs moved his briefcase aside and stood. He buttoned his suit jacket. Diggs, his black curly hair cut short, and his long dark sideburns neatly trimmed to near his ear lobes, stepped toward O'Neill. Light from photographers' flashbulbs reflected off the shiny red, black, and green Pan-African lapel pin Diggs often sported. Looking straight ahead, his dark brown eyes gazing through his thick eyeglasses, Diggs stood with his hands clasped together in front of him.[4]

Congressman Julian Dixon of California, a freshman member of the Congressional Black Caucus, could not bear to watch. He left the House floor. Earlier he told a reporter—speaking for many of Diggs's friends and constituents—"I am very much aware of all the things Congressman Diggs has done in the past to make things better for black people.... The man has done so much in years gone by and out of respect for all of that, I will not be there."[5]

O'Neill put on his glasses, looked down at Diggs, and began to slowly read the censure resolution aloud. The *Washington Post* reporter described it as an "almost mournful tone."[6]

> Resolved, that Rep. Charles C. Diggs, Jr., forthwith present himself in the well of the House for pronouncement of censure: that Rep. Charles. C. Diggs, Jr., be censured with the public reading of the resolution by the Speaker; that Rep. Charles C. Diggs, Jr., is ordered to execute and deliver to the House an interest-bearing demand promissory note for $40,031.66 made payable to the Treasury of the United States; that Rep. Charles C. Diggs, Jr., is ordered, for the remainder of the 96th Congress, to require his employees to certify to the Committee on Standards of Official Conduct that funds he or she receives from clerk-hire funds are received in full compliance with current House rules; and that the House of

Representatives adopt the report of the Committee on Standards of Official Conduct dated July 19, 1979, in the matter of Rep. Charles C. Diggs, Jr.[7]

When he finished, Speaker O'Neill slammed his gavel and pronounced, "The matter is closed."

After the reading of the resolution, several of the members crowded around Diggs, shook his hand, and patted him on the back. Over the next year, Diggs's lawyers filed court appeals, hoping to overturn his convictions. Finally, on June 2, 1980, the US Supreme Court refused to hear Diggs's appeal. The next day, Diggs resigned. In July 1980, Diggs began serving what would be a seven-month term in a federal prison near Montgomery, Alabama. It was the end of a remarkable political career.

I FIRST HEARD ABOUT Congressman Diggs when I was in high school and became interested in government and politics. In 1978, around the same time Diggs's payroll kickback scheme became public, ABC hired Black broadcast journalist Max Robinson to coanchor the *World News Tonight* broadcast; it was the first time a Black person anchored a national newscast. That so impressed me that every weekday evening I would race home in time to watch Robinson deliver the news of the latest events in the United States and around the world. I excelled in my high school civics and history courses and have long been convinced that watching Robinson each night piqued my early interest in government and politics.

While I first heard about Diggs on the TV news, I first *learned* about him and his contribution in the early 1980s, when I was an undergraduate political science student at Savannah State University, a small historically Black college in my hometown, Savannah, Georgia, where my principal professor and mentor was Hanes Walton Jr., an architect of the modern study of Black politics.[8] Walton taught many of the political science courses at Savannah State, and Diggs came up in nearly all of them—not as some second-string player, but as an essential member of the first team. When I went to graduate school to study political science, I learned still more about Diggs. After being familiar with the significance of his tremendous accomplishments and the tragedy of his end, I decided to write the first biography of Diggs.

This book details Congressman Diggs's extraordinary life. It describes his experiences as the son of the Great Migration, confronting racism as a young officer in the US military in segregated Alabama; his years as a successful funeral home director; his elections as state senator; his role at the trial of Emmett Till's white murderers; his friendship with Martin Luther King Jr.; his impact on federal civil rights policy; his role as founder of the Congressional

Black Caucus; his fight against apartheid in South Africa; and many other examples of his work as a public servant. And yes, as a serious biography, this book does not turn a blind eye to a less savory side of Charles Diggs—the collapse of his funeral home, his problems with women, the deep personal financial debt that plagued him, and the payroll kickback scheme that ended his illustrious career.

My hope for this book is it will enable us to see, and remember, Charles Coles Diggs Jr. in perspective, with clarity, as the stunningly effective, and sadly, almost forgotten, freedom warrior he was.

Abbreviations

ACOA	American Committee on Africa
AFL	American Federation of Labor
BFFP	Black Forum on Foreign Policy
CAA	Civil Aeronautics Administration
CBC	Congressional Black Caucus
CIO	Congress of Industrial Organizations
CIO-PAC	Congress of Industrial Organizations–Political Action Committee
CODEL	congressional delegation
CORE	Congress of Racial Equality
DNC	Democratic National Convention
DOD	Department of Defense
DSC	Democratic Select Committee
FAAP	Federal Airport Act Program
MFDP	Mississippi Freedom Democratic Party
NAACP	National Association for the Advancement of Colored People
OCS	Officer Candidate School
RCNL	Regional Council of Negro Leadership
SAA	South African Airways
SAG	South African government
SCLC	Southern Christian Leadership Conference
SNCC	Student Nonviolent Coordinating Committee

TAAF	Tuskegee Army Air Field
UAW	United Auto Workers
UAW-CIO	United Auto Workers–Congress of Industrial Organizations

House of Diggs

From the 1940s and into the late 1960s, the House of Diggs was one of the largest Black-owned funeral home establishments in the United States. When visiting Detroit, many Black Americans would tour the funeral home and mail House of Diggs's postcards to friends and relatives. Courtesy Charles C. Diggs III.

Introduction

CHARLES C. DIGGS JR. AND THE POLITICS OF STRATEGIC MODERATION

IN 1954, CHARLES C. DIGGS JR. became only the fifth Black man elected to Congress since Reconstruction. He would prove to be different, both in kind and in approach, from the four Black congressmen who preceded him, and he would exhibit a style of governance that would have a lasting and enduring impact.

When Diggs arrived in Washington, DC, there were only two other Black men in Congress. In 1942, William Levi Dawson, a Black Democrat and machine politician, won election representing a majority-Black district on Chicago's South Side; and in 1944, voters elected Adam Clayton Powell Jr., an activist minister and New York's first Black congressman, representing a majority-Black Democratic district in Harlem. Ten years later, Charles C. Diggs Jr. became the first Black congressman from Detroit, Michigan. For the first time since Reconstruction, three Black men would serve in the US House at once, only three out of 435 House members! None of the three was a Republican.

A few months after Diggs was sworn in, *Ebony*, Black America's premier magazine, published a glowing profile of the thirty-two-year-old Diggs on Capitol Hill, including a photograph of him smiling and posing with Dawson and Powell. "Inevitably now," *Ebony* reported, "young Diggs will be compared in Washington with Adam Clayton Powell and William Dawson, the only other Negroes in Congress. How he will measure up to them only time will tell."[1]

This book shows that Diggs strategically practiced a moderate politics that was quieter than the militant race politics practiced by Powell, more appealing than Dawson's conservative Chicago-style approach, and often more effective than both. Each of the three Black congressmen would create a political reputation for their times. But few Americans know of Diggs's contributions and accomplishments. Diggs put his shoulder to the wheel and got work done. In terms of tangible achievements, Diggs was far more consequential than the other two congressmen.

Dawson and Powell represented the continuum of conflicting Black leadership styles at the middle of the twentieth century.[2] Sponsored by Chicago's

Democratic machine, which was controlled by Mayors Edward J. Kelly and Richard J. Daley, Dawson was by instinct a conservative politician who avoided race issues. Yet he succeeded politically because Black voters admired his ability to extract favors from the political machine.

Reverend Adam Clayton Powell Jr. was the pastor of Harlem's Abyssinian Baptist Church, one of the largest Protestant congregations in the country with more than 10,000 members. Powell effectively made his case to voters. A militant on racial issues in his sermons as well as in the public arena, Powell frequently invoked racism and chastised America for promoting it. His Harlem district appreciated that he made the case for Black equality and had the audacity to "tell off white folks." Once elected, both Dawson and Powell were returned by voters to Congress, time and time again.

Dawson and Powell, coming from different political structures, responded to different constituencies and were socialized by their respective political environments; Chicago and New York City had produced two very different political actors. Yet apart from their ability to win reelection every two years, there remains the question whether they were *effective* in Congress. In other words, did they get anything done legislatively beyond casework for their voters?

Charles C. Diggs Jr. was different. He was neither the product of a highly organized Chicago-type political machine nor a flamboyant pastor dependent on a large congregation. In this book, I show that Diggs employed what I call a *politics of strategic moderation*, an approach that aimed to help Black Americans achieve political incorporation and become members of the governing coalition that dominated national policymaking on civil rights.[3]

It is important to be careful about the term "moderation." Today's politicians call themselves "moderate" to differentiate their positions from the extreme wings of their political parties. Diggs was moderate in that he believed Black Americans should actively work to achieve political incorporation into the Democratic Party, contribute to the party's post–New Deal coalition, and advocate for change in government policy in civil rights and related areas in Congress. As a moderate, Diggs sought to recruit supporters across the political spectrum. The framers of the US Constitution designed Congress to be an institution of bargaining and compromise, and Diggs found within this structure a pathway to effect change.

Diggs's politics of strategic moderation represents a pragmatic approach for a Black legislator in the 1950s and 1960s; he used the Democratic Party to change civil rights policies in Congress. For much of the second half of the twentieth century, the Democratic Party controlled the US Congress: establishing the rules for structuring the legislature, determining its leaders, selecting committee chairs, and determining which bills would likely become laws. Charles C. Diggs Jr. viewed his participation in the Democratic Party as a vehicle for achieving his goals in Congress in the areas of Black civil rights and US African policy.[4]

By 1950, the Democratic Party, led by President Harry Truman and Speaker Sam Rayburn, had become the party of social reform and civil rights. However, forging a coalition of House Democrats—many of whom represented disparate districts made up of poor farmers, blue-collar workers, unionists, Jews, and Catholics—to support legislation that would prohibit racial discrimination in education, employment, and housing was difficult. Prior to the 1960s Southern civil rights movement, Black-interest issues were often considered outside the policy concerns of white congressional Democrats. Conservative Southern interests were influential in the Democratic Party in Congress well into the 1970s. In addition, Congress operated under a complex set of rules and norms, and it required a certain set of political skills (and the right political environment) to "mark-up" a bill, get it through a committee, and win approval on the House floor. Diggs's moderate politics was a strategic approach by a "rational political actor" who sought to achieve his policy goals in a setting in which institutional considerations compounded the challenges of coalition formation.[5]

IN 1954, AT AGE SIXTY-EIGHT, William Levi Dawson was much older than Diggs, older even than Diggs's father. Born in Georgia in 1886, Dawson graduated from historically Black Fisk University in 1909 and moved to Chicago a few years later. He then fought in World War I in a segregated US Army combat troop in France. After the war, he completed law school and, angered by the racial discrimination and injustices he experienced in the military, soon entered politics as a "radical" Republican.[6] By 1939, however, Dawson recognized he could wield more influence as a part of Chicago's Democratic machine. He believed that the vote was the best weapon Black Americans had, and he switched parties, becoming a ward leader and building support in Black precincts for the Democratic machine. In 1942, white machine bosses rewarded him by selecting him to succeed retiring congressman Arthur W. Mitchell, another Black machine politician. Dawson became the embodiment of the "organizational" politician and "submachine boss."[7]

Dawson's strength came from the number of Black votes his submachine could deliver to the white-controlled Chicago machine in local, state, and national elections. Dawson controlled the largest bloc of voters to be found in the state. In 1948, Dawson played a key role in organizing and mobilizing Black voters across the nation for President Harry S. Truman. In Illinois and Ohio, the Black vote provided the margin of victory for Truman over Republican Thomas Dewey. Democratic leaders recognized Dawson's role in electing Truman by naming Dawson vice-chair of the Democratic National Committee.

Dawson became the first Black man to hold such a prominent position in the Democratic Party. Dawson and Truman remained allies throughout the remainder of his presidency.

On Capitol Hill, Dawson developed a reputation of being a competent and serious legislator, and he enjoyed the respect of Southerners as well as large numbers of Northern Democrats. Dawson seldom provided press interviews or crowed about his own achievements. In 1949, Dawson became the first Black man to chair a standing committee of Congress, the House Government Operations Committee, whose powers included the right to investigate the spending of public monies within every executive department and independent agency of the government. In that role Dawson garnered praise from his white colleagues for saving the federal government millions of dollars annually. Dawson, however, rarely used his committee to investigate racial discrimination in the federal government.[8]

Dawson is a complicated historical figure. Historian Christopher Manning describes Dawson during the 1930s and early 1940s as being popular in Chicago for arousing Black crowds on race issues.[9] With his entry into the Democratic machine, however, Dawson abandoned racial rhetoric. To maintain power, Dawson's submachine depended on patronage that was controlled by the citywide Democratic machine. Machine bosses prohibited politicians from elevating race over loyalty to the organization. Instead, Dawson delivered tangible, specific, and direct benefits to his Black constituents on matters that did not arouse the antagonism of whites. Dawson's submachine could help a mother get into public housing or find out why a constituent's welfare check had not arrived. It did not, however, address Chicago's systemic racial inequalities in housing, education, employment opportunities, and policing.[10]

When Richard J. Daley was elected Chicago mayor in 1955, Dawson retreated further into silence on race. Mayor Daley significantly diluted Dawson's power. Daley also installed his own preferred Black individuals as ward committeemen, over Dawson's objections. Dawson depended on Daley's support to retain his own clout.[11]

Meanwhile, the civil rights movement was shifting into a new phase—a period of heightened protest. In the wake of the 1955 murder of fourteen-year-old Black Chicagoan Emmett Till in Mississippi, Dawson came under fierce attack from Black activists for remaining publicly silent. Dawson's biographer observed that Dawson never recovered from his "unacceptable" silence over Till's murder.[12] Dawson's style of politics began to be viewed by critics as paternalistic and resistant to change.

According to Manning, by the time Diggs arrived in Congress in 1955, Dawson had developed a reputation as an "Uncle Tom."[13] Starting in 1957, the aging Dawson's health began to decline, but he continued to win reelection and held his seat for a total of twenty-eight years, until his death in 1970 at the age of eighty-four. Diggs was among the public officials who spoke at Dawson's funeral.[14]

BORN IN 1908 in New Haven, Connecticut, middle-aged Adam Clayton Powell Jr. was fourteen years older than Diggs.[15] Educated at Colgate College and later at Columbia University, Powell was the best educated of the three Black congressmen. He was also light-skinned and often mistaken for white. As the activist pastor of one of the nation's largest and most prosperous Black congregations that his father had pastored before him, Powell's base of support gave him considerable freedom to pursue independent politics. He embraced his role as a militant pastor, becoming an advocate for civil rights and leading boycotts and demonstrations to protest racial discrimination. In 1941 he won a seat on the New York City Council. Three years later, in 1944, Black voters in Harlem sent Powell to Congress as a Democrat.

Upon his election, Powell exclaimed, "I will represent the Negro people first."[16] Powell presented himself as "the militant, uncompromising fighter for civil rights," determined to use his office to advocate for Black civil rights.[17] Tall and handsome, Powell's flamboyant personal lifestyle of fancy cars, multiple homes, foreign travel, and beautiful women (he once married noted jazz pianist Hazel Scott) resonated with his Black followers who viewed him as a powerful Black man who had "made it" in racist America.

Powell was also a publicity-seeker, frequently grabbing headlines for his denunciations of bigotry and racial discrimination. He spoke his mind, and his good looks, charisma, powerful speaking voice, and theatrical talent brought him national media coverage. In the 1940s and into the middle 1950s, Powell stood "virtually alone" as a national Black figure in taking a "no-compromise position" on civil rights and in challenging racial bigotry.[18] As his biographer offered, Powell was "the one who believed that stirring up matters and creating tension were preferable to moderate, balanced calm appeals to patience and reason."[19]

While Dawson had quietly accommodated the House of Representatives' segregationist practices of separate facilities, Powell immediately and publicly contested racial segregation and demanded equal treatment for himself and his staff in the House cafeteria, barber shop, and other congressional facilities. "Within two years, Powell quickly became a national symbol of politics to all black people," according to Chuck Stone.[20] Part of Powell's appeal to Black voters was his willingness to say and do things other Black leaders were not prepared to say or do. To whites, however, Powell was nothing more than a racist demagogue. As political scientist Charles V. Hamilton explains, "He became the quintessential irritant within Congress, a role that suited him perfectly, and one he obviously relished."[21]

Although Powell introduced numerous civil rights bills, bills proposed before the 1960s to prohibit racial discrimination were dead on arrival, blocked by segregationist Southerners who controlled key committees in the House and stymied by the filibuster in the Senate. Beginning in 1955, Powell frequently offered an amendment to funding bills, denying federal funds to states and jurisdictions that practiced racial discrimination. Liberals and moderates supported the so-called Powell Amendment in principle but were angry that Powell forced them to support it while knowing it would ultimately be blocked.[22] Initially, Diggs supported the Powell Amendment; Dawson always opposed it.

Whereas Dawson was a strict party politician, Powell did not hesitate to go against the Democratic Party line. Due to his independent and sometimes contrarian approach, Democratic Party leaders refused to give him a House subcommittee chairmanship.

Powell developed a reputation for being a "show horse" rather than a "workhorse." Those who worked with Powell complained that he was irresponsible, self-centered, and seldom followed through on his rhetoric. As one congressional staffer recalled, Powell "could arouse people. He would make headlines and would say things to get headlines, but seldom had the time when it came down to the nuts and bolts."[23] "He just doesn't want to take time with legislation," complained a Democratic colleague.[24] Powell was also "afflicted by the travel bug," frequently taking trips to Paris and other foreign destinations at the government's expense, often accompanied by attractive young women staff members.[25] J. Raymond Jones, a Black Harlem politician, offered, "Adam doesn't like to work. He is lazy and he likes to lead the good life."[26] Privately, many leaders of the national civil rights organizations considered Powell unpredictable and unreliable. "He could not be trusted, his friends and adversaries lamented," writes Hamilton.[27]

Powell's voters, however, continued to reelect him. In 1961, following the election of Democratic president John F. Kennedy, Powell's seniority finally paid off, and he assumed chairmanship of the House Education and Labor Committee, a position he used to push through a significant body of social welfare legislation. Even Powell's critics had to acknowledge the masterful way he guided President Lyndon Johnson's Great Society programs through the House.[28]

However, Powell's militant style and high level of absenteeism eventually led to serious problems. In 1963, a jury found him guilty of defaming the character of a constituent and ordered him to pay $211,500 in damages. In 1967 Powell was expelled from the House on allegations of misusing his committee's budget; but in 1968 his constituents overwhelmingly reelected him to a twelfth term. The House then voted to deny Powell his seniority and to fine him for misusing payroll and travel finances. In 1969, the US Supreme Court ruled the expulsion unconstitutional. Powell remained in Congress until his defeat in the 1970 Democratic primary by New York assemblyman Charles Rangel. Powell died in 1972 at the age of sixty-three. Diggs also spoke at his funeral.[29]

IN A NOW-CLASSIC 1960 ARTICLE, political scientist James Q. Wilson showed that the differences between Dawson and Powell were functions of the differences in their respective local political organizations and in the nature of their approaches to maintaining political control.[30] Differences in organizational context and local political environment explain the differences in House member behavior.[31]

Diggs's politics of strategic moderation was shaped by his relationship with the liberal-Black-labor coalition that dominated Michigan Democratic Party politics from 1948 until the late 1960s. For Charles Diggs Jr., the single most important political socializing influence was the example set by his father, Charles Diggs Sr. Diggs Jr. had watched his father provide support to Detroit's burgeoning labor union movement and help forge alliances between labor unions, liberal whites, Black voters, and the Michigan Democratic Party. Young Diggs had watched white and Black Detroiters develop and share political power.

In the 1920s, the elder Diggs became a leader in Marcus Garvey's Universal Negro Improvement Association Detroit affiliate, and Charles Sr. was active in Republican politics. In 1932, he switched to the Democratic Party, and in 1936 he became the first Black Democrat elected to the Michigan State Senate from a Polish American majority district that included a substantial Black population.[32] In the state senate, Diggs, along with his friend, senator Stanley Nowak—a Polish immigrant and staunch supporter of civil liberties, Black civil rights, and organized labor—became one of the two strongest allies of labor unions in the Michigan Legislature.[33]

In 1936, Diggs Jr. was fourteen years old. Detroit, reeling from the Great Depression, became the epicenter of the burgeoning industrial labor union movement. Diggs Sr. emerged as one of a new generation of Black leaders working to forge an alliance between Black Detroit and the Congress of Industrial Organizations (CIO), of which the United Auto Workers (UAW) had the largest number of members. Diggs Jr. watched his father become one of Detroit's strongest Black supporters of the UAW's successful 1936–37 sit-down strike against General Motors.[34]

In 1941, when Diggs Jr. was twenty years old, his father was one of the leading Black supporters of the UAW's successful unionization of Ford Motor Company, Detroit's largest employer of Black workers and the last of the big auto companies to agree to collectively bargain with the union.[35] The union's victory over Ford signaled the end of the Black community's traditional skepticism toward labor unions. Black Detroit also broke away from Henry Ford's patronage grip. By the early 1940s, the UAW had become Black Detroit's "warmest and most dependable ally."[36]

In 1948, the CIO and UAW abandoned their official policy of nonpartisanship and resolved to "remold" the Michigan Democratic Party "into a real liberal and progressive political party."[37] In the 1948 gubernatorial election, a coalition composed of the CIO, UAW, party reformers, Black voters, and liberal whites helped elect Democrat G. Mennen "Soapy" Williams as Michigan's governor; Williams was a thirty-six-year-old liberal and "uncompromising" supporter of civil rights.[38] Williams remained in office until 1961.

During the 1950s and 1960s, the liberal-Black-labor coalition constituted a powerful alliance in Michigan politics. The coalition transformed the state Democratic Party into a reformist organization that embraced civil liberties, labor organizing, and Black civil rights. For example, Williams successfully pushed a reluctant, Republican-controlled legislature to adopt fair employment practices legislation; he oversaw improvements in housing and education, and he made historic appointments of Black Americans to top positions in state government. He placed Black people on most state commissions.[39] The number of Black Democrats in the legislature increased during Williams's tenure.

In 1951, at age twenty-nine, Charles Diggs Jr. won election to his father's old seat in the Michigan State Senate. Three years later, the liberal-Black-labor coalition helped elect Diggs Jr. to Congress in a district that was over 60 percent white.

At times the coalition was strained. In 1957, Black UAW members formed the Trade Union Leadership Council to emphasize Black workers' concerns within the labor movement.[40] Political tensions between Polish Americans and Black civic leaders in the First Congressional District, which encompassed most of Detroit's Black East Side and the predominantly Polish American town of Hamtramck, went back decades. Nevertheless, Diggs Jr. believed that, given Black voters' numerical minority status in Michigan and Detroit, the liberal-Black-labor coalition and the Michigan Democratic Party provided the highest likelihood of advancing the race.

DIGGS JR.'S BELIEF in the liberal-Black-labor coalition was tested with the rise of Black consciousness and Black nationalism in Detroit, spurred on by the Southern civil rights movement. In the 1960 and 1962 Democratic congressional primaries, Black leaders organized the "Elect 3" campaign, an effort to unseat two liberal, white, Detroit-area Democratic congressmen and replace them with Black Democrats and to reelect Diggs.

Charles Diggs Sr., who retained a Garveyite-perspective on race in America, led the 1960 "Elect 3" campaign, which gained the support of several prominent Black ministers and Black fraternal organizations.[41] Many Trade Union Leadership Council members opposed the effort but failed to convince the organization's executive board to denounce the campaign. Congressman Diggs neither publicly endorsed nor denounced it. Privately, however, Diggs Jr. broke with his father and strenuously opposed the "Elect 3" campaign.

Diggs Jr. wrote his father an eleven-page letter chastising him and emphasizing that the two Black "candidates CANNOT win."[42] In the letter, Diggs made it clear that he embraced the politics of strategic moderation as a pragmatic and rational approach to advancing the race. Diggs stressed that Black voters were a minority of the voters in the two districts, and he reminded his father that the two white congressmen had "unassailable voting records on Civil Rights." Diggs cautioned that a race-based campaign "would be a retrogression from the alliance which has been built between the Liberals, Labor, and Negro community since 1949" and "could very well backfire."

Diggs Jr. explained that there were ways that Black Democrats could work with their white coalition partners to achieve their goals that left "no scars" and that allowed Black leaders to "continue to get cooperation with respect to other objectives they can't obtain by themselves." He explained, "It takes cold, hard calculations and proper timing, not emotion and impulse, however, well meaning."[43] Black leaders had to employ a strategic approach.

The two white congressmen were easily reelected, and analysis of vote totals showed that both did well in heavily Black precincts, thus convincing Diggs Jr. that the vast majority of Black Americans embraced integrationist ideology and coalitions with liberal whites.[44]

The 1962 "Elect 3" campaign is significant because it was led by Reverend Albert Cleage Jr. who emerged as an early and articulate advocate for Black nationalism in Detroit.[45] Diggs Jr.'s endorsement by Detroit's leading Black nationalist affirmed that those who knew Diggs understood he was a "race man," a Black leader dedicated to advancing the race.[46] "Diggs still has the best political image in these parts. *He's a 'race-man' and a fighter*," Cleage opined in his Black nationalist newspaper.[47] Diggs and the two white Democrats were easily reelected.

Charles Diggs Jr. strategically employed a moderate approach, but he always pushed and maneuvered to advance the race, always mindful of the structure and function of the Congress and the Democratic Party, institutions he believed were the vehicles necessary to advance his policy goals. From the perspective of Black Americans, as a minority group working within majoritarian institutions like the Democratic Party and the US Congress, one cannot dismiss the practical logic of Diggs's politics of strategic moderation.

WHEN DIGGS JR. ARRIVED in Congress, it was well known that Dawson and Powell did not get along with one another. As Diggs recalled years later, "There was very little, if any, communication between Dawson and Powell."[48] Diggs's moderate politics allowed him the space to work with conservatives and militants. Diggs understood the institutional power bestowed on committee chairs and, like many House members, aspired to one day be called "Mr. Chairman." Diggs and Dawson were also both military veterans, and Diggs had a special appreciation for Black citizens who served in America's segregated military.

As a result, Diggs treated Dawson like a senior statesman. He respected Dawson for achieving the distinction of becoming the first Black man to chair a standing committee in Congress and for the high esteem he enjoyed among his colleagues. In terms of his stature in Congress, Dawson was the kind of model legislator Diggs desired to become. In 1958, as Dawson approached his tenth year as chair of the Government Operations Committee (and was under intense attack by Chicago's Black activists), Diggs even proposed sponsoring a "testimonial banquet" to honor Dawson.[49] Dawson liked the young congressman and accepted Diggs's role as the new congressman building a political brand. In 1956, Dawson used his influence as vice-chair of the Democratic National Committee to successfully lobby for Diggs's appointment to the party's presidential campaign platform and resolution committee.[50]

But Diggs was different from Dawson. In Diggs's view, being a model legislator like Dawson was necessary but insufficient to achieve his policy goals. He did not believe that all problems facing Black people could be solved solely through the committee system or the Democratic Party. Partnering with outside groups would also be necessary. He believed that it was necessary to organize at the local level to apply sufficient political pressure to get Congress to act. As Diggs told an interviewer in 1970, "The role of the black congressman is to educate the public" and "at given times get them to put pressure on the executive or to [pressure] their own elective representatives."[51]

Unlike Dawson, Diggs spoke out in support of Black civil rights and denounced bigotry. Diggs made clear demands of white leaders, and he protested vigorously against discriminatory treatment. At the same time, he was careful not to close channels of communication. Like Dawson, Diggs was not anxious to turn every slight into a public fight. For example, in early 1960, when Diggs overheard a Capitol Hill guide "denouncing the anti–poll tax legislation" to a large group of visitors on an official government tour, he immediately walked to the offices of the tour guide's boss to protest. Diggs demanded that the tour guide be told to keep his partisan policy views to himself.[52] He did not make a public statement about the incident.

Diggs also admired and respected Powell. Both were privileged men, born and reared in the North, who had benefited from their fathers' reputations as leaders in the Black community. "I had more contact with Adam," Diggs remembered. "He took me around. He was more social."[53] In the 1950s and early 1960s, Diggs and Powell often spoke at the same mass meetings and civil rights rallies. They became friends. Powell told others that Diggs was "not only ... his friend" but also "completely loyal."[54]

Diggs's and Powell's mutual respect held even when they disagreed. In 1956, Diggs publicly disagreed with Powell after the Harlem Democrat endorsed Republican president Eisenhower's reelection.[55] Unlike other Democrats, however, Diggs never questioned Powell's intentions. Diggs valued Black political leadership, writing Powell, "I will never be a party to any attempts to impugn your motives. Negro leadership on a national level is a rare and precious commodity. It must be protected from those who would destroy us by an irreparable division."[56] Instead of abandoning the party like Powell or remaining silent like Dawson, Diggs publicly criticized the leading Democratic candidate, Adlai Stevenson, for "pussyfooting on civil rights views"; and Diggs warned party leaders that a "moderate" candidate on civil rights would assure Eisenhower's reelection.[57] Diggs would not hold steadfast to party doctrine at the expense of his own beliefs.

In 1957, Diggs opposed the addition of the Powell Amendment to an education bill. Diggs was blunt and called it "a distraction."[58] Perhaps more than Powell, Diggs understood that an individual Black leader would not be enough to change government policy and advance Black civil rights. The need for Black House members to be working in solidarity was one of the rationales that ultimately motivated Diggs to form the Congressional Black Caucus.

Diggs was among many Black leaders and Black Americans who cried foul when Democratic leaders on Capitol Hill and in New York threatened to purge Powell from the party over his support of Eisenhower.[59] Diggs supported Powell when House Democrats stripped him of his seniority and refused to seat him; and in 1970, Diggs campaigned for Powell when Rangel defeated him in the Democratic primary.[60]

IN A 1961 ARTICLE, political scientist Nicholas Master described a model legislator who was likely to have the personal and institutional characteristics to be more effective than others. Diggs possessed the characteristics of what Master called a "responsible legislator," a member who is respected by fellow legislators, especially by party leaders, who has reverence and appreciation for the legislative process, who is willing to compromise even on difficult issues, and who "is moderate, not so much in the sense of his voting record and his personal ideology, but rather in the sense of a moderate approach."[61]

Throughout his nearly twenty-five years in Congress, Diggs had a reputation as a hard worker. A profile of Diggs published four years after he took office described him as "a quiet, hard-working sort."[62] In the spring of 1969, Ethel Payne, a Black journalist who had covered national Black politics since the early 1950s, observed that Diggs "manages to put in a prodigious amount of work," stressing that he "carries on a full schedule" as a member of Congress.[63] In 1974, the editors of the *Chicago Defender*, the legendary Black newspaper, observed that there had been criticisms of some Black members of Congress (there were seventeen Black members of Congress in 1974) for not paying enough attention to issues of basic interest to Black Americans. "Whatever the measure of truth of the criticism," the editors noted, "it is not applicable to Congressman Charles C. Diggs.... He keeps a close watch on matters that fall within the orbit of his responsibility."[64] Congressman Charles Rangel agreed, adding emphatically, "I never heard anyone attack the integrity of Charley Diggs as related to his legislative work."[65] Journalist Simeon Booker remembered Diggs as "one of the [twentieth] century's hardest working, most effective members of the House of Representatives."[66]

Diggs was a thoughtful and deliberative legislator. "His basic approach to a problem was to mull it over thoroughly. Never in my experience had I known him to make a decision without thinking it over carefully," remembered a former press secretary.[67] Ralph Matthews, a longtime Black reporter who covered Capitol Hill during the 1950s and 1960s, observed that Diggs "permits no misunderstanding of the question and pins reporters down.... When he gets the exact meaning he deliberates slowly, then answers the question."[68] Matthews added that Dawson, by contrast, seldom talked to reporters on the record. When he did, like Diggs, Dawson was "unambiguous and concise." Powell, on the other hand, "usually answers the question before you get it out" and is likely "to deny not only that he ever gave the answer, but that he ever heard the question.... Diggs is precise and concise—one story," Matthews stressed.[69]

Diggs's interpersonal behavior was deferential and respectful. He got along with people. Shortly after Diggs's election, Louis Martin, the former editor of the Black-owned *Michigan Chronicle*, correctly predicted that Diggs's temperament provided "great equipment for tackling the pros down in Washington who are usually very sensitive about their prestige and importance."[70] John Conyers (D-MI), who in 1965 joined Diggs as the second Black congressman from Detroit, remembered that Diggs "was a guy that never got upset, and he comported himself with a certain amount of dignity."[71] Representative Ronald

Dellums (D-CA), who arrived on Capitol Hill in 1971 with a reputation as a voluble Black militant, remembered Diggs as a "very thoughtful human being. To me he always seemed very polite and gentlemanly," Dellums recounted.[72]

Diggs, however, was no pushover. His personal demeanor and punctilious mannerisms muted his political aggressiveness. "He may be soft-spoken and amiable, but when it comes to manifestations of anti-blackness, whether it is domestic or foreign, Charlie Diggs wades right in to do battle," Ethel Payne correctly explained.[73] Diggs exhibited what another observer called a "quiet aggressiveness" that emitted "occasional outbursts of temper and passion.... Diggs walks the tight rope of an ambitious man who won't be pushed around but who knows how to avoid offending people."[74] Diggs had a buttoned-down audacity that matched his faux deferential facade that put even his political foes at ease.

Chapter 1

FROM THE DELTA TO DETROIT

ON THURSDAY, APRIL 28, 1955, an airplane bearing Charles Diggs Jr. and his father landed at the airport in Jackson, Mississippi. For the younger Diggs, Mississippi was like visiting another world. The nation's newest Black congressman had been invited to Mound Bayou, a small, all-Black town in the Mississippi Delta, about 130 miles north of Jackson, to be the keynote speaker at the annual convention of the Regional Council of Negro Leadership, the leading organization for Black civil rights in Mississippi. It was the younger Diggs's first time in Mississippi. Diggs Sr. was born in the Delta, in Issaquena County. In May 1950, he had returned to Mississippi for the first time in nearly forty years.[1] He was back now for a second visit, this time as the father of a congressman.

As they made their way through the airport, the men noticed signs denoting "Negro" and "White" restrooms, a reminder that segregation was an all-encompassing way of life in Mississippi. After renting a car from an agency that serviced Black drivers, the two had a late dinner and stayed at a rooming house.

The next day the congressman and his father rose early and drove west through the Delta. As they drew closer to Issaquena County, the elder Diggs began to point out the places he remembered from when he was a boy. People sitting outside, wondering who the strangers were, waved from a distance as they passed. The Diggs men smiled and waved back.

The congressman and Diggs Sr. first paid a solemn visit to the gravesite of James Diggs, the elder Diggs's father. Then Diggs Sr. directed his son to the Woodland Baptist Church, the modest church his father had founded in the unincorporated community of Tallula. They took photographs of the church, including the cornerstone, which reads, "Woodland Baptist Church, Dec. 17, 1899, J. J. Diggs, Pastor."[2] The church still stands today.

CHARLES DIGGS JR.'S IMPULSE to fight for change and his devotion to public service were part of his family's DNA. Diggs's great-great grandmother, Lilly Ann Granderson, worked as a house slave in Kentucky; she learned how to read and after she was sold to a Mississippi plantation owner, near Natchez, she established a secret night school for slaves, teaching reading and writing.[3] Diggs's great-grandfather, James J. Diggs Sr., served as a justice of the peace in Issaquena County during Reconstruction.[4] In 1877, Diggs's grandfather, James J. Diggs Jr., and his grandmother, Lilly Ann Granderson (she was named after her mother, the "midnight teacher"), were in the first graduating class of what is now Jackson State University.[5] Later, James J. Diggs Jr. became a Baptist preacher and traveled to Liberia for a year as a missionary.[6]

Upon his return to the United States, in the early 1890s, Reverend Diggs moved his family back to Tallula in Issaquena County, where he and Lilly Granderson Diggs eventually had eleven children.[7] Their third son, Charles Diggs, was born on January 2, 1894, and was given the middle name "Coles" in honor of his father's mentor, John J. Coles, America's best-known Black Baptist missionary to Africa, and a measure of the significance James Diggs attached to his missionary experience.[8] For much of the next century, Africa would remain of interest to the Diggs clan.

IT IS HARD TO CONCEIVE a more treacherous environment for a Black child to be born into than that faced by Charles Diggs Sr. and his siblings in Issaquena County in the later years of the nineteenth century. In 1890, Mississippi leaders held a constitutional convention for the primary purpose of disenfranchising Black voters. A suffrage amendment was adopted that required voters to be able to read and interpret the US Constitution to the satisfaction of the registration officials, who were white. Mississippi also adopted a poll tax that was required of all voters and that included a cumulative feature requiring the tax to be paid for each of series of years in order to qualify to vote. The new Mississippi constitution swiftly excluded Black residents completely and permanently from electoral politics.[9] "Once the Negro was disenfranchised," writes historian John Hope Franklin, "everything else necessary for white supremacy could be done."[10]

In Mississippi and the South, laws were passed that separated Black people and whites on trains and in depots. Black people were banned from white hotels, barber shops, restaurants, and theaters. Laws against intermarriage of the races were adopted in all Southern states. By 1885, most Southern states had laws requiring segregated public schools.

From the moment of their birth, Delta Black residents had to learn how to negotiate the etiquette of race relations in Mississippi. In the racially tense Delta, violence and terror were common. White offenses against Black citizens, including murder, went unpunished. Lynch mobs often acted with the full knowledge, and often the cooperation, of locally elected sheriffs. Faced with a repressive racial climate, caught in an agricultural system that offered no hope of landownership or economic advancement, and disillusioned by injustice, thousands of Southern Black Americans chose to leave. Between 1910 and 1970, 6.5 million Black Americans moved from the South to the North, pouring into Detroit, Chicago, New York, and other cities. Historians would come to call it the "Great Migration."[11]

Charles Diggs Sr. would be one of the many thousands of Black Mississippians who eventually felt compelled to leave the Delta. He was the most self-assured, confident, and uncompromising of the Diggs children. After attending public school, at about age sixteen, Charles Diggs left home to attend Alcorn State Agricultural and Mechanical College about 100 miles south of Issaquena County. He studied shoemaking and carpentry, but after his father died unexpectedly in 1911, Diggs returned home. He then worked as a dishwasher and waiter on the *Kate Adams*, a steamboat that made semiweekly trips between Memphis and New Orleans.[12] On one trip, Diggs encountered a white automobile company recruiter, or "agent," from Detroit who told him he should move North where he could "be somebody and do things."[13] Diggs took the advice.

Hoping to escape the Delta's racial repression and seeking better economic opportunities, Charles Diggs Sr. moved to Detroit in 1913. Diggs apparently first took a train to Tennessee where his brother Weston was working in Knoxville while attending school at Knoxville College. Charles visited for just a few days, but during this visit he met his future wife, Mayme Ethel Jones, a teacher. Born in 1898 in Chattanooga, Tennessee, Jones's father was a minister and leader in the African Methodist Episcopal Zion Church, and her mother was the daughter of a mixed-race marriage.[14]

Within a few years, all of James and Lilly Diggs's children would leave the Delta. By 1916, Lilly was also living in Detroit with her younger sons.[15] Weston Diggs left Knoxville and first moved to Chicago before eventually joining the rest of his family in Michigan. The Diggs's family roots may well have been deep in the soil of the Mississippi Delta, but their future would reside in the streets of Detroit.

THE CITY OF MANY INNOVATORS, including several pioneers of the internal combustion engine, Detroit was home to nearly seventy auto manufacturers by 1906.[16] Workers of every kind were needed, and people came from everywhere to fill the available jobs. Detroit's population expanded from 285,704 in 1900 to 465,766 in 1910. English Canadians crossed the border and were joined by immigrants from Poland and other European countries. Detroit also attracted large numbers of Southern white migrants, including many from Appalachia who brought their racism with them. In 1910, only about 6,000 Black people lived among the city's 466,000 residents; by 1930 approximately 120,00 Black people lived in Detroit, 7 percent of the city's 1,570,000 residents.

Detroit's swelling Black population crowded into the city's East Side, which became known as "Black Bottom." As the Black population increased, the community expanded into an adjacent area that became known as "Paradise Valley."[17] The area would be home to some of the Black community's most important and venerable institutions, churches, schools, social organization, and businesses. It also became the city's first racial ghetto, with all the social and economic challenges that characterize ghetto life. Restricted from living in other areas of the city, more and more Black people crowded into Paradise Valley and Black Bottom. Overcrowding and the lack of decent housing would remain a central challenge for decades. For the Black migrants living in Detroit's East Side during the height of the Great Migration, Paradise Valley was no paradise at all.

But things were better than they had been in the South. In Detroit, Black people could vote, sit next to whites on the bus and in streetcars, and drink from the same water fountains as whites. Southern migrants who made about three dollars a day back home, in Detroit earned between six and eleven dollars a day.[18] The higher wages offered in Detroit's industrial sector provided a chance for Black economic advancement and the potential for upward mobility.

As the number of Black residents living in Black Bottom and Paradise Valley grew, the opportunity for businesses catering to the Black community expanded. A growing business class, including Black doctors, lawyers, grocers, barbers, and morticians, were now able to serve the commercial markets created by Detroit's Black migrants. Charles Diggs Sr. was one of these men. Instead of pursuing employment with any of the automakers, Diggs opened a modest shoemaking and shoe repair business. Then, in 1917, Diggs used the meager profits from his shoe repair business to launch a more lucrative career as a funeral director. It was a great decision.

Diggs Sr. understood the Black American tradition of the open-casket funeral and reverence for proper burial, a cultural phenomenon that dated back to Africa. Looking good in death was important to Black Americans. Many Black Americans did not trust that whites would treat their dead bodies with care and respect, and most white morticians did not want to work on Black bodies. The mortuary business was highly segregated and would remain so throughout the twentieth century.[19]

Becoming a funeral director was one of the few professions available to Black men. Like preachers, funeral directors wore suits and ties, and were highly respected in the community, both for their bearing and because, like preachers, they were independent from whites. Booker T. Washington once pointed out that Black funeral directors were some of the most prosperous Black men in America during his time.[20] For Diggs Sr., the decision to enter the mortuary business set him apart in the community and, almost immediately, conferred on him a certain status, a status that he would eventually pass on to his son.

At the age of twenty-four, Diggs Sr. temporarily moved to Philadelphia and enrolled in the Eckels College of Mortuary Science. While attending school, he rented a room in the home of a local minister and worked as a bellhop in a downtown Philadelphia hotel; then, after the United States entered World War I, he became a carpenter at the federal shipyard on Hog Island. Whenever he had the chance, he took the train to Knoxville to visit his older brother Weston and court Mayme Ethel Jones.[21]

On June 17, 1918, Diggs Sr. and Mayme became husband and wife, beginning a marriage and partnership that would last nearly fifty years. Later that summer, his embalming training complete, the couple moved back to Detroit. In the rapidly growing Black community, Diggs's services were in demand.

When Diggs Sr. returned to Detroit with his new wife, the newlyweds did what many Black migrants in Detroit did during the Great Migration when in need of housing; they turned to the Black church. Reverend Joseph Gomez, the pastor of Detroit's Bethel AME Church, convinced a Black physician to let the couple stay in one of his apartments for a month, rent-free.[22]

Diggs Sr.'s next big break came when George Green, a Black undertaker based in Paradise Valley, hired Diggs as an apprentice. Green was considered "one of the leading [Black] undertakers in the State," and "his funeral parlors [were] said to be the finest in this section of the country."[23] Diggs and Mayme lived with Green and his wife upstairs over the funeral home at 1939 St. Aubin Avenue. Green, who was active in Detroit's civic affairs and who served as something of a mentor for Diggs, demonstrated that a successful businessman also had a larger responsibility to his community, an obligation Diggs Sr. would eventually pass on to his son.[24]

In January 1921, Diggs Sr. and Mayme opened the Diggs Funeral Home on the East Side. Later described by their son as "a mom-and-pop" business, Charles Diggs Sr.'s first funeral home was a storefront at St. Antoine and Adams Streets.[25] During the first two years that Diggs was in business, "he had a larger number of burials than any other undertaker has had during a corresponding period of one's business career."[26] In 1922, Diggs moved his growing business into a much larger building at Mullett and Russell Streets and lived with his wife in a second-floor apartment above the funeral parlor. This was the home they would share with their son. Charles Coles Diggs Jr. was born on December 2, 1922, at Detroit's Women's Hospital.

AS A YOUNG BUSINESSMAN, Diggs Sr. became involved in a variety of organizations and civil rights causes. Joining was always good for business, and the man his family would one day refer to as "Papa Diggs" became a joiner.[27] Diggs Sr. was a trustee of the Detroit affiliate of Marcus Garvey's Universal Negro Improvement Association. Garvey was the Jamaican-born Black Nationalist who in the early 1920s argued that Black people around the world should unite in solidarity to fight racially based oppression. Garvey stressed Black pride, opposition to European colonialism, and Black business development.[28] Garvey's example would profoundly shape Diggs Sr.'s worldview and, through him, that of his son as well.

Papa Diggs became the "prime mover" behind the formation in 1925 of the Detroit Memorial Park, a Black cemetery he helped plan and support.[29] Black funeral directors had for years been frustrated by the indignities that Black Detroiters faced from white cemetery owners. Few white cemeteries allowed Black burials. Those that did, often permitted such burials only on designated days of the week, overcharged Black families, and allowed access only through side or back gates. Congressman Diggs later told of one incident during which his father became exasperated with the treatment he and other Black morticians experienced. When a white attendant tried to block a funeral procession from entering the cemetery with his car, "my father came to the gate anyway, got out, knocked the man down and backed the car out of the way.... My father was not a big man, but he was just fed up with that kind of treatment."[30] As a result, in 1925 Diggs Sr, organized local Black funeral directors. With a $25,000 loan, they collectively purchased nearly 100 acres in Macomb County and sold stock in the new corporation. In fact, Detroit Memorial Park became Michigan's first Black-owned corporation.[31]

Diggs Sr. likely got involved in Detroit electoral politics in 1927, working on the unsuccessful city council campaign of his friend George H. Green. Two years later, Diggs supported incumbent mayor John W. Smith in the mayoral race opposite Charles E. Bowles, who was backed by the Ku Klux Klan. Diggs Sr. successfully organized the city's Black precincts in support of Smith's candidacy. In 1931, Diggs Sr. ran unsuccessfully for a seat on the Detroit City Council.

Meanwhile, Diggs Funeral Home continued to thrive. In 1926, Diggs Sr. purchased Dunbar Hospital, a former twenty-seven bed Black hospital, for an expanded funeral home and residence. Diggs Sr. appeared well on his way to dominating the Black funeral industry in Detroit. Then the stock market crashed, and the Great Depression came to Detroit.

Historian B. J. Widick observed that "the Great Depression was an experience most Detroiters could never forget. The devastation of human lives and hopes left a permanent scar on the people."[32] As a city dependent on one industry, Detroit was among the worst afflicted major cities during the Great Depression. The city suffered one of the highest unemployment rates in the country. "If the plight of the whites was desperate," observed historian Robert Conot, "that of the Blacks was very nearly mortal."[33] Black Detroiters were only 7 percent of the population, but over half the families on relief were Black Americans. As Detroit's economy tanked, Black workers were typically the first to lose their jobs. Unemployment among Black residents in Detroit reached 80 percent.[34]

Charles Diggs Jr. was seven years old when the stock market crashed and brought financial and personal pain to the Diggs family. Many Black families suddenly had no money to pay for proper burials. Unable to secure a loan to keep his under-capitalized business afloat, in 1929 the Diggs Funeral Home went bankrupt.

That wasn't the end of bad news for the Diggs clan. On July 18, 1930, Diggs Jr.'s Uncle Osmond, his father's brother, out of work and amid a divorce, barricaded himself in his apartment and turned on the gas stove, committing suicide.[35] Financial pressures also forced the Diggs family to admit Lilly Diggs's mentally challenged son, George, to Eloise Mental Hospital. By 1932, as Congressman Diggs recalled years later, "The devastatingly negative impact" of the Great Depression "prompted my mother and I to move to Chicago," where for a time they lived with Weston Diggs and his family. But as Diggs Jr. explained, "When my daddy called, we returned to Detroit."[36]

It was in Detroit where events, attitudes, and his family shaped his views about politics, and where he would meet his destiny.

Chapter 2

GROWING UP IN BLACK DETROIT

WHEN CHARLES JR. AND MAYME DIGGS returned to Detroit in 1933, the political terrain in the United States, Michigan, and the City of Detroit was experiencing dramatic and permanent change. Since the end of the Civil War the Republican Party had controlled Michigan's state government and all the federal patronage coming from Washington, DC.[1] When Black people were first granted the right to vote, they supported the Republican Party. In the wake of the Great Depression, that was changing. No one would be more affected than Charles Jr. and his father.

In early 1932, Papa Diggs began to question the relationship between Black voters and Michigan Republicans. He learned that despite the overwhelming support given to the Republicans in Michigan, Black Americans received only a few low-level patronage positions. Despite his bankruptcy, Diggs Sr. remained a respected voice in the Black community, and in the 1932 state-wide elections, he and two Black Democratic Party activists, attorneys Harold Bledsoe and Joseph A. Craigen, canvassed the state and led thousands of Black voters out of the Republican Party and into the Democratic Party. In a transformative and historical election, Democrats won many of Michigan's top elected offices, including that of governor. Sixty years of Republicanism in state government had come to an end. The new governor appointed Diggs Sr. to the state parole commission, a change that would help propel the Diggs family to newfound prominence and prosperity. For Charles Jr., his father's activism would provide a roadmap to his future.[2]

WHEN MAYME AND CHARLES JR. first returned from Chicago, Papa Diggs reopened his funeral business and worked hard to make up for lost ground. He convinced the National Negro Funeral Directors Association to hold its seventh annual convention in Detroit, and in 1934, he rented the former home of George Green's business on St. Aubin Street.[3] In addition to the funeral home, the building housed a drugstore and two apartments, one of which housed the Diggs family.

Diggs Sr. also stayed involved in politics. Between 1905 and 1930, no Black person held an elective office in Detroit.[4] Their small numbers (only 7 percent of the city's total population in 1930) and the city's structure of nonpartisan and at-large elections made it almost impossible for Black candidates to compete and win city council elections. However, because state legislators represented people living within specifically defined boundaries, the geographic concentration of Black residents on the city's East Side enhanced the possibility of Black representation from districts encompassing Black Bottom and Paradise Valley.

Diggs's home district, the Third District, which included Black Bottom and Paradise Valley, was only one-third Black residents. The district's boundaries stretched into Hamtramck, a small municipality of nearly 47,000 that was almost surrounded by the City of Detroit. Home to the Dodge Main plant that opened in 1914, thousands of Polish immigrants had moved there to work, and in 1926 and 1928, a Polish American was elected to the Third District state senate seat. However, in 1930, Charles Roxborough, a Black Republican, won the Third District state senate seat. He lost reelection in 1932 to a Polish American Democrat.[5]

In 1936, Papa Diggs was drafted by the women's auxiliary of the Michigan Federated Democratic Club, one of the first Black-led state organizations dedicated to incorporating Black voters into the Democratic Party in the nation and a group the elder Diggs helped create, to seek the Third District senate seat as a Democratic candidate.[6] Diggs Sr. claimed that the women of the Michigan Federated Democratic Club paid the filing fee and filed his name without his knowledge.[7]

Campaigning in a majority-white district, Diggs Sr. developed relationships with Polish American leaders throughout Detroit and in Hamtramck. He earned endorsements and support from various parts of the Polish American community, including from Michigan lieutenant governor Leo J. Nowicki and several Polish-language newspapers. With encouragement from Nowicki, the mayor of Hamtramck also endorsed Diggs.[8] The *Michigan Chronicle*, a new weekly Black newspaper, threw its support behind Diggs.[9] Diggs Sr. won the Democratic nomination and the general election.

ON JANUARY 6, 1937, Mayme Diggs and fourteen-year-old Charles Jr. witnessed the opening of the Michigan Legislature. The thirty-two state senators included small farmers, lumbermen, attorneys, automobile dealers, and, like

Diggs Sr., owners of small businesses. Many Republicans represented rural areas and small towns, while most of the Democrats were from larger cities. Charles Jr. witnessed his father make history as the first Black Democrat to serve in the Michigan Legislature and as one of only two Black state senators in the entire country, which instantly made Diggs Sr. a national figure in Black politics.

With Democrats in control of both legislative houses, in his first session Senator Diggs pushed through an antidiscrimination civil rights bill that made him a legend in Detroit. Popularly known as "Diggs's Law," the legislation outlawed discrimination in public places such as restaurants and hotels. Violators could be charged with a misdemeanor and subjected to a minimum penalty of twenty-five dollars, fifteen days imprisonment, or both. Over the next several decades, before the federal civil rights laws of the 1960s, Michigan's Black residents repeatedly invoked the "Diggs's Law" when confronted with instances of racial discrimination.[10] While not always effective—as the law required the victim of discrimination to take the initiative, and both juries and judges rarely enforced the statute—it nevertheless sent an important message. Congressman Diggs later called the legislation "the cornerstone" of his father's "active political career."[11] In the words of one contemporary observer, it made Senator Diggs a "'messiah of civil rights to his people.'"[12] He would be reelected in 1938, 1940, and again in 1942.

For much of the next three decades, "Senator Diggs" played a leading role in nearly all the major developments in Detroit related to the Black community, both legislatively and in helping to forge an alliance between the Black community and the local labor movement.[13] Senator Diggs was "very dynamic, daring, outspoken, [and] fair," remembered a nephew. Black Detroit "loved him," he added.[14] "He was a little Napoleon. He was hard-driving, aggressive and intelligent," an acquaintance of the Senator recalled.[15] Papa Diggs's legacy, however, would not be a single piece of legislation, his success as a businessman, or the role he played bringing Black people into Detroit's political mainstream. It would be his son.

IT WAS NOT EASY growing up in the shadow of Senator Diggs. By the time Charles Jr. was a teenager, his father's name had become well-known throughout Black Detroit. Charles Jr. soon learned the name came with both responsibility and expectations.

One summer day about a year after Senator Diggs was elected to the legislature, Mrs. Diggs gave "Junior" a dollar and sent him out to purchase fish from a nearby market. As he walked to the store, he saw a group of young men crouched together in an alley, laughing, and talking excitedly. One man was playing "three-card monte," while the others alternately watched and gambled. Young Diggs sauntered over and leaned in to watch. With a dollar bill burning a hole in his pocket, Charles Jr. couldn't resist and got pulled into the con game. To no surprise to anyone but himself, within only a few seconds he had gambled away the dollar. He had no choice but to return home, without the fish or the dollar bill, and explain to his mother what had happened. She told the Senator.[16]

Papa Diggs took his son firmly by the arm and led him back into the alley, where the game continued. Then, as Charles Jr. remembered, his father "demanded return of the dollar, but when the dealer refused, he began to take off his coat to fight for it. However, one of the dealer's allies quickly intervened, saying 'Hey man, this guy is Senator Diggs. Give him his dollar back.' My Father took the dollar with his left hand, but with his right hand hit me in the face, breaking my glasses and then ushered me back home. I never played '3-card monte' again."[17]

Charles Jr. grew up immersed in the full spectrum of the Black American experience in Detroit. Helen Nuttall Brown, who was about the same age as Charles Diggs Jr., lived with her physician father and her mother near the funeral home. She recalled, "We would walk and get almost anything we wanted—bakeries, hardware, cleaners, grocery stores."[18] There were also bars, movie houses, and poolrooms. Across the street from Diggs Funeral Home was St. John CME Church, a Black Methodist denomination. The neighborhood was also the headquarters of the Nation of Islam, a religious sect. After police harassment in 1934, the group relocated to Chicago.[19] On the other side of the street were the cleaner's and the tailor's shops owned by William and Ida Young. Although Black Bottom was generally safe, the Youngs' son, Coleman, who later became the first Black mayor of Detroit, recalls that the neighborhood was also home to "the slicker" and "the gambler."[20] Coleman Young remembered that their home was "just a block or two away from a strip that offered all manner of illicit backroom sin."[21]

The Diggs Funeral Home serviced the full spectrum of Detroit's Black community—the poor and the elite. Young Diggs saw his father treat customers with respect no matter their status, and he would grow up valuing the Black community's diversity. Papa Diggs was a generous businessman. When a fire destroyed a home, killing several young siblings, Papa Diggs buried them at no cost.[22] Whenever there was a need in the community, Senator Diggs was there. The funeral home sponsored children's sports leagues and an annual "Mother's Day" celebration, and it contributed to many community causes. Damon Keith explained that in Black Detroit "the Diggs's name was gold."[23]

"The Diggs just were really popular. People liked them. They were good people," recalled Roberta Hughes Wright.[24]

AND IT WAS FROM HERE, in the heart of Black Bottom, amid the Great Depression, as he grew from boy to man, that Charles Diggs Jr. bore witness as his father's business and civic involvement and responsibilities expanded. Over the next few years, the lingering economic challenges from the Great Depression, the UAW's victory over Ford Motor Company, and racial conflict around issues like housing, law enforcement, and public transportation as well as racism would begin to shape the younger Diggs.[25] His parents, especially his father, would be a major source of his political education and socialization.

"Diggs was special in his parents' eyes. Both parents were supportive of everything he managed to do."[26] Temperamentally, however, Charles Diggs Jr. was more like his mother, "quiet" and "introverted," traits that he carried into adulthood.[27] Always a private person and personally shy, young Diggs had a light complexion, was tall but slightly overweight, and was self-conscious about his thick eyeglasses. He shied away from most sports. One would never have picked him out as a future leader.

His transformation can be credited to Senator Diggs, as Diggs Jr. would later admit, "My father always had an influence on what I was doing."[28] As a busy and successful businessman and a prominent politician and civic leader, Diggs Sr. was constantly on the move. Their time alone was most often devoted to the family's funeral home business. Diggs Jr. remembered that he "frequently" rode along with his father in his hearse and funeral cars. By the time Charles Jr. was eleven or twelve years old, his father even began training and instructing him on how to assist during funerals. The experience of standing before large crowds of mourners as he helped his father is "why I matured professionally at such an early age," Congressman Diggs would later conclude.[29] Diggs Jr. also developed an emotional intelligence beyond his years from observing his father having personal, emotional conversations with families of the deceased.

In 1936, Diggs Jr. began attending Sidney D. Miller Junior High and High School. During the 1920s, Miller, a middle school that had once served as a feeder into Eastern High School, was racially integrated.[30] But by the time young Diggs attended, the school board transformed Miller into a senior high school and announced a liberal student transfer policy, effectively creating a segregated, Black high school in Detroit; Miller became the city's de facto primary Black secondary school.[31] "The school graduated scores of future professionals, including perhaps more teachers and school administrators than any high school in Detroit, as well as many future lawyers, police officers, doctors, and dentists," and a host of civic and political leaders.³²

In the fall of 1935, because of community protests, the first Black teachers were assigned to Miller. English teacher Alvin Loving, one of the first Black teachers at the school, became Diggs Jr.'s favorite teacher at Miller High, and Loving had a significant influence on the teenager. He was Miller's debate coach, and he taught the introverted young man the skills to speak confidently and in a persuasive style. Diggs Jr. soon became an outstanding orator and debater, and in 1938 he won the city and state oratorical contests. His shyness was gradually replaced with a quiet confidence, and he soon became a member of the student council, the editor/publisher of the school newspaper, and in 1940, his senior year, class president.³³

AFTER GRADUATION, in September 1940, Diggs Jr. enrolled at the University of Michigan, the state's premier four-year public university. Located thirty-five miles west of Detroit in Ann Arbor, the University of Michigan, unlike the state-supported white colleges in the South during this period, admitted Black Americans. Still, there were fewer than 100 Black students in a student body of nearly 25,000.³⁴

"The biggest problem in Ann Arbor was obtaining admission to the dormitory system, where no Black had ever penetrated," Diggs Jr. explained years later.³⁵ When university officials refused to assign Diggs Jr. to a recently constructed dormitory for men, Senator Diggs, who was still a member of the legislature, "confronted the president of University of Michigan."³⁶ It was only after his father talked with the university president that Junior was assigned to a single room in George Palmer Williams House, making him the first Black man to live in a men's dormitory at the university. Still, Junior remembered that most of the white students "would not even speak to" him.³⁷ "Racism," as historian Ruth Bordin explains, "flourished among the faculty, students, and administrators."³⁸

At the end of his freshman year, Diggs Jr.'s father encouraged him to get a job on campus to earn extra spending money. However, when he visited the campus office in charge of hiring students for summer work, he was told there were no jobs available—even though Diggs Jr. could see a stack of job announcements on the man's desk. Junior told his father, and Senator Diggs met with the person in charge. As Diggs Jr. recalled decades later, "I can remember my father snatching the box of employment [announcements] out of his hand and flipping through them ... indicating that obviously there were all kinds of opportunities around."³⁹ Senator Diggs then called the office of the president of the university and "marched right over there to the president's office. . . . I can assure you that a job came available pretty fast," Diggs Jr. added.[40]

At Michigan, Diggs Jr. dated Elsie Virginia Miller, a student from Culver, Indiana. "Although she looked white," Miller was biracial and seemingly identified as a Black woman.[41] "She *was very attractive*," Diggs emphasized decades later. "She became my girlfriend, and we would have been married had WWII not come," he recalled.[42]

After the December 1941 attack on Pearl Harbor, Diggs Jr. swiftly decided to volunteer. The bespectacled young man was disappointed to have his application to the Navy rejected because of his eyesight, although he would long maintain that recruiters used his poor eyesight as "just an excuse."[43] He believed the main reason for the rejection was that recruiters knew his father was a powerful civil rights leader and "figured Dad would raise a lot of hell" if the Navy officers were to discriminate against his son.[44]

Denied an opportunity to volunteer, Diggs Jr. returned to Ann Arbor and completed his sophomore year before deciding to transfer; he would later indicate that this decision was due to unnamed "racial incidents."[45] The environment at Michigan was clearly challenging for Diggs, and his transcripts show the university requested him "to withdraw because of poor scholarship."[46]

During the war, Elsie Miller moved to Detroit, not far from Diggs's parents. The couple continued to date and talked about getting married. However, as Diggs Jr. grew in both confidence and accomplishments, he found that women were increasingly available to him, and he began to take advantage of that fact. For much of the rest of his life, Diggs Jr. often carried on multiple relationships with women.

In the fall of 1942, Diggs Jr. transferred to Fisk University, one of the nation's premier historically Black universities, in Nashville, Tennessee. For young Diggs, the train ride from Detroit to Nashville was both memorable and eye-opening. Once the train crossed the Mason–Dixon line, he had to disembark and move to a segregated train, where he was seated in a dingy passenger car directly behind the engine. Although he had heard of Jim Crow, the South's separate-but-equal racial policy, this was Diggs Jr.'s first experience with such institutionalized humiliation. He would never forget it. Neither would it be his last experience with the policy.

While the raw nature of state-sanctioned racial discrimination would become more evident to Diggs Jr. during his time at Fisk, the Black college provided a dramatically different environment compared to the University of Michigan. Many of the students at the all-Black school were from the South, but there were also students from New York, Boston, Detroit, Chicago, and even from as far away as Maine. Many were the sons and daughters of upwardly mobile Black families. Constance Motley Baker, who later became the first Black woman appointed to the federal judiciary, recalled that she wanted to attend Fisk because it "seemed a part of the black Ivy League."[47]

Diggs Jr. found that Fisk provided a psychologically supportive atmosphere. Still, living in Nashville was revealing. If they remained on campus, the students at Fisk had few dealings with local whites and state-sanctioned separate-but-equal laws. A theater across the street from the main campus welcomed Black customers, as did the local drugstore. But if they ventured farther off campus, as they inevitably did, the students encountered segregation. Downtown restaurants refused to serve Fisk students, and in a letter home, Diggs Jr. explained, "There are only two theaters that admit Negroes downtown, and you have to go down an alley and sit in the balcony"[48]

But at Fisk, he found his place and began to flourish academically and socially. In fact, Diggs excitingly told his parents, "I'm going to pledge Kappa [Alpha Psi fraternity] next semester," before adding cautiously "if I haven't been drafted."[49]

Chapter 3
LIEUTENANT DIGGS IN THE JIM CROW SOUTH

IN THE SUMMER OF 1944, Lt. Charles Diggs Jr., accompanied by a few fellow Black servicemen, boarded a bus in Tuskegee, Alabama, home of the Tuskegee Army Air Field (TAAF) and of the famed Tuskegee Airmen, for an outing to the nearby town of Opelika. The young officer and his friends looked forward to the trip. "Tuskegee and surrounding environs were officially 'dry'; eating places were segregated and unsavory, and there was not a decent place to dance."[1] Opelika, with a population of 10,000, was nearly twice the size of Tuskegee.

But as Diggs Jr. boarded the bus, he made what was almost a fatal error; he addressed the white bus driver as "Buddy." The driver's eyes flashed with hate. According to Charles E. Francis, who was deployed to TAAF and who recounted the story in his book, *The Tuskegee Airmen*, "The driver whipped out a pistol that he had tucked under his belt and threatened to kill Diggs."[2] The young lieutenant froze in place. As a Northerner, Diggs Jr. still found the ways of Jim Crow jarring, and he sometimes let his guard down. The driver remarked, "If you weren't wearing that uniform, I would blow your brains out for calling me 'buddy.' I am not your buddy."[3]

The most frightening experience of his twenty-one years, he never spoke about the incident in any of his oral histories and kept it a secret from his family. Even in the service of his country it was impossible to escape the racist reach of Jim Crow and its accompanying white supremacy, where a bus driver felt it was permissible to threaten a man with death who simply had referred to him as a friend. Diggs Jr., like thousands of other Black servicemen in World War II, experienced widespread racism and violence at the hands of their fellow citizens. Historian Matthew F. Delmont explains that although Black Americans bravely helped the country defend its freedom, many white Americans still considered Black servicemen second-class citizens, "half Americans."[4]

IN FEBRUARY 1943, after only one semester at Fisk University, Charles Diggs Jr. was drafted into the US Army. He would remain in the military until June 1945, and because most military bases in the United States during this period were in the South, Diggs would have his first extended experience with Jim Crow-style racial discrimination. It would prove to be eye-opening.

Alabama was a state in which segregation laws were both legally binding and strictly enforced. As DuBose explains, Diggs Jr.'s "experience as an officer in Alabama in the forties was a turning point in his life."[5] In Alabama, Florida, and other places he lived during his army career, his behavior and lifestyle would be restrained by a social system that had a long history and active supporters. His military uniform did not insulate him from this racist environment in any of the states in which he served; in fact, it exposed to him the intractability of white supremacy policies. His experiences would strengthen his long-held belief that racial discrimination was inconsistent with American democracy.

After twenty-year-old Diggs Jr. reported to the induction center at Battle Creek, Michigan, in March 1943, he traveled to Kearns Field near Salt Lake City, Utah, for basic training. Although his stay was relatively uneventful, Diggs later recalled that the city "was very racially prejudiced in those days. Black theater patrons, even in uniform had to sit in the balcony."[6]

Promoted to private first class, Diggs Jr. scored well on the Army General Classification Test, a literacy and aptitude exam, and was sent to the Army Administrative School at Atlanta University, a historically Black university in Georgia. As he traveled to Atlanta from Utah by train, the experience of crossing into the South, again, made a lasting impression. "Once I crossed the geographic line into the South, I was transferred to the coach next to the locomotive," he recalled. "When I was seated to eat in the dining car, a green curtain was pulled around me technically separating me, even in a military uniform."[7]

One of the top two graduates in his class, Diggs Jr. spent two months at MacDill Field in Tampa, Florida, as "an Army classification specialist."[8] Once again confronted by Jim Crow, Diggs recalled that Black soldiers could congregate only on "the street perpendicular to the Black USO [United Service Organizations] or within that [USO] building."[9] Diggs was then transferred again to another Army Administrative School in Brookings, South Dakota, on the campus of South Dakota State College. He found the experience "revelatory, for it proved that racial attitudes were not confined to the South."[10] There were few Black residents in South Dakota. Diggs remembered white people staring and "a little kid at one point tugging at his mother's arm, exclaiming, 'Look, ma, there is a n——.'"[11] In September 1943, after successfully completing training in South Dakota, Diggs was promoted to sergeant and ordered back to

MacDill Field in Tampa, where he applied for admission into the recently established the Army Air Force Officer Candidate School (OCS).[12]

THE WINTER OF 1943–44 BEGAN as an exciting time for Charles Diggs Jr. In November 1943, his parents purchased a home at 505 East Boston Boulevard in Detroit's North End, one of the city's most exclusive neighborhoods. For the first time, the family was living away from the Black ghetto and in a home not physically connected to the funeral home. Known as the "Diggs's Mansion" to friends and relatives, it was a magnificent house designed by Louis Kamper, Detroit's premiere architect for affluent and wealthy families.[13] While Diggs was in the service, the Diggs Funeral Home had thrived. Eventually renamed the "House of Diggs" and well-known to most every Black Detroiter, the family business would continue to grow over the next decade.

In December 1943, after going home on leave and having a look at the house, Diggs Jr. learned that he had been accepted into OCS. Although the US Army Air Force had been segregated for two decades, because of the pressure applied by the National Association for the Advancement of Colored People (NAACP) and other Black civil rights organizations, the military leadership mandated that a share of the slots for OCS be granted to Black applicants.[14]

In January 1944, Diggs Jr. was ordered to the new training facility for OCS in Miami Beach, where he would learn to perform the administrative duties required of pilots. He was one of only twelve Black men in his OCS class of nearly 1,500.[15] Race relations were generally "good" in that there was "almost total integration" at the school.[16] However, white and Black soldiers were not allowed to room together, and, as Diggs would later explain, "When in formation, marching or otherwise, we were instructed to place ourselves on the inside in the rear, so we would not be easily seen."[17] Diggs also remembered that he and other Black students "under the supervision of a Black upper-classmen . . . were trucked into the city of Miami's Black USO and told to have a Black neighborhood barber cut our hair."[18]

As Diggs Jr. described in a letter to his parents, the course of study was rigorous. "The material is so abundant and the pace so fast," he wrote. "You find college professors, Ph.D.'s [sic], lawyers, Phi Beta Kappans, and all kinds of highly qualified people flunking out or taking 5 and 6 months to complete the course."[19] In addition, he told his parents about the preparation he and his classmates were making to spend ten days "out in the woods under simulated combat conditions."[20]

On April 29, 1944, Charles Diggs was commissioned as a second lieutenant in the US Army Air Force. At age twenty-one, he was the youngest member of his graduating class. Becoming an officer in the Air Force was a huge accomplishment at the time. In 1944, only 1,303 of the 375,973 Army Air Force officers were Black men—less than 1 percent.[21] "I'm not excited or puffed up about this matter," he wrote his parents. "Naturally, I take pride in my advancement and in the success of my undertaking. However, further than that I have not been affected, as so many I have observed. I am still cool and calm as ever. That trait is one of the greatest reasons for my success here."[22]

Unfortunately, his parents would not witness the ceremony in which their son earned his commission. In 1944, Senator Diggs was arrested and indicted four times for bribery. In 1943, a one-man grand jury—a peculiar institution in Michigan typically used to prosecute political corruption—had been convened in Detroit to investigate allegations of buying and selling of votes during the 1941 session of the Michigan Legislature. During the four-year investigation, 127 people were arrested. Kim Sigler, who would later become governor in 1946, ultimately secured sixty-two convictions, including twenty-three state legislators and a former lieutenant governor.[23]

Senator Diggs denied the allegations. Although prior to his indictment he had told "several personal friends" that he would not seek reelection in 1944, after the indictment he changed his mind.[24] Other factions of the Democratic Party, namely labor and white liberals, however, asked Senator Diggs to step aside and not seek renomination as the Democratic candidate. Diggs Sr. subsequently ran and was defeated in the 1944 Democratic primary. Meanwhile, in late April 1944, Lieutenant Diggs reported to TAAF in Alabama and was appointed a base classification officer.

WHILE THERE WAS already a long tradition of Black Americans serving in the military, in most instances Black soldiers had traditionally been segregated and engaged in menial tasks. Yet, as US involvement in World War II loomed, Black leaders and the NAACP turned up the political pressure on President Roosevelt to allow the full participation of Black soldiers in the military on a desegregated basis.[25] In October 1940, the White House announced that the military would train Black Americans as aviators. However, Black pilots would be trained at a facility separate from that of the white pilots and would be supported by an all-Black staff of mechanics, technicians, and administrative officers. In January 1941, the War Department announced that it would locate the segregated army airfield at Tuskegee, Alabama.[26]

The NAACP and Black newspapers across the country all strenuously objected to the decision. In the 1940s, perhaps only Mississippi could match Alabama in terms of the discrimination, prejudice, and lynchings that Black Americans had to endure. Like all towns in Alabama, Tuskegee adhered to state laws legalizing racial segregation. Those opposed to building the air base at Tuskegee argued that cadets, soldiers, and officers, many from Northern cities with no experience in the segregated South, would be subjected to the racial indignities of Alabama's Jim Crow laws.

The origins of TAAF are closely tied to the presence of the Tuskegee Institute, a historically Black college, and to the legacy of the college's first president, Booker T. Washington.[27] Many Black leaders were livid over the decision to house the new Black aviator training facility at TAAF, which revived the old debate between W. E. B. Du Bois and Washington over the best strategy for advancing the race. Washington advocated a conservative approach, while Du Bois favored more militant activism. A *Pittsburgh Courier* editorial noted that the segregated training facility "perpetuate[d] the 'American way' of racial segregation" and would expose the Black cadets to racial discrimination.[28] But Frederick Patterson, president of Tuskegee Institute from 1935 to 1953, contended that training Black military pilots—even in segregated conditions—gave Black men a foothold in the air corps and would in time lead to integrated air units.[29]

When Charles Diggs Jr. arrived in Tuskegee in April 1944, the new base commander, a "white liberal" who had arrived a year earlier, had been working hard to improve race relations at TAAF and gain the respect of the Black servicemen.[30] Diggs still experienced the racism and abuse that nearly all Black soldiers had to live through. He learned that not even Black officers were exempt from mistreatment and disrespect. White soldiers typically crossed the street to avoid saluting him.

Diggs Jr. often recounted his experience living in segregated Alabama, with its segregated public facilities, water fountains, and other public places. At a theater in downtown Tuskegee, Black soldiers had to enter through the back door and were "directed to go up in the balcony"; Black people were prohibited from sitting on the first floor.[31] To keep the Black soldiers entertained and to limit their visits into town, TAAF sponsored Black entertainment on the base. "As a 21-year-old second lieutenant," Diggs Jr. later recalled, "I remember shaking hands with Lena Horne at the Officers' Club."[32]

Still, the racial atmosphere at Tuskegee was always tense.[33] According to military historian Stanley Sandler, TAAF was "surrounded by hostile whites" who controlled the town and county although they were a minority of the population. Local people were on edge and especially "fearful of armed Blacks on the Tuskegee bases."[34] Black soldiers stationed at TAAF typically did not leave the base unless they had to.

Diggs Jr. also witnessed the most demoralizing experience: German prisoners of war, confined at the nearby Walterboro Airfield, permitted to eat with white soldiers and guards in places that refused to serve him and other Black servicemen because of their race. The notion that Black soldiers were risking their lives fighting for democracy abroad, yet subjected to Jim Crow laws at home, was glaringly inconsistent.[35]

On June 1, 1945, shortly after the fighting in Europe ceased, Diggs Jr. was honorably discharged. Diggs's military service, especially the time spent in Jim Crow Alabama, had a profound impact on him and would later characterize his service in the US Congress. But that was all still to come. First, it was time to head back to Detroit, return to school, and help with the family business while his father fought indictment. When Diggs Jr. returned to Detroit, he enrolled at the Wayne State University School of Mortuary Science. He completed the yearlong coursework in June 1946 and subsequently became a licensed mortician.

AS ONE LONGTIME Black resident and community leader explained decades later, the Diggs Funeral Home "was a thriving business and it was noted that if you died you were just going to Diggs to be buried. You just know they were going to bury you."[36] By the late 1940s, the Diggs Funeral Home handled more than half of the Black burials in Detroit. The Diggs family had prospered financially and rapidly and had become part of Detroit's Black elite. The funeral home would eventually provide a springboard for Diggs Jr.'s entry into both business and politics, just as it had for his father.

Papa Diggs's political connections gave his business tremendous advantages. His appointment to the parole board in the early 1930s initially allowed him the financial stability to re-open the funeral business, and then, becoming a state senator provided him advantages over other funeral directors. Of note was when, in 1937, Diggs Sr. was awarded a contract to bury the indigent patients who died while at Eloise Hospital, a 4,000-patient hospital and mental asylum in Nankin Township, in western Wayne County, twenty miles from Detroit. Although Diggs would later be criticized over the arrangement, the contract helped the Diggs tremendously. Between 1937 and 1941, Wayne County would pay Diggs nearly $30,000 (the equivalent of about $500,000 in 2024) for handling between 250 and 300 burials a year to cover the deaths that occurred at Eloise.[37] "That contract," Diggs Jr. recalled years later, "was another turning point in my family's life ... despite our modest compensation for these services, the accumulation of those funds helped my parents purchase" a new facility for their growing business on Mack Avenue, directly across the street from the Brewster Public Housing Project.[38]

In 1942, Papa Diggs added a burial insurance component to his funeral home business, the first funeral director in Detroit to do so. Diggs Sr.'s company, the Metropolitan Funeral System Association, provided an opportunity for Papa Diggs to expand his business and a means for poor and working-class Black families to pay for a proper burial. Sometimes called "burial societies," "funeral systems," or "burial associations," and modeled after the old fraternal organizations and mutual aid societies that had been a part of Black Southern life for generations, these associations collected from members weekly premiums ranging from ten to twenty-five cents. Although some believed the system allowed funeral directors to take advantage of customers and limit consumer choice, for only a few cents per week, members could pay toward a policy that would still guarantee them a proper burial.[39]

"The sale of those policies went like wildfire," Charles Diggs Jr. recalled years later.[40] The burial insurance soon helped make the Diggs Funeral Home the largest Black funeral home in Michigan. One newspaper article reported that "out of the 1,600 Negroes buried in 1948, the Diggs Funeral Establishment buried 801 persons."[41]

The funeral home built a reputation for providing outstanding service to their customers. An open-casket funeral has long been a Black cultural tradition, and it is not unusual for family members or friends to touch and even kiss the deceased body. "The cultural importance attached to an open-casket viewing required of morticians a particular skill with and attention to the appearance of the deceased," writes Karla F. C. Holloway, a Black cultural scholar.[42] In the Black cultural tradition, how one looks in death is almost as important as how one looked in life.

To that end, the funeral home employed some of the best embalmers in the state. Papa Diggs had a reputation for being "a hell of an embalmer."[43] Charles Diggs III, Congressman Diggs's son, also began working at the funeral home with his father and grandfather when he was a teenager. He was aware of the funeral home's reputation when he was growing up. "We had the greatest embalmers, and we were known for it. If you were in a car wreck or they found you floating down the river, or somebody shot you in the head fifty times," you could still have an open-casket funeral. "We had maybe the best embalmers in the country. That was the hook. You want 'so-and-so' to look like something, you better call Diggs."[44]

By the 1940s and 1950s, Black funerals had taken on the cultural tradition of a "show," in which matters such as "the type and color of the hearse and the type of cars that would transport the bereaved family had become an important detail for Black costumers."[45] Diggs Funeral Home staff never talked during a funeral, and training included learning hand signals so the staff—largely men in black suits, white shirts, and dark ties—could communicate. All duties were strictly choreographed. Everybody knew "exactly when to move and not to move," remembered Denise Diggs-Taylor, Congressman Diggs's daughter, who grew up around the family business and later became a licensed mortician.[46] Black Detroiters knew that if Diggs had the body of their loved one, the bereaved family would be provided a highly professional and well-coordinated funeral. As Weston Diggs Jr. explained, there was a "Diggs's way of directing a funeral."[47]

BY THE TIME CHARLES JR. returned to civilian life, his parents' social status had risen, and they had become members of Detroit's Black elite. It was nearly impossible to escape the Diggs Funeral Home in Black Detroit. The business even sponsored a weekly radio program. The brainchild of Papa Diggs, the program proved to be extremely popular. Junior, making use of his experience as a high school and college debater, would serve as the host.

If any of Senator Diggs's constituents had a problem or needed to reach him, they knew to come to the funeral home. Later, when Charles Jr. became first a state senator and later a congressman, he too would meet with constituents in the offices of the funeral home, simultaneously building his political base as well as a consumer base for the family's funeral business. "The funeral home was more than a funeral home," Charles Diggs Jr. recalled. "It was a community center."[48]

Chapter 4
A RELUCTANT POLITICIAN

IN THE SUMMER OF 1945, after he returned from military service, Charles Diggs Jr. moved into the Diggs's Mansion with his parents. He was just twenty-two years old, but Charles Jr.'s professional future was already obvious. He appeared eager to be back home to help his parents manage and operate their successful and growing mortuary business. It was like old times. Diggs Sr. was enthusiastic to have Junior back to take on positions of increasing responsibility in the family business, and Mayme was bursting with pride over her only child. As one close relative recalled years later, "The only thing she cared about was him. That was all. Charles Junior. That was her love and her life."[1]

While Charles Jr. was in the military, other members of the family had taken on larger roles in the Diggs Funeral Home. Mayme helped run the flower shop and Junior's Uncle Weston worked diligently at the funeral home. Well-liked by everyone in the family, Weston was also loyal to his brother and initially lived in an apartment in the Diggs's Mansion. When Weston later remarried, his son from his previous marriage, Weston Jr., eventually began working at the funeral home as well.[2]

Charles Jr. plunged into work at the Diggs Funeral Home. He kept busy organizing the format for the funeral home's Sunday night radio program. The radio program promoted the funeral home and left time for Charles Jr.'s commentary on national, state, and local issues of interest to Black Detroiters; in addition, he encouraged listeners to register and vote. Sometimes he invited speakers to talk about current affairs or Black history. The funeral home's choir provided musical selections. It was a popular broadcast. Charles Jr. would use the radio program as a platform to speak directly to political constituents in Black Detroit.[3]

In 1946, after completing the mortuary program at Wayne State University, Charles Jr. was named "general manager" of the Diggs Funeral Home. Family members recall that Diggs Jr. enjoyed the responsibility. His oldest daughter, Denise, would later explain that as a young man, her father "really wanted to be in the funeral business."[4] Juanita Diggs, Congressman Diggs's ex-wife, recalled years later how much her former husband enjoyed being before the crowd of a large funeral. "When he would walk into a church or the chapel, that was his time as if it was like a movie scene. That door would open, and he would come in with the casket. He'd be in the front of the casket and walk down the aisle. People talked about it, how he would walk. He had arrived. He was no longer 'Junior.'"[5] At the time, Diggs Jr. said that he had no interest in running for public office. "I'll stick to business and make my contributions there," he told the *Michigan Chronicle*.[6]

AS A YOUNG MAN in his twenties, life for Diggs Jr. was not all about work. A small group of his close friends included several other prominent and successful young Black men in Detroit, including Jack Barthwell Jr., whose uncle operated a successful Detroit-based drugstore chain. Another close friend, John Roxborough, was the son of Charles A. Roxborough, a prominent attorney who served one term as the first Black Republican member of the Michigan State Senate (the same seat formerly held by Diggs Sr.). John Roxborough eventually earned a law degree and later became an aide to Secretary of State John Foster Dulles. Another friend, Damon Keith, graduated from Howard University School of Law and got to know the Diggs family in his professional capacity at a prestigious Black Detroit law firm. As a congressman, Diggs Jr. would later play a central role in Keith's appointment as a federal judge.[7]

Diggs Jr. and his friends enjoyed the nightlife in Paradise Valley at places like the Frolic Show Bar, Café Bohemia, and Chesterfield Lounge. During the summer, many of Diggs's friends gathered at the Flamingo Club in Idlewild, Michigan, a Black resort town.[8] A heavy smoker, Diggs Jr. also liked to drink. "He wasn't an alcoholic, but he did a lot of drinking," recalled Damon Keith.[9] Coleman Young later represented a state senate district that was also in Diggs's congressional district. The two childhood friends and political allies often campaigned together, and Young recalls that Diggs "was one of the best drinkers I have ever seen. We'd hit nine or 10 bars along the north side of Mack [Avenue], buying a couple of drinks for the house in each one. And, of course, someone would buy you one or two back. By the end of the line, I would start feeling it. But Charlie would still be going strong. I don't know how he did it."[10]

Diggs Jr., suddenly finding himself the scion of a wealthy family, was having a great time, working hard, and playing hard. He received a regular salary as general manager, but he nevertheless often became "overextended," spending more than his established salary.[11] When Diggs asked his father for extra money, Papa Diggs typically declined and told his son, "'Look, you're getting a salary, live within your means.'"[12] However, all Junior had to do was ask his mother, and Mayme Diggs would give him the funds he wanted. Living beyond his means would prove to be a personal challenge for Diggs Jr. throughout his adult life.

Diggs Jr. was also one of Black Detroit's most eligible bachelors. Although Diggs maintained a relationship with his college sweetheart, Elsie Miller, he also dated other women. In letters to his parents, while in the army, he often mentioned dating.[13] Nevertheless, in December 1946, Diggs proposed to and presented Miller with an engagement ring.[14] A short time later, however, the situation changed. Elsie was stopped by a police officer while driving a funeral home limousine and issued a citation. When she gave the citation to Diggs to pay, he noticed that the officer noted on the citation that Miller was "white." He subsequently learned that Miller's driver's license also identified her as "white."[15] Although Diggs never spoke in detail about what happened, the incident ended the relationship. It is likely that Diggs suspected that Miller was trying to "pass" as white, no insignificant matter in the Black community during this time. Shortly afterward Diggs met the woman who would become his first wife.

AS GENERAL MANAGER of the funeral home, Diggs was responsible for hiring employees. In March 1947, nineteen-year-old Juanita Rosario, a graduate of the Lewis College of Business, a Black-owned trade school, interviewed for a "junior" secretary position at the Diggs Funeral Home. Her father was an immigrant from Bonaire, a small island about fifty miles off the coast of Venezuela, and her mother an Arawakan Indian. Juanita's parents had moved to Detroit in the 1920s. Typical working-class Black Detroiters, the only thing that distinguished them from other Black residents was that Juanita's parents spoke English with an accent.

Papa Diggs came into the office as Rosario was completing an interview with the chief secretary. They were introduced, and Diggs Sr. told an employee to "tell Junior he better get over to the office to see this one."[16] Years later Juanita recalled, "I don't even remember him [Charles Jr.] talking to me. I am sure he did. But she [the chief secretary] came out and said, 'You're hired.' I reported that Monday."[17]

Juanita began working at the funeral home in March of 1947. Within weeks, Diggs Jr., now twenty-four, took her on a date to see *The Mikado*, an opera, and soon the couple were dating regularly. In May 1947, the couple went to nearby Inkster, Michigan, to catch a show at a popular Black night club. That night Diggs told Juanita that they were getting married. As she recalled years later, "'We're getting married,' he said. I said, 'Getting married?' He said, 'Yes, we're getting married in June.'"[18] It wasn't so much a proposal as a statement of fact.

Her parents, residents of Detroit's West Side, had heard of the Diggs family, but her mother, Clarine, told her daughter it was "awful fast, it's awful early" in the relationship.[19] In the end, however, after the wedding was put off a few months, Juanita's parents gave their approval.

Juanita Rosario and Charles C. Diggs Jr. were married on August 2, 1947, only five months after they had met. Juanita was Catholic and over 500 people crowded into St. Benedict the Moor Catholic Church for the ceremony, one that the *Michigan Chronicle* described as "one of the city's more dazzling" events.[20] Afterward, in a huge display of the Diggs family's growing social and economic status, hundreds of guests gathered at the Diggs's Mansion for the reception, where they were entertained by Celeste Cole, a "world famous lyric soprano," accompanied by the popular Leroy Smith and His Orchestra.[21] All expenses, including a two-week honeymoon in New York City, were paid for by Diggs Jr.'s parents.

One night as they dined in a family-run Chinese restaurant called "the House of something," Juanita remembered that Papa Diggs wanted another name for Diggs Funeral Home. She told Junior the restaurant reminded her of the funeral home. "Charles, you're there, your father is there, Uncle Weston, cousins—James and Oliver—and your mother. I said, 'You know what, that is the House of Diggs.'"[22] On January 2, 1948, Diggs Funeral Home became "House of Diggs."

The young couple moved into Diggs's parents' home and in early 1948 received exciting news; they were expecting their first child. However, all was not well in the newly named House of Diggs.

In May 1948, the Michigan supreme court affirmed the bribery convictions against Diggs Sr. He continued to proclaim his innocence and in early October 1948, announced that his lawyers had asked the US Supreme Court to review the decision. On October 28, 1948, while he waited for his father's legal fate to be determined, Diggs and Juanita welcomed the birth of Charles C. Diggs III.

But 1948 did not end on a high note for the family. On December 6, 1948, the US Supreme Court denied a request to review Diggs Sr.'s bribery convictions, exhausting all appeals. On December 15, 1948, Charles Diggs Jr. watched as his father was transported to the state prison in Jackson, Michigan. Although Diggs Sr. would always maintain his innocence, he would nevertheless serve fifteen months.[23]

Before his father was imprisoned, a special meeting of the board of directors of the Metropolitan Funeral System Association, the growing insurance component of the family's business, named Diggs Jr. president, replacing his father. Diggs Jr., however, was not expected to run the firm's day-to-day operation. That responsibility fell to a longtime associate of Papa Diggs. Diggs Jr. was also not yet fully licensed and was therefore legally prohibited from performing all the functions of a funeral director. With her husband imprisoned, Mayme Diggs, with the help of Weston Diggs Sr., significantly expanded her role in the management of the funeral home. The volume of business had already prompted the hiring of several additional licensed funeral directors and embalmers, so despite Papa Diggs's imprisonment, the House of Diggs continued to thrive.

MEANWHILE, DIGGS JR. continued to plan for the future. In 1949, he and Juanita purchased their first home, "a two-family flat that I bought under the GI Bill," Diggs would later recall.[24] Diggs appeared to relish the notion of helping his father grow the family business. He thoughtfully considered how might he and his family benefit from the expanded opportunities Black Americans of his generation had gained following World War II.

To that end, Diggs helped create the Cotillion Club, a social organization for Black business and professional men. However, because racial discrimination was still so much a part of Black life in Detroit, shortly after its founding, the Cotillion Club leaders made the decision to directly involve the club in politics. John Roxborough served as the Cotillion Club's first president; Diggs was the second. The group sponsored social events like a debutante ball but also a lyceum that promoted Black speakers. Composed of about fifty to seventy members, many were up-and-coming attorneys. By the early 1950s, the Cotillion Club also became a launching pad for ambitious Black politicians.[25]

Around this time, Diggs Jr. decided he would obtain a law degree. He had witnessed his father consulting with attorneys on an array of legal issues related to the funeral home, and he knew his father could use a trusted in-house lawyer. Unlike many of his friends, Diggs had not yet earned a four-year undergraduate degree. His admission into the University of Detroit Law School was likely made possible through a special program for World War II veterans. With funds provided by the GI Bill, Diggs planned to attend night classes starting in the fall of 1950. Several months before, on March 17, 1950, Diggs Sr. was released on parole from Jackson State Prison.[26] About a month later, Diggs Jr. and Juanita welcomed the birth of their second child, a daughter they named Denise.

UPON HIS RELEASE, Diggs Sr. seemed like his old self. "Prison was good for me, mentally and physically," he told reporters.[27] His business had continued to prosper while he was incarcerated. Diggs Sr. was alleged to have bragged about the great increase in income tax he had to pay while he was away because of the growth of his business. When those reports surfaced in the local newspapers, Diggs Sr.'s political opponents asked the Michigan attorney general to invoke a little-used law that requires ex-prisoners with means to reimburse the state government for the cost of their incarceration, and Diggs Sr. was forced to pay $980.²⁸ That Michigan officials applied to him a law that had been invoked only in rare instances was an indication of the extent that some of Diggs Sr.'s political enemies went to weaken him. For Charles Diggs Jr., these legal challenges helped to convince him that attending law school was the right decision. But circumstances would soon interrupt his educational plans.

On June 23, 1950, Diggs Sr. shocked the local political world when he filed papers to once again become a candidate for his old Third District senate seat.²⁹ Although many Detroiters continued to refer to him as Senator Diggs, Diggs Sr. had not been a member of the state legislature since being indicted and losing the Democratic primary in 1944 to Henry R. Kozak. Now he was hoping to regain his old seat. And he had reason to believe that he could. The incumbent had decided not to run; even more Black residents had crowded into the city's East Side, which now comprised an increasing proportion of the district's electorate; and Diggs Sr. remained personally popular, especially among Black voters.

The Diggs name still meant a great deal in Black Detroit. This was made evident when Charles M. Diggs, a Black Pentecostal minister not related to Papa Diggs, had challenged Senator Kozak in the 1948 Democratic primary. He lost the election but had won 32 percent of the vote based on his name alone. Indeed, to the chagrin of Papa Diggs, in 1954 Reverend C. M. Diggs would eventually win a seat in the Michigan House of Representatives, which he held until he was defeated by Oliver Roosevelt Diggs, Papa Diggs's nephew.³⁰

On September 12, 1950, Diggs Sr. defeated eight other candidates (including Reverend C. M. Diggs) to win the Democratic primary with 45 percent of the vote. Then, in a stunning political comeback, Diggs Sr. overwhelmingly defeated his Republican opponent in the general election. Black voters stuck with Diggs Sr. He had been their voice for many years and, as Carolyn DuBose explains, "Many Black Detroiters believed that Diggs Sr. was the victim of harassment.... While no one condoned wrongdoing, the general feeling was that the system persecuted powerful blacks who sought change."³¹

Diggs Sr. appeared to be headed back to the state capital. However, when the Republican-dominated state senate convened in January 1951, it refused to allow Diggs Sr. to take his seat. The Republicans contended that Diggs Sr. was an unfit person to help make laws affecting the people of Michigan. Democrats, greatly outnumbered in the postwar legislature, supported Diggs Sr.³²

Black voters were outraged. "It seems that they are ganging up on Charlie and trying to crucify him," a Diggs's supporter told the *Baltimore Afro-American*.³³ Others also noted a racial double standard. Second District senator Anthony Wilkowski, a Democrat of Polish descent, also elected in 1950, had not been barred despite going to prison after a 1934 conviction. During debate a freshman Republican called out his Republican colleagues for treating

Diggs Sr. differently from Wilkowski, insisting that the only difference in the two cases "is one of color and that should not be."[34]

On January 11, 1951, to avoid the appearance of a racial double standard, the Republican-dominated state senate declared both Diggs Sr.'s and Wilkowski's seats vacant; this was the first time in Michigan history that the legislature used its constitutional powers to reject a candidate elected by the people.[35] Governor G. Mennen Williams ordered that a special election be held, and Diggs Sr. announced that he would consider running for the seat again. But if he did not, he told reporters, his son would be a candidate.

Diggs Jr. had just completed his first semester at the Detroit School of Law; he had a growing family and a third child, his daughter Alexis, on the way. He wanted to get his degree and, as one close family member recalled, he "was very reluctant" to enter the February 1951 special primary election.[36] Juanita Diggs remembered that her husband "talked to his father and told him that he was in law school" and wanted to continue attending classes.[37]

But Papa Diggs was persuasive and convinced his son to enter the race. As a family member explained, Papa Diggs "saw the potential in him and said 'Okay, he can carry on where I can't. He can pick up that rod and carry it forward for me.'"[38] Diggs Sr. also wanted to get back at the Republicans and his other political opponents. Papa Diggs likely reminded his son that if he did not run, Reverend C. M. Diggs, the "impostor," could possibly capture the seat. Finally, Weston Diggs Sr. also encouraged his nephew to run, telling him he had to do it for the sake of the family.[39]

On Monday, January 16, 1951, Charles C. Diggs Jr. filed papers as a Democratic candidate in the special election.[40] To display his support within the community, about 200 supporters accompanied him for the filing of the nominating petitions. Diggs Jr. told the crowd that he intended "to build upon the foundation laid by [his] father to further better race relations through a fair employment practices law and any other types of legislation which are needed."[41] Six other candidates also filed papers for the special election, including Reverend Diggs (who eventually dropped from the race).

Diggs Jr. won an impressive victory in the primary, garnering 63 percent of the votes cast. In March 1951, Diggs soundly defeated his Republican opponent, winning 82 percent of the total votes cast. When he assumed his seat in April 1951, Diggs Jr. was only twenty-nine years old and the youngest member of the Michigan Legislature. He was also one of only two Black members in the state senate (a Black Democrat won the special election for Wilkowski's vacant seat.). As Carolyn DuBose observes, "Diggs had been in law school for only one semester when the weight fell on his shoulders to run for his father's senate seat. Although he wanted to become a lawyer, a pattern of events seemed to conspire to push him toward a career in politics."[42]

Chapter 5

POLITICAL AMBITIONS

A Close Run for City Council

ONE EVENING IN OCTOBER 1951, the young legislator entered a restaurant on Detroit's East Side. In the shadow of Our Lady of Sorrows Catholic Church and the Roose-Vanker VFW Hall, the restaurant, owned by Ervin Steiner, was something of a local institution in the working-class Belgian American neighborhood, where the gigantic Briggs Manufacturing Company employed generations. The restaurant was just over a mile away from Black Bottom in a semi-industrial section of the city. In the restaurant's bar, Charles Diggs Jr. got the attention of a young bartender and ordered a drink, only to be told abruptly that he was not welcome to drink at the bar.[1]

It didn't matter that he was a member of the legislature and a veteran. He was a Black man, and the bar was for white patrons only. Refusal of service was a violation of the 1937 "Diggs's Law" passed by his father in the state senate. Diggs Jr. pressed charges—and according to statute, he had to press charges against the bartender, not the restaurant owner. Yet when the case came to court an all-white jury dismissed the charges, exposing the weakness of the statute.[2]

Unfortunately, the incident would prove to be something of a metaphor for Diggs's tenure in the Michigan Legislature. Although he was duly elected, he was not welcomed and would have little real impact on legislation. Just as his uniform had not protected him from Jim Crow laws in the South during his time in the military, neither did his status as an elected official protect him from discrimination in his hometown of Detroit. In the end, however, it would spur him to become even more politically active.

IN THE WAKE OF WORLD WAR II, Black Americans in general and aspiring Democratic Black politicians in particular were initially hopeful. In 1948, President Harry Truman made civil rights a priority in his acceptance speech and later unilaterally mandated an integrated federal workforce and US military. Yet the postwar political climate in Michigan, after leaning strongly Democratic under Roosevelt, swung back toward the Republicans. Although Democratic governor G. Mennen "Soapy" Williams tried to forge an alliance with organized labor and Black Americans to wrest control of the legislature, the GOP held a healthy majority in both the Michigan Senate and House of Representatives.[3]

When Diggs first arrived at the Michigan State Capitol in Lansing in spring 1951, Governor Williams was in the middle of a second effort to push a fair employment practices bill through the Republican-controlled legislature.[4] The forty-year old Williams was popular with Michigan voters, a progressive who, in his first inaugural address in 1949, had made civil rights his first priority.[5] He urged the legislature to adopt a fair employment bill in response to complaints of discrimination in hiring.

But in Michigan no bill could come before the full house or senate unless recommended by a committee, and the Republican Party held firm control over all such committees. Only seven of the senate's thirty-two members were Democrats and, in the house, Democrats held only thirty-four of the 100 seats. The phenomenal population growth of Detroit and its expanding suburbs were not yet reflected in the state legislature, which was still heavily weighted toward small towns and rural counties where the Republican Party was traditionally strong.[6] Six of the seven senate Democrats, like Diggs Jr., were from Detroit; the other was from Flint.

Diggs Jr. was appointed to the Corporations Committee and the Veterans Affairs Committee. He looked forward to working with Williams. Diggs Jr. was one of the highest-ranking Black elected officials in the state Democratic Party. Young, articulate, and a proven vote-getter, Diggs provided the party with a strong voice; he was a visible symbol of change. Williams and other party leaders consulted with him about expanding the party's reach within Detroit's growing Black electorate, and Diggs Jr. hoped to help other Democrats committed to incorporating Black voters into the state party.[7]

But Diggs Jr. quickly learned just how powerful the Republicans were in the senate. Partial to the business community and automakers, who opposed the fair employment bill, the legislation went nowhere as the Republican-dominated legislature easily blocked the popular governor from enacting his number-one policy goal. It would require several legislative sessions before the legislation was approved.

FOLLOWING THE INCIDENT at the restaurant, Diggs Jr. became a more active legislator in his second legislative session that convened in January 1952. He proposed a bill to bolster Michigan's antidiscrimination statutes, including the "Diggs's Law." However, senate Republicans allowed Diggs's civil rights bill and several others that touched on civil rights to die a slow death.[8]

Next, Diggs Jr. turned his attention to legislative oversight. The governing boards of the state's leading public universities held closed-door meetings from which the public, including newspaper reporters, were excluded. In response, Diggs introduced a senate resolution that would prohibit the allocation of state funds to public colleges and universities unless their governing boards held open meetings. However, as the *Detroit Free Press* reported, "Too few Republican senators would go along with the idea to make it a part of the appropriation bill," and even that modest reform was defeated.[9]

Despite these legislative defeats, in August 1952, Diggs Jr. easily won the Democratic nomination for reelection, defeating two challengers with 58 percent of the total votes cast, and in November he won the general election with 87 percent of the vote. Although he had entered the legislature as "Charles Diggs's son," he was becoming his own man. They now called him Senator Diggs.

He stood out among many of his colleagues for more than his race. As a former champion high school and collegiate debater, he enjoyed debating his colleagues. His wife, Juanita, recalled that during this period, "He enjoyed it. ... He had a wonderful voice. He was smart, he knew what words to use, when to use them, and when to emphasize."[10] Reporters began to quote him, his name appeared more and more in the local newspapers, and Diggs Jr.'s popularity among his constituents, especially among Black Detroiters, skyrocketed. "He began to enjoy the attention," his wife remembered.[11]

Legislative work in Lansing caused Diggs Jr. to spend more time away from home. The annual legislative sessions convened in January and typically ended in late May or early June, and the ninety-mile drive from Detroit to Lansing, nearly two hours, was demanding. Diggs eventually rented an apartment in Lansing during the sessions. This not only impacted his family life but interfered with his law school studies. Diggs would explain many years later that winning the senate seat "terminated me in law school"; the daily drive "was too physically exacting" to allow him to continue attending night classes.[12] He completed only one semester at the Detroit School of Law before dropping out.

Diggs Jr. soon realized the futility of his efforts to accomplish any meaningful change in the Republican-controlled state senate. In 1953 Diggs took aim at an office from which he felt he had a better chance of influencing policy. He decided to campaign for a seat on the Detroit City Council.

NO BLACK PERSON had ever been elected to the nine-member Detroit City Council. Other prominent Black leaders, including Diggs's father (twice), had tried, but under Detroit's "reform" system of city governance, all city council members were elected "at-large" representing the entire city rather than a single ward or district. The system was also nonpartisan. Since voters could select up to nine candidates, the system favored contenders with ample resources and citywide appeal.[13] In 1950, only 16 percent of Detroit's 1.8 million residents were Black, so a successful Black candidate needed to draw considerable support from white Detroiters.

Several years earlier, Reverend Charles A. Hill, the pastor of Hartford Avenue Baptist Church, which had the largest Black Baptist congregation on the city's West Side, nearly became the first Black councilor. In 1945, Hill benefited from the liberal-Black-labor coalition and finished ninth in the primary election, advancing to the general election. But the general election took a nasty racist turn. Mayor Edward Jeffries, who had once projected himself as a friend to Black Detroiters, employed an "effective race baiting" reelection campaign focused on housing. Hill lost, and ran unsuccessfully in 1947 and 1949, crushed by an avalanche of voters from the city's white neighborhoods.[14]

In the wake of World War II, simmering racial tensions in Detroit surfaced around the issue of housing. The explosion of the city's population during World War I, and again during World War II, created a housing shortage that was ongoing.[15] Racial tensions had been a particular concern among city leaders since the summer of 1943 when Detroit became the site of a two-day race riot. President Franklin Roosevelt sent in federal troops to quell the violence. Nine whites and twenty-five Black residents died.[16]

Despite the riot and its aftermath, Black people still poured into Detroit searching for work and exacerbating the city's already tight housing market. Housing for Black residents was especially inadequate, substandard, and overcrowded. White homeowners fought to keep their neighborhoods exclusively white, creating "neighborhood associations" that effectively prevented Black people from moving in.[17] As a result, in Detroit's municipal elections, the liberal-Black-labor coalition fractured as fear of housing integration triumphed over workplace solidarity.[18] Still, Diggs Jr. believed he had a chance to become one of nine city councilors and to effect change.

LATE IN THE SUMMER OF 1952, after securing his renomination to another two-year term in the state senate, Diggs Jr. began to position himself to run for a seat on the city council. He began to speak out more on issues directly affecting Detroit, like open housing, and in September, before a meeting attended by over 500 residents, Diggs argued in favor of keeping rent control in place.[19] The council would later vote five to four to allow rent control to expire. However, had Diggs Jr. been a member, rent control might have remained in place.

In the summer of 1953, Diggs Jr. became one of more than 100 candidates for the nine-member city council and one of only four Black candidates. Due to his seat in the state senate, Diggs was by far the most prominent. "When I ran for the city council, I did not have to give up my senate seat, because it was a separate year," Diggs explained years later.[20] He established a campaign committee composed of key Black leaders from across the city. He named his father as campaign manager.

Diggs Jr.'s campaign strategy was straightforward—turn out Black voters and appeal to as many white voters as possible. Since Black people constituted only 23 percent of the city's total population in 1953, victory required white voters' support. Diggs's campaign made an overt, biracial appeal to whites. His platform not only embraced urban reform, including addressing the city's slum housing, but also stressed policing in crime-ridden neighborhoods, expanding recreational facilities, abolishing the tax on the city-owned Detroit Street Railways, and providing adequate medical care for Detroit residents, policies that appealed to both Black and white voters.[21]

Diggs Jr. campaigned as a moderate candidate, appealing to voters across the city's political spectrum. Throughout the campaign, he stressed that "fair play" dictated Black representation on the nine-member city council, and he made direct appeals to white liberals.[22] His advertisements in the local newspapers included the caption, "Make our city government fully representative. Full representation is just plain good business," and prominently featured a picture of two hands—one Black, the other white—each with a firm grip on the other.[23] The powerful and influential CIO-PAC (Congress of Industrial Organizations–Political Action Committee) endorsed Diggs as did the American Federation of Labor (AFL), a more conservative union representing railroad and craft workers, and the campaign hoped the endorsements would help Diggs gain more white support.[24] Several white liberal activist groups, including the Americans for Democratic Action and Volunteers for Adlai Stevenson, also endorsed Diggs in the primary although none of Detroit's mainstream daily newspapers followed suit.[25]

In the September 1953 primary, Diggs Jr. finished sixth, receiving 57,626 primary votes, more than any Black candidate in history and enough to carry him into the general election, where the top eighteen finishers would run for nine open seats. The *Michigan Chronicle* called Diggs's primary finish "a startling run."[26]

The heavy turnout of Black voters helped Diggs Jr.'s performance immensely. The *Michigan Chronicle* observed that "Diggs's votes came primarily and overwhelmingly from the Negro wards of the city," while the *Detroit Free Press* noted that Diggs Jr. "maintained a steady front running position in the primary by bringing out the frequently apathetic Negro vote."[27] Diggs also benefited from "single-shot" voting in the heavily Black wards, a strategy in which the campaign quietly urged Detroit's Black voters to cast a ballot for Diggs only and for no other candidate. The tactic gave Diggs a "substantial boost" in the primary election.[28]

In the general election, the eight incumbent candidates were considered locks for reelection, leaving the question of the ninth seat up for grabs between Diggs and Blanche Parent Wise, a white businesswoman. Wise was a forty-six-year-old mother, wife, and former schoolteacher who in 1939 became the only woman to sell cars and trucks for Ford Motor Company. A racial conservative who opposed open housing, she had been involved in civic affairs for many years and presented herself as a spokesperson for small business owners. In several previous runs for office, she had run competitively and showed promise as a politician. All three daily newspapers endorsed Wise in the general election, as did many white civic organizations, and Wise publicly courted Republican voters.[29]

Meanwhile Diggs Jr., knowing he had to have white voters' support to win, continued to emphasize his interracial appeal, stressing interracial progress and brotherhood.[30] The liberal-Black-labor coalition again provided financial support to turn out voters throughout the city, including from the city's heavily white union households. Diggs labored to remind Black voters to return to the polls again in November, campaigning throughout Black Bottom and Paradise Valley. He also targeted Black voters on the city's West Side, a corner of Black Detroit that was not as familiar with the Diggs name. Diggs visited Black churches across the city. Black ministers endorsed him. The *Michigan Chronicle* observed that Diggs's candidacy had "whipped up considerable interest in an otherwise lagging campaign."[31]

On Election Day, November 3, 1953, Diggs Jr. felt confident. Diggs, his wife, and his parents joined a large crowd of white and Black supporters at the Black-owned Gotham Hotel to await the outcome of the election, hoping to celebrate. The first of the city's twenty-two wards to report results came from the city's East Side, and it was soon clear that the Black community had responded to the campaign's get-out-the-vote effort. Diggs Jr. finished in first place among all candidates in wards one, three, five, seven, and eleven, all wards Diggs Jr. and his father before him had represented in the state senate, all places where Black Detroiters had long struggled for safe, affordable housing, where city services were neglected, and where tensions between city police and residents had long simmered.

Early evening returns showed Diggs Jr. with an "impressive lead" as he outperformed both Wise and an incumbent.[32] When Diggs finished second in wards eight and nine, two majority-white wards, it looked like he was on track to victory. As Charles J. Wartman of the *Michigan Chronicle* explained,

"As precinct tallies rolled in from all sections of the city, Diggs jumped into one of the pacesetters' positions with less than half the precincts reported. His position improved to fifth with 1,000 precincts [out of a total of 1,480] reporting, and it appeared that the thirty-year-old legislator was on the verge of making political history in Detroit."[33] At the hotel, excitement filled the air among the throng of Diggs's Black and white supporters as they prepared to celebrate.

As his election seemed more certain, Diggs Jr. and Juanita rushed from the hotel with a newspaper photographer to have pictures taken of the newly elected councilman. As Juanita recalled years later, "We went home to take pictures with the photographer; to take pictures with the kids, they had told him he had won."[34] One such photograph of a visibly happy Diggs on the telephone receiving voting results, flanked by his smiling wife and parents, later appeared on the front page of the *Michigan Chronicle*. The caption under the photograph noted that at the time it was taken, Diggs "was running comfortably in fifth place and had been all but conceded a seat on the Council."[35]

While the photographer was snapping more pictures, the telephone rang. It was Papa Diggs. "We got a call from his father from the headquarters, where they were counting the tallies, saying he had lost the campaign," Juanita Diggs remembered.[36] As late returns came in from two predominantly white wards, wards strongly opposed to open housing, Diggs Jr.'s lead over Wise quickly evaporated. A close analysis of the election later concluded that "the all-out effort against Diggs" in these white wards "spelled Diggs's defeat."[37] As the *Michigan Chronicle*'s Wartman noted, Diggs failed to "overcome the racial and class prejudices which for so long . . . dominated elections to office in Detroit."[38] Diggs finished tenth, losing to Wise by just over 5,000 votes. After a recount, on Monday, November 23, 1953, Diggs conceded defeat.[39] Diggs had lost his first electoral contest, but this loss would only increase his resolve.

A glance at the front page of the *Michigan Chronicle* that day would show why: Diggs Jr. shared the front page with stories recounting instances of racial discrimination not only in Detroit and Michigan, but throughout the United States. Inspired in part by the emerging civil rights movement occurring in the South, Black Detroiters were adopting a heightened sense of racial consciousness. Diggs Jr. was young, ambitious, and talented. His speaking ability, his intelligence, his background, and his demeanor—everything about him—indicated that he was a future leader. The excitement in the Black community and the turnout of Black voters in his city council race proved that the Diggs name remained a potent mobilizing force.

In short order he would decide to run for the US Congress.

Chapter 6
I COULD BEAT THIS GUY

IN THE WEEKS THAT FOLLOWED his defeat in the city council race, Diggs Jr. pondered his political future and considered his next move. The Republican majority in the state senate frustrated his desire to effect change, and it would be four long years before another city council race. Although Diggs had lost, it was obvious to everyone that, at only age thirty-one, Diggs had a bright future in politics.

Diggs Jr. realized, too, that he had appeal outside the Black community, at least in those sections of the city where he was well-known. The Thirteenth US Congressional District comprised six wards on Detroit's West Side and the small city of Highland Park, an enclave city surrounded by Detroit. In the city council race, Diggs outperformed Blanche Parent Wise in four of those six wards even though, cumulatively, the voting population was over 60 percent white.

Examining the vote totals even more closely revealed something startling. Diggs Jr.'s vote totals from those six wards were nearly 10,000 more than the total number of votes the incumbent US congressman George D. O'Brien had garnered in the 1952 Democratic primary, even when one included O'Brien's votes from Highland Park. "I concluded I could beat this guy," Diggs recalled decades later.[1]

O'Brien, a fifty-one-year-old attorney and veteran of World War I, was first elected to Congress in 1936, riding the huge Democratic wave of support that reelected Franklin D. Roosevelt to a second term and defeating the thirteen-year incumbent Republican Clarence McLeod. A New Deal Democrat, O'Brien supported Roosevelt's programs, and his voting record was typically liberal. He had worked with Black leaders during the Sojourner Truth Housing Project controversy of 1942 to secure assurances from federal officials that the housing project would have Black occupants as originally recommended; he voted to extend rent control; and he supported the adoption of a permanent federal fair employment practices commission. Throughout much of his congressional career, the CIO and the AFL unions endorsed O'Brien's election campaigns.[2]

From 1936 through 1952, O'Brien won every Democratic primary in the Thirteenth District; but he had not been quite so successful in general elections. After winning the seat in 1936, in 1938, he lost the general election to McLeod. O'Brien regained the seat in 1940, but in 1946 he was defeated by Republican Howard Coffin, only to regain the seat again in 1948. As the district and state began to trend Democratic, O'Brien easily won reelection in the next two elections, and by 1954 the seat was considered reliably Democratic.

O'Brien was well-liked by the Democratic establishment, but he was not very dynamic.[3] The election losses in 1938 and 1946 had interrupted his seniority status in the House and O'Brien had not accumulated the level of political clout usually bestowed upon a veteran member of Congress.

The seat was ripe for the picking.

THE GREAT BLACK MIGRATION to Detroit and other Northern cities had transformed local Democratic and Republican Party politics. As Black voters were segregated into racially defined political districts, ambitious Black politicians began to realize that they finally had a legitimate shot at being elected to Congress.[4]

In Detroit, even though four of Michigan's seventeen congressional districts were centered in the city, and three of the four had sizable and growing Black populations, Black candidates were rare. The First Congressional District, comprising the city's East Side, had the largest Black population. However, Black candidates did not attempt to win election until 1932, when Charles A. Mahoney, a Black attorney, became the Republican nominee.[5] By 1930, the predominantly white, Polish American city of Hamtramck was added to the First District, making it difficult for Black candidates to win.

Charles Diggs Jr.'s decision to run for Congress in the neighboring Thirteenth Congressional District, on Detroit's West Side, acknowledged the city's changing demographics. The oblong-shaped district ran through the heart of Detroit, from the Detroit River to Eight Mile Road, bounded on the east by Hastings Street, a main thoroughfare in the heart of Detroit's Black community, and Wabash Street on the west. In the 1930s and 1940s, Black settlement had expanded beyond Black Bottom and Paradise Valley, west of Hastings Street, to parts of the lower West Side. A few Black people also lived in the Eight Mile–Wyoming area of the district, a neighborhood centered on the intersection of Tireman Avenue and Grand Boulevard. Collectively, the district was racially and ethnically mixed. In addition to Black voters, it included significant numbers of Greeks, Mexicans, Jews, Scandinavians, Chinese, Maltese, Lebanese,

Italians, and significantly, Irish, who were better organized politically than the other ethnic groups. The district was approximately 60 percent white.

Yet more and more ambitious Black politicians had thrown their hats into the Thirteenth District's Democratic primary. As the Black population continued to grow, O'Brien faced more challenges from Black Democrats. All were unsuccessful. But each time the Black candidates' percentages of the vote increased.

On January 20, 1954, Diggs Jr. announced his candidacy for the Thirteenth Congressional District.[6] Papa Diggs initially did not believe his son could win over enough white voters to defeat the veteran incumbent. Juanita Diggs was surprised by her husband's decision. As she recalled, Charles "probably came home and announced that he was running for Congress."[7]

From the beginning, Diggs Jr. took a global view regarding Black political leadership. His candidacy stressed that the country's continued treatment of Black people as second-class citizens tarnished America's reputation as an example of democracy, and he argued that his election would send a positive signal to people around the world about America's place as a democracy.[8]

However, Diggs Jr. focused on local issues, especially on the need to increase working-class wages. "Decent wages and working conditions for labor is the key to a healthier economy and we will not enjoy continued prosperity until the minimum level of our economy is elevated," Diggs announced.[9] He also promised to return more federal dollars back to Michigan to fund state roads and highways, all proposals that appealed to Black and white voters alike.

From the start, Diggs Jr. was clearly O'Brien's most formidable Democratic primary challenger to date. In addition to being well-known, well-qualified, and a proven vote-getter, Diggs had three accomplished political strategists guiding his candidacy. As campaign chair, the elder Diggs remained well-respected in the Black community. Asa Canadia, the campaign's general manager, worked for the House of Diggs and was "well-known in local Black political circles as a 'behind-the-scenes-man,'" while Lillian Hatcher, the campaign's assistant general manager, was a pioneer within the UAW-CIO.[10] In 1944 Hatcher had been appointed to the staff of the UAW's Fair Employment Practices Division, becoming the first Black woman to serve on the staff of an international union, and she was also active in Democratic Party politics. Those relationships made her invaluable.[11]

Diggs Jr. was also becoming his own man. It had been his idea to challenge O'Brien, and he had clear views about campaign strategy and how best to present himself to voters. Campaign plans in his own handwriting outline a two-fold strategy. He would try to run up massive majorities in the district's heavily Black precincts and simultaneously run a moderate campaign directed at liberal whites, women, and younger voters by focusing on issues such as unemployment and improving public roads.[12]

To help him raise the necessary resources, Diggs Jr. convened a twenty-member "finance committee," half of whom were women such as Hatcher.[13] Finance committee members included Dr. Robert C. Bennett (chair), the personal physician of former heavyweight boxing champion Joe Louis; night club impresario Sunnie Wilson who, along with Diggs Sr., Harold Bledsoe, and Joseph Craigen, had recruited Black voters into the Michigan state Democratic Party back in the early 1930s; Dr. Guy O. Saulsberry, the founder and medical director of Kirkwood General Hospital, at the time Detroit's only Black hospital; James Del Rio, owner of one of the largest Black-owned real estate companies in Detroit; Roderick G. Schuster, owner of a Detroit insurance agency; and Attorney William T. Patrick Jr., who in 1957 would become the first Black person elected to the Detroit City Council.

DIGGS JR. UNDERSTOOD he had to register as many Black voters as possible, and he focused his efforts not just on new voters but on making sure newer district residents changed their existing registration to match their current residency. The *Michigan Chronicle* reported he was "spending much of his time explaining that he [was] not running for reelection to the state senate."[14] Restaurants, pool halls and other Black businesses provided a public space for Black residents to discuss the historic campaign.

The campaign also made a concerted effort to mobilize the Thirteenth District's Black church community. Diggs wrote ministers of twenty-two "leading churches" personal letters asking them to encourage their parishioners to support Diggs and register to vote.[15] Among those congregations was the 7,800-member New Bethel Baptist Church, pastored by the Reverend C. L. Franklin, the father of legendary singer Aretha Franklin.[16] During Sunday worship services ministers often allowed Diggs to make a personal appeal before their congregants.

The *Michigan Chronicle* covered Diggs's campaign extensively. News articles and opinion columns about the campaign typically described Diggs Jr. as "the hardworking senator" who was "highly respected" among his colleagues for "getting things done."[17] The Diggs campaign naturally purchased political advertisements in the *Michigan Chronicle* as well.

The resources of the House of Diggs also played a key role in the campaign. Diggs continued to host the weekly Sunday radio program, and he urged his largely Black listeners to register to vote. If someone needed to register to vote, they could call the House of Diggs to arrange transportation, perhaps in a funeral home limousine.

To reach white voters Diggs Jr. had to negotiate the difficult terrain of biracial politics, just as he had in the council race. Diggs decided that the campaign would produce "two types" of campaign literature.[18] One would target Black voters with "positive emotional appeals to Negroes on the basis of group representation, group recognition, [and] Negro contributions to the development of the United States."[19] The other, aimed primarily at white voters, would be "strongly interracial, based upon the principles of goodwill, Diggs's legislative experience, training, and his statesmanship."[20] Diggs continued to emphasize the same interracial themes of "brotherhood" and "fairness" as he had in his city council campaign. Diggs also made certain that campaign literature featured two photographs of him: "One military picture and one civilian picture."[21]

Several other factors worked in Diggs Jr.'s favor. The UAW-CIO, the city's largest and most powerful labor union, chose to remain neutral in the Democratic primary, thus providing a major boost for Diggs. As a reporter for the *Detroit Free Press* noted, the UAW-CIO's neutrality made "the outcome more uncertain than ever."[22]

In addition, Diggs Jr. astutely timed his campaign. Although the US House was scheduled to adjourn on July 31, just before the August 3 primary, the Eighty-Third Congress stayed in session longer than usual. O'Brien was pinned down in Washington, DC, leaving him only limited time to campaign in Detroit.[23] Consequently, O'Brien was unable to respond quickly to Diggs's insurgent candidacy.

By late summer, Diggs Jr. seemed to have tremendous momentum. The *Michigan Chronicle* confidently reported that "experienced election forecasters" agreed that Diggs was "a certain winner" in the Democratic primary.[24] Yet Diggs remembered that he had lost the city council race by a scant 5,000 votes, and he did not want to fall short again. As DuBose notes, "Diggs campaigned with a vengeance. He was fiercely aggressive."[25] In the weeks leading up to primary election day, Diggs began to use the slogan "It's in your hands," reminding voters of the price of indifference from his close defeat in the past city election.[26]

ON AUGUST 3, the day of the primary election, Detroiters awakened to a beautiful summer morning, guaranteeing a good turnout from Diggs's enthusiastic supporters. When the results rolled in that evening, Congressman O'Brien did not know what hit him. Diggs Jr. trounced the incumbent, winning with 61 percent of the total votes cast versus O'Brien's 28 percent. Local observers were stunned by the margin and called Diggs's victory an "upset."[27] Charles J. Wartman, the editor of the *Michigan Chronicle*, reported that "those closest" to Diggs "expressed surprise at the great victory."[28]

A significant number of Democrats abandoned Congressman O'Brien in the primary. One observer emphasized that had the UAW-CIO supported O'Brien instead of staying neutral, Diggs might not have won the primary.[29] But Charles J. Wartman argued, "Somewhere along the line [O'Brien] had failed to represent the people of the Thirteenth district as they should be represented."[30] Change was necessary. Charles Diggs Jr. represented change.

Diggs Jr.'s primary victory overwhelmingly reaffirmed the Black community's trust and pride in his candidacy. They wanted Charles Diggs Jr. to serve as their voice in Washington, DC. Diggs's biracial appeal garnered enough white support to lead to a landslide, making victory in November appear within reach. With a victory in the general election, he would become the nation's third Black congressman—joining William Dawson and Adam Clayton Powell—and the only Black congressman ever elected to represent a majority-white congressional district.

Charles Diggs Jr. became the first Black man nominated by the Democratic Party for a US House seat from Michigan. The editors of the *Michigan Chronicle* offered that Diggs's nomination was "long overdue" and provided an opportunity for the state to demonstrate democracy at work. "That metropolitan Detroit, long the locale of one of the nation's largest Negro populations should finally get around to sending a Negro to the Congress, is in itself remarkable," the newspaper proclaimed.[31] John Roxborough, one of Diggs's closest friends, wrote a letter to the editor calling Diggs's nomination "a victory for Americanism," an affirmation "that the communist propaganda theme—that American Democracy is a sham and a fraud—is false."[32]

Across the country, Black newspapers reported on Diggs Jr.'s nomination with pride.[33] Yet despite all the excitement, Diggs projected his characteristic calm and even demeanor. He told the *Michigan Chronicle* that he was grateful that Democratic voters had given him "the best chance of any candidate to date of becoming Michigan's first Negro congressman."[34]

To make history, however, he would still have to defeat not only the Republican nominee, Landon Knight—the son of John S. Knight, editor, and publisher of the *Detroit Free Press*—but the tidal forces of racism that still ran through Detroit politics. There was a real sense that he could win, but Diggs Jr. and others in his campaign agreed with the editors of the *Michigan Chronicle* who predicted that the general election campaign would be "an all-out fight."[35]

The battle for a seat in Congress was not yet over.

Chapter 7
THE BATTLE FOR CONTROL OF THE HOUSE

ON FRIDAY EVENING, OCTOBER 8, 1954, hundreds of business and political power brokers from across Detroit poured into the main ballroom of the downtown Leland Hotel. They were there for a "kick-off dinner" to raise funds for Charles Diggs Jr.'s general election bid for the US Congress. The event was so well-attended, reported the *Michigan Chronicle*, that many of the guests "overflowed into the halls."[1] After all, a victory for Charles Diggs Jr., for those who dared dream it possible, would be historic.

Charles Diggs Jr. worked the crowd with his trademark solemnity; yet outside the hotel, there was trouble. Moments before, as Diggs and his guests arrived, they had been greeted by supporters of his Republican rival, Landon Knight, carrying placards denouncing Diggs Jr. as an "anti-labor" businessman, and passing out handbills attacking the business practices of the House of Diggs. Papa Diggs became enraged and believed that Knight's forces had hoped that someone would start a fight and generate negative press coverage for his son. Diggs Sr. called a couple of newspaper reporters to warn them about what might take place. No such disruption occurred, but an angry elder Diggs fired off a two-page statement to the *Michigan Chronicle* criticizing Knight's tactics as "a new low in political campaigns."[2]

Regardless of the opposition-supporters outside the hotel, as Diggs Jr. moved through a sea of well-heeled Democratic leaders and party faithful crowding the main ballroom, the air felt charged and upbeat as he reached out to shake all the hands thrusted toward him. Near the end of the evening a succession of speakers, including Roy Reuther, director of the UAW-CIO Political Action Committee and brother of UAW president Walter Reuther, lavished Diggs with compliments, praising him for his allegiance to Michigan's working class, his tireless fight for civil rights, and his solid moral character. Then the candidate stepped to the podium. As he did, the crowd of more than 500 Black and white movers and shakers roared its approval of the young politician.

Diggs Jr. waited graciously for the cheering to subside, and then, his tone resolute, issued a full-throttled critique of the Republicans' handling of the economy and urged "timely and courageous action to prevent further decline."[3] Some 142,000 people were currently out of work across Michigan. As Diggs emphatically told his audience, "We cannot afford to entrust our destiny to those who either do not understand or do not appreciate the basic tenets of the greatness that is America."[4]

DIGGS JR.'S PATHWAY to Congress would not be easy. It was hard enough already for a Black candidate to win a congressional election, but in 1954 it would be even more difficult. Congress was up for grabs and, therefore, so was control of the country. The Republicans, under President Dwight Eisenhower, held the White House and a majority in both houses of Congress. But GOP control of the Eighty-Third Congress was tenuous; their margin in the US House was only four votes, and they held the US Senate by only a single seat. As a result, national Republican Party leaders, desperate to expand their margin, were ready to stage a no-holds-barred fight for Michigan's Thirteenth District seat. Although Diggs Jr., with his silver tongue and his family's reputation, admittedly made a strong contender, Republican leaders figured thirty-year-old Landon Knight II had just the right stuff to beat him.

Landon Knight was the son of John Knight, owner, editor, and publisher of the *Detroit Free Press*, one of Detroit's three daily newspapers. His grandfather, Charles Landon Knight, the family patriarch, had been a Republican member of the US House of Representatives, representing Ohio's Fourteenth District from 1921 to 1923.[5] John Knight inherited the *Akron Beacon Journal* from his father in 1933 and purchased the *Free Press* in 1943. He would go on to organize the second largest newspaper group in the country, Knight-Ridder.

Other than being the son of the *Free Press* publisher, "Lanny," as many called him, had no significant record of personal accomplishment. Afflicted by polio as a boy, his mobility required the use of either crutches or a wheelchair. Knight was not a particularly good student and struggled through his courses in college, where he developed a reputation as a heavy drinker.[6] After working various editing jobs in Michigan and New York, by the spring 1950 he became a staff editor at the *Free Press*. In 1951, he ran for elected office for the first time, coming in second to former congressman Clarence McLeod in the Republican primary for the Thirteenth Congressional District. In 1954, after McLeod retired, Knight easily won the Republican primary. His birthright seemed to be the only logic to his candidacy; he was the quintessential "establishment" candidate—uncontroversial and easy to swallow, especially for voters looking for an excuse not to vote for a Black candidate.

Even though the Thirteenth Congressional District skewed Democratic, it was approximately 60 percent white, and Republicans thought Knight could defeat Diggs Jr. Knight portrayed himself as a supporter of labor, plugging his membership in the Newspaper Guild. "As a member of the CIO, I know the problems of those who work for a living," he told reporters.[7] Knight reached out to union members claiming that he "once risked his job attempting to organize a union in Syracuse, N.Y."[8] He hoped his candidacy would splinter the union vote and that traditionally Democratic white union voters who were reluctant to vote for a Black candidate would cast their ballots for him instead. Knight charged that Diggs had an "anti-labor record" as a businessman, and he urged union voters to break away from the liberal-Black-labor coalition and Democratic Party.[9] He challenged voters to "pick men, not parties."[10]

Diggs Jr. countered by laying out a vision rooted not in race, but in mainstream Democratic Party politics, hammering the Republicans on unemployment and the economy, painting them as a party of bigwigs indifferent or insensitive to the plight of unemployed workers and too self-absorbed to empathize with the struggles of everyday Americans.[11] He blasted Eisenhower and the Republicans in Congress for eliminating or cutting many programs that had helped average Americans. The GOP, Diggs claimed, had "curtailed" public housing programs and replaced them with a "cut-rate housing plan which leaves the poor and lower middle-class groups out in the cold."[12] Diggs supported a program that would extend federal housing programs into the private market, and he vowed to support an increase in the federal minimum wage from seventy-five cents per hour to one dollar and twenty-five cents per hour.[13]

Race, however, remained central in the election. In the wake of the recent Supreme Court decision in *Brown v. Board of Education*, issues of racial equality were part of the national conversation. Ever so slowly, the Eisenhower administration was showing signs of moving the Republican Party toward racial reconciliation.[14] There was, for instance, President Eisenhower's appointment of Black Americans to high-ranking government positions, such as Ralph Bunche as deputy secretary general of the United Nations. Eisenhower also pushed to end racial segregation in the District of Columbia, a city in which 35 percent of the population was Black, and he prodded military officials to implement President Truman's order to bring racial equality to the armed forces.

However, Eisenhower distanced himself from the *Brown* decision. He would not publicly endorse the Court's ruling and did not speak to the moral issue behind the *Brown* decision, which incensed Black voters; in addition, he refused Black leaders' request for a meeting to discuss Southern racial affairs. Consequently, Black Americans began to consider him insensitive or, worse, a supporter of Jim Crow. Black voter support for the Republican Party continued to deteriorate.[15]

Diggs Jr. took care not to present himself as a racial militant. One newspaper reporter who covered the campaign correctly described Diggs as embracing "middle-of-the-road principles."[16] Diggs sometimes would even "give due credit" to President Eisenhower for, as Diggs put it, "continuing to foster" efforts to improve race relations.[17] However, Diggs made clear that if he were elected to Congress he would "vigorously resist any effort to circumvent federal judicial decisions outlawing segregation" in education, housing, and other areas.[18]

Landon Knight traveled the district in a house trailer, speaking glowingly of President Eisenhower and his policies and linking his candidacy with the former war hero. "President Eisenhower has more feeling and warmth for people than any president in my lifetime," Knight declared. "His program has brought wide benefits to all classes of citizens."[19] Especially when speaking before Black audiences, Knight pointed to the number of Black Americans appointed to high positions within Eisenhower's administration. He reminded voters that segregationist Democrats in Congress were the major obstacles to the adoption of federal civil rights laws. "Both parties stand for equal opportunity. It belongs to you, the voters, to decide what man, not what party, will best represent you in Congress," Knight told the Black congregation at the Thompson Avenue Baptist Church.[20]

In mid-October Diggs Jr. and Knight met in a debate that was broadcast on local radio. Knight claimed that in 1950, during the Truman administration, 1.5 million more people were unemployed than under Eisenhower. He maintained that Eisenhower and the Republican Congress were "advancing a constructive program" to keep the economy moving.[21] Diggs countered that "wages and salaries were down 7.5 billion dollars from a year ago. Farm income has fallen two billion dollars in two years." Diggs said Knight and other Republicans "refused to admit we are in the midst of economic chaos."[22]

When Knight noted the relatively high number of Black appointees in Eisenhower's administration and argued that the *Brown* decision "had come after the Republicans moved into Washington," Diggs Jr., the experienced debater, was prepared.[23] He skillfully rebutted Knight on *Brown* and highlighted the issue the Democrats believed was the GOP's major weakness—the national economy. "I am sure Negroes are filled with pride as a result of the [Republican] appointments," Diggs retorted, "but they cannot eat them."[24]

Knight's appeal to union voters was hamstrung by the Republican Party's general antagonism toward labor unions. Meanwhile, the liberal-Black-labor coalition was fully behind Diggs Jr. The largest single contribution to Diggs's campaign came from the UAW-CIO, constituting nearly half of all the funds raised.[25] Diggs also got a big boost of union support when Ford Local 600, a largely white UAW local that represented more than 55,000 workers, threw its powerful weight behind his candidacy.

Diggs Jr. continued to work his base, mining the Black community for votes, writing personal letters to local clergymen, and visiting a different church every Sunday. In late October, the Black congressmen William Dawson of Chicago and Adam Clayton Powell Jr. of Harlem came to Detroit (on separate visits) to campaign for Diggs, each man appealing to a different set of voters.[26] From the pulpit of Ebenezer Baptist Church, Powell whipped up the crowd with his high-powered rhetoric and screaming, "Elect Charlie Diggs! Detroit needs him! Michigan needs him! The world needs him!"[27]

The campaign received another boost when Eisenhower's defense secretary, the former head of General Motors, Charles Wilson, came to Detroit for a Republican congressional campaign dinner. He told a partisan crowd that he opposed further government aid to the unemployed, saying, "I have lots of sympathy for those without jobs. But I have always liked bird dogs better than kennel-fed dogs myself, you know, one who'll get out and hunt for food rather than sit on his fanny and yell."[28] Wilson's intemperate comments made headlines, and Democrats and labor leaders jumped all over them, chastising Wilson for comparing unemployed workers to dogs.

Knight knew his best hope was to chip away Democratic support among white voters, and it appeared to be working. *Detroit Free Press* public opinion analyst Samuel Lubell wrote a series of articles about the 1954 congressional elections, and in the final weeks of the campaign Diggs Jr.'s campaign learned that Lubell's researchers had conducted thirty-nine interviews of "mostly white-collar whites" in an area of the Thirteenth District and reported that "of the 27 respondents who voted Democratic in 1952, 24 stated that they were splitting their ballot for Landon Knight. These twenty-four said that otherwise they would be voting a straight Democratic ticket."[29] In other words, if the interviews were to be believed, white Democratic voters appeared to be shifting to Knight.

During the final weeks, some Knight supporters also distributed what appeared to be overtly racist campaign literature. One letter urged voters "to split your ballot" and warned that, if elected, Diggs Jr. would be "primarily interested in the advancement of the negro [sic] race."[30] A campaign flyer was circulated that included a picture of Diggs that the *Free Press* noted was "smeared," the image defaced. Knight denied responsibility saying it was likely "a printer's error," before adding "I agree with the printed text but certainly not the pictures."[31]

Yet another anti-Diggs leaflet carried pictures of Diggs Jr. and three Democratic candidates for the Michigan Legislature. All but one was Black people.

The text, designed to tap into white voters' fears about Black people moving into their neighborhoods and taking their jobs, stated, "We believe all Negroes must have equal rights. They are entitled to live in any neighborhood, work in stores, offices, and any place of business. We Democrats, if elected, will work for the rights of all Negroes."[32] Community leaders condemned the flyer as an attempt to use race prejudices against Democratic candidates.

During the home stretch, both campaigns pulled out all the stops. On Monday, October 25, nearly a week before Election Day, Stephen A. Mitchell, chair of the Democratic National Committee, flew to Detroit and held a huge rally for Diggs Jr. and other Michigan Democrats in Highland Park.[33] Afterward, Diggs and Mitchell were greeted by more than 500 guests at the Gotham Hotel. Governor Williams, who was running for reelection, also stumped for Diggs, as did Philip Hart, the Democratic nominee for lieutenant governor of Michigan. Wrote Wartman, "Practically the entire Democratic slate campaigned throughout the Thirteenth District in a last-minute effort on behalf of Charles Diggs, Jr."[34]

Not to be outdone, on the Friday before Tuesday's election, the Republicans punched back. President Eisenhower came to Detroit to stump for GOP candidates, the last leg of a hastily arranged, one-day campaign swing to Ohio, Kentucky, Delaware, and Michigan.[35] With Charles Mahoney, the recently-named Black UN delegate and Michigan native standing with him on the stage at city hall, Eisenhower told the huge crowd that the economy was on the upswing and not to listen to the Democrats, whom he called the "prophets of doom and gloom."[36]

On Election Day, November 3, 1954, Detroit voters were greeted with snow flurries and frigid temperatures, a mix known for keeping voters away from the polls. Despite the inclement weather, lines began forming early that morning at voting precincts across the state. Diggs felt confident, and by late afternoon, as the snow flurries subsided, he began to hear good news from the polls.

Diggs Jr. won 66 percent of the votes cast, riding what turned out to be an off-year election wave that swept Democrats into office in Michigan and across the country. Although the outcome of the election was clear early in the evening, Knight waited all night before finally conceding defeat, a reflection of how nasty the campaign had been. Nationally, the Democrats added twenty-nine seats in the House and won the Senate with a two-vote majority. Unlike his experience in the Michigan State Senate, in Congress Diggs Jr. would serve in a majority party.

Diggs Jr. was characteristically calm in victory. Reporters described him as "composed and in a serious mood."[37] One *Detroit Free Press* reporter wrote that Diggs "displayed no evidence of triumphant exultation" about going to

Congress.[38] Rather he was "serious and expressed his determination to do his best to help solve the needs and problems of the people in his district."[39]

Now Diggs Jr. had to face the reality of what his election would mean for his young family, Charles III, age six; Denise, age four; and Alexis, age three. He and Juanita had recently acquired a larger home, and Diggs told reporters that he planned to commute to Washington, saying, "I intend to keep in close touch with the people of the 13th District. I do not intend to move out of the district. I intend to commute from Washington every weekend, and I intend to have an office in my district, competently staffed, where people may come with their problems."[40]

Also, Diggs Jr.'s election to Congress meant his dream of returning to law school would remain unfulfilled. He became resigned to the idea that he would likely never complete his education, later telling reporters that his election likely ended "a secret desire to go to night school to a get a law degree."[41]

Diggs Jr. was fully aware of the enormous responsibility the voters had just bestowed on him. He would go to Washington, DC, as one of just three Black members of Congress, joining Dawson and Powell. Their small number limited their political power and ability to influence legislation, but the prominence of their position on Capitol Hill gave each man a bully pulpit from which to advocate for reforms that would help Black Americans. Charles Diggs Jr. was fully aware he had suddenly become an important national figure. "A lot of people are amazed at our victory, and they wonder why we're not jumping up and down in glee. This is just the first step," Diggs told a Black reporter. "They don't realize just how much responsibility goes with being a pioneer."[42]

Diggs Jr.'s historic victory garnered national attention, worthy of a story from the Associated Press that appeared from Honolulu to Miami. No other House race in the country received such widespread notoriety. The report ran under a variety of headlines, most a variation of "Michigan's First Negro Congressman Elected," and noting his occupation as undertaker. "I intend to work for all these people," said Diggs Jr. to the Associated Press reporter, "It gives me a fine feeling to know I am the choice of such a truly American population."

The *Detroit Tribune* ran a banner headline on the front page that announced boldly "Diggs Jr. to Congress." Even Knight's own paper, the *Detroit Free Press*, could not ignore the significance of the election. The day after the election, Diggs's opponent's newspaper ran a modest but glowing profile of the winning candidate in his home alongside his wife as his three children "romped" nearby.[43]

Mr. Diggs Jr. was going to Washington.

Chapter 8

ABOARD THE DIGGS'S SPECIAL

The Arrival of a New Black Congressman

"THE OLD MAN LIKED to do everything big," a friend of Papa Diggs remembered.[1] Shortly after Charles Diggs Jr.'s historic election victory, the elder Diggs began planning to charter a train to bring hundreds of the younger Diggs's supporters to Washington, DC, to witness the swearing-in of Michigan's first Black congressman. After initially planning a trip for 300, the committee sold more than 400 tickets.[2] The "special excursion" train would leave Detroit the night before the swearing-in, and the $29.50 round-trip ticket included a sightseeing tour of Washington, an informal "congressional ball," and an opportunity to attend the swearing-in ceremony.[3] "The idea of a special train captured the imagination of everybody in Detroit," Papa Diggs's friend added.[4]

Some people warned Diggs Jr. that bringing "a whole train load" of largely Black voters to Washington "might not look dignified to the white folks," and that he risked alienating too many voters in his majority-white congressional district.[5] Diggs and his father, however, were adamant; they wanted Black Detroit to be a part of the celebration.

ON TUESDAY, JANUARY 4, 1955, shortly before 7 p.m., a huge crowd of Diggs Jr.'s supporters and friends gathered at Detroit's Michigan Central Station to witness the departure of the "Diggs's Special." Among the 400 or so passengers were a diverse group of family, personal friends, and business associates of the elder Diggs, Black professionals and working-class men and women from all parts of Detroit. As one auto worker declared, "I wouldn't miss this for nothing."[6]

As the final coach of the fourteen-car train lurched out of the station depot, the crowd of well-wishers seeing them off could see the red-white-and-blue "Diggs, Jr. Congressional Special" insignia mounted on the rear of the train illuminated in the night. Those aboard referred to the charter as "The Freedom Train," a big step forward in the Black American struggle for equality.[7]

"It was a jovial, care-free but extremely orderly group" aboard the Diggs's Special.[8] Sixteen members of the House of Diggs gospel choir and a male quartet provided entertainment. A reporter for the *Pittsburgh Courier* wrote that the refreshment bar "remained crowded but orderly throughout the night," and a special "beauty bar," staffed by professional cosmeticians, was to be available "for the convenience of the ladies during the entire trip."[9]

AT ABOUT NINE O'CLOCK on Wednesday morning, January 5, 1955, the Diggs's Special pulled into Washington's Union Station, and Diggs Jr.'s supporters poured onto the busy concourse and made their way to the east end of the station where a "special platform" had been erected with a podium and a loud speaker blared out the familiar chorus of the "Battle Hymn of the Republic"—"Glory, Glory, Hallelujah, his truth is marching on."[10]

More than 100 of Diggs Jr.'s supporters were already at the station to greet the train, including representatives from the Black republics of Haiti and Liberia and Congressman Adam Clayton Powell. "It was so crowded the regular trains could not leave on time. Other people could not get to their trains," recalled Val Washington, a Black Republican official, who was in Washington on that day.[11]

After William Patrick Jr., a Detroit attorney and friend of Diggs Jr.'s, introduced Powell to the roaring crowd, Powell dashed onto the platform. Powell called Diggs's election "a blow to Communism."[12] Powell told the largely Black crowd that Diggs Jr.'s election "proved to the world that democracy really works in the U.S. Congressman Diggs comes to Washington as a representative of all of the people of his district and not just a colored congressman!"[13] The crowd also heard from Max Osnos, a white Detroit department store executive and a strong supporter of Diggs Jr., underscoring that Diggs represented the entire district.

Charles Diggs Jr. soon arrived in a chauffeur-driven white Cadillac sedan.[14] Dressed in a blue overcoat, dark suit, and white shirt and tie, the young bespectacled congressman-elect received rousing applause when he finally appeared on the podium. As his proud father and beaming mother looked on, Charles Diggs Jr. described his arrival in Washington as an "electrifying and unforgettable experience."[15] Then, in prepared remarks, Diggs spoke with characteristic "earnestness and seriousness" about how his election was a significant step for Black America and a giant leap for democracy around the world.[16] "We must—none of us—forget for one moment that I am here to represent all of the people of my district."[17]

Diggs Jr. mentioned that he had received telegrams of congratulations from Japan, India, Africa, Sweden, and South America. He reminded the crowd that most of the people of the world were people of color who were eager to see if America's actions regarding its own people were consistent with her "pronouncements of equal rights." He called his victory "democracy at its finest hour, a victory for the Constitution, and the Bill of Rights." Said Diggs, "I am proud to stand before you today in the Capital of the United States as a representative of all the people—as a symbol of decent instincts in the hearts of men."[18]

After his speech, Diggs Jr. embraced Juanita and the children, then turned to greet his parents and other family members, friends, and dignitaries. He and his immediate family then piled into the white Cadillac and Powell's waiting car and were driven to the US Capitol building for his swearing-in ceremony at noon.

Most of the crowd from Detroit boarded waiting buses for the planned tour of Washington, DC, including historically Black Howard University, while a smaller group made their way toward Capitol Hill. At least some planned to take taxis. However, they were surprised when they were told that the taxis in front of Union Station were reserved for whites only. The Black taxis were around the corner.[19] Although by 1955 Washington was officially desegregated, in practice Jim Crow still lived on. Washington, DC, was still one of the most segregated cities north of Richmond.

CHARLES DIGGS JR. was the subject of great attention not just in the national press but also in the Black press. The *Baltimore Afro-American*, the *Atlanta Daily World*, and the *Chicago Defender* sent reporters to cover Diggs's arrival on Capitol Hill; the coterie of reporters included the *Defender*'s pioneering journalist Ethel Payne.[20] Trailed by reporters and photographers, Diggs Jr. took his family through "a round of handshaking and pop calling," his proud father "busy as a bee assisting 'Junior' and keeping a fond eye on him," Payne observed.[21]

Their first stop was Diggs Jr.'s new Capitol Hill office. Diggs also said hello to his new staff, including his Detroit-based staffers who had come to Washington for the big day. They included Dorothy Quarker, a thirty-two year-old Black Detroit native who had worked for many years at Detroit's Great Lakes Insurance Company, a Black-owned firm, where she supervised special personnel programs and "gained much recognition for her knowledge of clerical and business procedure."[22] Quarker was Diggs Jr.'s "administrative assistant," today's equivalent to chief of staff, and one of only a few women who held such high staff positions in Congress at the time. She quickly earned Diggs's trust and became his "right hand," reported Ethel Payne.[23]

Next, Diggs Jr. took the family by the suite of Sam Rayburn, the Democratic leader expected to be elected as Speaker of the House. Ethel Payne reported that "the gentlemen from Texas was not only cordial but warmly enthusiastic and even his staff seemed excited by the visit of the new Congressman."[24] Before leaving, however, Diggs asked Rayburn for a favor. Diggs's staff had learned that the hundreds of people who came from Detroit on the Diggs Special would not be able to witness the official swearing-in as the House gallery could not accommodate all his guests. So Diggs asked Rayburn if he would pose for a mock swearing-in that all his supporters could see. Rayburn readily agreed and told Diggs he would meet the group on the steps of the Capitol after the official swearing-in.[25]

INSIDE THE HOUSE CHAMBER, Ralph R. Rogers, the clerk of the House of Representatives, banged his gavel to begin the eighty-fourth session. "The House will be in order!" After the quorum call, the first order of business was the election of the Speaker of the House. Given the Democrat majority, the outcome was already known. Diggs Jr. cast his first vote as Sam Rayburn was elected on party lines over Republican leader Joseph Martin. At 1:30 p.m., Rayburn's small stocky body stood in the House dais toward the overflow crowd and asked Diggs and the other members to rise and to raise their right hand. Rayburn then read the oath aloud. "I do solemnly swear that I will support and defend."

With his six-year-old son standing next to him, Charles Diggs Jr. repeated after Rayburn. At age thirty-two, he was the youngest Black man ever to serve in the US Congress. After taking the oath, Diggs received congratulations from Adam Clayton Powel, William Dawson, Representative John Dingell Sr. (a Detroit Democrat and the longest serving member of the Michigan delegation), Michigan's Democratic governor G. Mennen Williams, and several others.

Then Diggs Jr., with his son in tow, headed out to greet Juanita and other members of his family and they all quickly proceeded outside to the east entrance of the Capitol Building. About 150 of Diggs Jr.'s supporters who had been waiting in "miserable cold drizzle" suddenly erupted in a huge cheer.[26] Soon Speaker Rayburn, wearing a topcoat and a black hat, and joined by Congressman Dingell, greeted the supporters on the steps of the Capitol. When he saw the huge sea of Black faces, Speaker Rayburn quipped, "My goodness, don't I wish I had all these good people in my district."[27] Flanked by Juanita, his parents, and large crowd of supporters, Diggs once again was given the oath of office by Speaker Rayburn. A photo of the mock ceremony later appeared in Black newspapers all over the country.

Diggs Jr. and his entourage then headed to Adam Clayton Powell's office, where the New York congressman held an "open house" in his expansive suite.

There, Diggs, Juanita, and their parents mingled among staff, House members, lobbyists, and others. The "open house" gave Diggs an opportunity to greet A. Philip Randolph, leader of the influential Black union the Brotherhood of Sleeping Car Porters.

Late that afternoon, Diggs Jr. and his party paid a visit to the headquarters of the National Council of Negro Women—an umbrella organization for Black women's membership associations—for a reception honoring the nation's three Black congressmen: Diggs Jr., Powell, and Dawson.

The men were greeted by National Council of Negro Women president Vivian Carter Mason and Mary McLeod Bethune, founder and president-emerita of the council.[28] For young Diggs, it was a tremendous honor to be welcomed by the famous Black educator and political leader whom he had admired for many decades. Long a proponent of interracial goodwill, Mrs. Bethune told the crowd that Diggs's election in a majority-white district was a living example of the progress made around race relations. She explained that "making Democracy work" remained "a challenge" for all those who believed in equality.[29]

Congressmen Powell also spoke and again reminded everyone that Diggs Jr.'s election was a huge victory for the United States in the fight against communism. Then, Congressman Dawson told the crowd that Diggs's election was evidence of the strength of Black voting power.[30]

Congressman Diggs then explained to the crowd of mainly Black women, that his mother was a significant partner with his father in the founding, expansion, and operation of the family's funeral home business. As Mayme Diggs looked on, Diggs told the crowd that his mother always recognized "the close relationship in business and political activity."[31] Then, according to the *Atlanta Daily World*, Diggs Jr. presented to the group "his attractive and youthful mother."[32] Mayme Diggs, so long in the background, was the center of attention and loved every minute of it as the crowd responded with warm applause.

The day ended with a huge celebratory ball at the downtown Dodge Hotel. Shortly after 8 p.m. most of the 400 supporters who came abroad the Diggs's Special began making their way through the entrance of the hotel and into the grand ballroom. As the crowd continued to swell, many of the hotel guests and employees were probably surprised to see such a large crowd of Black people, a rarity in a downtown Washington, DC, hotel. The men were dressed in business suits and many of the women wore elegant rhinestone-studded evening gowns.[33] Congressman Diggs, accompanied by his wife and parents, reportedly "managed to greet each person individually" at the ball.[34]

According to Ethel Payne, "the highlight" of the evening was the appearance of Governor "Soapy" Williams and his wife.[35] Black Detroiters adored the uncompromisingly liberal Williams. Sporting his famous green and white polka-dot bow tie, Williams was given a "rousing ovation" by the largely Black crowd. The governor shook hands for forty minutes before he and his wife took to the dance floor and mingled with the crowd for nearly two hours. Williams brought along several other white Michigan Democrats who were all key players in Michigan's liberal-Black-labor coalition. All came to pay tribute to America's newest Black congressman.

The party lasted past midnight. By 2 a.m. everybody had made their way back to Union Station and aboard the Diggs's Special for the return journey to Detroit, where the *Pittsburgh Courier* reported "the majority of the returning celebrants went straight to sleep . . . content because their 'man' was safely installed in Congress."[36]

After a long day, Diggs Jr. and his family stayed at the Congressional Hotel, across the street from the Cannon House Office Building. Diggs was the first Black lawmaker to live there on a permanent basis. He would live there for about a year.

The Diggs name was now a part of Capitol Hill, a long distance from the Mississippi Delta.

Chapter 9
RETURNING TO THE DELTA

WHEN CONGRESSMAN Charles Diggs Jr. stepped before the podium underneath the enormous canvas circus tent on the outskirts of Mound Bayou, Mississippi, on April 29, 1955, he must have found it difficult to believe. As far as the eye could see, in shirts and ties and Sunday bests, his gaze was returned by a sea of Black faces. Five thousand Black men, women, and children—sharecroppers, day-laborers, cotton farmers, teachers, ministers, and small business owners—crowded under the shade of the huge tent, and another 8,000 outside pressed in as close as they could get.[1] Some arrived by car, some by bus, some by wagon, by truck, or even by mule, and a few, like Congressman Charles Diggs and his father, by airplane to one of the most unique towns in the United States: Mound Bayou.

Although only about 1,300 residents called Mound Bayou home, for a Black man or woman, it was one of the safest cities in the nation, and certainly in the South. Mound Bayou, all 584 acres of it, was one of the few cities in the nation wholly owned and governed by Black Americans. It "stood out as an island of black self-rule in a sea of white supremacy," an example of what life could be if the laws of the land were truly for everyone.[2] Founded in 1887 by former slaves on land once owned by Jefferson Davis's brother, the small community was almost entirely self-sufficient, with its own stores, newspapers, insurance offices, a print shop, a drug store, and every other business one would find in any other small town in America, with one significant difference; in Mound Bayou all these businesses were owned and operated by Black people. Here was one of the few places in America where Black Americans were free to vote, speak their minds, and live without fear of reprisals from whites.

They came to hear Congressman Charles Diggs Jr. deliver the keynote address for the annual meeting of the Regional Council of Negro Leadership (RCNL), to hear a Black man speak his mind clearly and forcefully and without fear. In many ways it would be one of the most important and consequential speeches in Congressman Diggs's life.

THE RCNL, the leading organization for Black civil rights in Mississippi, was the brainchild of Dr. T. R. M. Howard, who also served as president of the organization.[3] A Kentucky native, Howard moved to Mound Bayou in 1941 to become the chief surgeon at the Taborian Hospital, a new facility built and supported by the largest Black voluntary organization in the state. A light-skinned, "tall, heavy man with a mustache, glasses, and a heavy booming voice," "Doc" Howard soon became a leading figure in Mound Bayou.[4] By the late 1940s, he began to use his wealth in a determined effort to defeat Jim Crow. Writing in the mid-1960s, Myrlie Evers lamented, "It is in the Delta that the status of the American Negro today most closely approximates that of slave."[5]

In 1951, Dr. Howard, joined by a group of Black community leaders, many of whom were veterans of World War II, formed the RCNL. The group included Aaron Henry, a Clarksdale pharmacist and a leader of the Progressive Voters League; Reverend George W. Lee, a minister in the small Delta town of Belzoni in Humphreys County; Amzie Moore, a gas station owner from nearby Cleveland, Mississippi; and Medgar Evers, who worked for Howard's insurance company and who had become something of a Howard protégé.[6] As president of the group, Howard became the state's most compelling advocate of Black civil rights.

By the early 1950s, working in careful collaboration with other local Black groups, like the Progressive Voters League, the RCNL claimed credit for the "gradual improvement in the racial climate" in Mississippi.[7] The number of local branches of the NAACP in the state rose, and the number of Black registered voters grew exponentially, rising to 22,000 by 1954 (but still just 4 percent of the eligible Black population). For the first time two Black persons had been selected as jurors for a trial in Greenville. In Indianola and Biloxi, white city officials had even hired a Black policeman to patrol the Black areas of town. The RCNL pressured the head of the state highway patrol to publicly promise that Black motorists would no longer be harassed by his officers.[8]

In this slowly improving racial climate, Dr. Howard and the RCNL began organizing its yearly convention. In 1952, 1953, and 1954, white Mississippi leaders seemed not to mind when thousands of Black people assembled in Mound Bayou to hear Black Northerners like Congressman William Dawson and Thurgood Marshall, the executive director of the NAACP Legal Defense and Educational Fund and lead attorney in the *Brown* case, speak about Black civil rights.

During the gatherings, the program typically featured workshops on civil rights issues and personal testimony from Black Americans who shared their experiences of the litany of barriers they faced in trying to register voters amid the daily humiliation dished out by racist white Mississippians. There was also a celebratory element to the gathering. For many, it was the first time they had ever met with so many others of their own race in an environment free from harassment and intimidation by the authorities. Bands played, food was served, and the attendees marched in a parade, their numbers swelling each year, from 7,000 in 1952 to more than 10,000 by 1954. According to historian John Dittmer, "Whites had not been aroused by these developments because they had become convinced that the racial status quo was no longer threatened."[9]

However, by the spring of 1955, that had begun to change. A year after its landmark school desegregation ruling, the US Supreme Court, in *Brown II*, ordered segregated school systems to comply with the first *Brown* ruling with "all deliberate speed." For white Southerners, this was a direct threat and was considered the first step toward social integration, interracial marriage, and racial equality. The backlash was swift, and nowhere more so than in Mississippi. Senator James O. Eastland declared, "The South will not abide by nor obey this legislative decision of a political court.... We will take whatever steps are necessary to retain segregation in education."[10] By early September 1954, just months after *Brown*, the Citizens' Council movement exploded onto the scene.

First formed in Sunflower County, Mississippi, Senator Eastland's home county, the Citizens' Council movement quickly spread throughout the South. Sharing the same goals as the Ku Klux Klan but claiming to operate "by legal means only," the Councils were led by "respectable" whites—bankers, attorneys, newspaper publishers, physicians, clergymen, and others.[11] "Their membership rolls soon included governors, legislators, and mayors and virtually all who aspired to those offices."[12]

Their strategy was blunt: to use economic pressure to punish anyone who pushed for racial integration or Black civil rights by making it impossible for them to keep a job, get credit, or renew a mortgage. Those who supported school desegregation or who attempted to register to vote were publicly identified. Those who held jobs lost them, found their rent suddenly raised, and their credit cut off. If the activists persisted, some received death threats. Despite Council leaders' public statements denouncing violence, the Councils inspired increasing incidents of violence against Black people. "Whites broke windshields in Negro-owned cars or broke windows in Black businesses, leaving a note in one case saying, 'You n——s paying poll tax, this is just a token of what will happen to you.'"[13] Recalled Aaron Henry, "If whites saw your name on the [voter-registration] list you just caught hell."[14]

On March 31, 1955, Congressman Diggs Jr. took to the floor of the US House and denounced the Citizens' Councils, warning of racial violence. He specifically mentioned the economic pressures directed at "those who are known to be active" in the NAACP and RCNL. The Citizens' Councils, Diggs said, were no different from "their Ku Klux Klan predecessors, kicking up clouds of terror dust." He called on the US Justice Department to conduct "a sweeping investigation.... The Federal Government by its silence... is abdicating its responsibility for the protection" of citizens who only wish to exercise their civil rights.[15] That same day Diggs Jr. wrote to President Eisenhower about his fears that Citizens' Council activities could lead to a race riot.[16] The letter was one of the first of hundreds Diggs would write to American presidents concerning the struggle for civil rights.

DR. HOWARD EXTENDED an invitation to Diggs Jr., and the young congressman readily accepted. Mississippi was Diggs's ancestral home, and the invitation provided him with the opportunity to see where he had come from, accompanied by his father.

After visiting the family graveyard and church in Issaquena County, Diggs Jr. and his father then drove north up Highway 61. When their car crossed the Bolivar County line, just a few miles south of the Mound Bayou town limits, "a contingent of white state policemen" followed them.[17] When they got closer to the center of downtown Mound Bayou, cars were parked along the highway (Main Street) in both directions as far as the eye could see, an indication of the huge crowd that had turned out for Diggs Jr.'s speech.

When Diggs Jr. and his father pulled into the driveway of Dr. Howard's expansive home (where they would spend the night), their host rushed over to greet them. Diggs Jr. shook Howard's hand then gestured at the state police officers. Howard told Diggs and his father not to worry. He said the troopers were there "ostensibly for their protection," but given the recent tensions, he believed "that the troopers were [also] there to monitor the event, and report back to their superiors in Jackson. It was disturbing but not unnerving, since the troopers didn't appear to be anything other than spies."[18] Still, their mere presence was a constant reminder that elsewhere in Mississippi Jim Crow was the law of the land.

Dr. Howard introduced his guests to several leaders attending the convention, a veritable "Who's Who" of the civil rights movement. Many were active in the RCNL, including Aaron Henry, Reverend George Lee, Amzie Moore, and Medgar Evers, who had recently been named director of the Mississippi NAACP.

The program was an all-day affair that began with a "morning session" held prior to Diggs Jr. and his father's arrival for the convention's 1 p.m. "general session."[19] The early session included a "panel discussion on desegregation," and RCNL officers presented committee reports on a wide range of issues, including child welfare, health, race relations, voter registration, and education. Several speakers addressed the crowd, entertainment was provided by the Rust College Singers, and a lunch of fish, chicken, and ribs was served.[20] When representatives of the RCNL passed out voter-registration forms there was a "near riot" as the crowd clamored to exercise their rights as American citizens.[21]

After lunch, Diggs Sr. joined his son on the rostrum with Dr. Howard and other leaders of the RCNL. The crowd sang "My Country 'Tis of Thee." Dr. Howard, himself a splendid orator, gave a powerful opening speech about school desegregation and civil rights. He then presented the Black victims of recent brutal attacks by whites. A schoolteacher from Indianola told how she was beaten after asking to use the restroom at a gas station; and Gus Courts, a local activist, told how the Citizens' Council had deployed economic pressure against him.[22]

One of the most dramatic speakers of the day was the Reverend George Lee, who had earned a reputation among the Black community as "the most militant preacher in the Delta," one who defied conventional standards by preaching about Black voting and civil rights.[23] The fifty-one-year-old Lee was a "tanned-skin, stumpy spell-binder" circuit preacher who pastored four small churches in the surrounding area.[24] In 1952, he became the first Black person since the end of Reconstruction to register to vote in Humphreys County.[25] Reverend Lee told the audience, "Pray not for your mom and pop. They've gone to heaven. Pray you can make it through this hell!"[26] Reverend Lee then made the crowd roar when he declared that Black voters in Mississippi could one day also send a Black man to the US Congress.[27]

Then Wiley A. Branton, one of the few Black attorneys in the South and the man who in 1956 became the principal lawyer representing nine Black children trying to integrate Central High School in Little Rock, Arkansas, stepped to the podium to introduce Congressman Diggs Jr.[28] The roar of the crowd nearly drowned him out as Diggs Jr. made his way to the microphone. A Black congressman was a big deal in Mississippi, where, outside of Mound Bayou, Black people held virtually no public office.

Clearly moved, Diggs Jr. waved to the crowd of 13,000 Black faces. Never had he spoken to a crowd this large and so hungry for his words. The former debate champion cleared his throat and addressed the crowd, speaking slowly and carefully. He began by thanking his hosts and then paid tribute to his father and "emotionally presented" the elder Diggs to the throng.[29] Looking over to his father, Diggs told them that his father was "the man who gave me the courage to continue" the struggle for Black freedom, and he "pledged himself to give his utmost in the fight for human dignity to live up to the dreams of his father and others liked him." The elder Diggs was visibly moved. Years later Congressman Diggs described it as "a thrilling experience," saying, "the Mound Bayou rally had a big impact on me because my father was there. It was the first time I saw my father cry."[30]

Congressman Diggs Jr. told the crowd that his election reflected true democracy and was a "living example" of the changes occurring in America and around the world.[31] Despite white state policemen "within earshot," Diggs spoke forcefully and encouraged the crowd "to fight with growing confidence and growing strength" for social justice and Black freedom.[32] He "challenged Negro leadership in the South to continue its forthright defense of justice for colored people, not only of America but all around the world."[33]

Simeon Booker reported on the convention for *Jet* magazine and later recalled that Congressman Diggs's "deep voice . . . stirred the crowd" as he encouraged them to keep up the fight against the Citizens' Councils.[34] Diggs urged them to contribute money to the emergency fund the NAACP and RCNL had established to fight the Councils' economic reprisals. Diggs also threatened national corporations that conduct business with companies affiliated with the Councils. "All the Negro wants is recognition of his personal dignity," Diggs proclaimed.[35] He pleaded with white people of goodwill to stand up against bigotry and racial hatred. "Man must be reborn in a new spirit or perish in his chosen concepts," he said.[36] "The time for segregation is running out in Mississippi. Victory will ultimately be ours," Diggs shouted.[37] "If we keep up the fight to make democracy live, we will get the justice espoused by Almighty God and the Constitution of the United States."[38]

The crowd roared its approval. The *Chicago Defender* called Diggs Jr.'s speech "a performance which gave proof" of Diggs's "fighting spirit" that left the crowd "spellbound."[39] The *Atlanta Daily World* carried the story on its front page with a huge banner headline, "Victory Will Be Ours, Diggs Tells Mississippi Group."[40] Dr. Howard described the mass meeting as "the most successful in Mississippi history."[41] Diggs later described it as his "first major speech" as a US congressman.[42]

ON MAY 3, 1955, after returning to Capitol Hill, Diggs Jr. again wrote President Eisenhower asking that the Department of Justice and the FBI to investigate the actions of the white Citizens' Councils.[43] The movement was dangerous, Diggs warned. "If the Federal Government does not intervene to protect the Negroes of Mississippi by stamping out these so-called Citizen Councils in the South, beginning in Mississippi, the people of that state will have one of the bloodiest race riots in the history of America."[44] Diggs added, "If the Federal Government stands passively by, it will be responsible for the consequences."

Four days later, on May 7, 1955, Diggs Jr.'s warning to President Eisenhower came to fruition. George Lee, the fiery Delta preacher Diggs had met in Mound Bayou, was murdered in Belzoni, Mississippi, as he drove home late one night; he was gunned down by several whites.[45] Dr. Howard immediately telephoned Diggs Jr. in Washington with the news. "My God," Diggs said to himself, "that's the man they've killed?"[46] Shocked, Diggs contacted the national office of the NAACP and the White House. He also apparently called the Justice Department to report that Dr. Howard's life might be in jeopardy.[47] No one was ever charged with Lee's murder.

The federal government was in no rush to lend a hand. A few weeks later, Deputy Attorney General William Rogers told Diggs Jr., "Our jurisdiction was limited." Rogers later explained, "Jurisdiction in matters such as this is limited to instances in which individuals are deprived of rights, privileges and immunities protected by the Constitution and laws of the United States."[48]

Diggs Jr. continued to speak out, addressing crowds over the next few weeks at the Hampton Institute and at Wilberforce University. He urged Black students to become involved in the political process, saying "Within the ballot box is the key to all doors of opportunity we seek to open."[49]

ON JUNE 24, 1955, Congressman Diggs was awakened in his Washington apartment by an early morning telephone call from Juanita. Papa Diggs had suffered a stroke.[50] He could not talk and was paralyzed on the right side of his body. Congressman Diggs hung up the telephone and arranged to fly back to Michigan to the bedside of his father. The elder Diggs, sixty-one years old, was hospitalized for several weeks. For a few days, "he could not speak, and he was crippled in one leg," Juanita recalled. [51] He was soon able to recover his speech, but his right leg never regained full strength. "His mind was not affected, but he did not have the energy" he had in the past.[52] From that time forward, he would rely more on his son and on others to run and manage his business. Diggs Sr. hired a chauffeur and would walk with a cane for the rest of his life.

When the House adjourned on August 3, 1955, controversial issues were left unsettled. The Republican White House and the Democratic-controlled Congress struggled to reach agreement over critical issues. Diggs had made an impact, but the inability of Congress to move forward on key issues demonstrated just how much work still needed to be done.

Congressman Diggs had been back in Detroit only a few days when he got a call on August 13 from Dr. Howard in Mississippi reporting on another sickening tragedy. Lamar Smith, a Black sixty-three-year-old World War II veteran, had spent Saturday morning distributing voting literature to Black residents in the town square of Brookhaven when he was gunned down in broad daylight on the courthouse steps. Howard told Diggs that Smith was a close friend and had attended Diggs's speech in Mound Bayou. Once again Congressman Diggs called on the Eisenhower administration to investigate the murder of a Black man attempting to exercise his civil rights. However, the White House continued to reply that it was the duty of the states to protect their citizens.

One evening, eleven days later, Emmett Till, a fourteen-year-old Black boy from Chicago who was visiting relatives in the Delta, went to the store to buy bubble gum.

Chapter 10

ON THE SCENE
Diggs at the Trial of
Emmett Till's Murderers

ON AUGUST 31, 1955, one week after Emmett Till went to buy bubble gum, his mutilated and swollen body was found floating in the Tallahatchie River. A huge industrial-size fan had been tied around his neck to anchor his body to the bottom of the dark waters. But he was already dead when he had been placed in the river.[1] "There was a bullet in the boy's skull, one eye was gouged out, and his forehead was crushed on one side."[2]

Precisely what happened remains as murky today as the waters of the Tallahatchie River. But we do know that when Till entered the store in Money, Mississippi, something took place. Carolyn Bryant, a twenty-one-year-old white woman, was alone in the store owned by her twenty-four year-old husband, Roy, when Emmett approached the counter. Bryant later claimed that young Emmett made a sexual advance toward her while showing her a wallet photo of a white girl.[3] However, Emmett's cousins claim that Emmett put the money for his purchase in Carolyn Bryant's hand instead of on the counter, violating a Southern racial custom.[4]

Whatever happened angered Carolyn Bryant to the degree that she ran out to a car to retrieve a gun. At that point, one of the boys yelled, "She's going to get a pistol," and they dashed for their car. Emmett then let out a "wolf whistle."[5] "To this day, I don't know what possessed Emmett to do that," recalled his cousin.[6] The children drove back home unharmed.

At about two in the morning on Sunday, August 28, 1955, Roy Bryant and his half brother, thirty-six-year-old J. W. Milam, armed with pistols, came to the home of sixty-four-year-old Mose Wright, the uncle of Till's mother, where the boy was staying. Wright was awakened from sleep and quickly came to the screened porch. "We're here to talk to you about the boy from Chicago, the one that done talking up at Money," Bryant told Wright.[7] The men pushed their way inside, went to a backroom where Emmett was asleep and forced him to dress. Wright and his wife offered the men money if they left the boy alone. Mose

Wright asked, "Why not give the boy a good whipping and leave it at that? He's only fourteen and he's from up North," hoping they'd excuse his failure to follow customs. Instead, the two men threatened to kill Wright if he made any trouble. They took the sleepy boy out the front door and put him into a waiting pickup truck and disappeared into the dark Mississippi night.[8]

RACIAL TENSIONS in Mississippi, already high, exploded after Till's body was discovered. On September 1, Roy Wilkins, the head of the national NAACP, said, "It would appear by this lynching that the State of Mississippi has decided to maintain white supremacy by murdering children. . . . The killers of the boy felt free to lynch him because there is in the entire state no restraining influence of decency, not in the state capital, among the daily newspapers, the clergy nor any segment of the so-called better citizens."[9]

Within a few days, the LaFlore County Sheriff charged Milam and Bryant with kidnapping and murder. The two admitted to taking the boy but claimed to have turned him loose unharmed. Still, they were indicted for murder by a grand jury in Tallahatchie County, where the alleged crime took place.

Wilkins's statement, coming on the heels of the Supreme Court's school desegregation decision, led many white Mississippians to believe that the trial of Bryant and Milam represented the last defense of white supremacy. Racial tensions were at their boiling point. J. J. Breland, one of the defense attorneys for the two accused men, declared, "If any more pressure is put on us, the Tallahatchie River won't hold all the n——s that'll be thrown in it."[10]

Emmett's body was shipped back to Chicago. Till's mother, Mamie Till-Bradley, chose to have an open-casket funeral, despite the disfiguration of her son's face. The decision would become a pivotal moment in the civil rights movement. Chicago officials estimated that as many as 250,000 people filed past Emmett Till's coffin during a four-day public viewing period.[11] Graphic pictures of Till's swollen and mutilated body appeared in the *Chicago Defender* and in *Jet* magazine. Black newspapers across the country carried the same pictures.

Not a single white newspaper followed suit.[12]

The *Michigan Chronicle* took special interest in Till's murder. In a front-page story under the blaring headline "Lynched Boy Lived Here," the paper reported that Till and his mother had lived for a time in Detroit before returning to Chicago in 1952.[13] Till's mother recalled that Emmett had been excited to go to Mississippi and looked forward to playing with his younger cousins at Mose Wright's home. Mamie Till-Bradley's parents, John and Adie Carthan, lived in Diggs Jr.'s congressional district. A neighbor remembered Emmett as "just a little boy full of life like any little boy."[14]

Even before Congressman Diggs learned of the family's Detroit connection, he "became immediately interested" in the upcoming murder trial.[15] "I think the picture in *Jet* magazine of the Till boy showing his mutilation after he was removed out of the river... was probably one of the greatest media products in the last forty or fifty years," Diggs said in 1986. "That picture stimulated a lot of interest and a lot of anger on the part of blacks all over the country.... The fact that the Till boy was just a child also added to this matter."[16]

On Sunday, September 18, Diggs spoke about the Till case on his weekly radio program. He reminded listeners that he had recently visited the Delta and noted the reprisals, threats, and violence directed at Black civil rights leaders by whites opposed to school desegregation. He announced that the House of Diggs was contributing $2,500 to the NAACP Legal Defense Fund and urged listeners to donate as well. Then Diggs said he "wanted to get a firsthand view at 'justice or lack of justice' in Mississippi" and planned to leave for Mississippi the next day to witness the trial.[17]

Congressman Diggs would be the only representative of the federal government to attend the trial. Diggs doubted whether the all-white jury would convict the white men for murdering a Black boy, saying, "No Negroes are on the Till jury because Negroes are not allowed to become registered [voters] in the county."[18] When the *Michigan Chronicle* informed the congressman that some Mississippians thought his presence at the trial would further "strain race relations," Diggs fired back, saying it is "obvious that relations are already strained, and my being on the scene would not make the situation any worse."[19]

DIGGS ARRIVED at the Jackson airport early Tuesday morning, September 20, 1955, the second day of the trial. He was accompanied by his staff attorney Basil Brown and James Del Rio, a thirty-one-year-old Detroit mortgage banker who had been active in Diggs's congressional campaign. The recent murders of Reverend George Lee, Lamar Smith, and now a fourteen-year-old boy, were reminders that Mississippi was a dangerous place for any Black person, including a member of the US Congress. Diggs would later tell others that because Brown and Del Rio were very light-complexioned, he believed they unknowingly provided him with protection from white Mississippians who thought they were white federal law officers assigned to protect him. Diggs later wrote about his experience for the *Pittsburgh Courier*, telling readers he "spent a harrowing week" in Mississippi "in fear of his life every moment."[20]

The trio was met at the airport by David Jackson, a *Jet* magazine photojournalist, who had traveled to Mississippi with Simeon Booker to cover the trial. Congressman Diggs noticed that Jackson was "trembling" as they loaded their luggage into the sedan.[21] As the car drove off north toward Sumner, in Tallahatchie County, Diggs, Brown, and Del Rio listened as Jackson "graphically" described the seething racial tension in the Delta.[22] During the two-and-half hour drive to the Tallahatchie County courthouse, Jackson filled Diggs and the others in on what happened at the trial the previous day.

Jackson also recounted an especially frightening encounter he and Simeon Booker had on Sunday, September 18, a day before the trial began.[23] Driving from Mound Bayou to Sumner, they had gotten lost. When Booker stopped on the side of the highway to check a map, a pickup truck suddenly pulled up to their car. "Stop, ya damn n——s," yelled a man. Then five white men, all with shotguns, jumped out of the truck and surrounded the car. "Get out," the huskiest one snapped and asked, "Who are you n——s and where are you going?" Booker told them they were reporters covering the trial and were lost. They were ordered out of the car, frisked and the car was searched before they were told "You n——s have no business around here. . . . You're just stirring up trouble." Jackson and Booker were then "'ordered'" to "'get the hell out [of here].'" Jackson told Diggs that he had never been so afraid and thought the men were going to kill them.

More than seventy newsmen, reporters, photographers, and cameramen from around the country covered the trial in tiny Sumner, including reporter James "Jimmy" Hicks, a correspondent for the Black National Newspaper Publishers Association and nearly a dozen other Black news reporters and photographers. The Black press corps stayed in the relative safety of Mound Bayou; many, like Diggs, stayed with Dr. Howard or in his small guest house. Others stayed in nearby Clarksdale.

Jackson told Diggs and his associates how the Black press had been treated by the local sheriff. Henry Clarence "H. C." Strider, the Tallahatchie County sheriff, was a rabid racist and openly hostile toward Black people. The 51-year-old, 270-pound white lawman was "the quintessential stereotype of a loudmouthed, racist Southern sheriff," remembered Booker. Strider told the press that Till was not dead and the whole thing was a stunt planned to drum up support for the NAACP and its civil rights activities. On the first day of the trial, he even tried to bar the Black reporters, telling them, "I ain't having no n—— reporters in my courtroom." Only after a white *New York Times* reporter complained to the judge did Strider allow the Black reporters inside. However, Strider made it clear to the reporters that the state's segregation laws applied to the county courthouse. Throughout the trial, the white reporters sat at a large press table near the jury while the Black reporters were segregated at a small card table in the back. Jimmy Hicks and the other Black journalists called it the "little Jim Crow" table.[24] After some members of the town's "local white establishment" became concerned that Strider was giving Tallahatchie

County a bad reputation, they asked that he "be more polite, especially to the black reporters."[25] In response, Strider began welcoming the reporters with the greeting, "Morning n——s."[26]

Jackson explained to Diggs that Circuit court judge Curtis Swango, a forty-seven-year-old graduate of the University of Mississippi, was presiding over the trial. Swango, a former member of the Mississippi House of Representatives, had been appointed to the bench in 1950. He was considered a "fair-minded jurist" who received "advance praise from both the prosecution and the defense."[27]

As the car got closer to Sumner, Diggs listened attentively as Jackson recounted how on Sunday night (September 18), the night before the trial was set to start, Frank Young, a Black plantation worker, told Dr. Howard that on the morning of Emmett Till's kidnapping (on August 28), he and "three or four" other Black plantation workers had witnessed a pickup truck that matched the description of J. W. Milam's drive onto a plantation in the town of Drew, Sunflower County, carrying four white men in the cab and three Black males in the back.[28] The plantation was managed by Leslie Milam, J. W.'s brother. One of the Black passengers was Till. Everyone got out of the truck and went into a nearby shed. "Soon thereafter Young and the others heard the unmistakable sounds of a vicious beating. . . . Someone then drove the truck into the shed, and the witnesses watched as it came back out with a tarpaulin thrown over the bed. Emmett Till was no longer visible."[29]

"Did the prosecuting attorney and law enforcement officials locate the other witnesses?" Diggs asked. "No," Jackson replied. Jackson explained that early on Monday, September 19, Medgar Evers, Ruby Hurley (the director of the NAACP southern region), Amzie Moore, Dr. Howard, and others had searched without success for the Black witnesses. Jimmy Hicks, the Black reporter, received a tip that two of them were being held under phony names at a nearby county jail, but he was unable to find them.[30]

SHORTLY AFTER 10 A.M., Diggs and the others pulled up in the car near Sumner's town square for day-two of the trial. About 1,000 spectators, nearly all of them white, gathered on the courthouse lawn and sat on the town square benches. A few wary Black residents stood on one side of the street. The locals appeared incredulous at seeing white and Black reporters greet each other and discuss the trial among themselves in a friendly manner. As Diggs walked across the town square toward the brick courthouse, a few Black spectators recognized him, and whites in the crowd wondered about the identity of the well-dressed Black man. Diggs felt a "great deal of tension" in the air, writing he could "almost see hatred oozing from pistol-packing, red-necked Mississippians who crowded around the streets and the steps leading up to the courtroom."[31] When a Black reporter accidentally bumped into a deputy sheriff, Diggs recalled, "The law officer's hand went to his gun holster and his threat to blow out the newsman's brains was emphasized with the unexpected unprinted epithets."[32]

As Diggs neared the courthouse, he was surrounded by reporters. "Mr. Congressman! Mr. Congressman! Why did you come to Sumner?" they yelled. Diggs stopped before a bank of microphones and told the press that he was attending the trial with the permission and approval of the judge as an "interested observer."[33] Locals watched in complete amazement as he spoke.

After answering the reporters' questions, Diggs Jr., Brown, and Del Rio walked into the courthouse. When they tried to enter the courtroom during a recess, a sheriff deputy blocked their way.[34] Black photographer Ernest Withers, standing near the courtroom door, noticed what was happening and rushed over to the Jim Crow press table. Hicks went out to talk to Diggs and took his business card to take it to Judge Swango. Blocked by another deputy who asked Hicks, "Where you going n——?" Hicks told him he was going to talk to the judge. "You can't go up there," he told Hicks. "Sir," Hicks replied, "There is a Negro congressman outside. I have his card." The deputy left and returned with another officer and explained, "This n—— here says there's a n—— outside who says he's a n—— congressman." The second deputy was incredulous. "A n—— congressman?" he asked, "It ain't possible. It ain't even legal!"[35]

Sheriff Strider then came over and took the card into Judge Swango's chambers. Swango told Strider to "bring Diggs right in."[36] Strider went over to the Black press table and said, "You got a n—— congressman down here who's coming to observe the trial. I'm gonna bring him over here and sit him down with y'all." As Hicks recalled years later, "And I'll be damned if he didn't make Diggs sit there at the Jim Crow press table with us."[37]

As one observer in the courtroom recalled, "Diggs maintained his composure and didn't seem bothered by the insult." He "appeared to have a rather reserved demeanor" when he stepped into the segregated courtroom.[38] Diggs later remembered that he could hear "a lot of buzzing" as he entered.[39] He noticed that although whites outnumbered Black spectators in the room, "I received gratification from the looks of relief and security which flooded the faces of Negro reporters and spectators when my companions and I walked into the courtroom. Why? Because here was a Negro Congressman, a representative of the Federal Government—one of their own—and he was on the scene with them."[40]

Seated with Diggs at the Jim Crow press table was Mamie Till-Bradley,

Emmett Till's mother. Not even she was allowed to sit in the main seating area. When court resumed, Diggs Jr. listened attentively as the two remaining jurors—all white men—were selected.

During a lunch break, the prosecution lawyers told Judge Swango about the potential surprise witnesses who had seen Till pulled into the shed. The judge subsequently recessed the trial until the next morning to give the state time to locate and, if the witnesses could be found, prepare their testimony.

Late on Tuesday night, Medgar Evers, Ruby Hurley, and Amzie Moore disguised themselves as plantation workers and began looking for the witnesses on plantations in Drew. Three potential witnesses were located: eighteen-year-old Willie Reed; Mr. Add Reed, Willie's seventy-four-year-old grandfather; and Amanda Bradley, Willie's forty-nine-year-old aunt. As Booker recalled, "All were frightened."[41] Amanda Bradley even refused to come out of her house when Dr. Howard and Evers arrived at her home. After Evers and Dr. Howard promised that each witness who agreed to testify would be given safe passage to Chicago, safe from reprisals, they all agreed to testify. In addition, there was some discussion about holding a press conference featuring Congressman Diggs and the witnesses. Ruby Hurley, the NAACP southern regional director, countered that any plan had to consider the deep fear that permeated Black people in the Delta. She argued that "the potential witnesses should be taken into hiding for their own safety before their names were revealed."[42] The group followed Hurley's plan.

ON WEDNESDAY MORNING, September 21, Diggs, Till's mother, her father and cousin, and the other Black witnesses were escorted from Mound Bayou to Sumner by a "well-armed" caravan organized by Dr. Howard.[43] When they arrived at the courthouse, the crowd outside was much larger and even more segregated than the previous day. Earlier that morning a cross had been set ablaze not far from the hotel where the jury was sequestered. Amzie Moore recounted, "The tension was so thick until, as the blacks and whites mixed on the courthouse grounds, you just looked for an explosion just any time."[44]

Local newspaper editors blamed the tension on the presence of Till's mother and claimed the appearance of Congressman Diggs only made it worse. "Many Deltans are convinced the two have hidden motives for being here," declared the *Mississippi Clarion-Ledger*.[45] "Diggs has about as much business being at the trial as he has being in Congress," wrote the editors of the *Jackson Daily News*. "Congressman Diggs, as well as many of the representatives of Negro publications, is interested only in the sensation they can create at the trial scene. Nothing would better suit his purpose than he be mistreated in some way."[46]

With the "encouragement" of Judge Swango, Sheriff Strider found a larger table for the Black press when the trial resumed. Yet seats were still so limited that Diggs brought "his own folding chair" from Dr. Howard's house.[47] Each day, he took his place at the press table with Emmett Till's mother and the others. As ceiling fans circulated the hot stifling air, the prosecution began to present its case against Milam and Bryant. The first witness was Mose Wright, Till's sixty-four-year-old great-uncle. A dramatic moment came when Wright stood and identified J. W. Milam as the person who took Emmett from his home. Congressman Diggs was in awe of Wright's bravery. "This is Mississippi in 1955 and with a long history of intimidation of witnesses, fear on the part of blacks to testify in the racial situations in particular. And for someone like Moses [sic] Wright ... to testify against white defendants in a situation like this was historical," Diggs later told an interviewer.[48]

One of the prosecution's responsibilities was to establish that the body pulled from the Tallahatchie River was indeed that of Emmett Till. Diggs listened closely as prosecution witnesses testified that it was in fact Till's body that was recovered from the river. LaFlore County sheriff George Smith and his deputy also testified that Bryant and Milam confessed to taking Till from Wright's home but claimed they "turned him loose" after determining he was the wrong boy.[49]

THURSDAY, SEPTEMBER 22, was perhaps the most suspense-filled day of the trial. Till's mother testified that the body pulled from the river and shipped to Chicago was indeed her son. Next, Willie Reed, the first of the surprise witnesses, testified. As the eighteen-year-old Reed stood and took the oath, his eyes met those of Congressman Diggs. Diggs gave him a reassuring smile. In her memoir—published under Till-Mobley, her new married name—Mamie Till-Bradley recalled that Reed had met Diggs the night before. "He had been impressed to meet a U.S. Congressman, a black congressman. He told Charles Diggs as such," she recounted.[50] "Seeing Congressman Diggs [in the courtroom] helped. The black congressman represented so much to Willie. Something he had never imagined before. In Diggs, Willie saw power, the power of possibility. He drew on that power source. It was the encouragement he needed to get through."[51] Reporters observed that Reed was "noticeably frightened, yet despite this, he held up well."[52]

His voice barely audible, Reed told the jury that on the day of the alleged murder, he saw Till in the back of J. W. Milam's pickup with two Black men at the plantation managed by Leslie Milam, J. W.'s brother. He also said he saw J. W. Milam leave the equipment shed where he had heard the beating and screams. Asked if the person he saw that morning was in the courtroom, Reed said yes. "He is sitting right over there," pointing to J. W. Milam.[53] Reed's testimony was the first to directly tie one of the defendants to Till's murder. Congressman Diggs thought that Reed "showed bravery of the highest type by daring to testify against white men accused of murdering a Negro."[54] The other plantation witnesses, Reed's grandfather and Amanda Bradley, both confirmed the young man's testimony. After their testimony, the prosecution rested its case.

Congressman Diggs was surprised by the sudden end to the prosecution's case. He and the others at the Black press table knew of the reports that two Black men were in the back of the pickup with Till; both were potential witnesses. They still believed the men were being held in jail under fictitious names and that Sheriff Strider was aware of the men's whereabouts. Prosecution attorneys, however, claimed to have checked into the matter and concluded the two men were not being held.

After a recess, the trial resumed, and the defense began to present its case. Carolyn Bryant was the first witness. Without the jury present, Bryant gave dramatic testimony about what happened in the store. She told the courtroom that Till grabbed her hands and asked her if she wanted to date him. He then chased her down the counter, she claimed, blocked her path, and put his hands tightly around her waist, asking, "What's the matter baby? Can't you take it?"[55] She said that Till intimated he had had sex with white women before.

Congressman Diggs could see the angry expression on the faces of nearly every white person in the courtroom. Many even gasped during Bryant's testimony. The jury, however, did not hear a word of Bryant's testimony. Judge Swango ruled that what happened at the store before the abduction and murder was immaterial to the case.

The defense then called several witnesses who raised questions about the identity of the body pulled from the river. A white doctor testified that the body was so badly bloated and mangled it was impossible to identify. Sheriff Strider testified that he could not determine if the body was that of a white man or a Black man.[56] At the end of the day, the defense announced it only had a few character witnesses to call for Friday's morning session.

Congressman Diggs and the others headed back to Mound Bayou. That evening, Black reporters received a tip that the two men seen in the back of J. W. Milam's pickup had been located. Once again, the reporters "began following this lead," and searched for the men. Basil Brown, with Congressman Diggs's approval, joined them.[57] They drove out to the nearby Charleston County jail but were unable to get anyone to look for the men.

Diggs at the Trial of Emmett Till's Murderers

ON THE LAST DAY OF THE TRIAL, Friday, September 23, a steady rain began early in the morning and seemed to come down harder throughout the afternoon. The defense called its final witnesses, character witnesses for J. W. Milam and Roy Bryant. All testified to the defendants' good character and that neither had a reputation for being violent.[58] Neither of the defendants testified. Just past ten o'clock, the defense rested its case.

There was great anticipation as the attorneys prepared to deliver their closing arguments. State prosecutor Gerald Chatham would give the state's summation, followed by four defense attorneys and a final summation by the state, presented by special prosecutor Robert Smith. As the rain picked up steadily, farmers, sharecroppers, and other country folk started coming off the nearby plantations to hear the verdict. They gathered close to the courthouse, trying to escape the rain and hear what was happening inside. The drama and tension in the courtroom were palpable. Diggs and others, however, were no fools. They had no confidence that Milam and Bryant would be found guilty.

CONGRESSMAN DIGGS, sweating from the heat in the stale courtroom air, lit a cigarette and took a deep drag as District Attorney Gerald Chatham began his summation. With his white shirt, wet with sweat, clinging to his large body, Chatham spoke passionately, occasionally pounding the table; reporters compared him to a country "Baptist preacher."[59] His voice could be heard outside through the open windows.

Chatham made a strong moral plea to the jury. "I am not concerned with the pressure of organizations outside or inside the state. I am concerned with what is morally right or wrong."[60] Chatham told the jury that the evidence was clear: Bryant and Milam kidnapped the boy. They did not come to take Till to "a card game," he declared.[61] "They murdered that boy," and it was a "cowardly act," he told the jury. There had been no need for them to kill the boy, Chatham said. If the boy did something wrong, the worst they should had done was "whip him." "You deal with a child as a child—not as if he is a man."[62]

Chatham reminded the jury of the testimony of the other witnesses and emphasized the bravery of eighteen-year-old Willie Reed. "Willie was telling the truth," Chatham declared.[63] Chatham also stressed the important testimony of Mamie Till-Bradley. Every mother knows their child, Chatham declared. He asked the jury, composed largely of unlettered country farmers, if they were to believe the testimony of so-called educated "experts" who claim the body is not Till's or would they take the word of the boy's mother, "someone who loved him and cared for him," he said.[64]

Chatham's closing summation "brought tears to the eyes not only of those seated at the colored press tables but to some of the white listeners as well."[65]

Mamie Till-Bradley described Chatham's closing statement as a "moving summation, filled with emotion and delivered with great passion."[66]

Then Congressman Diggs listened attentively as four defense lawyers argued that the body found in the river was not that of Till. However, it was defense attorney John W. Whitten's closing argument that Diggs and others would remember. Whitten, the first cousin of Diggs's colleague Congressman Jamie Whitten (D-MS), not only repeated the claim that the body pulled from the river was not Till's but also posited a theory that Mose Wright, working with the NAACP, had sent Till to Chicago, obtained a decaying corpse (perhaps from Dr. Howard's Mound Bayou clinic), and threw it into the Tallahatchie River! All this, he claimed, was a conspiracy by the NAACP to focus attention on segregation in Mississippi. "There are people who want to destroy the way of life of Southern people," Whitten shouted.[67] Whitten then told the jury that they had the authority to ignore the truth. "It is within your power to disregard all the facts, the evidence, and the law, and bring in any decision you like based upon any whim. . . . You are our hope and confidence to send these defendants back to their families happy." Finally, Whitten told the jury he hoped that "every last Anglo-Saxon one of you has the courage to do it."[68]

Special state prosecutor Robert Smith concluded with the state's closing argument. Smith reminded the jurors that Mose Wright had a reputation of being a "good old country Negro" preacher who would not tell a lie.[69] Acknowledging the bravery of the frightened young Willie Reed, Smith looked at the jury and exclaimed, "I don't know but Willie Reed has more nerve than I have."[70] Smith also pointed to the testimony of Mamie Till-Bradley, who positively identified her son's body. He called the defense claim that the NAACP threw another body in the river as "the most farfetched I've ever heard in a courtroom."[71] Smith concluded by telling the jury that "outside influences" like the NAACP wanted the murderers to go free. "If they are turned loose, those people will have a fundraising campaign for the next fifteen years."[72]

With that, the trial ended, and the jurors retired to deliberate. Nearly all the white spectators stayed in their seats as most expected a rapid acquittal. Roy Bryant's lawyer was heard telling him "to expect a deliberation of about twenty-five to forty-five minutes."[73] Some whites even went over to shake Milam and Bryant's hands and patted the defense attorneys on their backs.

CONGRESSMAN DIGGS remained seated next to Emmett's mother. He was surprised to see most of the Black spectators quickly leave. He pulled out a cigarette, began to light it, and suddenly Mrs. Till-Bradley turned to Diggs and the others and announced she was ready to leave. "What?" Congressman

Diggs said, "And miss the verdict?"[74] "The jury has retired and it's time for us to retire," she told them. "If that jury came back with an acquittal," she later recalled, "then white folks were going to know for sure that they could get away with murder. It was going to be open season on black folks and we were going to be prime targets. I was not about to wait around for that."[75]

Congressman Diggs came to the same conclusion. He gathered his belongings and said goodbye to Booker, Medgar Evers, and the others at the Jim Crow press table. Then Diggs, Mrs. Till-Bradley, her father and cousin, and Willie Reed made their way to a car with a driver provided by Dr. Howard. The car sped away toward Mound Bayou.

They were in the car about forty-five minutes out of Sumner, just a few miles from Mound Bayou, when a special news bulletin interrupted the car's radio broadcast.[76] A verdict had been reached: Not guilty.

As the report from the courtroom came across the radio broadcast, Diggs could hear the celebration in the background. As Diggs recalled decades later, "As far as a verdict was concerned, I was not surprised at that because that was typical of Mississippi justice at that particular time." He was nevertheless hurt and angered. "I was certainly angered by the decision although I was not surprised by it," he recalled. "I was certainly strengthened in my belief that something had to be done about the dispensation of justice in that state."[77]

When Congressman Diggs and the others arrived at Dr. Howard's house, news reporters were waiting. "What do you think of the verdict?" they shouted. Congressman Diggs offered that Judge Swango conducted the trial in "an objective manner. I was impressed with his fairness and the presentation of the case by the prosecution," Diggs told reporters.[78] However, Diggs added that justice was not served. "The deep-rooted prejudices of the jurors would not permit any kind of objective consideration of the case," Diggs declared.[79] A key problem, Diggs said, was that if Black citizens had been allowed to serve on the jury, the outcome may have been different. However, jurors were selected from the voter-registration rolls and in Tallahatchie County, although Black people composed 62 percent of the population, no Black Americans were registered to vote. "I think the basis of representation in Congress from Mississippi should be reduced," Diggs told reporters. "The total population is used for basing the number of Congressmen, but the Negroes, included in the total, are not permitted to vote."[80]

Late on Friday evening, Medgar Evers drove Congressman Diggs and Willie Reed, the brave plantation worker, to the Memphis airport. Diggs had arranged with Congressman William L. Dawson for Reed to move to Chicago to live with an uncle. "We felt Reed would be safer in Chicago. He would go to school and get a job there," Diggs told reporters.[81] Diggs respected Reed. "He was a young fellow; not very talkative, certainly determined to give a true story and I certainly admired him for that. I took him back to Chicago and that was the last I saw him," Diggs told an interviewer.[82]

Although most white Mississippians believed Congressman Diggs's purpose for coming to Sumner was to sow "seeds of hatred," and although the virulently segregationist *Jackson Daily News*, the state's largest newspaper, called Diggs "a meddlesome Negro politician" determined to castigate the South to win votes back home, Diggs was proud of his role at the trial.[83] "I went to Sumner, Miss. to give moral support to the abused and intimidated Negro citizenry of that community," Diggs wrote.[84] He succeeded, as his presence gave courage to several Black witnesses and elevated the issue of civil rights in Mississippi and throughout the South.

Diggs knew what he was doing, and he believed that his presence at the trial brought more national media attention to Black voting and civil rights. "I was the only congressman that was there. The fact that I was a Black congressman and just elected, I think it added a whole lot to the media interest," he told an interviewer.[85] A reporter who covered the trial remembered that Diggs "made a difference down there. When he went down there, people lined up to see him. They had never seen a black member of Congress."[86]

The Emmett Till murder case catapulted Charles Diggs Jr. into the national spotlight and revealed that he embraced the role as a representative of Black America. As Diggs wrote shortly after the trial, "I went to Mississippi because although I was elected a representative of the Thirteenth District of Michigan, I sincerely feel that the responsibility which I accepted in being sworn in was to serve the best interests of all people of the United States."[87]

Chapter 11

DESEGREGATING COMMERCIAL AIR TRAVEL

IN NOVEMBER 2007, the Smithsonian Institution's Air and Space Museum in Washington, DC, opened a permanent exhibit, *America by Air*, to tell the story of the development of commercial air travel in the United States. Included is a large display entitled "Air Travel and Segregation." It is the only public recognition of Charles Diggs Jr.'s pioneering efforts to desegregate commercial air travel, a little known but lasting aspect of his legacy.

WHEN CONGRESSMAN DIGGS traveled to Mound Bayou, Mississippi, in April 1955 it was his first opportunity to witness the impact of Jim Crow on all aspects of daily life in the South. While in the military he had been somewhat shielded from the full reach of segregation. But in 1955, when he first landed at the Jackson airport with his father, signs directed them to restrooms for "Negro" passengers. And on their return to Detroit, they learned that the airport's restaurant did not serve Black patrons, and they were required to sit in a "Negro" waiting area.

By 1955, air travel was becoming more commonplace even among Black travelers. The vast majority were, like Diggs, middle-class professionals whose work required them to be mobile.[1] Because federal regulations governed interstate travel and almost all air passengers were interstate travelers, Black air passengers enjoyed equal access in the aircraft cabins. However, the administration of airport terminals fell under the jurisdiction of local municipal officials. Black passengers using Southern airports were subjected to segregated facilities and discriminatory treatment. Waiting areas, ticket counters, restrooms, water fountains, restaurants, and other facilities were segregated throughout the South. Historian Anke Ortlepp notes, "Black and white air travelers who may have sat in adjacent seats on the same airplane became invisible to one another on the ground."[2]

National Airport in Washington, DC, was one of the many segregated airports. Black people could eat only at a small snack bar or use a basement restaurant. Black travelers began complaining about their treatment at National Airport as early as 1941, and it became the first airport to attract national attention as a segregated facility.[3] Although the airport was in Virginia, it was on federally owned land, and lawyers for the NAACP argued that because the airport was on federal property, Virginia's segregation statutes did not apply. They asserted that the Department of Commerce, which controlled the Civil Aeronautics Administration (CAA), had legal authority under the Interstate Commerce Act to compel the proprietors of the restaurants at National Airport to serve Black and white passengers on a nonsegregated basis. However, President Franklin Roosevelt's Commerce Department disagreed, and nothing changed.

Then in June 1946, the US Supreme Court ruled in *Irene Morgan v. Virginia* that segregation of bus passengers engaged in interstate travel was unconstitutional. In October 1946, considering the *Morgan* ruling, the NAACP again asked the Commerce Department to make the segregation of races inapplicable in all facilities at National Airport. In November 1947, the Truman administration asked Congress to permit white and Black travelers to use the same restaurants at National Airport despite Virginia's segregation laws.[4] Congress refused after Southern members strongly objected.

Despite this opposition, in December 1948, President Truman's CAA changed the federal regulations pertaining to the operation of National Airport and added an amendment that expressly prohibited racial discrimination. In January 1949, a federal district court in Virginia ruled that the CAA's amended regulations banning segregation held precedence over Virginia state law.[5] A few days later integration of National Airport became a reality.

However, the court ruling applied only to National Airport. In airports elsewhere in the South segregation remained the reality. New airports as well as airports being expanded or retrofitted, included segregated facilities. As more Black people discovered air travel to be a convenient and modern means of transportation, complaints regarding racial discrimination grew more common.[6] In July 1950, for example, Mamie Davis, regional manager for the national YWCA, wrote the NAACP that she experienced a great deal of "embarrassment, mental anguish, and unhappiness" when a policeman in a "very angry voice" told her to move because she was sitting in the wrong section of the Houston Municipal Airport.[7] Dobbs House Inc., a national business chain based in Memphis, Tennessee, that operated restaurants in several Southern airport terminals, including Atlanta, was notorious for denying service to Black people.[8] In 1955, Sidney Poitier, the Black actor, was told by Dobbs House Restaurant staff in Atlanta that he could be given a table at which to eat, "but we're going to have to put a screen around you."[9] Poitier walked away outraged and angry. Even Martin Luther King Jr. was regularly denied service at the Dobbs House Restaurant.[10]

Inconvenience and humiliation were made worse when travel delays and layovers often left passengers, Black and white, stranded in airports for hours. While whites could find a meal and a comfortable place to sit, Black passengers were left frustrated and hungry.

ON MAY 12, 1955, shortly after returning from Mississippi, Charles Diggs Jr. took up their cause, adding the state of the nation's airports to his list of civil rights concerns and writing the presidents of the nation's twelve largest national and regional airlines.[11] Ever the politician, Diggs started his letters by noting that he had been "heartened" during the early years of air transportation to see Black and white passengers treated equally. However, Diggs wrote that in recent years he noticed air transportation was "falling into the old pattern of segregation and discrimination established by railroads and bus lines [sic]." Diggs wrote, "A recent trip to the South . . . revealed widespread undemocratic practices." He made "a strong urgent request" to the executives that they bring an immediate end to segregation practices at municipal airport terminals.[12]

The executives hid behind the status quo. An industry trade group wrote, "We have no control over these facilities, and airline policy cannot be enforced upon them."[13] National Airlines, headquartered in Miami, was particularly hostile. National's president, George T. Baker, took a defiant tone, writing to Diggs that he "fail[ed] to see the substance" of Diggs's complaint about separate facilities for the races because "Negroes who live in the South want it that way. In Miami there are Negro jitneys and taxis which will not pick up white people—and no one objects."[14]

Diggs was undeterred and again focused on the federal government's role. Congress was considering amendments to the Federal Airport Act Program (FAAP), a grant-in-aid program designed to assist municipal governments in "airport development" with the goal of building a nationwide system of publicly owned airports. It provided a fifty-fifty match of federal and local funds to build runways and construct air towers and other airport infrastructure, including terminals. By 1955, hundreds of airports across the country had received FAAP funding, including airports in Atlanta, Memphis, and other Southern cities.[15]

Congressman Diggs believed this amended bill created an opportunity. On July 7, 1955, Diggs wrote Secretary of Commerce Sinclair Weeks to ask whether the amended bill would allow the Commerce Department "sufficient authority" to prohibit racial discrimination and segregation in airport terminals receiving funds from the FAAP.[16]

Philip A. Ray, the general counsel for the Commerce Department, acknowledged that the legislation did not "contain any specific authority to prohibit discrimination and segregation in the use" of airport facilities, adding that the "problem of ending discrimination and segregation in transportation should be considered separately" from the FAAP.[17]

Diggs also proposed a legislative change to the FAAP. He attempted to insert language explicitly prohibiting federal spending on segregated airport facilities. On July 14, 1955, Diggs testified before the House Committee on Interstate and Foreign Commerce's Subcommittee on Transportation and Communications. Current practices went against the tenets of democracy, Diggs testified, saying there was "widespread undemocratic practice" in many airports throughout the South.[18] "Congress has an opportunity to require common facilities open to all people," creating "little islands of democracy just like military installations."[19]

However, the FAAP had widespread support, and there was little appetite for making significant changes. The subcommittee voted down Diggs's amendment. The Federal Airport Act was passed and became law on August 3, 1955.

When Clarence Mitchell of the NAACP learned of Congressman Diggs's amendment and testimony, he asked the NAACP Washington bureau's chief legal counsel, J. Francis Pohlhaus, to send Diggs a copy of a legal memo Pohlhaus had prepared on discrimination in airport facilities.[20] The memo supported the NAACP's long-held view that Jim Crow airport terminals violated the nondiscrimination provisions of the Interstate Commerce Act and the CAA.[21] The CAA administrator could end segregation in Southern airport terminals by forcing compliance with the antidiscrimination provision of the FAAP.

THE FIGHT AGAINST segregated airport terminals got an unexpected boost. On August 22, 1955, the Indian Ambassador to the United States, G. L. Mehta and his personal secretary, sat down for a meal in the Houston airport while waiting for a connecting flight. They were asked to leave the main dining room and escorted to the dining room reserved for Black customers. The ambassador later said that at the time "he thought he and his secretary were experiencing special treatment for important visitors, not racial discrimination," and had he "understood the incident was a matter of discrimination he would have left the restaurant" in protest.[22] Secretary of State John Foster Dulles and the mayor of Houston apologized to the ambassador and the Indian government.

Secretary of Commerce Weeks ordered a detailed report of the incident from the CAA.[23]

Black leaders took notice. Benjamin Mays, the influential president of Morehouse College, wrote in an opinion column, "It is strange that millions of Negroes are embarrassed, segregated, and humiliated, day in and day out, and nobody apologizes."[24] The *Pittsburgh Courier* carried an editorial with a headline that read, "So Sorry, Thought You Were Negroes."[25]

On September 16, 1955, as Congressman Diggs prepared to again travel to Mississippi to attend the trial of Emmett Till's murderers, he again wrote Secretary of Commerce Weeks. "I am," Diggs wrote, "protesting the allocation of Government funds, under the Federal Grants-in-Aid Program, to any state or sponsoring agent for the purpose of improvement or construction of public airports, until such sponsor has shown evidence that there is no discrimination or segregation in the use of facilities at the airport concerned."[26] Diggs also addressed the same protest letter to the head of the CAA and to the two CAA administrators for the southern region. Diggs publicized the letter and sent it to the editors of the Black newspapers.[27]

Black leaders in Raleigh and Durham, North Carolina, read about Diggs Jr.'s protest and turned to him for help. A new airport serving the two cities was scheduled to open with separate restrooms for Black and white travelers. After their protest failed to convince local airport officials to reverse the plan, the chair of the Durham Committee on Negro Affairs wrote Diggs and asked if the congressman could "hold up the appropriation" of federal funds due to the new airport's segregated facilities.[28] "You may rest assured that I will continue to press this matter and I believe in the end, we will be successful," Diggs responded.[29]

Diggs then sent telegrams to local authorities protesting "separate toilet facilities for Negroes and whites" at the new Raleigh-Durham Airport and demanding that "the proposed separate facilities based on race be immediately eliminated."[30] He sternly warned local North Carolina authorities that the Jim Crow policy was a violation of federal regulations and that he would "fight the distribution of any Federal funds to your airport if you refuse to honor this request."[31] Diggs also sent a telegram to Secretary Weeks, reminding him that segregated facilities were a "direct violation" of the FAAP and demanding that he "order" the officials in North Carolina to "immediately" eliminate "the proposed separate facilities."[32]

The pressure on the CAA to do something increased when, in September 1955, a few weeks after the incident with the Indian ambassador, a Black Air Force officer entered the Dobbs House restaurant in Birmingham's Municipal Airport with nearly twenty white officers. After their Black colleague was denied service, all the white officers refused to eat there too; and together they all left the airport restaurant in protest. The incident was covered widely by the Black press.[33]

On September 28, 1955, Secretary Weeks informed Diggs that the CAA would launch an "official study" of airport segregation and the FAAP, and he assured Diggs the study would also include the recently renovated Raleigh-Durham Airport.[34] Diggs rightly received credit, and his office sent a press release to the Black newspapers touting his ability to get "results."[35]

A few days later, on October 1, 1955, the CAA quietly formulated a new policy on federal aid to local airports. Moving forward, local grantees had to explain and describe in their application for funding whether their facilities would be available to all patrons without regard to race. Airports that practiced segregation would continue to receive funds for facilities such as runways, control towers, and other operation projects, but would receive no federal aid for segregated waiting, dining, or restroom facilities. Only state and local dollars could be used to construct Jim Crow airport facilities.[36]

Diggs was critical of the new policy and pointed out its weaknesses to Acting CAA administrator Charles J. Lowen, asking, "Is not the Federal-Aid Airport Program still a party to segregation if *any* funds are allocated to a terminal whose governing authorities are willing to construct discriminatory facilities with local finances?"[37] He noted that the policy could set a "dangerous precedent" for other federal programs and that "Pro-segregationists have always been resigned to pay extra for the maintenance of their policy."[38] The NAACP also registered their criticism for similar reasons.

Although Diggs kept pressing the issue, the policy continued throughout the remainder of the Eisenhower administration. Diggs requested and received updates on the outlays of the FAAP. Regulators regularly heard from him about building projects at Southern airport terminals as the congressman used his oversight authority to continue to monitor the FAAP.[39]

In May 1960, when the FAAP was up again for extension, Senator Jacob Javits, a liberal Republican from New York who had been elected in 1956, saw an opportunity to attach an amendment that would prohibit the "disbursement of any FAAP payments to airport terminal building projects where segregated facilities were in the process of being constructed."[40]

The amendment failed to pass, but the debates surrounding the failed amendment had an impact. Months later, in October 1960, the FAA issued new regulations for the FAAP that "limited eligibility to projects related to airport safety operations."[41] Federal investment in local airports would be confined only to safety features such as towers, weather stations, and runways.

Diggs continued to exert pressure from his position in Washington, DC, a position strengthened after the election of Democrat John F. Kennedy to the presidency. By the early 1960s, federal aviation regulators began to question the utility of the FAAP as a tool to desegregate airport terminals; they were concerned that, if pushed, Southern authorities might forgo federal airport support if it required dismantling racial segregation.

In 1961, federal regulators, appointed under the new Kennedy administration, also held to the notion that it was safer for airports to be in the orbit of the FAAP. Air travel regulators now believed legal action against racial segregation at airport terminals was the most viable alternative to regulatory and statutory reform.

One of the earliest cases involved the notorious Dobbs House restaurant at the Atlanta Municipal Airport. H. D. Coke, a Black insurance executive from Birmingham, Alabama, brought a class-action lawsuit against the City of Atlanta, the Atlanta Municipal Airport, and Dobbs House for denying Black travelers access to the airport's restaurant. In January 1960, the US District Court ruled that the defendants violated the FAAP, the equal protection clause of the Fourteenth Amendment, and the interstate commerce clause. Significantly, in *Coke v. Atlanta*, the court ruled that because the city had hired Dobbs, the restaurant's refusal to serve Black customers amounted to state action. The *Coke* decision, however, covered only airports under the jurisdiction of the federal District Court in Atlanta.[42]

Over the next few years, the NAACP Legal Defense Fund took a case-by-case approach, successfully challenging the legality of Jim Crow airport terminals in Greenville, South Carolina; Tallahassee, Florida; and Memphis, Tennessee. In addition, beginning in 1961 under new Attorney General Robert F. Kennedy, the Justice Department initiated successful federal lawsuits against airport authorities in Montgomery, Birmingham, New Orleans, and Shreveport. Consequently, many Southern airport terminals were desegregated before the passage and implementation of the 1964 Civil Rights Act.

WHILE CONGRESSMAN DIGGS worked to dismantle Jim Crow airport terminals, he also quietly used his power as a member of Congress to change employment practices within the growing, nearly all-white airline industry. Diggs had noticed that Black people did not work as reservation clerks, stenographers, typists, or in any other white-collar positions at the downtown ticket offices or at the airports; instead, they served only as porters, ramp attendants, and plane cleaners. Throughout the industry Black men and women were barred from in-flight positions—as pilots, engineers, and flight attendants.

Such overt racism permeated the development of commercial aviation in the United States. Although flight attendants and Pullman porters—the widely popular male Black attendants used since the 1860s in sleeping cars attached to long-distance passenger trains—were "occupational parallels," when the airline industry started hiring flight attendants, its leaders decided to hire whites only.[43] Airline executives "linked whiteness to technological prowess in an industry widely hailed as being at the cutting edge of modern commerce and mechanical ingenuity," reasoning that white passengers were more likely to embrace air travel if they saw white faces in charge.[44]

By the mid-twentieth century, the airline "stewardess" had taken on the image of the "all American girl" and become a celebrated icon of American womanhood.[45] Although the airlines did not have an explicit written policy of not hiring Black stewardesses, "Supervisors, consciously or unconsciously, hired white women to match [the] dominant cultural images of the ideal American woman."[46]

In 1955, when Congressman Diggs arrived on Capitol Hill, there were 5,919 stewards and stewardesses employed in the United States on scheduled airlines. None was Black.[47] By 1955, both the NAACP and the National Urban League pushed to integrate hiring practices in the airline industry, paying particular attention to flight attendants and pilot jobs.[48] Diggs understood that government contracts and federal subsidies put the airlines within the scope of President Eisenhower's, and later President Kennedy's, executive orders prohibiting discrimination by companies with government contracts.

On June 4, 1956, Congressman Diggs wrote to many of the same industry executives he had a year before concerning segregated airport terminals, now asking instead, "Is it, in fact, your policy to discriminate against Negro applicants for hostess positions?"[49] Diggs referenced an editorial in the *Pittsburgh Courier* that claimed that airline executives had made it clear to the Urban League that "they will NOT hire any Negro hostesses under any circumstances."[50]

Diggs pressed the executives to explain why no Black workers were hired on flight crews. "I do know that World War II proved that color of skin was no bar to the ability to" be "pilots and other technical personnel."[51] Diggs explained that as an officer at Tuskegee Army Airfield he had seen "Negroes being trained and used in every technical capacity from pilot on down." Diggs also noted the "continuous advertising" of stewardess positions in the major newspapers, "which indicates that the need is there."[52] Diggs wanted to know why Black women were not hired.

The executives justified their policies in several ways. TWA, while acknowledging that no Black woman had ever been hired for a stewardess position, attributed this fact not to discrimination but to the "highly selective process involved in the procurement of hostess personnel."[53] In other words, no Black women were qualified.

Delta Airlines admitted that Delta discriminated against Black applicants for stewardess and other flight crew positions because, it claimed, Delta's customer base was largely in the South, and it had to "conform to the mores of the people we serve."[54]

That response prompted Diggs to contact the President's Committee on Government Contracts, formed in 1953 to make certain corporations receiving federal government contracts complied with federal government antidiscrimination clauses. Eisenhower tapped Vice President Richard Nixon to chair the committee. But when Diggs wrote Nixon nothing changed.[55]

The most effective action regarding fair employment practices in the airline industry took place with individual state fair employment laws that prohibited discrimination based on race, creed, color, or national origin. The New York State Commission Against Discrimination had the strongest arsenal with which to combat employment discrimination, allowing individuals to file complaints for both investigation and settlement.[56] In May 1960, after many complaints filed by Black people with the commission, and following years of public pressure, Capital Air Lines hired Patricia Banks as one of the country's first Black flight attendants.[57]

THE MAJOR NATIONAL AIRLINES—American, Eastern, TWA, Capital, Delta, and Northwest—however, continued to discriminate, catering to predominantly white passengers, as airline leaders argued they would not react favorably toward Black flight attendants. Despite mounting pressure, no major airline would employ Black stewardesses.

Once again, Diggs focused on the federal government's role and turned to President Kennedy's new Committee on Equal Employment Opportunity, headed by Vice President Lyndon B. Johnson. The committee was designed to take a tougher approach than Eisenhower's President's Committee on Government Contracts.

In March 1962, Congressman Diggs and Vice President Johnson spoke "at length" about the fact that none of the national airlines had Black stewardesses.[58] Johnson apparently agreed as Diggs's long-term campaign of subtle but relentless pressure, backed by an irrefutable moral argument, again bore fruit. Johnson told Diggs that he planned to push his committee more on the matter and assured the congressman, "You and I are in full agreement on the objectives, and I believe we will be able to attain them."[59]

By threatening to cancel existing federal contracts, Lyndon Johnson made hiring Black flight attendants a personal priority. "I just want you to know that I consider this matter a personal project on my part because I realize the symbolic significance and you may be sure that I will follow through," Johnson pledged to Diggs.[60] Johnson directed the committee's staff to keep Diggs abreast of its progress, and throughout the 1960s the number of Black employees in the airline industry, including in-flight personnel, would slowly increase, a pace that accelerated after Johnson ascended to the presidency and signed the Civil Rights Act in 1964, outlawing racial discrimination.[61]

A few years earlier, Sterling Tucker, the executive director of the Washington, DC, Urban League, lauded Diggs for his work on airline discrimination. "All of us appreciate the work you are doing to achieve a significant breakthrough in the airlines industry.... We, in the Urban League, are particularly pleased and impressed with the quiet, yet efficient and persistent, way you go about your very important work."[62]

Charles Diggs Jr.'s approach to the issue of discrimination in the airline industry would prove emblematic of his approach during his time in Congress; dogged persistence combined with moral certainty.

Chapter 12

FIGHTING DISCRIMINATION
IN THE US MILITARY
On-Base and Off-Base

THE LETTERS just kept coming.

Even before Charles Diggs Jr. was sworn in as a member of Congress, Black US servicemen, aware of Diggs's background, wrote him about their experiences with discrimination while serving in the US military. Now that he was in Congress and taking on a more prominent role in the national civil rights struggle, he began to hear from more and more servicemen recounting their experiences and looking to Diggs to act.

Diggs understood that despite President Harry S. Truman's Executive Order 9981, a controversial 1948 action that called for the immediate desegregation of the military, discrimination did not end. Although in October 1954 the Secretary of Defense had announced that the last racially segregated US military unit had been abolished, Diggs knew that equality remained elusive.

THE STORIES TOLD in the letters were both common and familiar. In fall 1954, William L. Clay, a St. Louis native, and his family, were transferred from an army base in Missouri to Fort McClellan, Alabama. When he arrived at Fort McClellan, Clay discovered that the military installation was "thoroughly and officially segregated by race."[1] For example, Black soldiers could get a haircut on Saturdays only, when a Black barber was brought to the base. "There would be maybe a hundred or two [hundred Black] people waiting to get their haircut," Clay remembered.[2] White soldiers had access to the base's barbershop throughout the week. On Thursdays when white girls from nearby Anniston came onto the base for dances, the NCO (noncommissioned officers') club was off-limits to Black soldiers. The restaurant in the PX was for "whites only," as was the base's swimming pool.

Clay (a future congressman) became the leader of a protest campaign.[3] Black soldiers at Fort McClellan organized pickets of the base restaurant, blocked the entrance into the NCO club, and refused to get their hair cut. When the base commander threatened Clay with a court-martial, the soldier wrote Congressman Diggs, telling him that commanders at Fort McClellan "still resisted" desegregation and asking him to investigate.[4] In early 1955 Diggs wrote US Army secretary Robert T. Stevens demanding an inquiry, asserting that continuing segregation and discrimination were "out of tune" with the Department of Defense's (DOD's) order to integrate.[5] Diggs planned to visit the facility accompanied by a reporter; but before he did, Clay was transferred back to Missouri.

Diggs eventually received hundreds of letters from Black servicemen and their families; all, like Clay, complained about racial discrimination throughout the armed services, in the South and overseas. The letters told of their humiliation due to the use of the N-word and other racial slurs by other soldiers, including by noncommissioned officers. One such letter signed by thirteen servicemen described a fight after a noncommissioned officer referred to Black soldiers as "N——s." After the fracas, the unit commander told the Black soldiers that while he was growing up his family "always referred" to his town's only Black family as the "'N—— family'" and that "he did not see why the word" should hurt them. An inquiry into the matter ultimately exonerated the white officer.[6]

Others complained about retribution. One woman wrote Diggs pleading for help after her fiancée, an army private, had written Adam Clayton Powell to report patterns of racial discrimination and was then charged with "maltreatment of prisoners" by an all-white group of soldiers. "Must one who has fought in the 2nd World War and Korean War and looked forward to a career in the Army see his future jeopardized because of prejudice?" she wrote. "You believe in justice and equality for our race. Please help me."[7]

Complaints also poured into Diggs's office concerning discrimination in assignments and promotion. The assignment of Black soldiers to food service, transportation, and supplies remained evident in each branch of the service. Military officials routinely explained away discrepancies, alleging the educational deficiencies of Black servicemen. Airman Herbert Jones described how he and other Black airmen were "being discriminated against on promotions" at Bolling Air Force Base in Washington, DC.[8] Less qualified white airmen were routinely promoted over more qualified Black airmen. "I am not a cry baby," Jones explained to Diggs, "but I think if a man deserves a stripe regardless of his race he should be promoted."[9] One airman wrote Diggs alleging that when qualified Black airmen approached a promotion, white commanders transferred them to another squadron so the Black airmen would have "to start all over again" to reach a new rank.[10]

Promotions were made by boards of senior military officers that included few Black officers, making promotions for Black servicemen hard to come by.

In 1954, Black Americans were 13 percent of all enlisted personnel in the US Army but only 3 percent of its officers, and Black Americans constituted less than 1 percent of the officers in the Navy, Air Force, and Marines.[11] Black soldiers were particularly galled by the fact that despite rampant discrimination, military service still offered Black citizens better opportunities than the civilian workforce.

Coupled with his own military experience, Diggs needed little convincing. He knew firsthand how both on- and off-base discrimination negatively affected the morale of Black troops. "What Diggs and other blacks found especially infuriating were the tendencies of commanders to ally themselves with local authorities in communities that enforced Jim Crow practices and refuse to investigate complaints by blacks that their rights were being denied," wrote military historian Bernard Nalty.[12] A Black Air Force major stationed at Maxwell Air Force Base in Montgomery, Alabama, complained to Diggs that he had been arrested for violating the state's segregation laws simply for accompanying two Ethiopian officers and an Air Force captain to a barbershop.[13] When Diggs complained, the inspector general responded that the Air Force's policy of equal treatment was restricted to military installations and did not apply off-base.

In response, in April 1959, Diggs proposed HR 6390, a bill to "prevent discrimination in any public or semipublic place or by any public or semipublic transportation against members of the Armed Forces because of race, color, or creed."[14] He reasoned that if Black and white soldiers could work and travel together, they could certainly eat a meal together. The bill never got a hearing.

Once again, these problems were prevalent not only in the South, where state laws required segregation, but also elsewhere in the country and even overseas. Journalists and other military observers noted that discrimination near US military installations abroad was "caused primarily by the pressures and actions of white GIs, not by the wishes of local proprietors."[15] In 1954, Adam Clayton Powell had asked President Eisenhower to declare "off-limits" any establishment that practiced racial discrimination. "We call a place off-limits if it breeds venereal disease. We should do the same to a place that breeds the disease of discrimination," wrote Powell.[16]

Discrimination extended even to off-base housing in private homes and apartments. Black servicemen often had a difficult time finding safe housing as many homeowners and real estate agents refused to rent to Black soldiers, often relegating them to segregated neighborhoods located far away from the base, sometimes in the most dangerous and undesirable parts of town.

Black service personnel feared reprisals if they brought up such matters related to equal treatment and race discrimination. Although they were supposed to be able to make confidential complaints about any violation of military policies to an inspector general, the system was inadequate for handling claims of racial discrimination. As a result, many soldiers said nor did nothing, and discrimination was allowed to fester. Writing to Diggs, Powell, or the NAACP was their only alternative.

That explains why many complaints Diggs received were made anonymously, while others, fearing retaliation, asked Diggs not to reveal their names. One Black member of the Air Force Reserves wrote, "I am asking you not to mention my name to the general because they might put me out. I have 10 years, and was in action over there in Korea, and I am trying to make 20 years."[17] At the end of the letter, the sergeant reiterated his fear in large handwriting, reminding Diggs, "Don't mention my name."[18]

TAKING HIS USUAL patient strategic and dogged approach, Diggs took up the cases of the Black servicemen, writing the secretaries of the armed forces to call attention to the servicemembers' complaints. Although allegations of racial bias in assignments were difficult to prove, Diggs maintained that the promotion process suffered from conscious and unconscious bias by white supervisors and promotion boards. Photographs and other racial designations were included in each candidate's promotion files, which Diggs believed influenced the board members' racial biases. Both he and the NAACP advocated their removal.[19]

But sometimes Diggs intervened personally. In April 1955, Diggs learned that a Black staff sergeant, a member of the NAACP, had been "dishonorably" discharged from the Air Force for being disloyal.[20] After reading a transcript of the disciplinary board's hearing, Diggs learned that several witnesses had testified to the airman's "loyalty and character" and that no witnesses were presented to support the charge against him. Diggs sent public telegrams and letters to the Air Force secretary calling the board's action "an injustice" and demanding another hearing for the airman.[21] A few weeks later Diggs's office announced that the Air Force had agreed to reconsider the case.[22]

Diggs consistently pushed the Eisenhower administration to remove discrimination and segregation from all aspects of the armed forces. In September 1957, after a football game between Tulane University and Army was transferred to West Point in deference to Louisiana's segregation laws, Diggs wrote Army secretary Wilbur Brucker, asking him to adopt a policy prohibiting the army from participating in any sporting event with a competing team that "practices and/or advocates policies of discrimination and segregation."[23]

Even as letters continued to pour into Diggs's office from Black servicemen, progress was limited. Then in January of 1960, a particular incident caused Diggs to immerse himself even more into military race relations. Diggs received a letter from a Black airman complaining about a story entitled, "Our Fighting Men Have Gone Soft," that appeared in an official Air Force publication. A reprint of a *Saturday Evening Post* article, the story claimed that racial integration of the armed services negatively affected military readiness, and it blamed Black soldiers for the military's problems. The airman reported to Diggs that he and his fellow associates were thoroughly demoralized by the article.[24]

On February 8, 1960, Diggs wrote Air Force secretary Dudley C. Sharp saying he was "absolutely shocked" and "amazed that the Air Force would expand the circulation of this erroneous propaganda."[25] The reprint gave credence to the hundreds of complaints his office had received and reinforced the fear soldiers felt about reporting on incidents of discrimination. Diggs circulated the letter to the Black press, which had an immediate impact.[26] Sharp ordered remaining copies of the publication with the offensive article removed from circulation, although he denied Diggs's claim that commanders targeted Black servicemen who reported violations of the Air Force's equal treatment policy.

IN APRIL 1960, DIGGS, accompanied by former Tuskegee airman Lt. Col. Daniel "Chappie" James Jr. of the Air Force, spent two weeks visiting six military installations in the US Pacific Command including Travis Air Force Base in San Francisco, and the Tachikawa Air Base and Army Installations in Tokyo, Japan. His investigation involved meeting with commanders and enlisted personnel at each base.[27] Diggs also held individual meetings with soldiers who, afraid of reprisals, preferred to discuss their concerns in private. All told, Diggs estimated that he addressed between 1,200 and 1,500 military servicemen.

On July 7, 1960, Congressman Diggs sent Air Force Secretary Sharp and Secretary of Defense Thomas S. Gates a twenty-five-page report of his investigation.[28] In the Philippines and Japan, Black servicemen reported encountering "shabby and offensive treatment" in clubs, restaurants, and other businesses near military bases. Restaurants, theaters, and recreational facilities near the bases discriminated against Black servicemen. Commanders repeatedly told the Diggs team they "can't tell owners of businesses what to do" and that the servicemen preferred to segregate. However, Black troops told Diggs that racial segregation was enforced "through a system of reprisal, intimidation, and physical violence." Meanwhile, local business owners told him they had no problem serving Black servicemen or integrating their establishments but were only responding to the prejudices and threats of boycotts from white American military personnel.

Diggs discovered "frequent" allegations of discriminatory practices in off-base housing everywhere he visited. Base commanders, Diggs argued, could "solve this." If commanders could declare brothels off-limits, they could do the same for places of businesses that practiced racial discrimination. "The failure to exercise such control is inexcusable," Diggs stressed.

Diggs also concluded that Black servicemen were at a disadvantage regarding promotions and assignments and filling "an obvious disproportionate number" of low-skilled, service-oriented assignments and holding "an inconsequential and unrepresentative proportion" of technical or skilled assignments. Diggs argued that white commanders employed "subtle" techniques that resulted in Black servicemen being "deliberately and arbitrarily kept in lower positions." The result of such entrenched discrimination was poor morale among Black servicemen.

To rectify this, Diggs recommended that commanders and enlisted personnel be better trained on the inspector general system and that the military encourage its use when violations were not solved at the base level. He also recommended that each base establish an "officers' program" to focus attention on full implementation of the military's equal treatment policy and to hold base commanders accountable for how well or not nondiscrimination and equal treatment occurred. Diggs advocated that base commanders and military officials play a role in preventing off-base housing discrimination by declaring private housing off-limits to all personnel unless it was equally available to Black and white military personnel.

CONGRESSMAN DIGGS was also determined to do his part to put more Black Americans in the officers' ranks. As a member of Congress, Diggs could nominate candidates for admission into military academies. Throughout his congressional career Diggs made a special effort to recruit young Black men to apply. One student Diggs supported in 1960 for the Naval Academy was Joseph Paul Reason, a third-year Howard University engineering major, who had already passed an examination for admission into the Naval Reserve Officers Training Corps (NROTC) at the University of Rochester.[29] Although Reason had finished second out of 300 applications, he had been rejected by the Southern regional NROTC admission board because he was a Black applicant. With Diggs's encouragement, Reason reapplied. In 1996, Reason became the first Black officer in the Navy to become a four-star admiral.[30]

Bonnie Gallagher, who worked for Diggs on constituent services, remembered that by the 1970s, recruiting and encouraging applicants for entrance into the military academies became one of her "biggest projects." Diggs "was very proud" whenever one of his Black nominees graduated from West Point or the Naval Academy, she recalled.[31]

Diggs was rapidly becoming a key advocate in Washington for fighting racial discrimination throughout the military. NAACP lawyers even began directing many complaints it received from soldiers and military personnel to Diggs, telling soldiers that because Diggs had "shown an interest in discriminatory practices against Negro servicemen" and "has some influence in such matters" they should contact him.[32]

ON JULY 13, 1960, just a few days after Diggs submitted his investigative report, the Democratic Party nominated Senator John F. Kennedy of Massachusetts to be the party's candidate for president. Kennedy felt he owed a debt to Black Americans, who supported him in large numbers. Despite this, Kennedy was not yet prepared to make civil rights the centerpiece of his administration; rather, the Kennedy administration used executive action to address concerns about racial policies and practices in the US military.

On March 6, 1961, the new president issued Executive Order 10925, ensuring equal opportunity for all qualified persons, without regard to race, creed, color, or national origin, employed or seeking employment with the federal government. That same day, Diggs wrote Secretary of Defense Robert S. McNamara, about continued off-base discrimination against Black troops in Germany.[33] McNamara, the former head of Ford Motor Company, approached military management from the perspective of modern systems analysis and knew some branches of the military were better integrated than others; he was concerned about the impact of Black troop morale on military efficiency. However, McNamara was not especially concerned about off-base discrimination.

The administration, however, could not ignore the growing momentum of civil rights activism. By 1962 McNamara had approved a series of policy directives focused on discrimination at military installations, among them policies prohibiting the use of DOD facilities by any organization practicing discrimination and barring military police from joining with local authorities to support the enforcement of segregation or other forms of racial discrimination.[34] The directives, however, were vague, providing wide discretion but little guidance to base commanders on how to handle race relations and the civilian community.

The flurry of directives did not ease Diggs's concerns. He remained vigilant, and on August 24, 1961, Diggs wrote McNamara asking him to give "paramount attention to the continuing problem of racial discrimination" in the military, including off-base.[35] Diggs also asked McNamara to examine continued discrimination against Black Americans in the National Guards, demanding that DOD force Southern states to allow Black soldiers to serve in their guard units. Given the continued racial challenges facing the US military, Diggs urged McNamara to do something bold to add meaning to equal treatment and form a "Citizen Study Committee" that "could make an effective study of the present status of the Equality of Treatment Executive Order on a service-wide basis, objectively delve into the situation and present problems they find with recommendations for their solution."[36]

On September 5, 1961, Assistant Secretary Carlisle Runge responded to Diggs's letter with the same tired excuses. "We cannot force a local community to accept any citizen, in or out of uniform," Runge wrote.[37] He dismissed the notion of the Citizen Study Committee. The response infuriated Diggs. On September 11, 1961, Diggs again wrote McNamara calling Runge's response "totally unsatisfactory and completely lacking in comprehension of the problems discussed."[38]

Congressman Diggs's strong reaction got the attention of McNamara and the White House. On Friday, September 23, 1961, Diggs met Adam Yarmolinsky, McNamara's special assistant, and Runge at the Pentagon to discuss "his recent correspondence with Secretary McNamara."[39] On February 12, 1962, the ever-vigilant Diggs wrote McNamara again, determined to push the DOD to expand the scope of the military's equality of treatment policies. Diggs's letter began, "The status of Negro Servicemen now serving in the United States Armed Forces at home and abroad is an international disgrace. The National Guard situation is even worse."[40] Diggs wrote that "within the past sixty days" he had received "well over 250 complaints" alleging "discrimination in job assignments, upgrading, promotions, and the use of housing and recreation facilities in communities in proximity to military installations."[41]

Diggs included in the letter an eight-page summary report of 255 complaints from Black service personnel that his office had received over the prior two months and an attachment of thirteen "exhibits" of specific complaints and incidents of racial discrimination in the US armed forces, including a newspaper article with the alarming headline: "Negro GI Finds Bamberg, Germany a Living Hell."[42] "I reiterate my strong contention that a Citizens Committee be invited by you to investigate the current status of integration in the Armed Forces, and the general allegations contained in complaints that have been made," Diggs wrote.[43]

Diggs did not yet know it, but his relentless pressure was beginning to have an impact.

Internal memoranda and letters indicate that Diggs's letter and exhibits were discussed by senior White House officials and were also forwarded to each branch of the armed services for comments.[44] McNamara recalled that Yarmolinsky "urged that we set up an outside group to examine the department's practices. I agreed to do so."[45]

On March 6, 1962, Deputy Assistant Secretary of Defense Stephen S. Jackson informed Diggs that the DOD had forwarded his letter of February 12 to the secretaries of each of the services and had directed them to investigate each of the cases Diggs mentioned.[46] "We feel that you will be happy to know that we are planning the establishment of a Citizens Committee, such as you have proposed, to consider the problems of our Service members," he wrote.[47] Although Yarmolinsky would later take sole credit for the idea, the record clearly shows that Diggs can claim authorship of the idea.[48]

On June 24, 1962, President Kennedy announced that he had appointed a Committee on Equal Opportunity in the Armed Forces. Gerhard Gesell, a prominent Washington, DC, attorney and future federal judge who played a central role in the Watergate investigation a decade later, was chosen to serve as chair.

On June 27, 1962, three days after Kennedy's announcement, Diggs wrote a lengthy letter to President Kennedy telling him that he "personally hailed" the announcement of the Gesell Committee.[49] Diggs also let Kennedy know it was he who "first urged the establishment of the Citizens' Committee you have commendably brought into reality."[50]

ON JUNE 13, 1963, the Gesell Committee confirmed many of the issues Diggs had reported to the DOD and the military secretaries. The bulk of the report, however, focused on off-base discrimination. Their recommendations mimicked those Diggs had long proposed: recommending that base commanders place "off-limits sanctions" on all businesses and facilities that refused equal treatment to all servicemen; and noting that the closing of bases in hard-core segregation areas that refused to comply would be considered as a last resort. The committee also concluded that equal treatment was a command responsibility that went beyond the military installation's gates, and it connected off-based discrimination to deteriorating Black troop morale and military efficiency.

Secretary McNamara agreed with many of the recommendations. In July 1963, he issued a directive ordering every military commander to develop a desegregation program to open to Black servicemen and their dependents all public accommodations in the vicinity of military installations in the continental United States, and he encouraged base commanders to work with civilian authorities to open restaurants and other private businesses to all servicemen.[51] Only the Secretary of Defense could authorize off-limit sanctions for racial discrimination. Nevertheless, DOD reports show that these voluntary efforts "achieved gratifying results."[52] Before the full implementation of the 1964 Civil Rights Act, local commanders helped open thousands of theaters, bowling alleys, and restaurants to Black servicemen and their families.[53]

Housing, however, would remain a problem for Black servicemen. McNamara embraced the philosophy of the Gesell Committee, one long advocated by Diggs, and in July 1967 issued a directive forbidding all personnel from leasing or renting housing in any segregated apartment building or trailer court near the Andrews Air Force Base, Maryland, in suburban Washington, DC. In September 1967, McNamara extended the sanctions nationwide. The DOD's open housing campaign was launched before the 1968 Fair Housing Act.[54]

Congressman Diggs was not satisfied. His advocacy for the expansion of civil rights would only grow stronger, as would his public profile.

Chapter 13

BROTHERS IN THE STRUGGLE

Diggs and Martin Luther King Jr.

THE MURDER OF EMMETT TILL and the trial's unjust verdict thrust Congressman Charles Diggs Jr. into the national spotlight. Throughout the winter of 1955, Diggs traveled the country speaking about the trial at rallies sponsored by the NAACP. And even as the White House maintained that the federal government lacked any legal authority to enforce civil rights in the states, Diggs continued to call on the federal government to protect the civil rights of Black citizens in the South.

In December 1955, when Black residents in Montgomery, Alabama, launched a boycott to protest segregated seating on city buses, the event propelled to prominence a twenty-six-year-old preacher, Dr. Martin Luther King Jr.[1] In February 1956, after King and nearly 100 others were indicted on state charges for violating the prohibition against economic boycotts, the young leader garnered attention and support from Black people across the country.

Over 800 miles away, Charles Diggs Jr. used his radio program to raise money to support the boycott. In March 1956, as Diggs recalled years later, "I contacted Dr. King . . . and he invited me to come down . . . to speak. I came down and brought this money. It was the first time I met Dr. King."[2] Diggs delivered $5,000 to King, stayed to observe King's four-day trial; Diggs returned again to Alabama a few weeks later, with nearly another $5,000, to speak at a huge rally with King and other boycott organizers.[3] In a letter, King later acknowledged that Diggs's visits helped bring attention to the boycott, saying, "I cannot adequately express our gratitude to you and other friends who are responsible for the tremendous interest shown in our behalf," King wrote Diggs.[4] It was the beginning of a friendship between the two men—one, the son of a preacher, the other, the son of a funeral director. Diggs and King became brothers in the struggle for Black civil rights.

"PRESIDENT EISENHOWER always had to be pushed" on civil rights, Diggs recalled years later.[5] No civil rights legislation had been adopted by Congress since Reconstruction. Blocked by Southern Democrats and some conservative Republicans, overcoming a filibuster in the Senate to pass civil rights legislation proved impossible. Diggs called the filibuster "the most potent weapon" used to oppose Black civil rights.[6]

In January 1956, in the wake of the Till verdict, the Montgomery bus boycott, and growing violence, President Eisenhower announced that his attorney general would send a civil rights bill to Congress. Eisenhower was up for reelection and advisers told him that proposing a civil rights bill could appeal to Black voters.[7] Even though Diggs found the proposed bill tepid, he was inclined to support it. He understood the urgency for any federal action and spent considerable time explaining the significance of the bill to colleagues.

On June 18, 1956, the House passed the administration's civil rights bill. But there was no time for the Senate to act before adjournment, which allowed both Democratic and Republican candidates to take credit for the symbolic passage of the bill in the House. In the 1956 elections, Eisenhower won by a landslide, yet Democrats maintained control of the House and held a slim two-vote majority in the Senate. After the inauguration, Eisenhower resubmitted the attorney general's civil rights bill. Meanwhile, the US Supreme Court ruled Alabama's segregated bus law unconstitutional, thus ending the yearlong Montgomery boycott.

In January 1957, King formed the Southern Christian Leadership Conference (SCLC), seeking to build from the boycott a national civil rights movement. Diggs agreed to serve on the SCLC's national advisory board.[8] The two men grew closer as Diggs had to navigate tensions between the upstart and activist-oriented SCLC and the established and more conservative NAACP. In March 1957, Diggs was a member of the US government's official delegation to Ghana for a celebration of the African nation's independence. Dr. King and his wife, Coretta, were also there. After Ghana, Diggs met up with the Kings in Paris, where they dined together.[9]

On May 17, 1957, Diggs spoke before a crowd of more than 25,000 at the Lincoln Memorial for the Prayer Pilgrimage, an event cosponsored by the SCLC, the NAACP, and A. Phillip Randolph, founder of the Brotherhood of Sleeping Car Porters, to urge for passage of the civil right bill. Diggs criticized Eisenhower for slow-walking civil rights and Lyndon B. Johnson (the Senate majority leader) for refusing to curtail use of the filibuster.[10] But Diggs and every other speaker were overshadowed by King's rousing "Give Us the Ballot" speech. Going forward, while King became the face of the civil rights movement, Diggs would become ever more prominent as a voice for civil rights in Congress. Over the next decade, as Diggs pushed for change in Washington, the two men grew closer and embarked on parallel tracks to effect change.

In early June 1957, the House again passed the civil rights bill. In the Senate,

Lyndon Johnson—believing that getting a civil rights bill through the Senate would aid his expected run for president in 1960—worked to weaken the bill enough to avoid a filibuster by Southern Democrats.[11] The Senate passed the watered-down bill. The House subsequently approved the bill, and in August 1957, Eisenhower quietly signed the 1957 Civil Rights Act into law.

Diggs and King would prove to be a potent and effective team. Before Diggs spoke in the South he often consulted with King.[12] And in late 1957, when the SCLC's first major initiative, a voter-registration campaign called "The Crusade for Citizenship," fell into organizational disarray, Diggs advised King on how to run an effective voter-registration effort.[13] "Rallies and speeches are fine for inspirational purposes, but a successful registration campaign demands skillful follow-up in the field."[14] King later told Diggs he was "deeply grateful" for Diggs's "wise and judicial counsel."[15]

In March of 1958, King came to Detroit to deliver several sermons at a local church. While there, Diggs took King to see Detroit's East Side, the economic hub of Black Detroit, and to tour the House of Diggs and Diggs Enterprises. "It was a great privilege to have you escort me through Diggs Enterprises," King wrote Diggs later. "Although I knew the Diggs Enterprises represented an important business setup, I had no idea it was so extensive until the other day. You and your father are doing marvelous work in the world of business."[16] By 1960, Diggs and King were addressing each other by their first names. Only close friends of Dr. King called him Martin or Marty.[17]

DIGGS CONTINUED to speak out against the violence perpetrated against Black people in Mississippi and in support of federal civil rights and voting rights legislation. During the summer of 1962, the Southern Regional Council in Atlanta sponsored a new voter-registration program and provided funding to the Council of Federated Organizations, an ad hoc coalition comprising the SCLC, the Congress of Racial Equality (CORE), the NAACP, and the Student Nonviolent Coordinating Committee (SNCC). The program targeted potential voters in several Mississippi Delta counties, including Coahoma and Leflore.[18] Whites in Mississippi responded with more shootings and bombings, and in the winter of 1962–63, white local officials in Greenwood punished Black residents by suspending the county's participation in the federal surplus commodities food program. Diggs successfully lobbied the US Department of Agriculture to resume distribution of basic foods to the county's poorest residents.[19]

In Clarksdale, Mississippi, the police arrested Council of Federated Organizations president Aaron Henry and other leaders on trumped-up charges. On April 3, 1963, someone tossed a gas bomb through the window of Centennial Baptist Church during a worship service, when it was full with 800 worshippers. Fortunately, the bomb did not detonate.[20] As the situation in the Delta worsened, Henry asked Diggs to come to get a firsthand look.[21]

Diggs arrived in Clarksdale on April 10. That evening, he addressed a "Freedom Meeting" sponsored by the Coahoma County NAACP, and he spoke at a huge mass meeting at the Jerusalem Baptist Church the following day. On April 12, Good Friday, as Dr. King wrote his famous letter from a cell in the Birmingham jail, Henry showed Diggs around Clarksdale and neighboring towns. That night, Diggs and Henry returned to Clarksdale where Diggs would spend the night at Henry's home with his wife and eleven-year-old daughter. Medgar Evers and Curtis Wilkie, a white reporter for Clarkdale's *Press Register*, came over. They all "sat around and drank beer" late into the night before Evers and Wilkie departed.[22]

At about 3 a.m., Saturday morning, when Diggs and the others were asleep, several Molotov cocktails came flying through the living room window. Henry awakened and "ran to the living room and found the curtains blazing and room quickly filled with smoke."[23] He rushed to his daughter and got her out of the house. Then another bomb exploded. Henry ran back in to check on his wife and Diggs. Diggs called the fire department as "the entire front part of the house was illuminated with flames, and the smoke was getting worse," Henry later wrote.[24] Diggs and Henry "started a water brigade from the kitchen to the living room, fearing every moment that another bomb would explode."[25] The two men managed to extinguish the fire, and another bomb in the carport failed to explode. No one was injured. Two white men were quickly arrested.

News of the bombing was printed in every major newspaper in the country.[26] Diggs told reporters he was "extremely upset.... The emotional impact of being awakened by a bomb out of the dead of sleep is tremendous."[27] The bombing "reflects the resistance of some white elements to the potentially of the voting drive."[28] Diggs said he planned to meet with President John F. Kennedy and would ask the House Judiciary Committee to conduct some of its upcoming civil rights hearings in the Mississippi Delta.

SINCE TAKING OFFICE in January 1961, Kennedy had moved cautiously concerning civil rights, fearful of alienating Southern Democrats. But the violence triggered after James Meredith's admission into the University of Mississippi, the seething scenes of terror in the Mississippi Delta, and the police dogs and fire hoses brought out by Bull Connor in response to King's nonviolent protest campaign in Birmingham in April and May of 1963, moved public opinion.

On June 11, 1963, President Kennedy gave an Oval Office address on national television, promising to send a civil rights bill to Congress; this was welcome news to Diggs and to other Black leaders. In Mississippi, Medgar Evers heard the president's speech while attending a NAACP meeting in Jackson. When he returned home, shortly after midnight, a sniper shot Evers in the back near his front door. Diggs would return to Mississippi days later to attend his funeral.[29]

The Birmingham campaign strained the SCLC's resources. King needed to raise more money. He turned to his friends in Detroit, Charles Diggs Jr. and Reverend C. L. Franklin, Aretha Franklin's father, who was nationally known as a gifted fundraiser.[30] On Sunday, June 23, 1963, Diggs, King, Franklin, Detroit Mayor Jerome Cavanagh, Walter Reuther, and other local leaders locked arms and marched down Detroit's Woodward Avenue for four miles to Cobo Hall. An estimated 125,000 participants, nearly all of them Black people, many carrying signs, followed in relative silence, as tens of thousands more watched from sidewalks and buildings. At the time, it was the largest civil rights demonstration in US history. At the end of the march, over 25,000 supporters stood elbow to elbow inside Cobo Hall. Diggs took the stage and gave King a rousing introduction, calling him "America's beloved freedom fighter." The crowd roared. Motown Records produced a recording of King's Detroit speech, and many Black Americans would listen to Diggs's forceful introduction and King's moving speech.

In his speech, Dr. King sketched out the origins of the burgeoning civil rights movement, stressing the power of nonviolence and endorsing Kennedy's civil rights bill. He talked about the "new militancy" in Black America, acknowledging the rise of Malcolm X and other Black Power advocates.[31] He also mentioned the murders of Emmett Till and Medgar Evers. As King concluded, he gave a longer version of the now-famous "I Have a Dream" speech he would deliver two months later at the March on Washington. He incorporated two important issues for Black Detroit—housing and jobs, saying, "I have a dream this afternoon that one day, right here in Detroit, Negroes will be able to buy a house or rent a house anywhere that their money will carry them, and they will be able to get a job."

Although Diggs welcomed the growing militancy within the Black community, he was concerned that some radicals would go too far; and he privately told White House officials he shared their concern about potential summer "public disturbances" occurring in the District of Columbia.[32] Perhaps the most dynamic new leader of the growing militancy was Malcolm X, a leader in the Nation of Islam.[33] According to an internal White House memo, "He [Diggs] also agreed that Malcolm X represented a potential threat, not only because of his potential ability to become a spokesman for large mass of Washington Negroes, but also because if he did so, or to the extent that he did so, he was not a person with whom one could deal on a rational basis."[34]

This rise of militancy made Diggs vigilant about plans concerning the March on Washington scheduled for August 1963. In late June 1963, Diggs expressed his concerns to King, writing that he worried that the march's organizers could not manage the "tremendous logistics problem" of bringing "100,000 to 300,000" people to Washington, DC.[35] Diggs warned that King had "considerable responsibility" in seeing that nothing went wrong during the demonstration.[36] Ralph Abernathy, King's top lieutenant, recalled that Diggs "even asked that the leadership reconsider the idea."[37] In the end, the march took place without disruption, becoming a seminal event in the civil rights movement.

The momentum Diggs and other Black leaders felt coming out of the successful March on Washington suddenly ended in November 1963 in Dallas, Texas, with Kennedy's assassination. The President never lived to see if Congress would pass his omnibus civil rights bill.

Diggs, like many others, had "a considerable amount of reservation" about Lyndon Johnson's commitment to civil rights.[38] However, sensing a window of opportunity in the grief for the martyred Kennedy, the politically astute Johnson pushed the civil rights bill through Congress. The Civil Rights Act of 1964 was signed into law on July 2, 1964. Diggs would later say that Johnson "kept that commitment" to civil rights "beyond even the wildest dreams of anybody that had any reservations about him."[39]

IN THE SUMMER 1964, trouble was brewing as the Democrats prepared to nominate their party's candidate for president, Lyndon B. Johnson, and announce at the convention the selection of Minnesota senator Hubert H. Humphrey, a liberal with a national reputation for supporting civil rights, as vice president. Diggs and King found themselves in the middle of it all.

Two different delegations from Mississippi arrived at the Democratic National Convention (DNC) in Atlantic City, New Jersey: One, an all-white, party-sanctioned segregationist slate; the other, an insurgent, racially integrated, yet predominantly Black slate representing the Mississippi Freedom Democratic Party (MFDP), organized by Robert Moses, Aaron Henry, and other SNCC activists. The MFDP hoped to convince the DNC to seat them.[40] To do so, they needed first to gain the support of 10 percent—*11 members*—of the 110-member DNC Credentials Committee, and then get 8 state delegations to vote to hear a "minority report" from the committee on the convention floor. Diggs was 1 of only 7 Black members of the DNC Credentials Committee.

Johnson, fearful of losing votes in the South, opposed seating the MFDP delegation, and privately, Diggs told Aaron Henry the MFDP should "think about alternatives" to replacing the entire all-white regular delegation.[41]

The Credentials Committee heard testimony from Martin L. King Jr., Roy

Wilkins, James Farmer, and Mrs. Fannie Lou Hamer in support of the MFDP.[42] Johnson eventually proposed a compromise that would allow the MFDP to be "seated as honored guests" and permit two MFDP delegates to cast votes as "special delegates-at-large."[43] Hubert Humphrey was charged with persuading civil rights leaders such as Dr. King to convince the MFDP to accept the compromise. The MFDP, however, rejected Johnson's proposal and a subsequent offer.

The White House, fearful that at least eleven members of the Credentials Committee were supporters of the MFDP and could bring the issue of the MFDP's seating to a potentially divisive floor vote of the delegates of the DNC, wanted to surreptitiously identify the MFDP supporters on the Credentials Committee and to pressure them to instead support Johnson's compromise proposal. Diggs played a big role in helping Johnson identify MFDP supporters among the Credentials Committee.

Diggs used his influence, his well-known reputation as a strong supporter of Black civil rights, and some pressure to obtain the names of the MFDP's supporters on the committee and then Diggs secretly shared them with the White House; Diggs concluded that Johnson's "two seats" proposal was "a good deal."[44] Johnson then had the FBI tap and bug the phones and hotel rooms of MFDP members and their supporters on the Credentials Committee.[45] James Forman of SNCC called the White House pressure campaign (that Diggs help facilitate) "the great squeeze."[46]

Meanwhile, UAW president Walter Reuther convinced Dr. King to support the compromise, arguing that a floor dispute would damage Johnson and might lead to a Democratic vice-presidential nominee who could be less sympathetic on civil rights. The MFDP, however, rejected Johnson's compromise.

In the end, it didn't matter. Johnson's "squeeze" worked. The Credentials Committee convened and approved MFDP leaders Aaron Henry and Ed King to be seated as "at-large" delegates—two additional votes. The other MFDP delegates could attend as guests, and the "regular" Mississippi delegation would be required to sign a loyalty oath to support the party's nominee. Significantly, party leaders pledged to eliminate racial discrimination in the selection of delegates in all future conventions.

Still, Aaron Henry felt betrayed by Diggs. Years later he wrote, "Charles Diggs, a longtime friend of mine who had been willing to sign the [minority] report was not to be found. He turned out to be a party man. . . . Perhaps this shows that the very best kind of people can become so much a part of the machine that they can only think in terms of the party's welfare."[47]

Diggs had no regrets. He believed what happened in Atlantic City would move Black Americans toward political incorporation into the Democratic Party. Diggs, King, and the other civil rights leaders were in alignment. A few weeks later Diggs explained, "Had a divisive floor fight developed the President probably would have been forced to select as his Number Two man a person less identified with the liberal wing of the party."[48]

By September 1964, the relationship between Diggs and King drew close enough that after the Atlantic City convention, Diggs felt comfortable enough to ask King to be the principal speaker at a testimonial dinner to be held in Diggs's honor. SCLC staffer Andrew Young responded to Diggs's request saying that because of the "personal friendship" between King and Diggs, "Dr. King would certainly like to share in the testimonial banquet" but that King's schedule would not allow it.[49]

King was preparing for a big battle over voting rights, which the 1957, 1960, and 1964 Civil Rights Acts had failed to guarantee. In many counties in the South, 90 percent or more of Black people of voting age were not registered to vote. President Johnson recognized the problem, and in his first State of the Union address, he directed the attorney general to draft legislation that would enforce constitutional guarantees to vote. Johnson, however, was "ambivalent about putting a voting rights bill before Congress in early 1965. Not because he doubted the value of giving blacks the ballot.... Rather, he was reluctant to force another confrontation with the South."[50] Events in Selma, the seat of Dallas County, Alabama, soon changed Johnson's calculation.

IN JANUARY 1965, Dr. King, now a Nobel laureate, brought the SCLC to Selma, a city with a population of 29,000; of these, 15,000 were Black residents of voting age, of whom only 355 were registered voters.[51] State law restricted voter registration to only two days per month and required a "literacy test." Black prospective registrants (including college graduates) were always told they failed.

Since July 1964, after Black people tried to desegregate Selma's restaurants and other public accommodations following the adoption of the Civil Rights Act, the city had been under a local circuit court judge's injunction barring more than three Black people from assembling.[52] Dallas County sheriff James "Jim" Clark was a rabid segregationist with an uncontrollable temper and a visceral hatred of Black people.

Beginning in January 1965, dozens of Black people peacefully walked each day to the courthouse to register to vote. Each day a handful were arrested for violating the judge's injunction. As the arrests increased, more protesters converged on the county courthouse, provoking Sheriff Clark. By early February, Clark arrested and jailed more than 3,000 demonstrators. Many were physically assaulted.[53]

On February 1, King and Ralph Abernathy intentionally got arrested. Determined to keep the national spotlight on Black voting in Alabama, King refused to post bond. Later that evening Sheriff Clark arrested another 700 demonstrators. King sent word to Diggs and asked him to organize a congressional delegation to come to Selma to help keep national attention focused on voting rights.[54] Diggs quickly agreed. Meanwhile, Malcolm X arrived in Selma to support voting rights. A few weeks later, he would be assassinated in New York City.

On February 4, President Johnson spoke forcefully in support of Black voting rights at a White House press conference, but he emphasized that he intended to use existing civil rights laws and the federal courts to protect voting rights for Black people.[55] Later the same day, Diggs held a Capitol Hill press conference and announced that he would lead an "unofficial" bipartisan House delegation to Selma to get "a fair and honest picture from all sides."[56] Members of the Alabama congressional delegation warned Diggs not to visit Selma. "I urge and implore my colleagues not to inject themselves into a situation that is critical and could be dangerous," cautioned an Alabama representative.[57] Diggs and the delegation went anyway, arriving on February 5 in a "caravan of funeral cars" arranged by Diggs to drive them from the Montgomery airport to Selma, across the Edmond Pettus Bridge, before arriving downtown.[58]

The fifteen-member delegation headed straight to the city jail, but Diggs was confronted by Joseph Smitherman, Selma's recently elected "moderate segregationist" mayor, who read a statement saying he did not want nor need any outside help.[59] Moments later King walked out of the jail with aides on each side. He was quickly greeted by Diggs. Diggs and the delegation met with King and his advisers. King pressed for federal legislation to eliminate literacy test requirements and to require the appointment of federal registrars in counties where discrimination against Black applicants was identified. King later told reporters he tried to make the congressmen "conscious of the terrible injustice" in Alabama.[60] Diggs and the delegation also met with local officials who all claimed that the backlog of voter applications and the long lines to register were the result of Alabama's two-day per month registration limit.

Andrew Young of SCLC and John Lewis of SNCC escorted Diggs and the congressmen to a meeting with Selma's Black leaders.[61] As Diggs later explained, the Black community was "greatly lifted by the fact that a delegation would come from Washington to try to help them."[62] The congressmen took depositions from Black individuals who testified about being denied the right to register and vote and from demonstrators who were arrested. Several members of the delegation came away convinced that federal voting rights legislation was necessary. "I think we've justified our presence here," Diggs told the press.[63]

Upon his return to Washington, DC, Diggs called the literacy test "the most damaging blow to voting opportunities" in Alabama.[64] He inserted into the *Congressional Record* the questionnaire used for voter registration in Dallas County, including the "literacy sections." Diggs also reported that there were "many examples of people who had been harassed, subjected to economic reprisals and other offenses with respect to their effort to register to vote."[65] Other delegation members joined Diggs on the floor to denounce the violence and to demand federal voting rights legislation. Swayed by Diggs's report, many other House members announced their support for federal suffrage legislation.[66]

On Thursday, February 11, Diggs sent a telegram to President Johnson on behalf of the fifteen-member delegation; he emphasized the need to "eliminate once and for all any racial restrictions on exercising the franchise."[67] The telegram urged Johnson to propose legislation to eliminate the literacy test, ban the poll tax in all local elections, and allow for the appointment of federal registrars.

Meanwhile, the SCLC and SNCC expanded their voting rights demonstrations into neighboring Black-belt Alabama counties. On February 17, Jimmie Lee Jackson, a Black veteran, was shot by Alabama state troopers dispersing a protest demonstration in Marion, in Perry County. Jackson died eight days later. A week after the shooting, Diggs and several delegation members met with Vice President Hubert Humphrey and Attorney General Nicholas Katzenbach.[68] Diggs stressed that "any voting rights bill had to be applicable not only to federal elections but to local elections also. Anything short of that is inadequate."[69]

Jackson's death strengthened King's resolve to continue the Alabama campaign until the federal government passed suffrage legislation. At Jackson's funeral on March 3, King announced that he and the SCLC would lead a march from Selma to Montgomery, the state capital, on Sunday, March 7.

A few days after "Bloody Sunday," when Alabama State Patrolmen attacked with clubs and tear gas the unarmed marchers attempting to cross the Edmond Pettus Bridge, Diggs sent President Johnson a telegram demanding federal protection for peaceful demonstrators. He also demanded that the president send to Congress legislation to protect the right of Black Americans to register and vote. Johnson's special assistant, Lawrence O'Brien, responded that the White House was "maintaining close touch with the situation in Alabama" and that the president would send legislation to Congress to secure the right to vote "in the very near future."[70]

Two days later, March 15, President Johnson delivered a dramatic address to a joint session of Congress calling for passage of the voting rights bill drafted by the Justice Department. In late May, after easily overcoming a filibuster, the Senate passed the bill seventy-seven to nineteen. The bill won passage in the House on July 9 by an overwhelming 333 to 85 votes. On August 6, Johnson signed the 1965 Voting Rights Act.

KING RECOGNIZED Diggs's role in the passage of the Voting Rights Act and agreed to serve as keynote speaker for an "appreciation dinner" to be held for him held at Cobo Hall on November 18, 1965, before several thousand members of the local community. It was the only time King ever spoke at "a testimonial gathering" for a public figure.[71]

By 1965, Black Americans were incorporated into Detroit's political and civic life, in many ways because of Diggs and his father. This was illustrated by individuals who sat at the "head table." Papa Diggs and Mayme Diggs were seated with the governor of Michigan, Republican George Romney, Mayor Jerome Cavanagh, Senator Philip A. Hart, Congresswoman Martha Griffiths, leaders of the UAW, and other powerful white civic and political leaders. They were joined by dozens of Black guests, including state senator Coleman A. Young, several other Black members of the Michigan Legislature, and attorney Damon Keith, Diggs's closest friend and cochair of the Michigan Civil Rights Commission, among others.[72]

King's speech foreshadowed his shift in focus from racism and segregation to poverty and unemployment. King was convinced that inner-city poverty and joblessness were the underlying causes of recent disorders in Philadelphia, Harlem, Rochester, and the Watts section of Los Angeles. King called for the federal government to implement "massive public works programs" to combat poverty with full employment.[73]

The speech proved to be both prescient and too late. The frustrations that led to the rebellions elsewhere would soon spark a rebellion in Detroit. Under liberal mayor Jerome Cavanagh, who took office in 1962, Detroit had developed a national reputation as a "model city" in race relations.[74] Few people thought what happened in Los Angeles would be repeated in Detroit.

The Detroit rebellion started in the early morning hours of Sunday, July 23, 1967, after the police raided a "blind pig," an after-hours club in a Black neighborhood, near Twelfth Street and Clairmount Avenue. A confrontation quickly metastasized as tensions between the Black community and Detroit's predominantly white police force exploded.

Diggs, John Conyers, Damon Keith, and other Black leaders could not calm the crowds. "I was on the streets right in the middle of the riot area from about eight o'clock in the morning on," Diggs remembered. "All day long it was just like a carnival. People were walking in and out of these stores that were being looted," Diggs added.[75] The rioters were angry. "Look at him," a Black rioter said to a reporter, pointing at Diggs. "'He ain't never been hungry.'"[76] When John Conyers climbed up on a car to address the rioters, they threw bottles and rocks at him and called him an "Uncle Tom."[77] By late Sunday morning, vandalism and looting were almost citywide. The fires grew throughout the day.

By Monday, July 24, the first full day of the rebellion, local and state officials had lost control of the city. Looting and arson escalated. Many of the Black-owned businesses in Diggs's congressional district were destroyed. On Monday evening Governor Romney and city leaders debated whether to request federal troops. Black leaders were initially divided. John Conyers "feared the army presence would 'inflame' the situation."[78] He opposed calling in federal troops. Damon Keith was old enough to remember the 1943 riot, when more than half of the Black victims who died were killed by law enforcement. Keith also opposed federal intervention. Diggs, however, favored immediate deployment of paratroopers. Diggs feared the damage inflicted on the city was so devastating that without an immediate cessation of the violence, the city might never recover. "That's when I realized we needed outside force," Keith remembered.[79]

President Johnson did not immediately activate the troops; he insisted that the governor first declare that Detroit was in "insurrection" and that he was "unable to enforce law and order in his state without the aid of the U.S. government."[80] Romney knew Johnson was playing politics. Romney was a leading contender for the 1968 Republican presidential nomination, and he felt that Johnson hoped to make him look weak on law and order.

As late as nine-thirty Monday night, Johnson had not yet decided to send in the federal troops. "I called the White House and told them of my concern. I didn't mince words and I didn't try to be diplomatic about it," Diggs told an interviewer.[81] "Diggs raised hell over the phone for about ten minutes about the failure to bring in the troops. He said that the blood was on the Administration's hands, that the Administration was playing politics with the situation," one White House aide recalled.[82] Diggs may not had known it, but by the time he reached the White House, Johnson had already approved the order to send in the federal troops, only a few of whom were Black troops.

The uprising left 43 people dead, nearly 1,200 injured, and more than 7,000 arrested. More than 2,500 buildings were destroyed, and financial losses were estimated to be as high as $500 million. Diggs told a reporter that the insurrection resulted from "the failure of the adult community ... to understand the dynamics and meet the needs of young people, white and Negro. It's something we must come to grips with if we're going to resolve this."[83]

In early August 1967, days after the rebellion ended, Diggs brought together sixty-five Black community and business leaders who agreed to form the

Inner-City Business Improvement Forum to plan for the restoration of the city's Black businesses. The forum advised Black businesses about economic development and provided economic and financial assistance to Detroit's Black businesses. For a short period, it even operated out of Diggs's West Side congressional office before being headquartered in a neatly renovated, two-story brick building in Diggs's congressional district. Within two years, Inner-City Business Improvement Forum provided loans totaling nearly $1 million to Black businesses, which created hundreds of jobs.[84]

Although a host of problems remained, the focus on jobs and economic opportunity advocated by King's lofty rhetoric and put into practice by Diggs and others on the ground made at least a measure of progress possible. In a sense, King's ongoing inspiration provided fuel for Diggs's consistent and pragmatic actions in Congress and as a leader in Detroit. Together, they were a potent team at a time of great change.

UNFORTUNATELY, their alliance and friendship came to an end with King's assassination in Memphis on April 4, 1968. Diggs, like millions of other Americans, was devastated. On April 9, an estimated 200,000 mourners took part in funeral services in Atlanta, followed by an emotional four-mile-long march. Long before the church service got underway, the Atlanta Police estimated that more than 50,000 people had crammed onto the sidewalks and streets surrounding King's church, the Ebenezer Baptist Church.[85]

Diggs was among the 1,300 who crowded into the church. The House of Diggs had never had a funeral of this size nor significance. "So many politicians and celebrities had come for the funeral that there wasn't room for all of Martin's friends and relatives," Ralph Abernathy remembered.[86] Many of the people were white. Vice President Humphrey headed a delegation representing President Johnson. Richard M. Nixon, the former vice president, running to replace the retiring Johnson, was there, as were a group of about sixty to seventy members of Congress, nearly a dozen governors, and celebrities like Marlon Brando and Paul Newman.

There were also civil rights leaders with whom Diggs and King had worked, including Jesse Jackson, Andrew Young, and Roy Wilkins as well as other Black public officials, UN ambassador-at-large Ralph Bunche, Justice Thurgood Marshall, and Senator Edward Brooke, the Black Republican Senator from Massachusetts, among others. There were many Black celebrities, including Diana Ross, Aretha Franklin, Sidney Poitier, and Bill Cosby.

Diggs was seated on the left side of the church, behind the family, with other government officials. He could see King's closed coffin, made of African mahogany, topped with a cross of white carnations. When Mahalia Jackson sang

"Precious Lord, Take My Hand," Diggs began to cry. Family members recalled that Diggs "was very sentimental and would cry at a moment's notice."[87] He dabbed his eyes with his handkerchief. The murder a few years earlier of Medgar Evers, with whom Diggs had worked, had shaken Diggs. Diggs had escaped an attempt on his own life in Mississippi. Now, the assassination of his friend Martin weighed heavily.

Diggs was also among the much smaller crowd of family members and close friends for the service at King's temporary gravesite. He sat in the front row, very close to King's coffin, opposite from the family. A video camera captured Diggs staring at the coffin in deep thought.[88]

Diggs lost not only a close friend but also a strong partner and fighter in the Black freedom struggle. Like many Black leaders, Diggs was likely wondering about the future of the civil rights movement, who would step forward in King's wake, and whether the movement would suffer from a void in Black leadership.

There would, however, be no single figure to replace King. The work was left to those he inspired and touched.

Charles Diggs Jr. soldiered on.

The Reverend James J. Diggs Jr. (1838–1911), Charles C. Diggs Jr.'s grandfather, was born in Mississippi and served as a Baptist missionary to Africa. He gave his son Charles the middle name Coles in honor of his mentor John Coles, America's best-known Black missionary to Africa. Courtesy Weston Diggs Jr.

Lilly Granderson Diggs (1862–1937), Charles C. Diggs Jr.'s grandmother, was in the first graduating class of what is now Jackson State University in Mississippi. Courtesy Weston Diggs Jr.

Charles C. Diggs Sr., a young business, civic, and political leader, ca. 1936. He became the first Black Democrat elected to the Michigan State Senate in 1936. Courtesy Weston Diggs Jr.

Congressman Diggs Jr. (*rear, center*) and his father (*front, center*), with House of Diggs funeral directors and Metropolitan Funeral System Association staff. *Rear, from left to right:* Robert Leatherwood (Congressman Diggs's public relations man), unknown man, James "Jimmy" Diggs, Charles T. Coles, Congressman Diggs, Boyd West, Felix Matlock (he later worked in Diggs's Detroit congressional field office), Carter Jones, Wilbur Hughes, and E. Earthmon Fort. Courtesy Weston Diggs Jr.

Charles C. Diggs Jr. was the second president of the Cotillion Club, a social club for Black businessmen and professionals formed in 1949. In the 1950s and 1960s, the organization became a political base for Black candidates seeking political office. With him are other Cotillion Club presidents. *From left to right:* William T. Patrick, Diggs, William T. Matney Jr., Damon Keith, and Edward Sylvester. Courtesy Weston Diggs Jr.

Front row, left to right: Charles C. Diggs Jr. with Alexis sitting on his knee, Charles III, and Charles C. Diggs Sr. *Back row, left to right:* Juanita, Denise, and Mayme Diggs. Courtesy Charles C. Diggs III.

Charles C. Diggs Sr. (*second from left, second row*) organized a special excursion train to Washington, DC, for 400 supporters to attend Congressman Diggs's swearing-in ceremony in January 1955. *Front row:* Charles III, Alexis, and Denise. *Second row:* Asa T. Canadia, Diggs Sr., Clarine Rosario, Carmelita Rosario, and Juanita R. Diggs. Courtesy Detroit News Collection, Walter P. Reuther Library, Archives of Labor and Urban Affairs, Wayne State University, Detroit, Michigan.

Speaker of the House Sam Rayburn (*center, right*) shakes hands with Charles C. Diggs Jr., on the steps of the US Capitol Building in Washington, DC, January 5, 1955, after a mock swearing-in ceremony for Michigan's first Black congressman. With them are Diggs's family and friends who came for the opening day program. *From left to right:* Charles C. Diggs Sr.; Bishop Raymond Jones, the congressman's uncle; and Charles C. Diggs III. Courtesy Associated Press.

Charles C. Diggs Jr. and Representative Adam Clayton Powell Jr., 1955. Diggs was overshadowed by the publicity-seeking and flamboyant Powell. Courtesy Johnson Publishing Company Archive, J. Paul Getty Trust and Smithsonian National Museum of African American History and Culture, Washington, DC.

Charles C. Diggs Jr. with Alvin Loving (*third from left*) and his wife and Congressman Gerald R. Ford (*right*). Loving was Diggs's high-school debate coach and taught the introverted young man the skills to speak confidently and in a persuasive style. Diggs and Ford were friends and longtime members of Michigan's congressional delegation. Courtesy Gerald R. Ford Presidential Library, Ann Arbor, Michigan.

William L. Dawson, the first Black man to chair a congressional committee. Dawson's conservative politics were frequently contrasted with the militancy of Adam Clayton Powell Jr. Courtesy Associated Press.

Charles C. Diggs Jr. attended the 1955 trial of Emmett Till's murderers in Sumner, Mississippi. Several Black witnesses later reported that Diggs's presence gave them the encouragement they needed to testify at the trial. *Left to right:* John Carthan, Walter Billingsley, Mamie Till-Bradley, Dr. T. R. M. Howard, Diggs, and Amanda Bradley. Courtesy Getty Images.

Charles C. Diggs Jr. in Oahu, Hawaii, with Lt. Henry W. Mack of Detroit on the first leg of a two-week tour of US military bases throughout the Pacific and Far East, April 1960. Courtesy Weston Diggs Jr.

In 1962, Charles C. Diggs Jr. authored legislation that designated Frederick Douglass's home in Washington, DC, as a part of the National Park System. Diggs looks on with Senator Philip A. Hart (D-MI) (*left*) and President Kennedy in the White House Oval Office. Courtesy John F. Kennedy Presidential Library, Boston.

In February 1965, Dr. Martin L. King Jr. asked Charles C. Diggs Jr. to lead a congressional delegation to Selma, Alabama, to observe the racial situation firsthand. Diggs (*left, first row*) and the delegation poses with King. Courtesy Associated Press.

Charles C. Diggs Jr. comforts his mother at the funeral of his father, who committed suicide in April 1967. Courtesy Weston Diggs Jr.

During the 1967 Detroit rebellion, Charles C. Diggs Jr. toured the affected areas of the city. Diggs favored immediate deployment of federal troops to quell the disturbances. Courtesy Tony Spina Photographs, Walter P. Reuther Library, Archives of Labor and Urban Affairs, Wayne State University, Detroit, Michigan.

On March 25, 1971, Charles C. Diggs Jr. and the Congressional Black Caucus met with President Richard Nixon at the White House. For over a year, Nixon had refused to meet with them. *Left side, left to right:* Parren Mitchell (D-MD), Shirley Chisholm (D-NY), Diggs, Nixon, Augustus Hawkins (D-CA), William Clay (D-MO), Ronald Dellums (D-CA), unknown man. *Right side, left to right:* Charles Rangel (D-NY), Louis Stokes (D-OH), John Conyers (D-MI), Robert Nix (D-PA), and Walter Fauntroy (D-DC). Courtesy Richard M. Nixon Presidential Library, Yorba Linda, California.

Charles C. Diggs Jr. with his second wife, Anna Johnston Diggs, September 1970. They divorced in 1971. In 1979, Anna Diggs was confirmed as a judge on the US District Court for the Eastern District of Michigan. Courtesy Detroit News Collection, Walter P. Reuther Library, Archives of Labor and Urban Affairs, Wayne State University, Detroit, Michigan.

Together with Amiri Baraka and Gary, Indiana, mayor Richard Hatcher, Charles C. Diggs Jr. cochaired the National Black Political Convention in Gary, Indiana, March 10–12, 1972. The convention brought together 8,000 Black civil rights activists and Black Power leaders with the goal of unifying the integrationists and separatist camps around a common Black political agenda. Reverend Jesse Jackson (*right*) was among the convention's keynote speakers. Courtesy Associated Press.

In 1970, as chair of the Foreign Affairs Committee's Subcommittee on Africa, Charles C. Diggs Jr. held hearings that examined South Africa's refusal to grant Arthur Ashe (*left*), the twenty-six-year-old Black American tennis star, a visa to play in the South African Open. Courtesy Associated Press.

In March 1977, President Carter invited Congressman Diggs (*third from right*) and other House and Senate members to the White House for a bill signing ceremony repealing the Byrd Amendment and restoring economic sanctions on Rhodesia's illegal government. Diggs had advocated and organized for years to reverse the Byrd Amendment. *From left to right, standing in the front row:* Senator Clifford P. Case (R-NJ), Senator Hubert H. Humphrey (D-MN), Senator Dick Clark (D-IA), Diggs, Senator Edward Brooke (R-MA), unknown man. Courtesy Associated Press.

Randall Robinson, who worked as Congressman Diggs's chief of staff from August 1976 to May 1978 and who organized what became TransAfrica, may have been the confidential informant who reported Diggs's payroll violations to the US Department of Justice. Courtesy Getty Images.

As a freshman congressman, Newt Gingrich (R-GA) targeted the convicted Congressman Diggs as an example of Democratic Party corruption and pushed for Diggs's expulsion from Congress. On July 31, 1979, the House voted 414–0 to censure Diggs. Courtesy Associated Press.

On May 14, 1980, sitting in his Capitol Hill office, with a trove of books and memorabilia from his many trips to Africa, Charles C. Diggs Jr. announced his retirement. He told reporters he hoped his "accomplishments . . . will not be forgotten." Courtesy Detroit News Collection, Walter P. Reuther Library, Archives of Labor and Urban Affairs, Wayne State University, Detroit, Michigan.

Charles C. Diggs Jr. arrives at the US District Court in Washington, DC, to wait for jury deliberations to begin in his trial on corruption charges, October 6, 1978. The jury convicted him on all twenty-nine charges. Courtesy Associated Press.

In 1974, Charles C. Diggs Jr. (*right*) authored legislation that established the University of the District of Columbia. He considered it one of his most important legislative contributions. In 1995, Charles C. Diggs Jr was recognized as the "Father of UDC" and was congratulated by UDC president Tilden J. LeMelle (*center*) and Michele V. Hagans (*left*), chair of the UDC Board of Trustees. Courtesy University of the District of Columbia.

Chapter 14
THE FOUNDING OF THE CONGRESSIONAL BLACK CAUCUS

WHILE MARTIN LUTHER KING JR. served as the leader of the Southern civil rights movement that began in the 1950s, by the middle and late 1960s a new generation of Black leaders had emerged, and these new leaders expressed a radical militancy of cultural pride and racial solidarity. Between 1964 and 1968 in New York, Baltimore, Newark, New Jersey, Detroit, and other cities, "urban rebellions" became a mechanism whereby the Black dispossessed expressed their impatience with racial oppression. Stokely Carmichael, a former leader of SNCC, emerged as a leader of the Black Power Movement. Huey Newton and Bobby Seale, leaders of the Black Panther Party for Self-Defense, based in Oakland, California, received widespread media coverage and quickly became nationally known for their militancy.[1] The Black Power Movement was a call for racial unity. It sought organizational and political change and would lead to the development of Black interest groups and racially exclusive organizations.

Few observers of Black politics anticipated that Richard Nixon would eventually win the presidency in 1968 by pandering to the white racist vote in the South. As Eisenhower's vice president, Nixon was viewed as a moderate but constructive supporter of civil rights.[2] Yet after Nixon lost narrowly to Senator John F. Kennedy in the 1960 presidential election, Nixon responded to growing Black militancy not by embracing civil rights but by embracing white fear. During the 1968 presidential race against Democrat Hubert Humphrey and former Alabama governor George Wallace, who ran as a segregationist third-party candidate, Nixon campaigned on "law and order." He opposed school busing and unfairly criticized Lyndon Johnson and the Democrats for creating what he called welfare dependency as he pandered to white fear stemming from the widespread civil disturbances.

None of this could have been foreseen when Charles Diggs Jr. entered Congress. He understood Black Power and its extraordinary and positive potential in mobilizing Black communities to address a growing "urban crisis."[3] Yet

Diggs's position as a member of Congress and an "insider" in the existing political system required an approach that differed from the words and deeds of civil rights leaders of the era. Diggs also concluded that combating the urban crisis and outmaneuvering President Richard Nixon required something quite different from working the committee system in the hope of changing federal policy. Much more was needed. The creation of the Congressional Black Caucus would be the result.

ON JANUARY 23, 1957, John H. Johnson, the influential founder and publisher of *Ebony* and *Jet* magazines, wrote Diggs, Adam Clayton Powell, and William Dawson and asked the three Black congressmen, "Are we using the representation we have in a way to get the best results? I say, no."[4] Johnson suggested they "create their own committee," with its own staff, so they could act in one voice. "Once a statement is made to America signed by three, not just one great congressman. It will be three-fold in every way," Johnson offered.[5] Powell, who preferred to work individually, responded dismissively with a short note.[6] There is no record of a response from Dawson.

Diggs, by contrast, recognized the significance of Johnson's proposal. He thanked the media mogul but explained, "There are only three of us ... I do not believe it would be wise for us to isolate ourselves into a 'Negro bloc.'"[7] Significantly, however, he did not rule out forming such a committee in the future. His electoral experiences in Michigan had made him acutely aware of the significance of coalitions and timing, and Diggs would move on the "Negro caucus" idea only when it made sense to advance his political goals, perhaps, as he wrote to Johnson, when the "complexion" of the House of Representatives changed.[8]

The "complexion" of the US House did change—and rather rapidly. By the late 1960s, millions of Black Americans had migrated from the South to Northern cities, expanding the Black electorate in many congressional districts. In addition, a series of US Supreme Court rulings dealing with reapportionment and culminating in the "one person, one vote" principle bolstered opportunities for Black representation in Congress. The passage of the 1965 Voting Rights Act enabled large numbers of Black people in the South to both register and vote, resulting in the expansion of Black elected officials in the South, and this contributed to the growth of the Black delegation in Congress.

In 1958, fifty-five-year-old Democrat Robert C. Nix won election as the first Black person to represent Pennsylvania in the US House of Representatives. Nix, "a long time wheel-horse" in Philadelphia's political machine, was "handpicked" by the party's white bosses to fill a vacant House seat in a predominantly Black section of the city.[9] A conservative in the mode of Dawson, Nix told reporters after his election that while he admired his congressional Black colleagues, he planned to follow his own course, saying he was a "congressman first, a Democrat second, and a Black third."[10]

In 1962, fifty-five-year-old Augustus "Gus" Hawkins, a veteran California assemblyman, was elected to represent a newly created majority-Black congressional district encompassing central Los Angeles. In 1965, he was joined by John Conyers, a thirty-five-year-old lawyer with deep familial ties to the Michigan labor movement, representing a new district that encompassed large parts of Detroit.

Diggs soon convinced the five Black House members to meet in his office after hours, "informally, if irregularly," to discuss issues facing Black Americans.[11] He often provided sandwiches and always "threw open his private stock of spirits to move things along."[12] Diggs, Conyers, and Hawkins were most enthusiastic, while Dawson and Powell shared an "aversion to group work."[13] Dawson preferred working behind the scenes, and Powell was his own man. Nix, a heavy drinker, "very rarely" participated.[14]

While Diggs initially had no plans to formally organize the group into a "Black caucus," after the 1968 national elections, several factors intersected to change Diggs's mind. In 1968, three more Black members were elected to the House. Diggs sensed the new members—William "Bill" Clay from St. Louis, Shirley Chisholm from Brooklyn, and Louis Stokes from Cleveland—all Democrats, were eager to work together. Diggs concluded that a "'critical number' for an organization seemed to have been reached."[15] Diggs also feared Nixon's assault on Lyndon Johnson's Great Society programs and concluded that forming a caucus would allow the Black members to enhance their political bargaining power. "It was not only the number. But it seemed we had the chemistry at that point," Diggs explained. "The timing was right," Diggs recalled.[16]

In early January 1969, Diggs called a meeting of the nine Black members of the House for the purpose of creating an organization of Black members of Congress. "I thought that there were many things which we could engage collectively that could influence the course of events that were pertinent to the black community," Diggs later told an interviewer.[17] In a letter to the group, Diggs stressed their "commonality of interests" and proposed a "loosely organized confederation" to coordinate communication among the nine members and between them and the Democratic leaders in the House.[18] No rules, bylaws, or leadership positions were adopted. There was neither staff nor budget.

Diggs called the group the Democratic Select Committee (DSC). The naming of the organization aligned with Diggs's politics of strategic moderation. A strong supporter of the Democratic Party, Diggs knew Dawson and Nix were tied to influential local Democratic organizations that frowned on Black separation in politics, and he sensed that Democratic House leadership, though not informed of beforehand of his plans, were "somewhat leery" of a "Black" caucus because of its separatist implications.[19] Although Clay and Stokes believed the group should be called the "Black Caucus," lacking seniority, they went along with Diggs.

By consensus, Diggs became the group's leader and chief spokesperson. They met periodically with House Speaker Carl Albert to discuss DSC concerns such as committee assignments and the treatment of Black Capitol Hill employees, and they also met with the chair of the Democratic National Committee to advocate for the fuller incorporation of Black members into the party.[20] Then in September 1969, eight of the nine Black members signed a statement opposing President Nixon's first Supreme Court nominee, Clement Haynsworth Jr., a conservative federal judge accused of being anti-labor and an opponent of civil rights. Only the conservative Dawson balked. He told Clay, "Listen, I told you before—don't bring any more Black stuff to me. I am tired of this Black shit!"[21]

Diggs, Chisholm, Clay, Conyers, Hawkins, and Stokes appeared before the Senate Judiciary Committee to oppose Haynsworth, the first time a group of Black House members appeared before the committee to oppose a Supreme Court nomination. The Senate later rejected Haynsworth, and the DSC also opposed and helped defeat Nixon's second nominee, G. Harrold Carswell.

Clay and Stokes pushed to formalize the DSC, arguing that it was "foolishness" to continue to "shy away" from calling the group the "Black Caucus."[22] They approached Powell about their ideas, hoping to gain his support, and they floated the notion that he could lead the group. Powell, however, had no interest. "But what I'll do," Powell told them, "is have Charlie Diggs lead you on this. You should designate Diggs as chairman."[23]

Clay and the others sensed that despite their differences, Diggs was the right man at the right time to lead the group. Decades later, Stokes recalled that Diggs was "an outstanding businessman" with demonstrated leadership skills and a stellar reputation as a legislator.[24] Moreover, he was well-known outside Michigan, his interpersonal behavior was deferential and measured, and his white colleagues, including House Democratic leaders, respected him. Diggs was also not Adam Clayton Powell, whom white members dreaded for constantly pointing out their racism.

DIGGS AND THE OTHERS knew that the DSC had to establish itself as a political voice and were alert for opportunities to gain visibility. In December 1969, Diggs accepted an invitation for the DSC to hold a day-long hearing in Chicago concerning the killings of Fred Hampton, the twenty-one-year-old leader of the Illinois Black Panthers, and twenty-two-year-old Mark Clark, another

Panther member. After the hearing, Diggs remarked, "I think a lot of people look to us as an emerging national force to voice the sentiments of black people. And they are going to be looking more and more, because there will be more and more of us."[25]

Diggs understood the influence of the national news media and was not shy about bringing his concerns directly to the nation's president. On February 18, 1970, acting alone, Diggs wrote President Nixon a two-sentence letter that read, "The Black Members of the House would like to confer with you on a range of questions representing the concerns of our constituencies. We would, therefore, appreciate your granting us such an audience."[26] Nixon's congressional liaison responded quickly, informing Diggs that the White House would "be in touch with you at the earliest possible date."[27] Diggs's letter would prove to be the opening scene in a national political drama that would cement the new group as a force in Washington, DC.

Six days after sending the request, Diggs starred in a dramatic scene that made national news headlines. Georgia's segregationist governor Lester Maddox came to Capitol Hill to testify on a voting rights bill. While having lunch in the House dining room, Maddox distributed to visitors a violent symbol of segregation, his now infamous pick handles.[28] When Diggs heard about it, he and a few colleagues dashed from the House floor to confront him.

When they entered the dining room, Maddox was seated with a Georgia State patrolman. Diggs stood over the smaller Maddox and told him "it was improper for him to be handing out the pick handles."[29] Diggs explained to reporters, "I told him it offended me, because the handles were a symbol of racism, and that they were an insult to me and other members of the House. I told him I didn't want to forget I was a gentleman and be forced to throw him out."[30] Then the confrontation got loud. Maddox turned red and screamed that Diggs was "acting more like an ass and a baboon than a member of Congress." Both men had reportedly reached "the boiling point" when a plainclothes police officer showed his badge and intervened.[31] Maddox paid for his lunch and stormed out of the dining room.

The incident was widely reported in the national news, even earning a segment on the *CBS Evening News* with Walter Cronkite.[32] There is little doubt that the confrontation got more attention in part because of Diggs's public image as a calm and collected congressman.

The timing of the Diggs-Maddox skirmish got the attention of the White House staff considering Diggs's request to meet with Nixon. Some warned that Diggs and the other Black House members, many of whom had publicly criticized Nixon's policies, could use the meeting to denounce the administration. They pointed to the fallout after Nixon met with Reverend Ralph Abernathy,

Dr. King's successor as president of the SCLC, to discuss issues related to poverty, after which Abernathy had harshly criticized Nixon.[33] Nixon was outraged, and Diggs learned the president allegedly had an "almost pathological fear" that Black leaders would leave a White House meeting and publicly criticize or "blast" his administration.[34] After the Abernathy meeting, it became "routine" for White House aides "to extract no-blast pledges" from Black leaders before granting them an audience with Nixon.[35]

While White House aides argued that Nixon's "minority affairs" adviser, Leonard Garment, should meet the Black delegation instead, Garment himself advised in a White House memo, "I think it would be a serious mistake, particularly at this time, to deny the request of this group of Black congressmen (and to offer me instead). They would be bound to take offense at this kind of treatment."[36]

Daniel Patrick Moynihan, a top domestic policy adviser, met with Nixon in late February 1970 to discuss civil rights and other racial issues. After the meeting, a controversial memorandum from Moynihan was leaked to the press suggesting that Black Americans had made significant progress over the past decade and that the "time may have come when the issue of race could benefit from a period of 'benign neglect.'"[37] John Ehrlichman, the president's senior domestic adviser, recommended the president meet with the Black congressional delegation "as a follow-up" to the meeting with Moynihan. Nixon ignored his recommendation.[38] In mid-April, White House congressional liaison William E. Timmons, discouraged Nixon from meeting with the Black delegation, warning that they would criticize the president afterward.[39] Nixon refused to meet with the DSC.

A few days later, Nixon aide Hugh Sloan informed Diggs, "The President's schedule has been such that we just have not been able to work it in.... We do not foresee an opportunity in the immediate future."[40]

NIXON WAS SHREWD. Refusing to meet the Black members of Congress fit into Nixon's larger political strategy of appealing to white Southerners and conservatives. Division and bitterness between the races helped him politically.[41] His refusal to meet with Diggs and the DSC became a public fight and reminded white voters that the Democratic Party was the party of Black Americans and civil rights, reinforcing the notion of Black people as "uppity" and impatient.

The standoff itself became a story in Washington media circles, one the White House tried to counteract with press releases touting the administration's record on race and highlighting the number of Black presidential appointees. In response, Diggs recruited a group of Black professionals highly knowledgeable about government workings who issued their own press releases that explained the negative impact of the administration's policies on Black America. Colleagues described Diggs's "shadow cabinet" tactic as a "brilliant coup."[42]

MEANWHILE, the number of Black House members increased. In November 1969, George Collins joined the House after winning a special election held to fill a Chicago seat, bringing the number of Black members in the House to ten. In 1970, Ronald Dellums of California and Parren Mitchell of Maryland, both liberal activists, expanded the number of Black congresspersons to twelve. Also in the 1970 election, Charles Rangel, a Black New York assemblyman, defeated Adam Clayton Powell. And after William Dawson died just a few days after the 1970 elections, Ralph Metcalfe, handpicked by Chicago's Mayor Richard J. Daley, replaced him. All were Democrats.

On December 31, 1970, William Clay wrote Diggs and other members of the soon-to-be twelve member DSC, warning, "Without adequate programming and planning, we might well degenerate into a Kongressional Koffee Klatch Club."[43] Clay wanted to formalize the DSC and rename the group. Reporters already referred to the DSC as the "Black Caucus."

In early January 1971, when Diggs convened the first meeting of the twelve Black members, the first order of business was to consider Clay's recommendations.[44] The group agreed to a formal election of officers—chair, vice-chair, and treasurer—and to the establishment of an executive committee and policy subcommittees. Then the group turned to the name of the organization. As Clay recalled, "Some wanted a kind of all-inclusive nomenclature so that at a future time Chicano, Puerto Rican, and Jewish members could join."[45] Shirley Chisholm's Brooklyn district, for example, included a significant Puerto Rican population. Others, like Hawkins, the Californian, argued that the group should not be racially exclusive but open to all who shared it goals.[46] Rangel, the New York freshman, suggested the group be named the "Congressional Black Caucus," arguing that such a designation would allow for admission of a Black Republican and that, perhaps, Senator Edward Brooke of Massachusetts, a Black Republican, would change course and join the group. "That ended all of the discussion, there was not any debate," recalled Clay.[47] The adoption of the name "Congressional Black Caucus" (CBC) reflected the growth and depth of the Black Power Movement and its newfound strength across a broad spectrum of Black America.

Diggs, forty-eight years old and the most senior Black member in Congress, was unanimously elected chair. As Clay later explained, "All of us respected him."[48] Diggs "was chosen as the first chairman of the Congressional Black Caucus because of his ability to keep older members like Nix and Dawson in a cordial mood [and] to relate to younger members like Chisholm, Stokes, and me," he wrote.[49] Hawkins was elected vice-chair and Clay, treasurer.

A few days after the CBC was formally organized, it was catapulted onto the national stage.

ON JANUARY 21, 1971, the day before President Nixon's State of the Union address, Congressman Stokes suddenly suggested that the CBC boycott the speech. "If the president won't meet with us, then we ought not to meet with him," Stokes remembers telling Clay.[50] "It sounds good to me," Clay replied.[51] Clay quickly left the floor to call members of the CBC and other political contacts. "We never had a meeting on it, but we got the word to the others that we thought the Caucus should do this," Clay remembered.[52]

The CBC released a letter sent to Nixon: "As you have consistently refused audience to the black members of Congress—the elected and legitimate representatives of 25 million Americans—we now refuse to be part of your audience when you deliver your 'State of the Union' address." All twelve CBC members signed the letter; Senator Brooke was not asked to be a signatory.[53]

The next day, news articles about the planned boycott appeared from Washington to Paris. When Nixon spoke, Senator Brooke was the only Black member of Congress in attendance. The next day, Brooke called Diggs and told him that Nixon had sought Brooke's advice on whether to meet with Diggs only or with the entire CBC. Brooke advised Nixon to meet with the entire group, although no date was offered as the president needed time to "save face."[54] Diggs saw this as a partial victory.

On February 7, 1971, Diggs departed for a scheduled month-long trip to Africa and Europe. Before he left, he asked a group of Black experts to develop policy recommendations on health and welfare, education, criminal justice, employment, and other issues. The recommendations were to be presented to Nixon if a meeting ever occurred. Input was sought from dozens of civil rights leaders and activists including Coretta Scott King, Roy Wilkins, and Bayard Rustin.[55]

On February 16, 1971, a year after Diggs first asked for a meeting, the CBC wrote to Nixon, once again requesting a meeting.[56] The next day, at a White House press conference, Nixon committed to a meeting in mid-March.[57]

DIGGS MADE ARRANGEMENTS for the meeting with Nixon aide Clark MacGregor, who demanded a "no-blast" pledge.[58] Diggs again agreed, refusing to let anything deter a White House meeting and stressing that the CBC members would make their case with "facts and figures and would speak frankly with the president." Diggs maintained it was "not the intention of the Caucus to embarrass the President."⁵⁹ Some younger CBC members, especially Clay, later grumbled that Nixon got to establish the parameters of the meeting "on his terms and at his time."⁶⁰

On Thursday, March 25, 1971, at 4:45 p.m., Diggs and the other CBC members were finally escorted to the White House Cabinet Room. As Diggs and the group entered the gigantic room, they were greeted by members of Nixon's cabinet and staff. Nixon had scheduled the meeting for 5 p.m., too late for coverage on the nightly television news. No members of the media were present. Diggs took a seat at the huge oval mahogany table, his back facing the Rose Garden. To his left was a taller, empty chair. Nixon would sit there. Other members of the CBC and administration officials took their places at the table.

Shortly after 5 p.m., Nixon and several aides stepped into the Cabinet Room. Nixon, ever the savvy political veteran, was gracious, congenial, and prepared. He smiled widely and greeted the room, walking around the table to shake hands with each member, adding personal comments. Nixon asked Diggs about his widowed mother who had recently undergone surgery. Diggs replied that the surgery was successful, and his mother was recuperating well.⁶¹

After everyone was seated, Nixon stated how much he welcomed meeting with the CBC (everyone knew that was not true) and that he and his staff had read through the documents the CBC had sent. After introducing members of his cabinet and staff, Nixon turned to Diggs.

Diggs thanked the president and read from a prepared statement. "We sought this meeting, Mr. President, out of a deep conviction that large numbers of citizens are being subjected to intense hardship, are denied their basic rights, and are suffering irreparable harm as a result of current policies."⁶² Diggs took a firm stand. "Our people are no longer asking for equality as a rhetorical promise. They are demanding from the national administration and from elected officials without regard to party affiliation, the only kind of equality that ultimately has any real meaning—equality of results."⁶³

When Nixon went around the table and asked to hear from the group, each CBC member spoke for two or three minutes about specific policy proposals highlighting specific CBC recommendations such as expanding low-income housing, combating discrimination in the US military, aiding those addicted to narcotics, providing federal grants to support expanded college access, and ending the war in Vietnam. Diggs told Nixon that the CBC recommended home rule for Washington, DC, increased US foreign aid to Africa, and sanctions against the apartheid government in South Africa.

Nixon told the group he appreciated their candor. "You know, if I were black, I'd be just as angry as you are about what's happening around our country today," he added.⁶⁴ Nixon promised to look into the issues the CBC members raised.

At the end of the hour-and-a-half meeting, Nixon thanked Diggs and the CBC members. Diggs requested that the president respond to the recommendations by May 17, 1971, by no coincidence the anniversary of the *Brown* school desegregation decision.

Then Diggs and the other CBC members appeared before White House reporters. As promised, there was "no blasting" of Nixon's policies. Diggs characterized the session as "candid, fruitful, and historic," adding, "Of course, implementation will be the important factor in our judgment."[65] Other CBC members said little and refused to go into detail about their reactions to the meeting.

It did not matter. As one observer noted, "The Nixon meeting marked the turning point in the modern history of blacks in Congress. Almost overnight the CBC was transformed from an episodic, informal protest group within Congress to a highly visible, legitimate vehicle that could speak for the black community."[66] The next day, Diggs told reporters the Nixon meeting "established the caucus as an instrument of national leadership of black concerns" and suggested that the new organization filled the Black leadership void left by the assassinations of King and Malcolm X.[67]

In early April 1971, Diggs wrote Nixon proposing that specific CBC members meet with Nixon's staff about "their respective areas of special interest" to discuss some of the CBC's sixty recommendations.[68] Nothing ever happened. Diggs hoped to open a dialogue with the administration to see if some policy outcomes could be achieved. But Nixon's response minimized the concerns the CBC members had raised at the White House meeting, claiming there was "a basic accord between the CBC's recommendations and his administration's policies.... We are already making significant progress ... to realize our shared goals."[69]

A month later, Diggs lunched with MacGregor, Garment, and Robert Brown, Nixon's "race" advisers. Afterward MacGregor informed the White House that he "anticipated no" future request for the president to meet with the CBC, "at least no request which we cannot successfully deflect," he added.[70]

On May 23, 1971, Diggs, Clay, and Hawkins appeared on the prestigious NBC Sunday television program *Meet the Press* and called Nixon's response "deeply disappointing."[71] As Watergate later showed, Nixon was not interested in a policy agenda; his interest was in gaining power and hanging onto it.

AS THE FIRST CHAIR of the CBC, Diggs needed to establish an institutional foundation for the organization's long-term existence. In May 1971, the CBC announced that it would sponsor an elegant $100-a-plate dinner to raise money to hire a full-time staff. Diggs, CBC treasurer Clay, and other members of the CBC met with lobbyists and executives from major corporations such as Coca Cola and others to solicit support. Several of the corporations purchased tables for the event.[72] Albert L. Nellum and Associates, one of the nation's first Black-owned management consulting firms, absorbed most of the administrative costs of organizing and publicizing the dinner.[73]

On June 18, 1971, nearly 3,000 people (about 80 percent Black), jammed into the grand ballroom of the Washington, DC, Sheraton Park Hotel; the hundreds of notable Black elected officials, political figures, educators, business leaders, and entertainers included Georgia State representative Julian Bond; Coretta Scott King; Reverend Jesse Jackson; Amiri Baraka; and Malcolm X's widow, Betty Shabazz. John H. Johnson, who in 1957 first suggested to Diggs the idea of forming a Black caucus, did not attend but purchased a table where Simeon Booker and other representatives of Johnson Publishing Company were seated. *Essence* magazine described the event as "a posh, emotional affair, a kind of March on Washington with gowns and tuxes."[74]

Congressman Diggs was the lead speaker. Diggs told the crowd that Black Americans had "mounted a quiet revolution through their ballots—a revolution which is changing both the direction and complexion of city halls, school boards and state legislatures."[75] Diggs declared the night's event a "Black America's political coming of age." Diggs emphasized the "value of coalitions" to attack racial inequality, eradicate poverty, address drug addiction, and provide good jobs. Embracing his politics of strategic moderation, Diggs told the crowd that Black people must join with "white, rich and poor, from every segment of skill and concern in our society" to achieve their goals. Diggs also touched on the theme of political independence, a major component of the Black Power Movement. Diggs said that the CBC would be "seeking to enter coalitions only as equal partners," stressing that Black America would "develop [its] own agenda, select [its] own leaders." He added, "After three hundred years it is high time black people call some of the tunes and take the lead in some of the dances." The crowd roared with approval.

The successful dinner raised $250,000, establishing CBC's financial footing, and as Diggs remarked, it "dispelled the notion that Black people are unwilling or unable to help causes that deal with their own interests."[76] The dinner eventually evolved into a weekend-long conference featuring a gala dinner and a series of forums, speakers, and policy workshops, an important source of the organization's revenue. Its first permanent headquarters was at 415 Second Street, four blocks from the US Capitol Building.[77]

IN JUNE 1971, *Newsweek* magazine featured Diggs and the CBC on its front cover, declaring them examples of the "New Black Politics." All members of the

CBC also eventually landed on Nixon's "enemies list"; if nothing else, this was evidence that the CBC had quickly become a potent symbol of Black Power.

The idea was for the CBC to influence the legislative process. The group developed a policy document, the "Black Agenda," that would form the basis for the CBC's legislative agenda inside Congress and that could be presented to candidates in both parties running for president in 1972.

Chapter 15
THE 1972 NATIONAL BLACK POLITICAL CONVENTION

THE MORNING AFTER the Congressional Black Caucus's successful fundraising dinner, Diggs and the CBC met with dozens of other Black elected officials who had remained in Washington overnight.[1] The meeting ended with the announcement of a conference of Black leaders to be held in Washington, DC, in November. The meeting would bring together Black integrationists and Black nationalists to confront a central question about the future of Black politics: whether Black voters should work separately *or* in coalition with other racial minorities and liberal whites to achieve favorable electoral results, particularly in the 1972 presidential election.[2] For Black political activists, the 1972 presidential election presented an opportunity. It would be the first presidential election in which the full effect of the 1965 Voting Rights Act on Black Americans could be demonstrated.

Although the CBC had evolved to speak as one voice and was beginning to wield outsized influence, there was no such unanimity among the larger Black body politic. Diggs, most Black elected officials, and the leaders of civil rights organizations like the NAACP and the National Urban League were "integrationists" who embraced Bayard Rustin's influential 1965 essay, "From Protest to Politics." Rustin argued that given that Black Americans were a numerical minority, "coalitions are inescapable"; he insisted that Black people could not "win political power alone. We need allies."[3] His essay urged Black Americans to join a progressive coalition of trade unionists, liberal whites, and Northern religious groups and to work within the Democratic Party.

By contrast, some Black nationalists, like Amiri Baraka, inspired by the African liberation movements, embraced the idea of an independent Black politics, including the formation of an all-Black political party. They were influenced by Black Power activist Stokely Carmichael and political scientist Charles V. Hamilton who, in *Black Power: The Politics of Liberation*, cautioned Black Americans about the "myth of coalitions," insisting that coalitions risked subordinating Black people's interests.[4] Black nationalists called for an independent Black politics and for Black voters to be skeptical of casting their lot with one political party.

Charles Diggs's politics of strategic moderation embraced coalition building and the recruiting of supporters across the political spectrum. The challenge for Diggs and other Black integrationists was how to direct growing demands for Black Power toward a politics devoted to Black Americans gaining incorporation into the Democratic Party.

STRATEGY SESSIONS to develop a unified Black political strategy for the 1972 presidential election and beyond began in earnest in September 1970, when Black leaders participated in the Congress of African Peoples in Atlanta, Georgia.[5] Organized by Amiri Baraka, the most visible Black nationalist in the country, the Congress of African Peoples was the first significant meeting of the two ideological camps. Among the 4,000 participants were Betty Shabazz, Malcolm X's widow; Louis Farrakhan of the Nation of Islam; Kenneth Gibson, mayor of Newark; Richard Hatcher, mayor of Gary, Indiana; Georgia State representative Julian Bond; Whitney Young of the National Urban League; and Ralph Abernathy and Jesse Jackson of the SCLC. Diggs did not attend.

The Congress of African Peoples adopted a series of resolutions, the most important of which was to develop a Black agenda for the 1970s and to form a Black political party. Baraka, who had played a central role in Gibson's historic election as Newark's first Black mayor, was behind both resolutions.

One year later, in September 1971, Diggs participated in a subsequent strategy session with a diverse group of Black leaders representing virtually every major ideology and institution in Black America. Convened by Mayor Hatcher at a hotel near Chicago's O'Hare Airport, Diggs was a co-host of the meeting, along with Bond, Jackson, Coretta Scott King, Baraka, and Willie Brown, the future mayor of San Francisco (although he did not attend). CBC members Walter Fauntroy, John Conyers, and Augustus Hawkins were also present. Shirley Chisholm sent a representative. Atlanta's vice mayor Maynard Jackson; Manhattan Borough president Percy Sutton; and Texas State senator Barbara Jordan were among the other Black elected officials in attendance. Vernon Jordan of the Urban League, Andrew Young of the SCLC, and Roy Innis of CORE were longtime civil rights leaders in attendance.[6]

No consensus emerged about a strategy for the 1972 presidential election. Bond recommended a "favorite son" strategy in which a popular Black candidate would run for president in their state primary, with the goal of winning committed delegates who could be used in bargaining at the Democratic convention in May 1972. Conyers made a strong case for supporting a Black candidate for president, namely Congresswoman Shirley Chisholm of New York, who planned to enter the Democratic nomination contest.[7] Diggs and Hawkins urged attendees to adopt the sixty recommendations the CBC had presented to President Nixon as the agenda for Black America, and to require presidential candidates to state their position on each of the recommendations.[8]

Although Baraka preferred forming an independent Black political party, he knew there was little support for the idea. He pushed instead for a "national Black convention" to bring together Black moderates, liberals, conservatives, and nationalists to develop a "Black agenda."[9] Others were cool to the convention idea. With no clear consensus, the group agreed to continue its discussions.

ONE MONTH LATER, on November 18, 1971, more than 300 Black elected officials and other Black leaders gathered at the Sheraton Park Hotel in Washington, DC, to attend a multiday conference sponsored by the CBC. Diggs hoped the conference would introduce the CBC to more Black elected officials and become a springboard for a series of CBC-sponsored hearings that would lead to the creation of the "Black Agenda." Diggs had no intention in calling for a national Black convention.

Controversy erupted on the first day during discussion on a panel titled "Development of Black Political Power in the Seventies," chaired by Congressman Clay.[10] Florida State representative Gwendolyn Cherry interrupted the discussion by asking why expected presidential candidate Shirley Chisholm was not a member of the panel. Chisholm accused Clay and the others of deliberately leaving her out of the discussion. Taken aback, Clay gave Chisholm the microphone. She unleashed, in Clay's words, a "broadside of immeasurable venom" at several members of the CBC, glaring at Clay and the others and telling them they had "better wake up!"[11] As she later told the *St. Louis Dispatch*, Clay's hometown paper, "I don't expect them to follow me or even endorse me, but at least they might recognize me."[12]

Tensions around Chisholm's candidacy were now in the open, exposing the fact that there was not even agreement within the CBC members about the best strategy for 1972. Clay, Louis Stokes, and others in the CBC didn't believe Chisholm was the right candidate to run nationally, while Baraka, sensing an opportunity, asked if Chisholm would be willing to run on a third party or Black party ticket if she did not get the Democratic nomination. Chisholm replied she would have to think about it.[13]

Diggs's hope for creating a united Black political strategy for 1972 was spinning out of control. Yet Baraka knew that there could be no meaningful Black national convention or Black political party without the active input of the CBC. Coming on the heels of its meeting with Nixon, the CBC now symbolized

Black electoral power. As Baraka recalled, questions concerning the CBC's viewpoint continually "bedeviled" the strategy sessions.[14]

Baraka then pushed the idea of a Black political convention, but most elected officials pushed back, seeing potential political minefields if Black elected officials were to endorse "way-out positions" developed by Black militants at a convention. In Baraka's words, "Confusion and chaos reigned."[15]

Then Congressman Diggs took the microphone and quieted the room. He announced that the entire CBC would meet alone in a sort of executive session with Richard Hatcher, Jesse Jackson, and Baraka to discuss a way forward.

Assembling in another conference room, Diggs led the group through a discussion of the ideas put forth. Baraka again advocated for a Black political party, but there was no appetite among the CBC members, all Democrats, to abandon their party. When the discussion turned toward supporting a single presidential Black candidate, attendees could not agree on a candidate, and Chisholm told Diggs and the others she did not want a vote on endorsing her candidacy for president. Meanwhile Clay, Stokes, and Hawkins stressed their belief that Black people had to work in a coalition with other groups, including whites, to have any influence on national candidates.[16]

With the group at loggerheads, Baraka again pushed his idea of a national Black convention. Diggs and the CBC were under pressure to come up with a plan; in the end, Diggs concluded that the convention was a reasonable way out of the stalemate. Before the convention idea was finally approved, Diggs appointed Clay; James Gibson of the Potomac Institute of Washington; Antonio Harrison of the National League of Cities/National Conference of Mayors; and Howard Robinson, executive director of the CBC, to consider the ideas discussed in the strategy sessions and make a recommendation. After several hours, the committee reached a compromise, approving a Black national political convention and the formation of the "Black Agenda," but rejecting a Black political party.[17]

That evening, Saturday November 20, Diggs made his way to the dais following the keynote speaker from *Ebony* magazine. From a prepared statement, Diggs read the call for a Black national political convention. "For 300 years Black people have been the victims and pawns of the American political process. The political representatives of the Black community, meeting in Washington, DC, in November 1971, has concluded that we still wear the shackles of political bondage. Tonight, the Congressional Black Caucus issues a call to the Black people of the United States for a national political convention to be held in April or early May of 1972, for the purpose of developing a national Black agenda and the crystallization of a national Black strategy for the 1972 elections and beyond."[18]

Many in the crowd burst into applause and raised hands in a clenched Black

Power fist symbol. Diggs quieted the crowd, and after Walter Fauntroy, an ordained minister, gave the benediction, he and Diggs raised their fists, too. Everybody in the audience, including nearly all the 300 Black elected officials, followed their lead.[19]

Diggs, Mayor Hatcher, and Baraka were later named co-chairs of the convention, which was scheduled for March 10–12, 1972, in Gary, Indiana. Newspapers across the country carried an Associated Press report headlined "Has Time Come for Blacks to Build Party?" and asking, "Would this turn out to be the first step toward formation of a national black political party?"[20]

Later, a few weeks before the Black convention would take place, CBC treasurer Clay, concerned that the CBC would be left to pay for the cost of the convention and be held responsible, helped convince other CBC members to vote to refuse to financially support the convention and to withdraw the CBC as an official sponsor.[21]

In the months leading up to the Gary convention, Diggs, also a member of the House Committee on the District of Columbia and chair of the House Foreign Affairs Committee's Subcommittee on Africa, was very busy. As chair of the CBC, invitations to speak around the country arrived almost daily. Diggs was becoming overwhelmed and began to tell friends that "he was involved in more activities than he felt he could adequately handle."[22] "Diggs was involved in so many things that one day he showed up at his [Capitol] Hill office with stubble on his chin," recalled a former press secretary. When she asked him if he was growing a beard, Diggs "stroked his chin absentmindedly and remarked, 'I forgot to shave.'"[23] Diggs was, indeed, extremely busy.

As a result, on February 8, 1972, a month before the Gary convention, Diggs resigned as chair of the CBC; he was replaced by Louis Stokes, a move that generated speculation in the press that he had been pushed out by younger and more militant members of the CBC.[24] Stokes called those rumors "false and ridiculous" and an attempt "to show divisiveness" in the CBC "where there [was] none."[25] Simeon Booker reported that the "heavy demand for personal appearances throughout the country" played a key role in prompting Diggs's decision to give up the chairmanship.[26] "Diggs could have been chairman as long as he wanted to," New York congressman Charles Rangel stressed.[27] Diggs's resignation "seemed like a sensible idea at the time," recalled Diggs's press secretary.[28]

ON MARCH 3–4, 1972, Diggs met with Baraka, Hatcher, Walter Fauntroy (chair of the convention's Platform Committee), and others at Howard University to plan the convention's program and agenda.[29] Diggs asked Ronald Walters and other Howard University professors to assist. In what would become a source of contention in Gary, the group completed nearly 90 percent of what would become the convention's "Black Agenda."[30] A few days before the convention, Diggs was hopeful that it would bring the disparate groups together. "The agenda will be a statement of principles," Diggs told the *Baltimore Sun*. "We expect to circulate it among various political aspirants for president, and based upon their reaction, to educate the black nation as to who their friends are. The national black political movement is shapeless and tenuously connected. The convention will be a long step toward giving the movement some form."[31]

Diggs arrived in Gary a few days before the March 10 convention opening. At Hatcher's home, Diggs met with Baraka, Fauntroy, and others for a final planning session. As Hatcher recalled, "The three of us did not know each other very well. But, in the process we got to know each other very well. And I think we got to like each other quite a lot. We understood each other better and I think particularly between Congressman Diggs and Amiri Baraka, I think they came much closer together."[32]

Baraka and his supporters were the "backbone of the Gary convention," organizing the logistics of the convention and putting their prior experience with the Congress of African Peoples meeting in Atlanta to productive use.[33] Mayor Hatcher directed his administration to do all they could to support the convention, placing red, black, and green flags, African liberation colors, on sign posts throughout the city and making a local high school gymnasium available as the convention hall. Baraka and his team planned for all the delegates to be seated under state banners as if they were at a Democratic or Republican nominating convention.

On Friday, March 10, the first day of the convention, Diggs, Hatcher, Baraka, and Jesse Jackson held a press conference at Gary's city hall to explain what they expected to take place over the next two days. Jackson, now the president of his own People United to Save Humanity (having recently left the SCLC following a dispute with Ralph Abernathy), hoped to use the convention to elevate his national political profile. Long percolating divisions between Black nationalists and radical leaders, and Black moderates and integrationists again resurfaced. Diggs, now fifty, was the senior statesman. He asserted that the convention was similar in significance to the 1905 Niagara Movement that led to the founding of the NAACP, saying, "We must liken this to the first truly black movement."[34] Mayor Hatcher's comments, though more forceful, aligned with Diggs's, while Baraka, dressed in a dashiki, emphasized Black unity. "We will be dealing with the shaping of a concrete and specific means of gaining political power for black people," he said.[35] Jackson, sporting a huge Afro and wearing a large medallion with the image of Martin Luther King Jr. around his neck, then told the press "the convention may very well evolve into a black political party."[36] The disparity among the group's remarks would serve as a prelude to the tensions between Black nationalists and mainstream Black politicians at the convention.

Friday was a working day for the convention's various committees, many of which were disrupted by controversy. The Credentials Committee faced heated questions from nationalists who wanted to know who chose Diggs, Baraka, and Hatcher to oversee the convention. Meanwhile, in the Resolutions Committee, Chair Barbara Jordan struggled to ease tensions between nationalists and integrationists over the issue of busing.[37] Simmering tensions also surfaced during the Platform Committee's meeting, when delegates complained that much of the platform and the "Black Agenda" had been developed without their input. Heated divisions also began to rise within state delegations as well.[38]

On Friday evening those divisions became public after the NAACP denounced the Platform Committee's convention draft preamble, calling it a separatist document. Titled "What Time Is It: The Gary Declaration—Black Politics at the Crossroads," the preamble declared that the American political system "does not work" and was "designed to operate for the benefit of the white race," and it called for an "independent Black political movement."[39] The NAACP released a statement saying the draft preamble "is one of revolution rather than reform. . . . If the 'agenda' adopted by the Convention turns out to be consistent with the draft preamble, the agenda also will be impossible for the NAACP to endorse."[40]

That Friday night Diggs met with the heads of state delegations to try to ease the tensions. He also met with Hatcher and Baraka to work out a response to the NAACP's opposition to the draft preamble. On Saturday morning, the men released a joint statement emphasizing that the NAACP was just one organization. "Other groups and organizations at the convention can be expected to take positions spanning the full spectrum of values and opinions held by the nation's blacks," the statement read.[41]

ON SATURDAY, MARCH 11, 1972, about 8,000 Black people, roughly 4,500 of whom were delegates from 42 states and the District of Columbia, gathered inside Gary's West Side High School gym. Men and woman of all ages, some dressed in business attire, many wearing dashikis, colorful head scarves, and other African-inspired attire, browsed the hundreds of Black vendors selling Afro-centric art, souvenir t-shirts, posters of Dr. King and Malcolm X, bean pies, and a large assortment of "soul foods." The attendees were supplemented by more than 500 members of the media. All the major newspapers, including the *New York Times* and *Washington Post*, had dispatched reporters to Gary.[42]

At 1:15 p.m.—four hours later than scheduled—Congressman Diggs opened the general session of the convention.

Diggs, by now widely respected as an expert on Africa, gave a short keynote speech about Africa and US African policy. "It is now time to set the record straight—to say that black people in America understand that our African past is intimately bound up in our African future and that the revolution we seek in our relationships to Americans is ultimately reflected in the struggle between African and European peoples in the world." He declared, "It is time now to sound the warning that no longer will the movement for justice and change in America stop at the water's edge."[43] The crowd erupted in thunderous applause. For Diggs, the huge ovation provided evidence that there could be an organized Black political movement devoted to improving the conditions of Africans and to altering US African policy.

Mayor Hatcher spoke next and criticized the failure of both political parties to deal effectively or sincerely with issues confronting Black Americans. Hatcher, however, stopped short of calling for a Black political party and told the delegates that Black voters should "give the two major parties one more chance" in the 1972 presidential election.[44] Yet, when Hatcher talked of forming coalitions with other groups, the crowd booed.

Jesse Jackson then stole the show with a rousing speech invoking the nationalist call for unity. "Brothers and sisters, what time is it?" Jackson asked. "Nationtime," the crowd responded. Jackson also fully embraced the formation of a Black political party, saying, "Nationhood is the politics of multiple options. One of those options must be a black political party."[45] Jackson brought the convention to its feet when he warned the Democrats and Republicans, saying, "Cut us in or we'll cut out." The speeches and the varying reactions of the crowd underscored the difficulty of reaching a consensus on a Black agenda.

Diggs again took the podium as presiding officer. One of the first orders of business was for the delegates to name the permanent chairs of the convention. Edward Sylvester quickly nominated Diggs, Hatcher, and Baraka. Diggs, determined to use *Robert's Rules of Order* to guide his actions, quickly called for a motion to close the nomination. When Diggs called for the "ayes" and "nays," an overwhelming number of delegates voiced opposition, but Diggs ruled the motion had passed. As Simeon Booker described, "In a matter of a few words the Convention exploded. There were jeers, boos, and a sudden outpouring from the delegations."[46] Some yelled that Diggs had tried to rig the outcome of the nomination process. Shortly afterward, members of the New York delegation stormed the stage to take the microphone from Diggs.[47] Security personnel prevented them from doing so.

Diggs, under enormous pressure in front of thousands of Black Americans, was caught off-guard. Benjamin Chavis of Oxford, North Carolina, was in the audience at the time and claimed the reaction of the delegates was not personal. He observed, "People were insulted because they didn't want the Convention to start on a point which they had just left in all the repression. We wanted an open Convention, not an oppressed Convention. And so, Diggs got himself in some hot water."[48]

Realizing he was losing control, Diggs announced a short recess and "instructed state caucus chairmen to poll their delegates."[49] When the convention resumed, Diggs quickly revoked his earlier ruling and allowed delegates to nominate others as permanent convention chairs. Eight other delegates were eventually nominated, but Diggs, Baraka, and Hatcher were still elected as permanent chairs. Then Diggs, reportedly "in desperation," gaveled Saturday's session to an end.[50] Throughout the remainder of Saturday evening and into early Sunday morning, tensions remained high. Diggs tried to recover and at a press conference explained he was not "trying to railroad the election" and that he was surprised by the reaction to the initial vote. He said that in his experience the confirmation of the chairs was a "routine" procedure for conventions.[51]

The draft of the "Black Agenda" was released to several convention leaders on Saturday evening. Scholars give Baraka credit for working Saturday night and into early Sunday morning to keep the convention together and garner consensus.[52] However, according to those who were there, Baraka did not do the job alone. Diggs was also up all night, meeting with nationalists, heads of state delegations, and various caucuses. Simeon Booker, reporting shortly after the convention, observed that "Diggs, even after the criticism of his poor ruling, stayed in the battle."[53]

DIGGS DID NOT PLAY a prominent role in Sunday's final session. Baraka presided, moving discussion and debate along, and remaining focused on the goal of adopting the "Black Agenda." Delegates voted on a host of resolutions, many approved without debate. The integrationists and nationalists agreed that the convention would not endorse a candidate for president and would not vote to form a Black political party because both issues were simply too divisive. Instead, the convention voted to establish the National Black Political Assembly as a "permanent political structure" that would continue to bring the Black community together and operate as the chief broker in dealing with America's white political leadership structure.[54] Diggs was later elected the first president of the National Black Political Assembly.

At 3:30 p.m. that Sunday, a bomb threat caused the evacuation of the gymnasium. When the convention restarted and with two-thirds of the delegates still away, the convention adopted (with little debate) a controversial antibusing resolution drafted by CORE's Roy Innis and leaders of the South Carolina delegation. "Busing is obsolete and dangerous to Black people. We are ready to control our own destiny," Innis told the press afterward.[55] The resolution repudiated the long-held position of the NAACP and most of the nation's Black elected officials, including the CBC, and aligned the convention with the Nixon administration's policy opposing busing to desegregate public schools.

The convention also adopted a pro-Palestine resolution that called on the US government to "end immediately its economic and military support" to Israel.[56] Black moderates and integrationists saw this as an affront to a valued coalition partner; American Jews were traditional allies with Black people on civil rights causes.

The "Black Agenda" called for proportional representation in the US Congress, based on the Black percentage of the population (fifteen Black US Senators, for example); proportional Black employment in the federal government; home rule for residents of Washington, DC (something Diggs would soon champion); and a plank calling for the end of the FBI's Counterintelligence Program (COINTELPRO), a surveillance initiative used to spy on Black radicals. Economically, the agenda called for reparations to Black Americans for slavery and state-sanctioned segregation, demanded tuition-free college education, Black control of neighborhood public schools, the creation of a system of publicly owned day care centers, the elimination of the death penalty, and the creation of a government-run national health system. It also called for financial aid, land reform, and health policies to further develop Black rural communities in the South. Environmental racism was also included in the agenda, as were racial issues related to the fledgling cable television industry and the future of Black-owned media outlets.

The document also denounced America's complicity in European colonialism in Africa and Asia and called for Black Americans to assist Africans in their struggle for self-determination.

Congressman Clay and other critics pushed back and said Black nationalists had taken over the conference as evidenced by the "Black Agenda."[57] Many Black elected officials were furious. The 260-member Michigan delegation (the second largest among the delegations), dominated by members of the UAW and staunch adherents to the coalition approach, was especially agitated. State senator Coleman Young, Diggs's political ally and a future mayor of Detroit, was the most vocal.[58] He denounced the "Black Agenda" from the floor of the convention as "completely off-target and unacceptable . . . ; a blatantly separatist document. . . . Separatism is asinine and suicidal," Young shouted.[59] Young declared the document too long to digest and vote upon and asked Baraka if the delegates could take the document home to read and consider.

"The Baraka gang refused to allow that, which made it clear to me that they were trying to ramrod the thing through," Coleman Young recalled.[60]

Late Sunday evening, after many of the delegates had already left or were preparing to depart, the convention formally adopted the controversial anti-busing and pro-Palestine resolutions. Coleman Young and nearly the entire Michigan delegation quickly staged a dramatic walkout in protest. As Young recalled years later:

> Poor Charlie Diggs didn't know what to do. He felt committed to the caucus [convention] as one of its organizers, but he had obviously been misled by Baraka. Taking note of his ambivalence, I used the occasion to say, "Charlie, I always told you I'd never run against you. But if you're going to run as part of this black political party, let me know, because I'm interested in being the Democratic candidate for Congress in your district." I didn't want to be any goddamn congressman; I just wanted to shake Charlie up, which I did.[61]

At about 9:30 p.m., Baraka gaveled the convention to a close. The leaders of the convention announced that a steering committee—with Diggs, Baraka, and Hatcher as co-chairs—would work on revising the "Black Agenda," promising to release a final version on May 19, Malcolm X's birthday.

Diggs and Hatcher then held a postconvention press conference. Hatcher announced that the convention was a success because it brought together "every spectrum of political thought and political ideology" in the Black community to discuss shared issues and concerns. Diggs told reporters that he was "very much gratified" with the results, saying, "Both the Democrats and the Republicans are going to have to take this new black political force into consideration. The two major political parties will have to reexamine their attitudes toward black people. They will have to reckon with us now."[62]

Diggs also held a press briefing with Betty Shabazz in which both praised Shirley Chisholm. Chisholm did not attend the convention, but Diggs said her bid for the Democratic nomination should be taken seriously and announced that he planned to endorse Chisholm in the Michigan Democratic primary.[63]

MOST BLACK POLITICAL COMMENTARY viewed the convention a success simply because so many Black people and leaders of diverse backgrounds and ideologies had come together. Congressman Diggs also viewed the convention favorably. "I think the convention was a great success in terms of our objectives and in view of the limitations of our resources and the time element. I think it was a great organizational feat."[64] He saw the convention not as representing the culmination of Black unity but as only one step toward unity. "There is a lot of work to be done," he said. "The unity is admittedly fragile. I believe, however, that our goal of unity was achieved by the very fact that we got together, and remained together, for three days. These were obviously the first steps in a unifying process."[65]

However, soon after the close of the convention, Jewish leaders and supporters flooded the NAACP's national office and the CBC with letters critical of the "Black Agenda"—critical, in particular, of the resolutions related to busing and Israel. Three days after the convention, the CBC denounced the busing resolution. A few days later, the CBC released a second statement disassociating itself from the anti-Israeli resolution.[66]

Years later, Congressman Clay repeated his view that the CBC made a strategic error by calling for the Black convention. "The CBC had made many mistakes in its brief history, but calling for a national convention and then losing control of the administrative apparatus was probably the most regrettable blooper.... By lending legitimacy and respectability to the function, we were held responsible for outcomes that we had no part in."[67]

On May 16, three days before the final version of the "Black Agenda" was set to be released, the NAACP followed the CBC and withdrew from the convention. Roy Wilkins said the withdrawal was "primarily because of a difference in ideology as to how to win equality for the Negro minority in the United States."[68]

On May 19, 1972, on Malcolm X's birthday, Diggs, Hatcher, and Baraka, joined by other members of the steering committee, issued the fifty-eight-page "National Black Political Agenda" at a press conference in Washington, DC. Diggs and Hatcher had failed to convince the steering committee to remove the two controversial resolutions. Now they released a written "disclaimer" and spoke out against the resolutions on busing and the Israeli-Palestinian conflict, saying they "are not representative of the sentiments of the vast majority of black Americans."[69] When the "Black Agenda" was released, it received little attention. No major Black leader endorsed it. Baraka was the only person with a national following to embrace the "Black Agenda."

In early June 1972, Diggs joined Louis Stokes, William Clay, Charles Rangel, and other members of the CBC at a Capitol Hill press conference to present another document, the "Black Bill of Rights," a series of "nonnegotiable" demands for the Democratic nominee for president.[70] The document was an abbreviated form of the set of demands the CBC presented to President Nixon a year before, but "eerily similar" to and "a watered-down version" of the "Black Agenda" without a mention of Israel and urging Black Americans to move beyond the busing issue.[71]

CBC chair Louis Stokes threatened to withhold Black support for the Democratic nominee for president if the party refused to endorse the Black Bill of Rights. Diggs asserted that if the party did not accept their demands, "the Democratic National Convention might be just an academic exercise," adding, "There certainly would be less enthusiasm to participate in the national campaign. Some people might concentrate on local campaigns."[72] When a reporter suggested that the CBC's release of the "Black Bill of Rights" violated the "spirit" and "strategy" of the Gary convention, Clay replied that "any group could get together and adopt anything they wished, but that didn't commit either myself or the Caucus to that position. This is a statement of our position."[73]

The CBC moved to consolidate Black support behind US Senator George McGovern's (D-SD) candidacy before the August DNC in Miami. On June 26, Clay, Stokes, and Fauntroy held a press conference with McGovern and announced that enough of the 450 Black delegates expected at DNC supported McGovern to give him the party's nomination. McGovern supported the "Black Bill of Rights" and most of the "Black Agenda" (except for the busing and Palestinian resolutions) and promised "to name Blacks to the Supreme Court, to his Cabinet, to sub-Cabinet positions in proportion to their percentage in the general population."[74]

Baraka was outraged. He saw the move as a selfish power play by those who supported McGovern to position themselves as the chief Black brokers before the Democratic Party Convention in August.[75] He called the group members "sellouts," saying, "Black people are not for sale. We must negotiate to expand our power, like any nation."[76]

IN THE END, the coalition approach won out. Black voters helped McGovern win the Democratic nomination. Diggs and other Black elected officials across the country stumped for McGovern, hoping a progressive coalition could defeat Nixon in the general election and that Black Americans would benefit from meaningful political incorporation into the federal government. White America, however, had other ideas. Nixon, still fueling white fears, was reelected in a landslide. Black leaders were left with little to show from the strategy sessions and the Gary convention.

However, the Gary convention had settled the question of whether Black politics would take the independent-separatist route espoused by Black nationalists and militants or the coalition-school approach embraced by Diggs and other moderates and integrationists. Diggs's experience with Black nationalists in Detroit a decade earlier had convinced him that most Black voters supported the fundamentals of the coalition approach. "The separatism concept has very little support in the Negro community. The new-found pride of black people, and their insistence on equality, should not be read as a desire for separatism of some fashion. The vast majority of black people in the United States are for a pluralistic society," Diggs said.[77]

A pragmatic national strategy for Black advancement involved solidifying the Black electorate behind a progressive coalition within the Democratic Party, Diggs concluded. After all, this coalition had organized the March on Washington, adopted the Civil Rights Act and Voting Rights Act, and supported Lyndon B. Johnson's 1964 landslide election. Organizing and delivering the Black vote to the Democratic Party offered Black Americans the best strategy for addressing civil rights and other policy goals.

Charles Diggs Jr. cemented his reputation as an adept coalition strategist and political visionary. From his perspective, Black nationalists were all bark and no bite. Black nationalists had a loud voice but no vehicle or institution to advance their political goals. Diggs's strategic toleration of Baraka resulted in Baraka and the other nationalists becoming too hoarse to be heard. Moving forward, the convention motivated many Black militants to throw themselves into local electoral campaigns and into supporting Democrats. In 1984 and 1988, Jesse Jackson ran for the Democratic nomination for president. With the Gary convention, Black Power would have its greatest impact not in the streets but at the ballot box.

Chapter 16

RESTORING HOME RULE IN WASHINGTON, DC

AT 3:30 P.M. ON WEDNESDAY, January 30, 1974, Charles Diggs Jr. was joined by his wife, mother, children, and other family members; hundreds of friends from Detroit and Washington, DC; House and Senate colleagues; and local government officials in the Longworth House Office Building for the unveiling of his official "chairman's portrait." Diggs had been chair of the House Committee on the District of Columbia for a little over a year. In keeping with House tradition, as chair, a portrait of Diggs would be on permanent display in the committee's hearing room.[1]

A few weeks earlier, President Richard Nixon signed into law the Home Rule Act of 1973, legislation that restored an elected municipal government to the District of Columbia for the first time in nearly 100 years. Ancher Nelsen (R-MN), the senior Republican on the House District of Columbia Committee, reminded the crowd that Diggs had sponsored the law and had guided the legislation through Congress, restoring local democracy to DC's 750,000 residents, over 70 percent of whom were Black.

After Nelsen's remarks, Diggs's sons, twenty-five-year-old Charles III and ten-year-old Douglass, walked up to the portrait and removed its black draping. The crowd applauded. The photographic portrait framed in a four-inch wide, hand-carved basswood frame that cost $2,500 would one day prove to be almost as controversial as home rule itself.[2]

After the unveiling, Diggs's House and Senate colleagues offered words of praise for his leadership of the District of Columbia Committee. Senator Thomas Eagleton (D-MO), chair of the Senate Committee on the District of Columbia, who had guided the Home Rule Act through the Senate, spoke admiringly of Diggs. "This is a remarkable man, this Charles Diggs," Senator Eagleton told the crowd. "His is not the most flamboyant member of Congress. He is not an arm waver. He is a quiet, patient, deliberate man, who sets a goal and then measures both himself and those with whom he is working in terms of achieving that goal. When the story of home rule is written . . . the name of Diggs will be emblazoned on the record. The name of a quiet man, a very effective man, and I think the highest praise I can give to any fellow politician, a damned good man."[3]

THE US CONSTITUTION, namely Article I, Section 8, Clause 17, gives the Congress "exclusive" authority over the District of Columbia, which was carved from Maryland and Virginia, two states with significant proportions of Black inhabitants.[4] During its formative years, municipal affairs had been handled by locally elected officials, and for the next half century, local democracy (such as it was) took place in the nation's capital. Then came the Civil War and Reconstruction. Thousands of former slaves migrated to the District, joining the city's already sizable Black population. The District soon had the largest Black population of any city in the nation, comprising largely of unskilled laborers but also a sizable Black middle-class community.

In the summer of 1874, a combination of mismanagement and an economic depression led Congress to abolish the local District government and replace it with a "temporary" three-member commission appointed by the president. It was the beginning of what would become a nearly 100-year-old political battle to regain local self-government, or home rule.[5]

While most white voters supported home rule, influential white elites, importantly, the Metropolitan Washington Board of Trade, the city's powerful business interest group, staunchly opposed home rule.[6] Historians George Derek Musgrove and Chris Myers Asch maintain that white elites believed home rule would lead to Black people gaining political control, just as they believed had happened during Reconstruction. Black voters, they argued, would support huge spending increases and raise taxes, and businesses and wealthy residents would leave.[7] The prospect of a Black-controlled District government played a significant role in consolidating opposition to restoring home rule.

Every post–World War II president voiced support for self-government for Washington, DC, and the Senate passed home rule legislation several times. But self-rule was blocked each time by the House District of Columbia Committee. Established in 1808, the House District of Columbia Committee took the lead over the Senate Committee on the District of Columbia in overseeing the District. Hardly a plum assignment, the House committee was usually dominated by conservative white Southern Democrats and a member or two of either political party from suburban Virginia and Maryland. Each group used its position to appoint its constituents to patronage jobs in DC government, another major factor in the opposition to home rule. Many committee members also enjoyed cozy relationships with the city's local business community, including members of the Board of Trade, who generously donated to reelection campaigns and feted them with lavish parties and receptions.[8]

Committee chair John McMillan, from rural South Carolina, ruled the committee—and DC—with an iron fist.[9] The *Washington Post* described him as the "holder of ultimate authority for almost every aspect of life in the city from parking space assignments to public employee payrolls."[10] McMillan wouldn't allow home rule bills out of committee, which many Black residents attributed to his racism.[11]

In the 1960s, Black activists, galvanized by the civil rights movement, mobilized DC's Black community around home rule. In 1966, Julius Hobson, a militant leader of the Washington chapter of CORE helped form the Black United Front to provide a more confrontational approach to the fight. Around the same time, Marion Barry, who came to DC in 1965 as a leader of SNCC, launched the Free DC Movement. Barry started a controversial boycott of downtown businesses that did not support local self-determination and made the restoration of home rule front-page news.[12]

Over the next few years Congress grudgingly gave residents aspects of local control and political power. District voters cast ballots for the first time in a presidential election in 1964. In 1967, after nearly a year of intense criticism and mobilization by Black activists, pressure mounted on Congress to respond to demands by Black activists for an elected school board. President Johnson proposed replacing the three presidentially appointed District commissioners with a single mayor and a nine-member commission—though also appointed by the president.

Calling the proposal a "reorganization" of a governmental agency, Johnson bypassed the House District of Columbia Committee in favor of William Dawson's House Government Operations Committee, and in August 1967, the House voted 244–160 to approve the plan. By this time the District's population was two-thirds Black, and Johnson appointed Walter Washington, a Howard University graduate and director of the District's public housing authority, as the first Black mayor of Washington. He also appointed a Black majority to the city commission, including Walter Fauntroy as vice-chair.

The April 1968 rebellion that followed the assassination of Dr. Martin Luther King Jr. left DC with nearly $25 million in property damage, over 7,600 arrests, thousands of injuries, and seven deaths. Local leaders looked for answers to the disturbances, leading to increased interest in home rule.[13]

In November 1968, voters across the city's eight wards cast ballots in the school board election, the first local election since 1874. Marion Barry and Julius Hobson were among those elected. Then, in 1970, at the behest of President

Nixon, Congress restored the nonvoting congressional delegate for the District. In 1971, Walter Fauntroy was elected the District's nonvoting delegate to the House of Representatives.[14]

DIGGS WAS WELL ACQUAINTED and familiar with the District's Black community, even if initially he had little interest in serving on the House District of Columbia Committee. He had lived in the city since 1955 and was often seen about town at venues frequented by the city's Black civic and political elite. "Charley Diggs was a well-known and well-respected civic and political leader in Washington which had no leaders," remembered Congressman Charles Rangel.[15]

Shortly after the 1962 congressional elections, Speaker Carl Albert asked Diggs to join the House District of Columbia Committee. Diggs had authored the legislation that established the Frederick Douglass National Historic Site in 1962 in DC. A still-reluctant Diggs said, "I'll be just one voice, and [committee chair] McMillan runs that committee with an iron fist. It will never change. It's almost a waste of time to even consider it." After some arm-twisting Diggs caved, saying, "I'll accept the appointment," adding, "I must be out of my mind."[16]

Diggs's appointment was welcomed by local Black leaders although, as the *Pittsburgh Courier* correctly noted, "The addition of Diggs to the committee [left] the unit still tightly in control of Southerners and conservative Republicans."[17] Once he joined the committee, Diggs began advocating for change and challenged McMillan's iron-rule leadership.[18]

The passage, in 1965, of the Voting Rights Act, resulted in a gradual increase in the number of Black voters across the South, including in McMillan's South Carolina District. McMillan, who had been in office since 1939, soon saw a slow erosion of his support. In 1972, McMillan was defeated in the Democratic primary by John Jenrette, a thirty-six-year-old white state legislator, who argued that South Carolina voters were being short-changed because of McMillan's preoccupation with the District.[19]

After McMillan's loss, momentum for DC home rule increased, and when the second ranking Democrat resigned and the third ranking Democrat was convicted of bribery, Diggs suddenly became chair of the House District of Columbia Committee and quickly became a powerful figure in DC politics. On Saturday, January 27, 1973, about 800 people stood elbow to elbow beneath the domed ceiling of the huge House Ways and Means hearing room to witness the special "installation" ceremony of Diggs as chair.

Once in command, Diggs moved quickly, firing McMillan's staff, restructuring the committee and naming Dorothy Quarker, his longtime administrative assistant, chief of staff, making her the first Black woman to serve as chief of staff of a full House Committee.[20] Diggs also hired many other Black staffers, including Robert B. Washington Jr. as the committee's chief counsel; Ruby G. Martin as an associate counsel; and his high school debate coach, Dr. Alvin Loving, as a special consultant. He later named Azie Taylor Morton, who worked for the DNC, as staff director. A few years later, President Carter would appoint Morton as US Treasurer, the first and only Black woman to hold the position.

Becoming a committee chair changed the relationship between Diggs and his colleagues. Now Diggs was part of the House leadership, and he attended meetings to discuss Democratic Party policy. This gave Diggs an opportunity to work directly with and get to know Speaker Carl Albert and other Democratic leaders.[21] It also gave him opportunities to make his points with party leaders away from the commotion on the House floor.

DIGGS EXPLAINED to Ronald Dellums (D-CA) that he knew that "home rule was not ultimately the answer" for the District's "colonial" status and agreed that only statehood could bring full citizenship rights to the District's residents.[22] In 1971, when Dellums introduced a statehood bill, Diggs did not discourage the junior congressman. As Dellums recalled, "We both kind of realized statehood was not going to happen, but he did not discourage me and dissuade me from championing the cause." Dellums trusted Diggs. He was convinced that "at end of the day," Diggs would push "the curve as far as he could push it."[23]

Diggs knew that to pass a home rule bill that President Nixon would sign into law, he would have to traverse the delicate balance of restoring local self-government while preserving Congress's constitutional authority over the District. As historian Lauren Pearlman observed, Diggs "knew he had to walk a cautious line. He felt a sense of duty toward the Washington residents to craft home rule legislation that provided them real representation and afforded the local government meaningful powers."[24] Diggs had the support of the Democratic leadership in the House, including Speaker Carl Albert. Nixon also endorsed self-government for the District of Columbia.

Diggs could also count votes. Early on he identified eleven votes for home rule from the House District of Columbia Committee's liberal bloc and was convinced that several others could be swayed. "This is enough to pass the bill to the floor," Diggs predicted.[25]

As chair, Diggs shaped the contours of what would become the home rule bill. He believed that the mayor and legislative body should be elected. Diggs also proposed that the mayor appoint local judges and that control over planning, transportation, and housing development be shifted from the federal government to city officials. Diggs's proposal became H.R. 9682, the District of Columbia Self-Government and Governmental Reorganization Act.

Diggs then assigned the bill to Congressman Brock Adams's (D-WA) subcommittee. A gifted attorney and politician and a tenacious supporter of home rule, Adams chaired the hearings and played a huge role in guiding the bill through the Congress. Diggs also made sure meetings were scheduled to accommodate community groups, that meeting rooms were available, and that there was a quorum at meetings so the bill could move forward.

Beginning in early February through early June 1973, Adams chaired subcommittee hearings and received testimony from local leaders, neighborhood and community organizations, representatives of interest groups, community activists, and experts on municipal affairs about home rule, all mostly in support. Even the Washington Board of Trade was now on board.

After the subcommittee hearings, Diggs convened three days of additional hearings before the full committee, where amendments to have an appointed mayor and designate a "federal enclave"—a geographic area including the Capitol, the White House, and other federal buildings, and national monuments, to be administered by a presidential appointee—were debated. Both amendments were soundly defeated in the committee.

On July 30, 1973, the House District Committee approved the District of Columbia Self-Government and Governmental Reorganization Act, 20 to 4. The elected city council and mayor could raise local revenues through taxes and fees, which would allow District officials to control their own expenditures. The bill explicitly prohibited a commuter tax. Authority over housing, planning, transportation, and urban redevelopment matters would transfer from federal agencies to the municipal government. Diggs called the vote "a historic occasion"; it was the first time since 1948 that the committee had approved home rule legislation. Although he was "cautiously optimistic" the bill could make it through the House, there was opposition among House members.[26]

IN EARLY SEPTEMBER 1973, after Congress returned from recess, Diggs began to lobby his colleagues in his trademark fashion. As one reporter observed around that time, "Diggs does much of his work quietly over lunch, in elevators, or on walks to and from the Capitol. His soft touch is felt even as he jostles with colleagues on the underground shuttle train that takes members from their offices to the hill."[27]

"During the Home Rule discussions, I made a list of the real influential members," Diggs later explained. "There are 435 people in Congress and you have to know where the pressure points are or you can have the best piece of legislation and it won't go anywhere.... The first person I went to for support was Jerry Ford."[28]

As House Republican leader, Gerald R. Ford had considerable influence on how members of his party voted. Diggs and Ford were longtime members of the Michigan delegation. Although Ford had voted for amendments to weaken 1960s civil rights legislation, the two men were friends.

Ford's concern centered on the District's proposed authority to levy taxes, and he worried that an ongoing public dispute among members of the DC school board foreshadowed similar trouble in an elected city government. Diggs reminded Ford that the home rule bill explicitly prohibited the city from imposing a commuter tax and that heated debate among elected officials was to be expected.[29] A few days later, Ford told reporters, "I'm not going to go out and round up votes against home rule."[30]

Diggs also aggressively lobbied William Natcher, a conservative Kentucky Democrat whom Diggs described as "an extremely influential member of the House ... respected regardless of party."[31] As chair of the House Appropriations Committee's Subcommittee on the District of Columbia, Natcher effectively controlled the District's budget, and he knew the city's finances better than anyone. Natcher insisted that delegating full legislative and budgetary authority to a locally elected mayor and city council would violate the requirement that Congress have "exclusive" legislative rights over the District. He told Diggs he could support home rule but only if Congress retained control over the city's budget.[32]

ON OCTOBER 2, 1973, the House Rules Committee, which decides how bills will be considered by the full House, signaled to Diggs that there was opposition to his bill among House Democrats. The committee passed a rule that allowed for reconsideration of amendments that the District Committee had previously rejected. Although Diggs thought the Rules Committee's action was "terribly unfair and unjust," he knew he had to make changes to the bill.[33]

He quickly met with key members of the House District of Columbia Committee and obtained their approval for a substitute amendment that allowed Congress to keep control of the city's budget, including approving or rejecting line items added by the city council. The other significant change, made at the behest of Nixon and the Republicans, allowed the president, and not the mayor, to continue to appoint local judges and to assume emergency control of local police. Diggs also added a provision requiring a "layover" of thirty legislative days before any action by the city council action could become legal, giving Congress time to review and possibly veto any local legislation.[34]

Some home rule advocates and statehood supporters were critical of the compromises. David Eaton, the senior pastor of All Souls Church and host of a popular radio show, accused Diggs of selling "our souls [and] our ability to control our own lives."[35] But Diggs did not back down. "I am prepared to take my lumps from the home-rule, self-determination purists . . . who think anything short of statehood represents a deficient, imperfect product. . . . We're not going to get anything through Congress like the purists want. This is a practical tactic," he stressed.[36]

Critics called the concessions the "Diggs's Compromise."[37] But Walter Fauntroy and other key Black leaders announced their support. "We support it fully and with no reluctance," said Sterling Tucker, local chair of DC Committee for Self-Determination.[38] Dick Clark, the committee's national chair, praised Diggs. "He's willing to fight, but also recognizes the need to compromise to save the bill," Clark told the *Washington Post*.[39] "Had it not been for Charley, putting together the compromise," Ronald Dellums believed, the bill would not have gone "forward as strongly as it did. . . . Charley fashioned the solution that brought the legislation to the floor of Congress."[40] Diggs's politics of strategic moderation structured the home rule legislation.

ON OCTOBER 9, 1973, the House galleries were unusually crowded as the bill was scheduled for debate. As the *Washington Post* observed a few days before the debate, "A wrong move by members of either side could result in their measure being completely amended or not even discussed."[41]

Diggs first had to release his bill from the straitjacket that the Rules Committee and the bill's opponents had tried to put it in. He prepared a "committee substitute" containing the entire text of the home rule bill plus the critical compromises the District Committee and local leaders had endorsed. Next, Diggs hurriedly distributed copies of this "committee print" to members on the floor. Republicans objected, complaining that Diggs's last-minute changes had not been approved by the full District Committee, the document had no page numbers, bore no date, and was out of order.[42] When Gerald Ford rose and repeated the complaints on the floor, Diggs responded, "As the distinguished minority leader knows, the substitute does not have to be numbered." "I concede that," Ford admitted.[43]

Diggs's tactic was a parliamentary move borne of an experienced legislator. He had outmaneuvered the opposition as the tactic ensured the House would debate his original home rule bill as a substitute amendment rather than those amendments approved by the Rules Committee.

On Wednesday October 10, floor debate shifted to the substance of the bill. Speaker Albert, one of the first to speak, passionately favored passage of the bill. Other Democrats, and some Republicans, followed the Speaker and voiced their support, including Natcher and James "Jim" Wright (D-TX), a member of the House leadership. Diggs and home rule proponents, however, were unable to stop the House from approving a Republican-backed amendment giving the president power to nominate local judges, a big setback for home rule activists.[44]

Though rarely spoken of, race and politics fueled the debate. Diggs acknowledged the racial dynamics, telling the *Baltimore Afro-American* "That the race element is formidable," and "the historic opposition to home rule has been based on the highest degree of racism."[45] Race entered the debate over Ancher Nelsen's amendment for an elected city council with an appointed mayor—so the White House could continue to influence the appointment of the city's police chief. Several members supported Nelsen's amendment, stressing that it would alleviate "some fear" or "trepidation" members had about relinquishing policing to a locally elected government.[46] When Fauntroy urged members to vote "not on the basis of racial prejudgments" but on the bill's merits, Congressman Joel Broyhill (R-VA), known "for his consistently anti-District views," criticized Fauntroy, saying he did "not think anybody else has looked upon this matter as a racist matter."[47] The amendment was defeated.

A passionate debate then occurred when Congresswoman Edith Green (D-OR) put forth Broyhill's "federal enclave" proposal as an amendment. Green was a veteran and formidable legislator, and she was an early supporter of civil rights. She also supported home rule but characterized Diggs's bill as "'crypto-colonialism at best'" because it did not provide DC with full representation in the Congress.[48] Green's amendment designated a geographic area for a "federal district"—including the Capitol, the White House, and other federal buildings—to be administered by a presidential appointee with funds from Congress. She argued that her amendment, in the long run, would benefit the DC statehood movement. If Congress were ever to decide to grant the District's residents full citizenship and consider statehood or retrocession to Maryland, the constitutionally required federal "district" would already be designated.[49] Republicans embraced the amendment. While Diggs and other supporters of home rule opposed Green's amendment, arguing that it created an unnecessary layer of oversight and bureaucracy, the enclave amendment narrowly passed, 209 to 202.[50]

Eventually, the House voted 343 to 74 to approve the District of Columbia Self-Government and Governmental Reorganization Act. The audience in the galleries jumped to their feet and applauded. A few days later, a conference committee (chaired by Diggs) comprising both House and Senate members was appointed to work out the differences between the House and the Senate bills. On November 27, the conferees agreed to a final bill. A few weeks later, the House and Senate gave their final approval. On Christmas Eve, with little national fanfare (it made the front page of the *Washington Post*), President Nixon signed the bill into law. Nixon sent Diggs "a ceremonial pen" in recognition of his "diligent efforts" in passing the legislation.[51]

A FEW WEEKS LATER, at the ceremony unveiling Diggs's "chairman's portrait," Gerald Ford, just a few weeks into his new position as Nixon's vice president, spoke last. Ford described the role Diggs had played as chair of the House Committee on the District of Columbia and recounted how Diggs had assembled "an outstanding staff," developed an "exceptional rapport" with Republicans on the committee, and met with other key House members, "including a couple hours" with Ford and his staff. "If there is one person who can claim success for this [home rule] legislation the credit accrues to you, Charlie. The robe should lie on your shoulders." Before departing, Vice President Ford told Diggs, "I am honored to have you as a friend."[52]

In early May 1974, voters in the District of Columbia approved the new home rule charter by more than 80 percent, setting the stage for party primary elections in September and a general election on November 5, 1974. The newly elected mayor and city council would take office on January 2, 1975.

While statehood for the District remained the goal, DC residents would, at last, elect their own government again.

Chapter 17
LEARNING ABOUT AND DISCOVERING AFRICA

CHARLES DIGGS OFTEN WORE a small pin on the lapel of his suit jacket. Most observers probably thought the pin, a red and white striped flag, like the American flag, featuring a single white star in a field of blue, was a symbol of his patriotism and love for the United States.

It was not. Diggs was a patriot, but the pin represented the national flag of Liberia, the African nation founded by former enslaved people and where Diggs's paternal grandfather, Reverend James J. Diggs, had served as a Baptist missionary. The pin served both as homage to his grandfather and as a symbol of Diggs's enduring interest in Africa, an interest that would only grow and become what might be his most significant and lasting political legacy. While Diggs was fighting for a host of issues from civil rights to home rule for DC, the continent of Africa and its fight for freedom was as close to his heart as that pin on his lapel.

Diggs would become one of the first American legislators to demonstrate a genuine and continuing interest in Africa.

DIGGS'S INTEREST in Africa was an anomaly in Congress. Few members of the House of Representatives knew or cared deeply about foreign policy, and even fewer had an interest in Africa. Traditionally, most are concerned primarily with reelection and claiming credit for improvements in their home districts to secure another term.[1] Neither William L. Dawson nor Adam Clayton Powell served on committees focused on foreign affairs.

American presidents delegated Africa policy to State Department bureaucrats and national security agencies, giving it a low priority. In 1958, the US State Department formed a Bureau of African Affairs. Congress followed by creating Africa subcommittees in both the House and the Senate, but these subcommittees were largely inactive and ineffective.[2]

Outside of government, there was little US interest in Africa. From the 1940s through the 1960s, the NAACP, focused almost exclusively on issues affecting Black Americans and exhibited only "informal" interest in Africa.[3] During the 1940s and 1950s, the leading voice for Black Americans on Africa was the Council of African Affairs.[4] In 1955, the year Diggs entered Congress, the council dissolved leaving no other Black-led US organization devoted to Africa and US-Africa policy.

Meanwhile, the American Committee on Africa (ACOA) emerged as the most significant US organization focused on Africa. Formed in 1953 by a biracial group of liberal civil rights activists connected with CORE—including Bayard Rustin, A. Phillip Randolph, and George Houser, a white pacifist minister—the ACOA eschewed the radical approach of the Council of African Affairs and embraced the anticommunist sentiment that dominated the Cold War era.[5] Over the next twenty years, Diggs became the leading voice advocating that Black Americans form a lobby organization to exert influence on US-Africa policy, not unlike the way American Jews pressed for policies related to Israel.[6]

BETWEEN 1957 AND DECEMBER 1960, eighteen African countries gained independence from their colonial rulers, and during the 1960s another fifteen African countries joined them. These new nations aligned with recently independent Asian nations and formed an important anti-colonialism bloc in the United Nations. In Southern Africa, however, Portuguese colonizers deepened their determination to maintain white rule in Guinea-Bissau, Cape Verde, Angola, and Mozambique; and South African whites strengthened their resolve to sustain apartheid, the system of discriminatory laws designed by the white minority to control the country's Black majority.

South Africa won its independence from Britain in 1910. In 1948, the former colony instituted apartheid, imposed by the all-white Nationalist Party. Black people constituted 70 percent of the population while whites (most of them Dutch settlers, or Afrikaners) made up only 20 percent of South Africa's population. Under apartheid, however, Black people had no public policy voice. Apartheid mandated the strict separation of Black, White, Colored (mixed-race), Indian, and Asian persons. Whites held most skilled jobs. Only about 20 percent of Black people in South Africa were literate in 1960 compared to a nearly 100 percent literacy rate among whites.[7]

Despite these obvious inequities, the United States developed strategic and military ties to South Africa. And Portugal, which steadfastly maintained its colonial presence on the continent, was a founding member of the North Atlantic Treaty Organization (NATO) and leased to the United States strategically important military bases on the Azores Islands.

As Diggs pressed for civil rights in the United States, altering US-Africa policy to bring about Black-majority rule in Africa soon became another focus of Diggs's interests.

IN LATE 1956, the US government was invited to attend the freedom ceremonies of Ghana, the first sub-Saharan African country to gain independence. The prime minister, forty-seven-year-old Kwame Nkrumah, a graduate of Lincoln University, a Black college in Pennsylvania, had strong ties to the United States. Conscious of the importance of the Black vote in the upcoming presidential election, the Eisenhower White House included Black leaders in the official delegation to Ghana, hoping to garner Black votes and signal to Africans the US commitment to Black freedom.[8]

After some discussion, Diggs was asked to be part of the delegation.[9] He joined Vice President Richard Nixon and other US officials. Diggs realized the significance of Ghana's independence and saw it in terms of the Black freedom struggle in America. The trip, Diggs's first to Africa, would change the course of his Capitol Hill career.

On March 3, 1957, the delegation landed at the airport in Accra, Ghana. More than 10,000 Africans cheered their arrival. In addition to the US delegation, Prime Minister Kwame Nkrumah personally invited several prominent Black Americans, including Martin L. King Jr., Coretta Scott King, Adam Clayton Powell, NAACP chief Roy Wilkins, Ralph Bunche, and others to witness the ceremonies. Their presence was a signal of just how significant Africa was becoming to Black Americans.[10]

On the evening of March 5, Diggs and the others witnessed the last meeting of Ghana's Parliament under British rule. Then, just before midnight, Nkrumah, members of his government, and other dignitaries marched out of the Parliament Building. Diggs, Powell, King, and the other Americans, all jovial and smiling, followed them. Outside, a huge crowd of more than 50,000 Ghanaians jammed the main square. Nkrumah stepped toward the podium. "At long last," he announced to the huge crowd, "the battle has ended; Ghana, our beloved country, is free forever." Nkrumah, a Pan-Africanist, stressed that Ghana's "independence is meaningless unless it is linked up with the total liberation of Africa."[11] Then he asked the crowd to pause and be silent for sixty seconds. Diggs looked up into the dark sky and watched as the Union Jack was hauled down from the flagpole atop the Parliament Building. Shortly thereafter, the red, yellow, and green flag of Ghana was slowly raised in its place. Ghana was now an independent nation.

Diggs later remembered that "Adam [Clayton Powell] and I stood out there with tears coming down our cheeks as we saw the British flag come down and the other flag go up."¹² The ceremony was evidence of racial progress and took on a spiritual meaning for what the future might hold for the civil rights struggle in America. As Diggs and the others turned to walk away, they heard a mighty roar rumble through the streets of Accra. "Freedom! Freedom! Freedom!" "Ghana is free!" the people yelled. "Ghana is free!"

Diggs's trip rejuvenated his interest in Africa. Upon his return to the United States, Diggs requested reassignment to the Foreign Affairs Committee. Explaining he had a "consuming interest" in Africa, Diggs offered that as a Black American, he would bring a unique understanding of the "international significance of the racial situation" in Africa.¹³

In December 1958, Diggs returned to Africa as an "official observer" at the first All-African People's Conference in Accra, the largest gathering of African leaders ever assembled and the first such assembly held on the continent. Called by Prime Minister Nkrumah, the All-African People's Conference brought together 300 delegates from twenty-eight African countries, most of them still colonized. The delegates embraced Pan-Africanism and the view that anyone living in Africa, Black or white, could be part of Africa so long as the basic principles of democracy were accepted. They also endorsed a neutral position and nonalignment in the Cold War, a position the American administration was unwilling to support.¹⁴

When Diggs again returned to the United States, he sought to engage others in African affairs and found that the NAACP did not consider it a priority.¹⁵ Next, Diggs held a press conference about US-Africa policy, during which he directly criticized the US government for equating African nationalism with communism. "They [the Africans] don't view Communism as the same evil we do. Right now, they think racialism is worse than communism," Diggs stated.¹⁶

IN JANUARY 1959, Diggs became the first Black American assigned to the House Foreign Affairs Committee. In the 1950s and 1960s, the annual foreign aid bill dominated the Foreign Affairs Committee's work over any other policy issue. This laser-focus on foreign aid left the subcommittees essentially inactive.¹⁷ Diggs took advantage of the frequent membership turnover. By 1960 he was already the Subcommittee on Africa second-most senior Democrat. News reporters sometimes even referred to Diggs as "vice-chairman" of the subcommittee.

Diggs acquired books about Africa, a collection that resembled a required-readings list in a graduate seminar—anthologies and monographs by reputable scholars on the history and politics of Ghana, Nigeria, Rhodesia, and other African countries as well as on Portuguese colonization.¹⁸ Using his repeated visits to Africa as fieldwork, Diggs quickly developed a reputation as a congressmember with a deep interest in and knowledge of Africa. Over the next two decades Diggs would make more official trips and fact-finding missions to Africa than any other member of Congress. Diggs's self-directed study of Africa became so comprehensive that it showed up the superficial knowledge of many "Africanists," both Black and white.

Diggs wasted little time applying his expertise to push the Eisenhower administration on US-Africa policy. As more African countries gained independence, an increasing number of diplomats and ministers from the continent encountered difficulties obtaining housing and service in restaurants and barbershops in the Washington, DC, area. Diggs warned the Eisenhower administration that racial discrimination created challenges in developing favorable relations with new African nations. In September 1960, using the same tactics that had eventually resulted in changes to housing policies of the US military, Diggs wrote Secretary of State Christian Herter and suggested that Herter work with local real estate leaders to develop and maintain a list of "approved" housing in the DC area open to all, regardless of race.[19]

At the same time, Diggs watched events in South Africa with growing concern. In 1958, the ruling Nationalist Party elected Hendrik Verwoerd, the leading intellectual voice of apartheid, as prime minister. The Verwoerd regime rapidly instituted new racial laws and regulations restricting Africans and other non-whites. These racial policies provoked Black demonstrations in South Africa.

In March 1960, at Sharpeville, an all-Black township, what began as peaceful protest turned violent after police, without warning, fired upon demonstrators, killing 69 Black protestors and wounding over 180, including some 50 children and women. The Sharpeville massacre led to outrage and denunciations of apartheid. The editors of the *New York Times* called apartheid "immoral."[20] The NAACP and the AFL-CIO urged the United States to institute an official economic boycott of South Africa.[21]

The uproar forced the Eisenhower administration to depart from its previously unqualified support for the South African government (SAG) and, in April 1960, the United States supported a UN resolution that "deplored the policies and actions" of the SAG and called upon South Africa to abandon apartheid.[22] Yet the public denunciation of apartheid did not mean a change in policy. The American government continued to work with the SAG in furtherance of the Cold War imperative.

Still, Sharpeville made Africa an issue during the 1960 presidential election year. The close race between Vice President Nixon and Senator John F. Kennedy made the Black vote significant for victory. Nixon had a good reputation among Black voters and was viewed as the person most attuned to civil rights within the Eisenhower administration.[23] Kennedy, by contrast, was considered weak on civil rights and had only lukewarm support among Black Americans. Diggs initially supported the candidacy of former Michigan governor G. Mennen Williams. When Williams dropped out, Diggs backed liberal Missouri senator Stuart Symington for president.

Kennedy hoped to avoid a nomination fight at the convention in Los Angeles by capturing the nomination on the first ballot. He reached out to Williams, asking the popular former governor to release Michigan's huge delegation to vote for him. In response, in June 1960, Williams arranged for Kennedy to meet with Black leaders from Michigan's powerful liberal-Black-labor coalition. Kennedy told the group he would sign an executive order ending segregation in federally assisted housing, and he signaled he would tap liberal Symington to be his running mate. Although Diggs did not attend, he threw his support behind Kennedy even after Symington was pushed aside and Senator Lyndon Johnson of Texas joined the ticket.[24]

In the end, Kennedy garnered enough Black votes to ensure his election. While some observers credit Kennedy's victory to a telephone call he made to a pregnant Coretta Scott King while her husband was jailed in Georgia, others have suggested that Kennedy's focus on Africa was critical to his razor-thin victory.[25] In the last three months before the general election, Kennedy mentioned Africa 167 times in speeches and statements. By contrast, Nixon did so only twenty-three times. Kennedy even announced he would form a "Peace Corps" to send American volunteers to work in developing countries, including those in Africa. The clever political tactic allowed Kennedy to appeal to Black voters within the context of foreign policy without alienating Southern whites opposed to civil rights for Black Americans.[26] Black voters, in fact, gave Kennedy a winning margin in New Jersey, Michigan, Illinois, Texas, and South Carolina, states that had supported Eisenhower in 1956.

WITH A DEMOCRAT in the White House, Diggs soon detected a change. Kennedy's appointment of liberals, such as Dean Rusk as secretary of state and Adlai Stevenson as ambassador to the United Nations, put Diggs at ease, and Diggs became an early supporter of the president's Peace Corps legislation. Diggs was especially delighted when President Kennedy appointed G. Mennen Williams as the assistant secretary of state for African Affairs. Williams became a voice in the administration for Black freedom in Africa. Williams visited all the African countries (except South Africa) and generally made Africans feel that Washington supported their goals, even as Williams came under fierce criticism from European allies and those in the United States who believed that an "Africa first" policy threatened Europe's and NATO's security.[27]

However, it soon became clear to Diggs and others that the substance of

Kennedy's Africa policy was little changed from that of the Eisenhower administration. Key members of Kennedy's foreign and national security team opposed significant change in US-Africa relations. As the growing war in Vietnam consumed both attention and the US government's budget, spending and direct aid to Africa fell from $315 million in 1962 to $198 million by 1964.[28]

In 1962, working closely with Williams, the leaders of America's largest civil rights organizations pushed the Kennedy administration to provide more support for Africa. Calling themselves the American Negro Leadership Conference on Africa, their efforts met with mixed results. As civil rights at home consumed its leaders' time, the conference soon dissolved.[29]

After Lyndon Johnson assumed the presidency in November 1963, the Vietnam War occupied his attention and "became a consideration in judging all other problems and nations." African opposition to the war "made the administration less than zealous in its commitment to African concerns."[30]

FOR OVER A DECADE, the notion of economic sanctions against South Africa had been unsuccessfully pushed by African and Asian delegates to the United Nations. Events in Rhodesia in 1965 then elevated the debate. Ian Smith, the Rhodesian prime minister, defied Britain, the United States, and the United Nations when he unilaterally declared the country an independent nation and, emulating South Africa, instituted a new constitution that kept whites, less than 10 percent of the population (and terrified by the rapid movement toward decolonization), in control of the government. The United States soon instituted voluntary sanctions against Rhodesia, including an embargo on Rhodesian tobacco and sugar, an end to investments, and nonrecognition of the Smith government.[31]

In December 1965, Diggs led a bipartisan congressional delegation (CODEL) study mission to Africa, during which congressmembers met with seven heads of state in eight African countries. The African heads of state told Diggs and his colleagues that ethnic tensions were a major obstacle to government stability in many African nations and that—compared with Southeast Asia and Latin America—they felt devalued by the United States. The leaders told Diggs that America's racial problems were harmful to African diplomacy, that African liberation and Black nationalism were not tied to any political ideology, and that racism, not communism, was the major security threat in Africa. Afterward, in his CODEL report, Diggs pressed for a "greater awareness of and interest in Africa on the part of the Congress and the public."[32]

Yet, in December 1965, the United States, Britain, and France still abstained on a UN General Assembly resolution condemning apartheid. Barrett O'Hara (D-IL), chair of the House Foreign Affairs Committee's Subcommittee on

Africa, was so outraged that in March 1966 he held two weeks of hearings on apartheid and the issue of economic sanctions. It was the first time the Subcommittee on Africa held hearings on the United States' relationship with South Africa. Diggs used his time at the hearing to criticize US policy in South Africa.[33]

The hearings generated little coverage in the US media, but in South Africa, they were criticized as "a violation of the generally accepted international principle of noninterference in the affairs of a sovereign state."[34] William Roundtree, the new US ambassador to South Africa, said that South Africans were "anxious" about the hearings and potential changes in American policy. Yet he also secretly told the SAG "that no such changes are contemplated."[35] Diggs wanted to make a fact-finding visit to South Africa, but on May 1, 1966, the SAG denied Diggs's request for a visa and barred all members of the Subcommittee on Africa.[36]

With the US government unwilling to change its approach to South Africa, Diggs and others turned to economic disengagement and divestment by the private sector as methods to force change. In July 1966, A. Phillip Randolph, working closely with the ACOA, formed the Committee of Conscience Against Apartheid to encourage individuals and organizations to withdraw deposits from major US banks that made loans to South Africa. Diggs agreed with the "principle of economic sanctions" and told Randolph that he believed divesting funds from the banks would bring attention to "our country's significant involvement in the economy of South Africa" and expose "the hypocrisy of American policy, both in the public and private sectors."[37]

By December 1966, reportedly more than $23 million had been withdrawn from major US banks. The bank campaign soon expanded as student organizations pressured their colleges to end their relationships with banks conducting business in South Africa. Some Christian religious denominations also joined the divestment movement.[38]

Policy debates about US economic disengagement were elevated in December 1966, after the United States voted to support a UN resolution declaring an international embargo on Rhodesian exports; it was the first time the United Nations adopted economic sanctions against a nation.[39] The resolution also forbade UN nations to sell oil, arms, motor vehicles, or airplanes to the territory or to provide it with any form of economic aid. In January 1967 and July 1968, President Johnson signed executive orders sanctioning Rhodesia and barring the importation of Rhodesian goods into the United States with few exceptions.[40]

Soon, however, conservatives questioned why the United States would impose sanctions on a country that stood against Soviet communist expansion in Africa. Over the next few years, conservatives would work to ease sanctions against Rhodesia. Meanwhile, United States' involvement in Vietnam escalated, and Africa was again relegated to its traditional low-level status in US diplomacy.

WHEN RICHARD NIXON took office in January 1969, pulling US troops out of Vietnam in an "honorable" way was his central foreign policy concern. Both President Nixon and his national security adviser Henry Kissinger had little knowledge of Africa and were relatively uninterested in the continent.[41]

Almost immediately upon entering office, Kissinger ordered the National Security Council to develop a series of country evaluations with the intention of reviewing policy and developing long-term policy options. National Security Study Memorandum 39 (NSSM 39) focused on Southern Africa—Rhodesia, South Africa, and the Portuguese territories, with some discussion of Zaire and Tanzania.

NSSM 39 listed five options for US policy in Southern Africa, ranging from the normalization of relations with the white minority–ruled regimes to severing all US ties with the region. All five options assumed that the Black liberation movements would fail, and that violence would not produce permanent change in Southern Africa. Kissinger recommended "option two" to Nixon which called for the selective relaxation of US policy toward the white regimes to encourage change in their current racial and colonial policies.[42] David Newsom, Nixon's assistant secretary of state for African Affairs, concluded that Nixon was determined to "tilt" US policy toward more communication and engagement with white-ruled states in Southern Africa.[43]

Diggs, however, was in the fight for the long haul. That Liberian flag on his lapel was much more than decorative. He was prepared to fight any movement by the United States that might be seen as leaning back toward the white regimes in Southern Africa. Diggs believed such a move would seriously damage US relations with Black Africa. He was ready for a battle, and when the ninety-first session of Congress convened in January 1969, Diggs's influence on US-Africa policy on Capitol Hill increased exponentially.

Chapter 18

AWAKENING AMERICA

Diggs and the Africa Subcommittee

PERSISTENCE.

If one word encompasses Charles Diggs's approach in Congress, that word is persistence. That would never be truer than in his approach to South Africa and apartheid. Diggs used the same tactics that, over time, had impacted US policy regarding segregation in the US military and the airline industry and had brought home rule to the District of Columbia. He made a moderate moral argument, framed as an extension of American democratic ideals. Applied with consistent and unyielding pressure, he helped create a coalition of support that resulted in change that had once seemed impossible. As one close staff member noted, "Diggs believed in the art of the doable. . . . We weren't going to get a comprehensive anti-apartheid sanctions bill through the Congress; so, Diggs chipped away."[1] South Africa would prove to be both his greatest challenge and his greatest achievement.

In August 1968, eighty-six-year-old congressman Barrett O'Hara, chair of the Subcommittee on Africa, whom Diggs called a "constant inspiration," lost in the Democratic primary.[2] The forty-six-year-old Diggs thus became the chair of the Africa subcommittee, providing greater opportunities to advance his policy views. Diggs could now call hearings, set agendas, select witnesses, organize trips, question State Department and executive branch officials, call press conferences, and commission studies.[3]

Diggs told Clarence Mitchell, the NAACP chief lobbyist on Capitol Hill, that the Subcommittee on Africa had "a great deal of potentiality" for influencing US-Africa policy.[4] Diggs believed that "too many Americans still have the old Hollywood concept of Africa as a hot, humid country of jungles and wild animals. They do not think of it as a continent offering tremendous investment opportunities, exciting experiments in social progress, and a political development that closely parallels the growth of our own United States."[5] Similarly, the congressman believed that many Black Americans had only a superficial understanding of Africa. Most knew little about apartheid in South Africa or the freedom fighters in Angola, Guinea-Bissau, and Mozambique.

Yet Diggs was not naive. He knew that assuming the chair of the subcommittee would not be enough to move Congress and the White House. Diggs again emphasized the need for a Black American–led organization focused on US-Africa policy. "Our lobby has not been too effective," Diggs told Mitchell.[6]

DIGGS GOT BUSY right away and exerted his new oversight authority. In his first months as chair, he sent letters to every cabinet department requesting information about agreements or pending agreements with the SAG.[7] Nearly every department had agreements with the SAG, ranging from SAG-sponsored conferences to a DOD agreement placing a National Aeronautics and Space Administration tracking system on South African soil. Over the next decade, Diggs would send hundreds of such letters, memoranda, and telegrams to American presidents, their cabinet secretaries, and federal agency heads demanding answers to questions about African policies. He was determined to publicize what he considered US complicity in the subjugation of the Black majority throughout Southern Africa.

Diggs's first move was to question the US government's decision to grant South African Airways (SAA) landing rights at John F. Kennedy Airport in New York City. Only two days after Nixon's election victory, President Johnson quietly approved the Civil Aeronautics Board's decision to permit SAA to provide service between Johannesburg and New York City. The decision fulfilled a twenty-year bilateral agreement between the United States and the SAG, which owned SAA. Diggs contended that the SAA was bound to follow apartheid policies of race separation. He telegrammed President Nixon demanding that he direct the Civil Aeronautics Board to reverse their decision and prohibit his cabinet members from participating on SAA's complimentary inaugural flight.[8] Diggs also organized "a special order" for members to speak on the House floor about the issue. And Diggs emphasized that the decision was a "grave insult" to Black Americans.[9]

On April 2, 1969, Diggs chaired his first hearing as head of the Subcommittee on Africa to explore the Nixon administration's refusal to reverse the Civil Aeronautics Board's decision. The administration argued it had no authority to intrude on the existing bilateral agreement. However, George Houser of the ACOA testified that the United States was viewed throughout Africa as a "partner in apartheid" because of the agreement.[10]

On April 7, SAA flew a group of prominent US residents to South Africa for an all-expenses-paid week-long vacation; participants included Congressman

Samuel A. Friedel, a seventy-two-year-old Baltimore Democrat and chair of the House Commerce Committee's transportation subcommittee. Two months later, with twenty-three cosponsors, Diggs introduced a bill to prohibit flights to and from countries that discriminated against American citizens. Friedel blocked the bill, and it never received a vote.[11]

Still, America's South Africa policy was under scrutiny. The ACOA organized days of protest demonstrations at JFK International Airport, and Diggs's fight also caused the Organization of African Unity to adopt a resolution condemning the SAA agreement and appealing to the US government to reconsider. Newspapers around the United States and in South Africa covered the hearing and the airport protests. The hearing demonstrated that the Subcommittee on Africa could publicize an issue and educate the public.[12]

A few weeks later, Diggs held a subcommittee hearing on a program that guaranteed South Africa a percentage of the US sugar market. Diggs criticized the policy and its larger implications, saying, "I view it as part of a larger program, which should call for the disengagement of the United States from South Africa in both the private and public sectors."[13] Diggs pressed the US Department of Agriculture official Tom O. Murphy, who oversaw sugar policy, on the working conditions of sugarcane workers in South Africa. When Diggs told Murphy about how Black South Africans in the sugar industry earned less than a dollar a day, and about the "tot" system, by which some were paid with alcohol, Murphy claimed ignorance.[14] While Deputy Assistant Secretary of State Julius Katz testified that US government abhorred apartheid, he also said it was important not to isolate South Africa, that the United States was "carrying out a relatively normal relationship" with a country that it disagrees with on internal matters, much as the United States did with other countries.[15]

In April 1969, Representative Jonathan B. Bingham (D-NY) and Senator Edward Kennedy (D-MA) introduced companion bills in the House and Senate to delete the sugar quota for South Africa. Diggs testified in support of the bills; however, the bills were defeated. In June 1971, a second attempt by Diggs to open debate and strip the sugar quota from South Africa also failed in the House.[16] Although the hearing failed to change US policy, the issue began to gain traction and media attention.

DIGGS THEN EMBARKED on a fact-finding visit to Africa, leading a bipartisan CODEL traveling to seven countries in Southern Africa: Angola, Mozambique, Swaziland, Lesotho, Botswana, Malawi, and Zambia, and East African Tanzania. Diggs initially intended to visit South Africa, but Prime Minister John Vorster, who succeeded Verwoerd in 1966, granted Diggs only a conditional visa that restricted him from making any public statements while in the country. Diggs chose not to visit South Africa at all and claimed the SAG had denied him an unconditional visa solely because of his race.[17] During the trip, Diggs made contacts not only with African political leaders but with the leaders of liberation movements in Southern Africa, including Rhodesia, many of whom were now exiled in Tanzania and Zambia. The liberation leaders emphasized to Diggs that by cooperating with South Africa and Portugal in the leasing of the military bases on the Azores Islands, the United States was working against Black Africans.

Upon his return to Washington, DC, Diggs argued that US policy in Southern Africa was wrong-headed and based on erroneous reports of the scope and nature of the Black insurgency in the Portuguese territories, Rhodesia, and South Africa.[18] Diggs reported that liberation movements in Angola and Mozambique were armed, well-organized, and assisted by the Soviet Union and China. He stressed that the insurgents were not communists but nationalists who would accept assistance from communists and noncommunists alike. He predicted that liberation movements throughout the region would succeed, saying, "It's just a question of time."[19] Diggs's goal was to make sure economic and security concerns would not result in American support for government-sanctioned institutionalized racism.

Although the CODEL did not visit South Africa, many proposals in Diggs's final report to Congress were directed at the SAG. The report recommended a "step-by-step plan to isolate" South Africa and Rhodesia politically and economically, and it called on the United States to discontinue military aid to Portugal. The report also proposed an economic development program "comparable in scope" to the Marshall Plan to address the needs of Black-ruled nations in Southern Africa.[20]

OVER THE NEXT FEW YEARS, through study missions to Africa and public hearings, Diggs continued to challenge Nixon's Africa policy and pressure the United States to continue supporting full economic sanctions against Rhodesia. Diggs's outspokenness about Africa thrust him into the limelight among African leaders, many of whom would interact with Diggs regularly over the coming years. He built lasting relationships with leaders like Seretse Khama, the president of Botswana, and Kenneth D. Kaunda, the president of Zambia. In July 1969, Simeon Booker reported that Diggs's "African stance" made him "the most popular embassy guest" among African diplomats.[21]

In 1970, Diggs held hearings that garnered considerable media coverage. The first examined South Africa's refusal to grant Arthur Ashe, the twenty-six-year-old Black American tennis star, a visa to play in the South African

Open.[22] And in February of that year, Diggs chaired a hearing on the liberation struggles in the Portuguese colonies in Africa.[23]

Beginning in mid-March and ending in December 1970, Diggs led thirteen days of extraordinary hearings on US-Africa policy, taking testimony not only from US government officials but from prominent Black Americans representing academia, business, labor, pro-African liberation groups, and civil rights organizations. Never had so many Black Americans appeared before a committee in Congress to present testimony about Africa and US-Africa policy.[24] The hearings highlighted what Diggs and others believed was US hypocrisy.

Diggs slowly began to use the Subcommittee on Africa to help mobilize the Black community against apartheid and move Congress toward altering its US-Africa policy, for the first time articulating that goal as a defining principle. Diggs also continued to believe that a Black-led Africa lobby organization was necessary. As Diggs wrote in September 1970, "No one can doubt that there are powerful lobby groups supporting white domination over Black peoples in this country.... That being so, it is difficult to see why there should not be a Black lobby for Africa just as there are pressure groups for a host of other causes and nations."[25]

IN MAY 1971, Diggs hired Goler Teal Butcher, a Black lawyer, as staff consultant and legal counsel to the Subcommittee on Africa. Butcher had "a brilliant mind [and] a ferocious appetite for knowledge," and the two worked in tandem on Africa issues, something they both cared deeply about.[26] Butcher had worked in the legal office on Near East and South Asian Affairs for several years before moving in 1969 to the State Department's Africa Bureau. *Jet* magazine called Butcher "one of the best trained and smartest individuals in African affairs."[27] "I hired her because she was so focused on South Africa," Diggs recalled years later.[28]

When Butcher started, the Subcommittee on Africa had begun what was planned to be a week of hearings on US business involvement in Southern Africa; but only four American corporations had agreed to testify. Butcher stepped in and expanded the list of witnesses to include anti-apartheid activists, representatives from major church denominations, and the heads of relevant government agencies. She also scheduled the hearing to run intermittently throughout the entire summer, thus keeping the issue in the news.

In his opening statement, Diggs again linked American business investment in South Africa to the maintenance of apartheid. Diggs maintained that American businesses should be using their considerable power to bring about change in South Africa. If they could not or chose not to help bring about change, Diggs asked, should the US government not force American businesses to leave South Africa?[29]

Most corporations offered responses like that of Thomas H. Wyman, a senior vice president of Polaroid Corporation. He told the subcommittee that Polaroid believed the best way to oppose apartheid was for the company to stay and help expand opportunities for African employees and their families. The subcommittee also heard gripping and poignant testimony about the brutality of living under apartheid from Professor Daniel Kunene, a forty-eight-year-old Black South African exile whom Diggs had met at the University of Wisconsin. "For the black man in South Africa, life is one long nightmare of proving that you have obtained the necessary permission to be where you are," Kunene testified.[30]

Reverend Leon Sullivan, a Philadelphia-based Black Baptist minister who organized successful boycotts against Philadelphia businesses that refused to hire Black people, told the subcommittee that the only solution was for the United States and its allies to support a full economic embargo. When Reverend Sullivan finished his statement, members of the audience applauded.

Jennifer Davis and Charles Hightower of the ACOA testified that American companies doing business in South Africa made an average profit of twenty to 25 percent on their investment, gains based primarily on the exploitation of Black labor. Facilities at the American plants were racially segregated. Administration officials repeated the mantra that it "neither encouraged nor discouraged" business investment in South Africa.[31] They testified that the best way to change South Africa was not to abandon it but try to change the system from within.

Never before had a congressional committee explored and questioned the scope and nature of American business investment in South Africa. Yet there was little newspaper coverage of the hearings. Nevertheless, Diggs believed the hearings accomplished the goal of getting the implications of American business involvement in South Africa on the record. Transcripts were published under the title *U.S. Business Involvement in South Africa*. People were beginning to pay more attention to the work of the Subcommittee on Africa, and an "unprecedented number of requests" for copies of the transcripts poured into Diggs's office. Within eleven months, the stock of 1,440 copies had "been completely depleted."[32] Diggs then introduced a House resolution requesting a reprint of 1,500 additional copies.

IN THE SUMMER OF 1971, two unexpected events enshrined Diggs in history as a champion of African freedom. First, Diggs's application for a visa as part of a bipartisan and biracial CODEL to visit South Africa and the disputed territory of South-West Africa (Namibia) was approved by the SAG. Second, President Nixon appointed Diggs as a delegate to the United Nations; he was the first Black member of Congress to be named a delegate.

The visa decision by the SAG was unexpected. SAG officials were sufficiently concerned about the House hearings and the threat of US corporate withdrawal that they did not wish to antagonize Diggs any longer. He would become the first Black member of the US Congress to visit South Africa. Diggs and the CODEL planned to focus on "the people" of South Africa.[33] They planned to talk to Black, white, Colored, and Asian people; church groups; student leaders; families of detainees; and other "banned" people. Diggs hoped to meet Winnie Mandela, the wife of the jailed African National Congress leader. The delegation also planned to visit American businesses in South Africa.[34]

On Thursday August 5, 1971, the delegation met in New York with UN officials who urged Diggs to produce a study report about South Africa that could be easily digested.[35] The trip began in Portugal where the delegation was told that Portugal had implemented programs to give greater local autonomy to its African territories and that it had no plans to relinquish the African territories.

Then it was off to South Africa.

On Wednesday August 11, when the plane landed at Jans Smuts Airport, just outside of Johannesburg, there was immediate controversy. Diggs was met on the plane by Robert S. Smith, the deputy assistant secretary of state for African Affairs. He told Diggs that the SAG changed its mind and would no longer allow Diggs and the CODEL to visit Namibia without a SAG escort. Angry, Diggs first told Smith he would return to the United States immediately; but after learning it would be several hours before the next flight back, Diggs decided to proceed as originally planned, and he visited Soweto without a SAG escort.[36]

Soweto, the huge, all-Black township near Johannesburg, housed Black laborers who worked at industrial sites miles away from the city center. At least 70 percent of Soweto's population lived in extreme poverty. Diggs's itinerary included a tour of a training institute allegedly designed to provide Africans with "advance technical training." However, when the CODEL visited, the students were learning only to make toys.

Diggs next visited the Johannesburg Urban Bantu Council, a Black-led local council with limited administrative authority. Council head David Thebehali risked prosecution when he bluntly told Diggs that American businesses should disengage from South Africa; but if they were going to stay, he believed American businesses should improve the pay and overall conditions for Black workers. Diggs offered that in the short term the hearings and CODEL would result in direct changes to the wages and fringe benefits American corporations provided their African workers.[37]

While Diggs met with the Bantu Council, word spread throughout the slums of Soweto that an important Black American had come to help them. A throng of Africans of all ages congregated outside the municipal building and exploded in applause and cheers as Diggs left the building. A large group of school-age children, many of them teenagers, burst into a song of praise, singing in their African language, "Here is a black man who is lionhearted. And he is here with us today. Perhaps he'll help us. With the difficulties we have. Amen!" Diggs, visibly moved, addressed the crowd and said, "You are the future of [South] Africa. With the resources that this country has, natural, industrial and human, I can only say that I will be proud to say I knew you when."[38] Diggs smiled widely and then raised his hand in the clenched-fist Black Power salute.

The delegation then left Soweto and drove northeast to the US embassy in Pretoria. Diggs was again greeted by a mob of Black South Africans thrilled to see him—a Black man—moving about South Africa and going places unencumbered as no other Black person had before. US embassy officials told Diggs of the large crowd. "They had never seen anything like it."

At the embassy, Diggs and the other CODEL members were guests for dinner at the home of the US ambassador John Hurd. The fifty-seven-year-old Texan oil man, who had contributed generously to the Republican Party, was commonly known to refer to Africans as "Nigras."[39] Diggs told Hurd to focus more attention on Africans and that the US mission must reform its own employment practices. Diggs stressed that there was no justification for not assigning a Black Foreign Service Officer to South Africa.[40]

On Friday, August 13, Diggs held his first press conference since arriving in Africa. He said it was "with great surprise and deep disappointment" that he learned of the SAG's objection to his visit to Namibia.[41] He rejected the explanation for the reversal—the SAG claimed there was a lack of accommodations because of the short notice—calling it "ludicrous." South Africa barred him from Namibia, Diggs stressed, because he asked to be escorted by an American embassy guide rather than by one supplied by the SAG. "They just didn't have the guts" to admit it. Diggs shared that he was "deeply moved" by his reception in Soweto.[42] Diggs again called on the United States to do all it could to "accelerate the changes taking place in this country." The US government ought to be an example, he pointed out.

Tossing aside his official itinerary over the next eight days, Diggs kept up a "brutal pace, sometimes working eighteen-hour days" crisscrossing the country.[43] He wanted to hear the views and perspectives of all South African people. The study mission, Diggs said, had become a "people-to-people mission."[44]

He toured the National Aeronautics and Space Administration tracking station about thirty miles from Johannesburg and later described it as "one of the emotional experiences" of his visit.[45] The station employed 280 South African workers, sixty-one of whom were Black; the others were white. Diggs was deeply disturbed to find "all the trappings and marks" of South African apartheid in place at a facility financed by the US government.[46] The restrooms were segregated; Black workers were barred from the station cafeteria and were not eligible for technical or supervisory positions.

Diggs met with a group of largely white students organized by the National Union of South African Students, the anti-apartheid group led by liberal whites; with leaders of the Indian and Colored communities; and with leaders of the Labor Party, the dominant party for Colored people in Cape Town. In Durban, Diggs visited the nearby Phoenix Settlement, where Mahatma Gandhi had spent his formative years in the early 1900s, and visited with Gandhi's granddaughter and family.

Durban was also the headquarters of the American-subsidized South African sugar industry. The South African Sugar Association, a trade group, sponsored a tour of a plantation, and Diggs was shown a fifteen-minute film of its activities. Diggs would later describe the film as the most patronizing, racist, and insulting depiction of Black workers that he had ever seen.[47] Diggs later returned to the sugar plantation unannounced, and he learned that the sugar fieldworkers labored in deplorable conditions, six days a week, from 6 a.m. to 6 p.m., and earned fourteen dollars a month in cash. "You must help us," one worker told Diggs. "We work ourselves to death and get no money." Others told him bluntly, "The white people are killing us."

Diggs next met with a group of Black university students, led by Stephen Biko, a twenty-four-year-old medical student. Biko, an extremely bright and extraordinarily gifted public speaker, embraced the ideology of Black Power developed in the United States. In July 1969, he broke away from the National Union of South African Students and formed the South African Students' Association as a vehicle through which African students could mobilize to end apartheid.[48]

The climax of Diggs's South Africa visit was a visit to the General Motors and Ford auto manufacturing plants in Port Elizabeth.[49] Diggs got into "a heated exchange" with R. J. Scott, the managing director at Ford, who a few years earlier had told researcher Tim Smith he did not mix with Black people in South Africa or the United States; Scott justified his position, telling Diggs, "I've got to live with these people. I have got to conform. I can't make any waves."[50] Diggs was livid.

Next, Diggs visited the General Motors plant where he had a "hot" discussion with managing director William G. Slocum, a University of Michigan graduate who had come to South Africa in 1965. Diggs asked Slocum if GM's wage system provided "equal pay for equal work" and whether the company was doing all it could within existing apartheid laws to help its Black employees. Slocum responded defensively and pointed out that when the plant opened in 1926, only whites worked there. Now Colored people and "Bantus" work in the plant, Slocum explained, using a term Black South Africans generally considered offensive. Colored people could hold supervisory positions but could supervise only other Colored and Black workers—not whites. "Anything else is not allowable under the system in effect," Slocum added.

The exchange became heated when Diggs noted the signs denoting separate bathrooms and other facilities throughout the plant for "Blacks" and "Whites" and asked Slocum if such segregation turned his stomach. Slocum replied, "I feel our company being out here is doing a useful service to all persons." Slocum claimed he would be arrested if he tried to enact change. As they spoke, Diggs got increasingly upset. He was "mad as a hornet," Slocum recalled years later. According to Slocum, Diggs told him, "GM can do a hell of a lot more and they are just not."[51]

After a return trip to Johannesburg, where Diggs met with more Black leaders, on Thursday, August 19, an exhausted Diggs held a departing press conference at Jans Smuts Airport. "There is an appalling amount of racial injustice in South Africa, a blatant, ever present and all persuasive discrimination, based on race, color and creed," Diggs told the reporters.[52] "We are unalterably opposed to racial injustice wherever it occurs—whether in our country or in this country," Diggs pointed out. If South Africa "should repeal its repressive laws and change its apartheid policies, it would have one of the greatest potentials of any country in the world of comparable area and population." Diggs said, "We leave South Africa hopeful that efforts to improve the lives of the nonwhite population of this country will continue."[53]

Diggs stressed that American businesses were not doing all they could do within South Africa's laws. He "personally believed" American companies "should lead the way" in promoting racial equality and fair employment.[54] A reporter asked Diggs if he had changed his position about American corporations divesting from South Africa. "I have never made a flat statement that American enterprise ought to disengage from involvement in this economy," Diggs responded. "It has always been a conditional statement. . . . That they ought to justify the continuation of their engagement here; that they ought to share some of the benefits of their productivity; and that if they could not justify continuations here then they ought to disengage under those circumstances."[55]

State Department officials, especially the Africa Bureau, considered Diggs's mission a success. They liked Diggs's public challenge to Ambassador Hurd about racial discrimination at the US embassy. Kissinger and the White House, however, likely did not appreciate that Diggs's view challenged the administration's plan to "tilt" more toward white-led regimes in Southern Africa.

Diggs's position on American business involvement in South Africa thus began to crystallize. At a conference sponsored by American Society of International Law, Diggs provided a cogent argument about how American corporate presence in South Africa negatively impacted US policy in Africa.[56] He pointed out, there were "things that our government [could] do . . . to make it awfully uncomfortable for them" to stay in South Africa.[57] Diggs understood that there was little support in Congress for legislation demanding that American businesses disengage from South Africa. The Nixon administration was in no mood to change US-Africa policy. But that did not mean Diggs was powerless. He became more aggressive.

Chapter 19
MR. AFRICA

BEFORE HE LEFT for South Africa in the summer of 1971, President Nixon had appointed Charles Diggs to the US delegation to the United Nations. Even though UN delegates were expected to follow the policy lead of the administration, the Nixon administration soon learned that Diggs was not a rubber stamp. Diggs was his own man.

Diggs was concerned not only about South Africa but also about American economic involvement in Portugal and the Portuguese colonies of Angola, Guinea-Bissau, and Mozambique. In October 1971, Congress had voted to permit the importation of Rhodesian chrome into the United States, despite Rhodesia being ruled by an illegal white minority–rule government. With the adoption of the so-called Byrd Amendment (named for its sponsor Senator Harry F. Byrd [I-VA]), the United States joined Portugal and South Africa as the only nations openly violating sanctions against Rhodesia.

Diggs had made up his mind.

On Friday, December 17, 1971, Diggs arrived at the UN press room, which was filled with more than 200 reporters. He told the reporters that he "only undertook the [UN] assignment after being assured that there would be opportunity for input," but that he had been ignored.[1] Diggs followed with a blistering critique of the administration's policy toward Southern Africa, citing the recent UN abstentions and terming Washington's relationship with Pretoria "stifling hypocrisy." Diggs said he could not sit silent about a policy that supported Portugal using nearly half its budget "to fight wars against the legitimate aspirations of Black people in Africa for freedom and independence." After a dramatic pause he announced, "I am therefore submitting my resignation to the President," becoming the first American delegate ever to resign from the UN General Assembly.[2]

After the shock set in, nearly everyone in the room stood and applauded. Diggs's press secretary remembered that the resignation made Diggs "look like a hero."[3] Diggs's resignation received extensive media coverage, and he received support from the CBC, the Michigan House of Representatives, and a host of Black activists. Letters praising his principled stand flooded Diggs's Capitol Hill office.

By the early 1970s, a growing grassroots movement of Black activists, anti-apartheid activists, pan-Africanists, scholar-activists, and anti-imperialists concerned with Africa slowly emerged with Diggs as its titular head. Diggs's colleagues on Capitol Hill dubbed him "Mr. Africa" because of his knowledge of and interest in Africa policy. However, his influence was tempered by conservative congressional support for Nixon's tacit backing of South Africa. Privately, Nixon wanted closer relations, even as Pretoria continued to detain, ban, and arrest opponents of apartheid.[4] Although the State Department opposed the Byrd Amendment, seeing it as a danger to the country's standing in the United Nations, Nixon remained silent and had not heeded Diggs's call to veto the bill.[5]

In December 1971, Diggs developed an "Action Manifesto" containing fifty-five recommendations that, if followed, he believed would raise the United States' credibility with Africa and the other countries in the world. The manifesto was the only comprehensive document on US policies in Southern Africa that came from a member of Congress.[6] Diggs sent a copy to Henry Kissinger and when the two met, Kissinger brushed off the recommendations.[7] A few weeks later, Diggs resigned from the United Nations

The CBC, during the Ninety-First and Ninety-Second Congresses, put forth legislation aimed at divesting American corporations from Southern Africa and forcing all US businesses out of Namibia, Rhodesia, and the Portuguese-controlled territories.[8] To no surprise, the bills went nowhere. In March 1972, Diggs introduced the Fair Employment Practices Bill, his legislative attempt to dismantle apartheid. Like his approach toward discrimination in the commercial airline industry, the legislation required American corporations and subsidiaries operating in South Africa to apply American fair employment practices in their South African operations in order to qualify for US contracts elsewhere in the world. Diggs argued that the government had the right to set rules for granting contracts and that after passage of the 1964 Civil Rights Act, asking a US corporation to adhere to fair employment practices was unassailable. Once again, the legislation went nowhere.

Stymied by the indifference, Diggs sought other means to apply more pressure to get Congress to change US-Africa policy, including pushing the CBC to mobilize around Africa, filing court challenges, and encouraging Black leaders and organizations to agree to raise the funds to achieve his vision of a Black-led lobby focused on Africa. The organization would become TransAfrica.

IN EARLY APRIL 1972, Diggs, CBC chair Carl Stokes, and Congressman William Clay went to Harvard University for a long-planned conference with representatives of the nation's major newspapers.[9] One day earlier, Stokes and Clay met with Randall Robinson, a thirty-one-year-old Black Harvard Law School graduate active in Boston's anti-apartheid movement and someone who would later become the country's premier anti-apartheid organizer. The relationship between Diggs and Robinson would one-day prove to be transformative for both men. While the two shared many of the same goals, their approaches and temperaments differed.

Robinson was born on July 6, 1941, in segregated Richmond, Virginia, the son of public schoolteachers. Like Diggs, Robinson favored his own father's political and moral worldview; but where Papa Diggs had advocated coalition building and incremental progress, Robinson described his own father as "a moral absolutist," writing, "He would teach us by word and example to take stands on moral principle notwithstanding the price."[10] There were no gray areas.

Robinson, whose older brother, Max Robinson, became the first Black American to anchor ABC's nightly national newscast *World News Tonight*, had been drafted into the army after dropping out of the all-Black Norfolk State College in Virginia. He served two years and enrolled in Virginia Union, a Black college in Richmond, before winning a scholarship to attend Harvard Law School. Working with Christopher Nteta, a Black South African attending Harvard Divinity School, Robinson formed the South African Relief Fund to provide support to African freedom struggles; Robinson even spent months in the East African country of Tanzania. He then returned to Boston, to work as a community organizer in the Roxbury neighborhood and continued to support African freedom fighters.[11]

In February 1971, Robinson informed Diggs that the South African Relief Fund would focus on opposing American corporations operating in Southern Africa. He wrote, "It is our feeling that you might have ideas on how this problem might be tackled on a larger scale."[12] A few months later, Robinson, Nteta, and two Harvard law students formed the Pan-African Liberation Committee. Then, due to Gulf Oil's extensive operations in Angola, the committee demanded that Harvard divest its 700,000 shares of Gulf stock. Harvard took no immediate action.

Robinson met with Stokes and Clay to complain that the CBC's presence on Harvard's campus "gave official, albeit indirect, sanction to" Harvard's Gulf Oil policy and demanded they change the conference location.[13] Taken aback, they told Robinson that it was too late to change the venue but agreed to appear the next the day with Robinson at a press conference.

The next morning, Diggs, Clay, and Stokes, joined by Robinson and Harvard student James Winston, held a press briefing, and Diggs met Robinson in person for the first time. Diggs endorsed their demand that Harvard divest from Gulf Oil, and Robinson, comfortable before the media, emerged as the public face of the Pan-African Liberation Committee. Diggs was impressed and told the young lawyer "to get in touch" if he ever relocated to Washington.[14]

A MONTH LATER, in May 1972, Diggs convened the African American National Conference on Africa at Howard University. In his keynote address, Diggs stressed the connection between racism in the United States and African liberation movements. "There is no difference between the oppressor we face in America and the oppressor our African brothers face in the Motherland," Diggs pointed out.[15] The conference adopted a resolution that included supporting boycotting corporations with investments in Southern Africa and urged attendees to support the repeal of the Byrd Amendment.

The next day, Saturday, May 27, about 12,000 Africans and Black Americans marched in Washington, DC, on African Liberation Day, the "largest all-black demonstration" in the city's recent history and one of the largest displays of Black solidarity in opposition to white rule in Africa.[16] The Howard University conference and African Liberation Day demonstrated, as the *Baltimore Afro-American* editorialized, "on the streets how unhappy" Black Americans were "with their own government's involvement with racist southern African minority regimes."[17] Diggs, wearing a purple dashiki, spoke and delivered another blistering critique of US-Africa policy. He urged attendees to pressure members of Congress to support a more progressive foreign policy. Diggs also made clear his embrace of Pan-Africanism. It is "time for the people in America and Caribbean to see that our African past is connected to the African future," Diggs shouted. "No longer will the movement for justice stop at the water's edge!"[18] The crowd roared in approval.

The African Liberation Day demonstration showed that a Black constituency in the United States could organize and mobilize to change US-Africa policy. Black activist-scholars Ronald Walters, Willard Johnson, Herschelle Challenor, and others in the African Heritage Studies Association worked closely with Diggs.[19] "In the 1970s, African-Americans who wanted to do policy work on Africa hitched their wagons to Congressman Diggs's star," Randall Robinson later explained.[20]

While Diggs and a growing number of activists attempted to break the bond between the United States and white-ruled regimes in Southern Africa, the Nixon administration and conservative members of Congress tried to bring them closer together.[21] In addition, efforts to repeal the Byrd Amendment failed again, and another of Diggs's amendments, this one to eliminate South Africa's sugar quota, lost in the House.[22] Congress seemed largely uninterested in apartheid in South Africa and white minority–rule in Rhodesia and Portuguese Africa.

In June 1972, with little hope for congressional action, Diggs successfully pushed for planks in the Democratic National Committee platform to press US corporations in South Africa to end racial discrimination, repeal the Byrd Amendment, and end military aid to Portugal. It was the first time a major political party included Africa policy in its national platform.[23]

Diggs, the CBC, and other plaintiffs also filed suit to reverse the Byrd Amendment. Initially, a lower court had ruled that they lacked the standing to sue. But in July 1972, a higher court reversed that ruling.[24] *Diggs v. Schultz* is considered a landmark case as it broadened access to the courts in suits concerning the authority of government action.[25] Nevertheless, citing legislative prerogative, the court still upheld the Byrd Amendment.

RICHARD NIXON'S RESIGNATION on August 9, 1974, elevated Vice President Gerald R. Ford to the presidency. Ford already had a relationship with most CBC members, and Diggs's friendship with Ford promised to provide more access to the White House. Indeed, on August 21, the CBC met with Ford and his top aides in the White House Cabinet Room.[26] Diggs gave a "brief history" of Ford's relationship with the CBC but also noted Ford's weak civil rights record in the House. However, Diggs declared that the CBC was "wiping the slate clean" and would work with the new administration.[27] Diggs spoke first and, predictably, he focused on Africa.

Diggs was blunt. He told Ford that the United States should "refocus" its foreign policy to gain better insight into Africa and other parts of the developing world and advised the president that his daily briefings on foreign policy should include more matters related to Africa.[28] Ford defended his approach to Africa and told Diggs that in foreign policy meetings "Africa is discussed, but not every day."[29] Still, Diggs had gotten his concerns about US-Africa policy across to the new president.

However, US-Africa policy did not change. And Ford's policy in Angola created a huge conflict between Diggs and the new administration. In April 1974, after thirteen years of costly African wars and internal demoralization, a bloodless military coup overthrew Portugal's authoritarian government. The independence of Angola, Mozambique, and Guinea-Bissau soon followed. While the transition to Black rule went relatively smoothly in Mozambique and Guinea-Bissau, in Angola a bloody civil war for control of the new government ensued.

In January 1975, Ford, at the urging of Kissinger, authorized clandestine US involvement in Angola's civil war in opposition to the Movement for the Popular Liberation of Angola, which supported liberation movements throughout Southern Africa and had appeared to be headed toward becoming the successor government. The Soviet Union and Cuba had provided weapons and training to the Movement for the Popular Liberation of Angola. In turn, the United States and South Africa secretly provided money and arms to the National Front for the Liberation of Angola and later the National Union for the Total Independence of Angola. The Ford administration shrugged off warnings about any damage to America's image in Black Africa if it became known that the United States and South Africa were conspiring against the Movement for the Popular Liberation of Angola.[30]

In January and February 1975, Diggs led another study mission to Zaire, Angola, Mozambique, Zambia, Botswana, Swaziland, Tanzania, Kenya, and Somalia. In each country, a main topic of concern was the civil war in Angola. The United States' covert operation in Angola was no secret to African leaders, and Diggs left Africa deeply concerned. He was convinced that US policy had alienated the likely successor government in Angola and had offended the rest of Black Africa.[31]

By the Ninety-Fourth Congress (1975–77), the CBC had grown to seventeen members, including three members from the South—Harold Ford (D-TN), Barbara Jordan (D-TX) and Andrew Young (D-GA)—a first since Reconstruction. Young, an ordained minister who had gained worldwide fame as a close aide to Martin Luther King Jr., took an early interest in US-Africa policy, which he had seen as a moral issue. Young's first real foreign policy initiative in Congress was an amendment to prohibit Portugal from using any US foreign aid for military purposes.[32]

In August 1975, the CBC held a historic meeting with Kissinger; it was the first time a US Secretary of State officially met with a group of Black legislators about Africa policy.[33] Diggs called out Kissinger for his lack of interest in Africa and said the Ford administration, lacking a clear Africa policy, was continuing a historical pattern of indifference. He urged Kissinger to make a "comprehensive statement" on Africa.[34] Playing to Kissinger's alleged huge ego, Diggs said there was still time to accomplish something significant in Southern Africa.

Kissinger, who viewed African countries simply as pawns in the struggle between the United States and the Soviet Union, admitted that he and Ford "[hadn't] known what to say" about Africa.[35] Further, he let the CBC know that the State Department had completed a study of Africa policy and that within the coming year he would like to visit Africa. Kissinger also suggested that Diggs write a white paper on the proposals and principles the administration should include in an African policy. Although Diggs and the CBC spoke positively in public about the meeting, Diggs had mixed feelings. The meeting had not resulted in any tangible results beyond speeches and symbolic gestures.

IN THE FALL OF 1975, Diggs decided that the time had come to consider forming a new organization devoted to lobbying on behalf of Africa and pushing for change; the new organization would include many high-profile Black leaders. Herschelle Challenor, who had replaced Goler Butcher as the senior staff member on Diggs's Subcommittee on Africa, chaired a planning committee to form the new organization and decided to create a "forum" for the "exchange of ideas and information" about Africa.[36] Challenor kept Diggs, who was busy with other matters, informed about the progress of the new organization, the Black Forum on Foreign Policy (BFFP). The decision to include "Black" in the name was intended to discourage whites from becoming involved.[37] In October 1975, prominent Black figures such as Julian Bond, CBC members Andrew Young and Parren Mitchell, labor leader William Lucy, Randall Robinson, and several academics were invited to join as "founding members" of the BFFP.[38]

Robinson would play a key role in shaping the BFFP. In spring 1975, Robinson had moved to Washington, DC, to work as Congressman William Clay's chief of staff but resigned after just six months when Clay was investigated for illegally putting friends and relatives of important political families on his congressional payroll. The case was dropped for lack of evidence, but Willard Johnson remembers Robinson telling him that "he was disgusted by the moral climate in the office" and the verbal abuse Clay dished out to the office secretaries.[39]

On January 11, 1976, Diggs attended a meeting of the Organization of African Unity in Addis Ababa, where he again delivered a searing attack on US policy in Angola. "American intrusion in the Angola conflict is the biggest blunder in the history of its relations with Africa and may be the most serious foreign policy miscalculation it has ever made," he said.[40] He denounced the covert nature of the activity and emphasized that a policy that "converges with that of white supremacist South Africa" could only damage the United States' reputation internationally. He emphasized that the key to solving the Angolan crisis was for South Africa to end its intervention in the civil war. In addition, he predicted that a final government composed of the Soviet-backed Movement for the Popular Liberation of Angola and the National Union for the Total Independence of Angola was likely, and he advised that the United States should recognize the coalition as the legitimate Angolan government. Finally, Diggs told reporters that when he returned to America, he planned to recommend that the CBC form a Black American-led lobby focused on Africa.[41]

The following day, a front-page *Washington Post* headline blared "Rep. Diggs Hits Ford on Angola." At an Oval Office meeting, Kissinger confided to Ford, "Our position is basically hopeless in Angola." He then added, "It is unbelievable that Diggs would go there and attack us that way—when his specific proposal is in fact ours."[42] An angry Ford responded, "He is a lightweight and listens to the wrong people."[43]

A DECADE AFTER its illegal and unilateral declaration of independence, Rhodesia had survived economic sanctions and worldwide condemnation. But the illegal regime, led by Ian Smith, was now under tremendous military and economic pressures. The two main Black liberation movements, led by Robert Mugabe and Joshua Nkomo, had escalated their guerrilla attacks from Mozambique's western border in an uneasy alliance known as the Patriotic Front.[44]

Concerned that Rhodesian Black nationalist movements would turn to Moscow or Cuba, and become another Angola, Kissinger turned his focus on Rhodesia. Kissinger asked Diggs for some direction on policy. The congressman and CBC members met with Kissinger and gave him a five-page memorandum on issues Kissinger should consider as he embarked on his first trip to Africa.[45]

In April 1976, Kissinger began a two-week, seven-nation tour of Africa, and in Lusaka, Zambia, he announced America's "unequivocal commitment" to "self-determination, majority rule, equal rights, and human dignity for all the peoples of southern Africa."[46] The editors of the *New York Times* called the speech "an impressive if belated attempt for past blunders in Africa."[47] Guerrilla warfare had increased significantly in Rhodesia. Diggs noted that Kissinger "remained as vague as ever" with respect to Namibia and South Africa; and Diggs remained "unconvinced that Ford was in fact sincere" about repealing the Byrd Amendment.[48]

On June 16, 1976, in Soweto, the brutality of South Africa's apartheid policy was made obvious. What started as a peaceful demonstration resulted in a massacre. While the government claimed that twenty-three students were killed, an estimated 700 people, many of them children, are believed to have died, and more than 4,000 were injured.[49] Global anti-apartheid sentiment intensified as the horrifying images from Soweto were featured on nightly television news and plastered on the front pages of newspapers around the world. In the United States, national church denominations, labor unions, civil rights groups, and other organizations all denounced the shootings and called on the United States to reconsider its policies in South Africa.

On September 19, 1976, Kissinger and Ian Smith met in Pretoria. Kissinger presented the British plan to transition to majority rule in Rhodesia within two years and for the immediate appointment of an interim government, followed by independence. The plan included constitutional protections for Rhodesia's white minority and a foreign trust fund to help Rhodesians hurt economically by the transition to a Black majority. Smith agreed but stated the interim defense and justice ministers both had to be white for his parliament to endorse the plan.

A few days later, Ian Smith announced that he accepted majority rule. Predictably, the plan was unacceptable to the Patriotic Front. While they applauded Smith's announcement, they pushed for an earlier date for independence and maintained that white control of the military, police, and judicial system was unacceptable and nonnegotiable. Meanwhile, guerrilla warfare and vicious fighting in Rhodesia continued.

In Washington, election year politics killed any chance of repealing the Byrd Amendment as Ford never lifted a finger; this left Diggs and others to prepare to fight for its repeal in the next congressional session. The November presidential election was approaching, and the Democrats nominated Georgia governor Jimmy Carter. Congressman Andrew Young was one of his strongest supporters and advisers. Carter made "human rights" a central theme of his foreign policy planks.[50]

IN THE MEANTIME, the BFFP struggled to clarify its purpose. Diggs still believed a Black American-led African lobby organization was necessary, but he was uncertain whether the BFFP fulfilled that need. In August 1976, he hired Randall Robinson as chief of staff for his congressional office. The hiring signaled that Robinson would be organizing Diggs's vision of a Black American-led lobby focused on Africa. That goal was among the subjects on the agenda of a historic conference on Africa.

The Black Leadership Conference on Southern Africa, called by Diggs and Andrew Young, was held in Washington, DC, on September 24–25, 1976, as part of the CBC's annual legislative weekend. More than 3,000 Black people, including nearly 1,000 Black elected officials, attended the sixth annual CBC fundraising dinner.[51] Diggs and the other Black leaders discussed Kissinger's trip, questioned US policy in Southern Africa, and debated what should be done to end apartheid.

During the conference, Robinson, Challenor, and Charles Cobb (a former staffer for Diggs) developed *The African-American Manifesto on Southern Africa*, a forceful statement of Black American solidarity with Africans fighting to overthrow white minority-rule in Rhodesia, Namibia, and South Africa.[52] The *Manifesto* also called for the creation a new organization, a professional African lobby, staffed full-time by Black experts.

The conference unanimously endorsed the *Manifesto*, and dozens of leaders enthusiastically made pledges to donate money to launch the new organization that would one day become TransAfrica. Diggs was thrilled by the response. Years later, he fondly remembered the moment, "I can see them [excitingly waiting] to make their pledges."[53]

Afterward, Diggs asked Robinson to chair a working group charged with forming the new organization. Diggs freed Robinson from his routine chief-of-staff duties, and Robinson tapped into Diggs's huge Rolodex of national and international contacts. As Congressman Clay later recalled, "Diggs was not the founder" of what would become TransAfrica, but "Randall Robinson, its executive director and founder, cut his wisdom teeth on black African issues" by working with Diggs.[54]

One week later, Diggs and Robinson led a delegation of Black leaders, including Jesse Jackson, to meet with Kissinger at the State Department. Diggs told Kissinger about the new organization and said the group had "great reservations" about the financial trust fund planned for white Rhodesians.[55] They pressed Kissinger to use the leverage of the US government to force South Africa to take concrete steps to dismantle apartheid and to take an initial step by releasing Nelson Mandela and other political detainees and by ending South Africa's illegal administration of Namibia.

On Election Day, Democrat Jimmy Carter defeated President Ford by less than 2 percent of the popular vote, winning a narrow victory in the Electoral College by taking every Southern state except Virginia. The Black vote provided the margin of difference in Louisiana, South Carolina, North Carolina, and surprisingly, Mississippi, giving Carter the edge.

Days after the election, Diggs flew to Geneva, Switzerland, to confer with the principals trying to reach a settlement in Rhodesia. Diggs told the negotiators that President-Elect Carter fully supported the Ford administration's policy of establishing Black-majority rule in Southern Africa. In addition, Diggs said that Carter was comfortable having Kissinger come to Geneva to break the deadlock before the new administration took over in January.[56] Upon his return to the United States, Diggs, in a twenty-two-page letter to Cyrus Vance, Carter's secretary of state–designate, wrote that Ian Smith had "refused to participate in good faith" during the Geneva talks.[57]

DIGGS MADE HIS SECOND VISIT to South Africa in late November 1976, on his way to a conference in Lesotho. The Lesotho conference was co-chaired by US Senator Dick Clark (D-IA) and the foreign minister of Lesotho Charles D. Molopo, and it included representatives of twenty-three African countries and the leaders of five Southern African liberation movements.[58] Among the other Americans were Dororthy Height, the president of the National Council of

Negro Women, Senator Joseph Biden (D-DE), and Congressman Charles Rangel. Diggs introduced Robinson to many of the African leaders and made a major speech in which he again indicted South Africa.

The most significant outcome of the conference was the adoption of a statement of commitment by the Black American participants to work with Africans "to reverse the historic patterns of exploitation of Africa and African peoples." The Americans pledged to "intensify" their effort "to develop a forceful lobby on Africa" that would "work to influence American policy toward achieving the isolation of the apartheid society in South Africa from all public and private support."[59]

Before returning to the United States, Diggs, Biden, Rangel, and Robinson returned to Cape Town, South Africa, to meet with a small group of English-speaking white South African businessmen thought to be more liberal on race. However, only thirty minutes into the meeting, the discussion became explosive when Diggs brought up apartheid. "We've been talking around the real issue here and that is the franchise. When will black South Africans get the right to vote?" Diggs asked.[60] Robinson remembered that the room went silent and the "businessmen appeared stunned." Finally, one spoke up, saying, "But, Congressman Diggs, giving blacks the vote would be like putting a gun in the hand of five-year old." Diggs and the other Americans could not believe his words. Senator Biden was livid, asking, "Do you all know how the world sees you? Do you know that this country could burn to the ground and the United States would not lift a finger to help you? You don't have clue about what you're doing here, do you?"[61]

NEVERTHELESS, Diggs returned to the United States hopeful that President Carter would bring real change to US-Africa policy. After Carter nominated Andrew Young to become the US ambassador to the United Nations, Diggs believed America's relations with the African nations would improve. Diggs was so excited about Carter's victory that he named his sixth child, born on Inauguration Day, Cindy Carter Diggs.

Carter supported Young's bill, introduced before he resigned from the House, to restore sanctions against Rhodesia. In March 1977, Congress finally repealed the Byrd Amendment. In early April 1977, Randall Robinson, and others finalized the structure and function of the new African lobby. At Herschelle Challenor's suggestion, Robinson named the organization TransAfrica.[62]

Carter's emphasis on a foreign policy based on "human rights" collided with apartheid. Secretary of State Vance and Ambassador Young condemned apartheid directly. However, the administration still did not support economic sanctions against South Africa. Carter and Young believed that American corporate presence in South Africa could still serve as role models for other South African businesses.

A settlement to bring majority rule to Rhodesia, however, proved difficult as Ian Smith continued to lobby for disproportionate white influence in the interim government, while Nkomo and Mugabe insisted on control of the transitional government and the military. Guerrilla warfare escalated. The Carter administration worked hard to develop a joint US-British plan to resolve the issue, but a final resolution would not come until after Margaret Thatcher's election in 1979 and then without American involvement. In April 1980, Robert Mugabe became prime minister of independent Zimbabwe.

Meanwhile, the CBC sent Carter several specific proposals directed at South Africa, including Diggs's Fair Employment Practices Bill. Most were rejected. The administration's rejection of most of the CBC's South Africa proposals was considered one of many shortcomings Black leaders saw in Carter.[63]

TransAfrica was officially incorporated in Washington, DC, in July 1977, and it initially operated out of Diggs's congressional office. Diggs, although frustrated by the pace of change, had finally achieved his goal of helping create a Black American-led lobby focused on Africa.

By then, the Justice Department's investigation of Diggs had become public knowledge.

Chapter 20
THE FALL OF
THE HOUSE OF DIGGS

BY THE MID-1970S, Charles Diggs Jr. was the most powerful Black politician on Capitol Hill. He was the most senior of the seventeen Black members of Congress in 1976. Although never "one of the boys" who blindly acquiesced to House leadership, Diggs was well-respected, a quiet and hardworking legislator, and he had won reelection nearly a dozen times. His work in civil rights, as founder of the CBC, as champion of home rule for DC, as titular head of the anti-apartheid movement and his role in the creation of TransAfrica appeared to secure his legacy as the most important and consequential Black American politician to date. In Washington, DC, where everyone struggled to wield their considerable political muscle, Charles Diggs was at the peak of his power.

Yet, while Diggs was bringing change to America and Southern Africa, his role as a businessman, a father, and a husband—indeed, the foundation of his home—was crumbling.

When Diggs went to Congress in 1955, the House of Diggs was one of the largest mortuaries in the United States. In 1955, amid great fanfare, Diggs Enterprises was incorporated. Diggs Enterprises included a monument company, a livery service division, a flower shop, and a real estate firm.[1] At its peak in 1957, Diggs Enterprises and the House of Diggs employed as many as 450 employees, more than any other Black-owned enterprise in Michigan. At the annual company picnic for staff and family that summer, Papa Diggs announced that he was donating his Lake Erie summer house to his employees as a vacation home.[2] And in November 1957, the House of Diggs opened its first branch mortuary, Southwest Chapel, to serve Black clients who had moved into neighborhoods distant from Black Bottom. Papa Diggs's nephew James "Jimmy" Diggs successfully managed the Southwest Chapel.

Papa Diggs and his son were on top of the world, Papa in Detroit, and his son in Congress. Yet all was not what it seemed.

THE FIRST CRACKS in the House of Diggs date back to 1949, when Papa Diggs was imprisoned for bribery. While he was incarcerated his competitors in the Wolverine Funeral Directors Association, an organization of about thirty Black morticians, took aim at Diggs.[3] The organization complained that Diggs had created a "monopoly" because he was also engaged in the burial insurance business. They noted that the House of Diggs handled half of the nearly 3,000 Black funerals in the state each year.[4] The group convinced the Michigan Legislature to pass a law prohibiting an owner of a funeral home from also owning a burial insurance company. The new law also required that a burial insurance company's benefit be paid out in cash only and not as an in-kind funeral service, allowing bereaved families to select a funeral home other than the House of Diggs. The law directly targeted Diggs's Metropolitan Funeral System Association, reportedly the only burial insurance company of its kind in Michigan.[5]

In 1954 the burial society was turned into a mutual insurance company and renamed the Detroit Metropolitan Mutual Assurance Company. However, thousands of Black Detroiters still held old policies for $150.00 and $250.00 from the burial insurance business. House of Diggs's accountants had determined that the face amount on those policies did not cover the actual cost of a burial.[6] However, instead of raising the face amount of those contracts, the House of Diggs honored the old burial policies at substantial losses. In 1979, Congressman Diggs told the *Detroit News* that many of the funeral services his father provided "were so reduced by discounts through insurance policies that we hardly covered expenses."[7] Such small profit margins demanded expanded sales volume, yet once burial insurance was outlawed, the House of Diggs's case volume was negatively impacted.

Absentee-ownership also began creating problems. The state refused to restore the elder Diggs's mortuary license following his bribery conviction; and after his stroke in 1955, Papa Diggs slowed down considerably and was rarely at the business. In 1948, he hired Reverend J. S. Williams, a licensed funeral director and embalmer, as the general manager of the House of Diggs. And in the summer of 1954, Congressman Diggs became the president of the House of Diggs, but he left the business to be managed by others. In 1955, Charles T. Coles, another licensed mortician and a House of Diggs employee since 1950, succeeded Reverend Williams. Both the father and son trusted the people who worked for them; perhaps they trusted them too much.

Without the attention of either Papa Diggs or his son, the quality of service at the funeral home dropped and complaints rose. As the *Detroit Free Press* later observed, "There was a time when people bragged about relatives having been buried by the congressman. But the absentee congressman-owner and mismanagement did in the Detroit institution."[8] Customers even wrote to Diggs Jr. in Washington, DC, to complain. Frederick Brown of Detroit wrote him a scathing letter to complain about the funeral of a friend, calling the service "one of the worst conducted [and] ever given to the dead." He complained that there "was no prayer offered at the chapel" and that, "in violation of state law," the funeral procession sped along the expressway at a "speed of 75 mph." Once at the cemetery, prayers were offered before family and friends gathered around the grave site, and cemetery attendants did not remove their hats during burial. "It was a mess," Brown exclaimed. "I ask you in the name of decency, is this a proper way to be buried?"[9]

Part of the problem was that, with neither Diggs Jr. nor Sr. present, some newer employees were not well trained. Some of the House of Diggs's most valued employees went to work for competing funeral homes or left to form their own businesses. Charles T. Coles, for example, would later launch a funeral home. Writing to his father, Diggs Jr. emphasized that "keep[ing] our staff from spiraling off and going into business either for themselves or with our competitors" must remain a focus. "They need to constantly feel there is a future for them with us. . . . We must take all reasonable steps to assure their retention," Diggs stressed to his father.[10] At one point, Congressman Diggs proposed a "profit sharing plan" he hoped "would assure the retention of our professional staff."[11]

But the problems went even deeper. In 1959, Richard Austin and Ernest Davenport, CPAs for the House of Diggs, warned Diggs Jr. and his father that "general expenses" at the funeral home had increased at "an almost alarming rate" over the past year.[12] The increase was not related to salaries or benefits. The accountants suspected theft and pilfering by employees.

New tires and car batteries ostensibly purchased for the funeral cars ended up in the private automobiles of employees. Workers also took the opportunity to fill up their personal vehicles with gas and charge the fuel to the House of Diggs. Carpeting for the funeral home ended up in the homes of employees, while cases and cases of expensive embalming fluid were stolen and, presumably, sold at a discount to other funeral homes. "Nobody was keeping track of that stuff," lamented Charles C. Diggs III decades later.[13] "These people that were running the place were just doing what the hell they wanted to do," Weston Diggs Jr. explained.[14] One former employee even started a funeral home with equipment purchased for the House of Diggs. Before the House of Diggs's general manager Reverend Williams was replaced, the elder Diggs accused him of stealing.[15]

In the spring of 1959, Austin and Davenport warned that "cash is being used for purposes other than payment of goods. This situation cannot be permitted to exist. Effective measures must be taken—and taken at once." They "urgently requested" implementing internal controls "in order to return to a profitable pattern of operations."[16] Austin and Davenport warned that the cashier had "complete control" over account receivable records, a situation "fraught with danger."[17] A year later, Austin noted there was still a lack of effective internal controls at the House of Diggs, and he mailed the congressman a copy of a pamphlet called "25 Ways of Stealing and How to Stop Them."[18] Cash flow became a serious problem for the House of Diggs. The accountants warned, "There can be no compromise. The cash situation and the profit results demand action."[19]

Detroit's changing political economy also impacted the House of Diggs. Between 1949 and 1960, Detroit experienced four major recessions, and the restructuring of the auto industry in the 1950s and expanding automation in the 1960s led to plant closures and layoffs. Black Detroiters were disproportionately affected. In 1960, nearly 16 percent of the city's Black workforce was unemployed compared to only about 6 percent of the white workforce. Economists called it deindustrialization. Others referred to it as an "urban crisis" created by limited housing, high unemployment, poor public schools, and reduced economic opportunities.[20]

The impact trickled down to Black-owned businesses like the House of Diggs. Fewer Black Detroiters could pay the full cost of funerals, and the House of Diggs had difficulty collecting payments owed for past services. Accountant Richard Austin acknowledged it was "no easy task" collecting from "marginal cases."[21]

Diggs Jr. later claimed Black morticians in general have a difficult time collecting debts. "It's an institutional problem, a professional problem," he offered, a product of the unique place the funeral home fills in the Black community.[22] The "demand of the market is much different" for Black funeral directors, he said, later acknowledging that accounts receivable "had really always been a problem with the House of Diggs" and that his father "never pressed for collection" from many poor clients.[23]

Additionally, the federal urban renewal program of the 1950s and 1960s bulldozed much of Detroit's Black East Side. In spring 1958, after reading plans showing the proposed Chrysler Expressway (Interstate 75) coming through Mack Avenue and Hastings Street, Congressman Diggs wrote to the Michigan highway commissioner to learn how the House of Diggs and adjacent properties would be affected.[24] The urban renewal steamroller would eventually flatten Black Bottom, razing homes and businesses in its path and displacing thousands of Black residents. As more and more residents were displaced, the financial strain on the House of Diggs increased, intensifying the need for the business to relocate.

Diggs Jr. and his father sought advice from their accountant Richard Austin, who recommended the company have at least $100,000 in liquid assets to finance the purchase of a building and take on any reconstruction project.

However, in the fall of 1959, Austin confirmed there was only $25,000 in operating capital available, and he could not provide a viable scenario by which the House of Diggs could obtain the additional $75,000.[25]

Congressman Diggs looked into securing financing for capital expansion. At one point he inquired about a contract to bury deceased patients from the Veteran Affairs hospital in Dearborn, only to learn the contract had been given to a white-owned mortuary that in turn had subcontracted the work to the McFall Brothers, one of the House of Diggs biggest competitors.[26] In 1962, the Detroit Metropolitan Mutual Assurance Company merged with St. Louis–based Mammoth Life and Accident Insurance Company and provided a much-needed—albeit temporary—financial lifeline for the funeral home at a critical time. The liquidation of the insurance policies reportedly paid House of Diggs more than $300,000, finally allowing the company to open a new facility.[27]

In late 1962, the grand opening of the East Grand Boulevard mortuary drew "more than seven thousand visitors" who toured the new chapel on a Sunday afternoon. Congressman Diggs was on hand to greet them and to do a live broadcast of the House of Diggs radio show.[28] A few years later another funeral home opened on Dexter Avenue. Even after the bulldozer finally demolished Diggs Enterprises and the House of Diggs on Mack Avenue in 1971, the business continued at three locations. Nonetheless, Detroit's declining economy and problems with internal financial controls had weakened the House of Diggs.

THE DETERIORATING SITUATION was made worse by Congressman Diggs's personal failures and weaknesses. Just as he had done after his military discharge, when he entered Congress, he again began to live beyond his means; it was a problem that would grow worse with each passing year. Despite earning salaries as a legislator and in business, the congressman burned through money. At the time, the House Finance Office allowed members to collect their two-year salary over the first eighteen months of their term.[29] Diggs Jr. typically did just that, meaning that during the last six months of an election year (in other words, every other year), he received no congressional salary.

He made up for it by dipping into the rapidly dwindling coffers of the House of Diggs, which he used to pay for many of his personal expenses (he used company credit cards in his name).[30] At one point, Austin prepared a new "Handbook of Standard Travel Rules and Procedures," including processes for submitting vouchers and receipts for reimbursements to better account for the charges Diggs Jr. presented as "business expenses."[31]

Congressman Diggs was likely the person responsible for much of the missing cash. He got into the habit, especially after his father's stroke, when Papa Diggs no longer paid close attention, of coming to the House of Diggs and requesting cash for personal use. He would "tell the lady in charge to give me three, four, five thousand dollars. . . . Of course she would give it to him. He's the boss. And that happened all the time," remembered Weston Diggs Jr.[32] In April 1959, Papa Diggs wrote to Charles Cole to remind him not to "lose sight" of expenses; but he told Cole he recognized there were some things he "apparently [had] no control over. . . . I have in mind in saying this, the lack of financial help and control from the family angle," a reference to Junior using the funeral home as his personal bank account.[33] Papa Diggs eventually became so concerned about his son's spending that he asked attorney Damon Keith, the younger Diggs's best friend, and Richard Austin to hold an intervention and "sit down with Charley and find out what he is doing with his money."[34]

One weekend the four met at the Diggs's Mansion. Papa Diggs pressed his son about his spending, but as Keith recalled, "We came away empty handed. . . . Charley could never articulate what he was doing with the money."[35] No one was ever able to explain precisely how he spent his money. "His father couldn't, Dick Austin couldn't. I couldn't. We were closer to him than anybody," Keith added.[36]

Diggs Jr.'s uncontrolled spending was likely a combination of poor choices. Maintaining two households was costly, and while in DC, Diggs may have felt pressure to maintain a lifestyle that was financially beyond his means, entertaining and fulfilling his concept of how a congressman—an ever more important one—should live.[37] Diggs was also known to gamble at the suburban Maryland racetracks. Simeon Booker, the *Jet* magazine reporter and a close friend of Diggs Jr.'s, later wrote that Diggs "indulged a passion for gambling, to the point where it seemed to be an addiction."[38] Diggs also began to drink more heavily and have affairs. He had always been something of a womanizer, and as his public profile and self-regard increased, he regularly succumbed to temptation. He was "living large," and all that cost money—money he didn't have on his own.

IT WASN'T JUST the House of Diggs that was crumbling. As his stature rose, the congressman's home life was also falling apart. As he spent more and more time either in Washington or away on congressional business, he spent less time at home. His devotion to the cause of civil rights and to improving the world collided with his capacity to be a good husband and father. In December 1958, Diggs Jr. and Juanita separated; and in July 1959, Diggs filed for divorce, charging his wife with "cruelty."[39] Juanita contested the divorce, telling reporters she wanted to keep her family together. In court papers, Juanita claimed Diggs had grown tired of her and "wants someone with a greater cultural background."⁴⁰ She claimed Diggs was living lavishly in Washington and that he spent great sums of money on "personal entertainment and enjoyment."⁴¹

Diggs Jr. apparently spent little time with the children. "I don't think he really was a father.... He loved the kids ... but to actually spend time to go out and play baseball or do things like that with them, he didn't," Juanita reflected.⁴² "I don't remember him being around a lot. He was always away," Diggs's daughter, Denise, explained; and Charles Diggs III recalled, "Once he started going to Washington, we saw less of him."⁴³ When he did come home, Diggs was typically busy with mortuary business, meeting with political groups, attending as many churches as he could, and taping the weekly broadcast of the radio program. Juanita, however, publicly vowed never to divorce Diggs.

Diggs Jr.'s worlds would soon collide. In late August 1959, an attractive twenty-four-year-old former waitress, Jacqueline Marion Gibbs, claimed that Diggs was the father of her five-year-old daughter, Angela.⁴⁴ Gibbs claimed that in 1953 when Diggs was campaigning for the Detroit City Council, the then-eighteen-year-old had sex with him in the back seat of a car.

Diggs and Juanita had known about Gibbs's allegations for some time. Diggs called the charge "ridiculous" and a part of a "program calculated to discredit" him.⁴⁵ He also claimed that Gibbs was emotionally unstable. Damon Keith represented him in the paternity suit and remembers that Gibbs "was so convinced" Diggs was the father, she insisted on a paternity test.⁴⁶ When the test excluded Diggs as the father, Gibbs insisted on a second test. It too ruled Diggs out as the father. The court dismissed Gibbs's paternity suit, and Keith then asked Diggs if he had sex with the young woman. Diggs admitted he didn't know, saying, "I was drunk."⁴⁷

In late January 1960, Juanita was granted an uncontested divorce. Diggs's lawyers presented sworn financial statements showing him nearly $18,500 in debt, including $7,000 of advances on his congressional salary. Diggs was ordered to pay $750 per month to support his three young children, plus $600 per month in alimony, and he was directed to continue making mortgage payments on the family home, pay city and county taxes on the property, maintain payments on the new Cadillac awarded to Juanita, and pay the private school tuition for the three children.⁴⁸

Diggs then made an appeal on his radio program and asked his constituents to pray for him as he balanced his "responsibilities as a legislator" with family duties. Diggs tried to justify his problems by saying he belonged "completely to the people.... Although I think constantly of the needs of my own family, my own children, I cannot think of them without thinking of the other countless colored families and children who are starving, physically, politically and socially because of civic injustices."⁴⁹ In essence, he was saying that his commitment to political causes and the well-being of the Black community justified his lack of attention to his own family.

On March 3, 1960, just a little over a month after divorcing Juanita, Diggs Jr., now thirty-seven years old, married twenty-seven-year-old Anna Katherine Johnston after what Diggs called a "whirlwind courtship."[50] Anna, whose late father had for many years been the treasurer of Howard University, came from an elite Washington, DC, family. She graduated from boarding school, Barnard College at Columbia University, and Yale University Law School before becoming an attorney for the US Labor Department. The couple first maintained an apartment in Southwest, Washington, DC, with full views of the Potomac River.[51] Anna passed the Michigan bar, soon moved to Detroit, became a prosecutor, and later worked as a legal adviser in Diggs's Detroit office (before Congress prohibited members from hiring family members). In January 1964, the couple had a son, Douglass, and in April of 1967, they welcomed a new daughter, Carla. Supporting another family and maintaining another home only increased Diggs's financial difficulties, even though his wife earned income on her own.[52]

Then the bottom fell out.

EARLY ON MONDAY, APRIL 24, 1967, Weston Diggs Sr. was alone with his younger brother, seventy-three-year-old Papa Diggs. The founder of the House of Diggs had been hospitalized at Detroit Memorial Hospital for about a week after suffering another stroke. Already partially crippled from his first stroke, the family patriarch appeared depressed and despondent. The family was so concerned that they decided someone must be with him day and night.

Weston went down the hall to get a drink of water, and he returned to find Diggs Sr.'s hospital bed empty. Weston became frantic and then noticed an open window. He ran over to it, looked down from the fourth floor and was horrified. Just steps away from the hospital's front facade, on the bloodstained sidewalk, lay his brother's broken body. Papa Diggs, the visionary who built the House of Diggs and the man to whom Congressman Diggs owed so much, had committed suicide.[53]

The funeral procession, a ten-block motorcade, traveled with a police escort through Black Bottom, past the Diggs's Mansion, to Calvary Baptist Church, where Papa Diggs had been a member since the 1920s, just a few blocks from where he started his first funeral home. As bystanders watched, the pallbearers lifted Diggs Sr.'s body encased in a solid African mahogany casket out of the hearse and in solemn precision rolled the casket into the jammed church. As the House of Diggs choir sang a hymn, Congressman Diggs, holding his mother's hand, followed, as did other members of the family, all taking their seats in the pews reserved for family.[54]

Inside, "nearly 1,000 persons," a "true cross section" of Detroit, were "packed to the rafters" of the church.[55] Politicians and dignitaries from across Michigan were present, including Senator Philip Hart, Congressman John Conyers, Congresswoman Martha Griffiths, state senator Coleman Young, and state Democratic Party chair Neil Staebler. Regular working-class people from Black Bottom also came to show their respect.

Before giving the eulogy, Reverend L. Juan Burt read a telegram from President Lyndon Johnson to Congressman Diggs. "I know the heartache and grief you are suffering and I pray God will give you and your family strength and comfort," it read.[56] The president also sent a bouquet of yellow carnations and chrysanthemums. The House of Representatives sent a huge display of red roses.

Diggs Jr. listened expressionless, as Reverend Burt declared that Papa Diggs had a "rich outlook on life and his concern for people. He was a gateway for struggling souls. He lived in depth." The reverend only alluded to the tragic nature of Papa Diggs's death, saying, "It is often harder on those who are left behind" who must ask "why he died such an untimely death."[57] A soloist then sang Papa Diggs's "favorite" hymn, "We Are Climbing Jacob's Ladder," to a "nearly hushed" church.[58] Papa Diggs was buried in Detroit Memorial Park Cemetery, the Black-owned cemetery he had played a central role in forming.

Although personal pressures on Congressman Diggs increased exponentially following his father's death, he did not change his behavior.

IN THE SUMMER OF 1960, Congressman Diggs had met Janet Hall, a Detroit native, when he presented the high school graduate with a House of Diggs Foundation college scholarship.[59] Janet had also graduated from Barnard College and later Georgetown University, and in April of 1970 the fluent French speaker was working as a Foreign Service Officer in Dakar, Senegal, when Diggs encountered her during an "airport stop" in Dakar.[60]

Diggs, although still married to Anna, pursued the younger woman and went to "great lengths" to have the State Department assign Hall as an "escort officer" on his congressional delegations to Africa.[61] "From past experience I have found a French-speaking escort invaluable," Diggs wrote to the State Department.[62] Soon afterward, in January of 1971, Anna filed for divorce after eleven years of marriage.

Diggs and Janet Hall first traveled together a few months later. Hall served as Diggs's interpreter during "countless" trips to Africa.[63] A few years later, investigative reporters obtained State Department cables about Diggs's travels and accused Diggs of "courting" Hall using taxpayers' money.⁶⁴

In late October 1971, Diggs's staff and close friends were shocked to learn he planned to marry Hall within the week. Wedding invitations had already been mailed. But there was a huge problem. Diggs's divorce from his second wife, Anna, had not been finalized and would not be finalized until Diggs paid a $5,000 property settlement. The story became public, and when asked about Diggs's marital status, the judge in the divorce case said, "He's still married in the eyes of the law."⁶⁵ Anna, a highly skilled attorney, insisted that Diggs keep his obligation to help care for Douglass and Carla. Just five days before the wedding, Diggs paid up and the court finally approved the divorce decree.

Diggs pulled out all the stops for the wedding. More than 100 family and friends attended on November 6, 1971, at the Riverside Church in New York City and the "impressive" reception at the elegant St. Moritz Hotel across from Central Park.⁶⁶ Congressman Charles Rangel of New York served as Diggs's best man. "I did not know him that well" at the time, Rangel recalled. "And quite frankly, me being selected as his best man for one of his marriages indicated more of his lack of friends than his fondness for me."⁶⁷ Nevertheless Rangel and Diggs would become friends. Hall was only twenty-nine years old, and Diggs just shy of fifty. The couple would live in Washington, DC, and eventually, in 1977, welcome a new daughter, Cindy Carter Diggs.

AFTER PAPA DIGGS'S DEATH, even more business responsibility fell on Diggs Jr. Increasingly, however, Diggs Jr. was in Washington, DC, or traveling abroad. He became chair of the House Subcommittee on Africa two years after his father's death, and three years later he became chair of the House Committee on the District of Columbia. More and more, Diggs relied on others to manage and operate the House of Diggs's three funeral homes.

Cousin James "Jimmy" Diggs had initially kept the Southwest Chapel thriving. A dynamic personality who connected well with clients, Jimmy was also a heavy drinker, and it eventually affected his work. The funeral homes were hemorrhaging financially. By the summer of 1971, Diggs asked Juanita, with whom he remained friendly after the divorce, to go to the House of Diggs and assess its financial health. "By that time, it was too late to save it. It was too late. It was gone," Juanita lamented.⁶⁸ Bills were not being paid, including taxes to the IRS. The accounts receivable were all terribly delinquent. The pilfering and stealing had continued unabated. "There was nobody to watch them. . . . It killed the business," remembered Weston Diggs Jr.⁶⁹

For nearly all his adult life, Charles Diggs Jr. had depended on the family business to supplement his penchant for overspending and his inability (or unwillingness) to properly manage his personal finances. Now, family members on the House of Diggs's payroll were forced to alternate when each would get paid. The money was no longer there.

Rumors that Papa Diggs had died a millionaire were just that—rumors. Although the estimated value of his estate was $178,000, after federal government tax liens and other debts were paid, the value was reduced to $71,000.[70] He left the Diggs's Mansion to his wife, but Papa Diggs left nothing for his son. His will reads, "I have made no provisions for my son, Charles C. Diggs, Jr, under my Last Will because during my lifetime I have already made possible that he will have security for the balance and remainder of his life by virtue of investments and positions having been arranged for him and created by my efforts."[71]

The House of Diggs had received a temporary lifeline from the federal government by way of a $145,000 loan in 1971 from the Small Business Administration and another loan of $100,000 in 1974. Using the loans as guarantees, Diggs had then borrowed $200,000 from City National Bank in Detroit as he struggled to keep the funeral homes afloat.[72] None of it was enough. In the fall of 1975, the House of Diggs quietly merged with James A. Stinson Funeral home, creating the Diggs-Stinson Funeral Home. Although it was announced that Diggs would be chair and his daughter Denise would be vice-chair, Diggs had no financial interest in or involvement with the business.[73]

All that remained of the House of Diggs was debt. The two outstanding debts from loans totaling about $96,000, backed by the Small Business Administration, still needed to be repaid. Stinson assumed control of the assets of the House of Diggs and responsibility for the balance of the Small Business Administration loans, but Congressman Diggs was personally responsible for paying the taxes owed to the City of Detroit, the state of Michigan, and the US government. In addition, he still owed the federal government a debt of $36,223 for taxes owed on Papa Diggs's estate.[74]

The funeral business that had buried so many Detroiters no longer existed. Sadly, apart from the family, few people even noticed, and fewer still mourned its passing. The House of Diggs became a memory. All Diggs had left, apart from debt, was his work.

Chapter 21
THE CHAIRMAN'S PORTRAIT AND THE INDICTMENT OF CONGRESSMAN DIGGS

AFTER PAPA DIGGS'S DEATH in 1967, responsibility for operating the House of Diggs fell upon Congressman Diggs, and his reliance on others to manage the business created tremendous problems. The once booming business became a huge financial burden and eventually collapsed. Diggs, now middle-aged, was also on his third marriage and the father of five. Personal, private, and public responsibilities pulled at him from every direction.

Diggs had long depended on the House of Diggs to pay some of his personal expenses, but those resources were no longer available. Diggs became desperate. This does not excuse what happened next, but it may explain it.

In July 1972, Diggs and his wife, Janet, purchased a federal row house for $70,000 ($467,000 in 2024) on Second Street in Washington, within walking distance of the Cannon House Office Building. Within a year, Diggs took out a $2,500 "second trust" on the home, pledging the house as collateral at a high rate of interest.[1] A year later, when the second trust came due, Diggs again borrowed money to pay it off. By 1975, the row house would face foreclosure.

The *Washington Star* later reported that between 1972 and 1977, "Diggs, or Diggs and his wife jointly, [were] frequently in debt, frequently delinquent in payments and frequently sued."[2] By late 1974, Diggs's finances "got progressively worse."[3] He continued taking advances on his congressional salary and, as a result, later claimed that at times, he had "no income" from Congress as his paychecks were withheld to reimburse the US Treasury for the advances.[4] Family members said Diggs "got so underwater" financially that he would ask his widowed mother to pay some of his bills.[5] Only a few people outside the family knew he was in serious trouble. "Charlie was intensely proud and private," Coleman Young correctly told a reporter in 1979.[6] Diggs "hid his emotions" and rarely opened up, recalled a cousin.[7] The consequences of Diggs's inability or unwillingness to manage his finances soon closed in on him.

DIGGS'S LEGAL TROUBLES began in late 1972 as Diggs and longtime administrative assistant, Dorothy Quarker, prepared for big changes. In January 1973 Diggs would become the first Black chair of the House Committee on the District of Columbia and only the third Black man to chair a full committee in Congress. Quarker would serve as its chief of staff. Diggs planned to backfill Quarker's position with new staff when she moved to the DC committee.

Congress appropriates a "clerk-hire" allowance to compensate staff members in the discharge of their official duties. In the 1960s and 1970s, members pressed leaders for additional staff to meet the demand for constituency services that skyrocketed after the expansion of federal social programs.[8] In 1976 the allowance went up from sixteen staffers at $157,092 to eighteen staffers, with an allotment of $205,116.[9] Congress also appropriated allowances for standing committees. As chair of the DC Committee, Diggs had a clerk-hire allowance for a total of about thirty staff members. Members and committee chairs had some flexibility in setting staff salaries within the prescribed allowance, although there was a ceiling on individual earnings. Unused allowances were returned to the US Treasury, providing strong incentives for members to use the full amounts.

In October 1972, Diggs hired Jean Stultz, a Black staffer, as a "legislative assistant."[10] Stultz soon became Diggs's personal secretary, making deposits into his checking account and, on Diggs's direction, completing personal checks for his mortgage and other personal bills, presenting them to Diggs for his signature and then mailing them. After Quarker resigned, Stultz also supervised staff and maintained the office's budget.

Members of Congress operated like a collection of "small" businesses or member "enterprises" and exercised unusual discretion over their own actions.[11] Each could decide how many staff members to employ on Capitol Hill and in their home district office. Job titles and duties varied. With help from Quarker and later Stultz, Diggs regularly juggled the clerk-hire allowance to suit his needs.

Members also received a travel allowance for up to eighteen annual trips between home and Washington, DC, an annual allowance of $2,000 for district office expenses, and up to $1,200 a year to rent space in their district if none was available in government buildings.[12] Diggs used the allowance to pay the House of Diggs rent for an office suite above the funeral home.

To help pay expenses not covered by allowances, members often tapped into their personal funds. Before campaign contribution laws requiring disclosure became more stringent, many House members also used "unofficial office accounts," typically funds contributed by lobbying organizations and private individuals within their districts, for this purpose. Journalists called them "slush funds."[13]

Diggs believed use of such resources threatened a members' independence and did not have a "slush fund." He accepted "modest" contributions from the UAW but claimed to "have never solicit[ed] any funds" from General Motors or other big corporations in his district.[14] He rarely held fundraisers as he never faced a serious challenge to reelection, sometimes raising less than $1,000 during an entire campaign cycle. According to a study conducted in 1972, "Diggs' own campaign finance statement reads like a high school class treasurer's report."[15]

House members without a "slush fund" still found ways to cover expenses and other desires. For example, Congressman J. Irving Whalley (R-PA) got into legal trouble trying to make ends meet. Specifically, Whalley was involved in a payroll kickback scheme. He used his clerk-hire allowance to pay operatives in Pennsylvania to perform political and campaign work and paid chauffeur expenses from the driver's inflated salary. Several aides also deposited portions of their salary in special bank accounts that Whalley had access to.[16]

Whalley announced his retirement, but in July of 1973, he was indicted and charged with fraud. The congressman claimed such arrangements were common. In response, on July 12, 1973, the House Ethics Committee released an "advisory opinion" that clerk-hire allowances were not for personal services and that members should not enter into any agreement whereby staff members pay any salary or any benefits directly to the member of Congress or on his or her behalf. In August 1973, Whalley pleaded guilty, paid a fine, and was given probation.[17] Diggs would soon follow Whalley's path, but the fallout for Diggs would be more devastating.

In April 1973, Diggs hired as a consultant Ofield Dukes, a former editor of the *Michigan Chronicle* then working in public relations. In June 1973, Diggs, increasingly cash-strapped, paid Dukes using the congressional clerk-hire allowance. Over the next three years, Dukes earned between $12,000 and $20,000 annually as Diggs increased Dukes's salary to pay the cost of political advertisements, WJLB for broadcasting Diggs's weekly radio program, and travel expenses for trips made on Diggs's behalf. As the Whalley case demonstrated, the payments were illegal.

WHEN DIGGS BECAME CHAIR of the House Committee on the District of Columbia, there was no congressional allowance for the traditional "chairman's portrait." Normally, the chair solicited private contributions to pay for the portrait that would be displayed in the committee's hearing room. In late 1973, Dorothy Quarker told Diggs that Black portrait photographer Joseph Daniel Clipper would produce a portrait of Diggs for between $2,000 and $2,500. "But where are we going to get the $2,500?" asked Diggs. "You know I don't have that kind of money."[18]

A few days later, Diggs called Jean Stultz into his office. He told her there were "certain bills that needed to be paid, and he wanted to increase" her salary. The increase would go toward paying the bills.[19] "Oh no. I don't think that is legal." Stultz told Diggs, "I don't want to be involved in that."[20] Diggs took a drag off his cigarette, rested it back on the ash tray, and explained it is "permissible," that a person "can do anything she wished to do with her own salary."[21] The two went back and forth and Diggs told her that Quarker had agreed it was allowed and that she had suggested the arrangement. "All right, I will do it," Stultz agreed, adding, "I don't want to do this for long."[22] Diggs assured her, "It will only be for a couple of months."[23]

Days later, Stultz's salary more than doubled from $14,000 to $34,000. The extra money, allocated for Diggs's obligations and expenses, went into Stultz's personal checking account; but she took meticulous care to keep her own money isolated from this "special account."[24] On November 2, 1973, Stultz used funds from this "special account" for a cashier's check of $1,000 as an initial deposit to the photographer for Diggs's "chairman's portrait." It was the first payment Diggs directed Stultz to make from her inflated salary.

Although Diggs promised Stultz the arrangement would last only for "a couple" of months, the kickback scheme went on for two-and-a-half years. Each month Stultz would sit with Diggs in his office, and he would direct her to pay certain bills from the "special account." Initially, she paid reimbursable expenses related to Diggs's district office in Detroit, but over time the scope of expenses paid from the "special account" expanded to include expenses such as tickets to *Ebony*'s annual fashion show, flowers Diggs sent to colleagues and constituents, and catering for his lavish swearing-in ceremony as chair of the House District Committee. As Stultz later explained, the money "was used for whatever purposes the Congressman indicated to me."[25]

In early 1974, Dorothy Quarker became ill with cancer. By the summer of 1974, Diggs's personal bills were piling up, and many were delinquent. He had exhausted his salary advances and became more desperate. In June 1974, Diggs directed Stultz to pay his personal bills from the "special account." Now each month, Stultz made a list of Diggs's personal bills, and Diggs would tell her which bills to pay from the "special account." Using cashier's checks, money orders, and her own personal checks, Stultz would pay Diggs's creditors. Occasionally, Diggs's even directed her to give him cash. Stultz recorded the payments in a ledger and filed it away.

Diggs also misused clerk-hire funds to pay for House of Diggs debts. When accountant George Johnson threatened to sue after not being paid, Diggs had Stultz add Johnson to his congressional staff. From July 1973 to December

1974, Johnson earned over $15,000, paid by the US Treasury. He later admitted that he did not do any congressional work for Diggs.[26] Still, the financial noose of the funeral home continued to tighten around Diggs's neck.

In 1974, he took out another Small Business Administration loan, this time for $100,000, and in July he placed Jeralee Williams Richmond, a former House of Diggs bookkeeper, on the congressional payroll. Although Diggs would later claim Richmond worked in the Detroit field office, her primary assignment was to collect delinquent payments for the House of Diggs. In early August 1974, Dorothy Quarker died of cancer. The noose kept getting tighter.

Diggs soon shifted Stultz to the House DC Committee's clerk-hire allowance payroll, setting her salary at $36,000, near the maximum allowable amount. The next month, Diggs shifted Stultz back onto the payroll of his congressional staff at the same salary. Yet her duties never changed.

In September 1975, Felix Matlock, a longtime staffer in Diggs's Detroit office, also began receiving an inflated salary to offset Diggs's congressional expenses. Each month, Diggs would tell Stultz which office expenses Matlock should pay, and he authorized an increase in Matlock's salary to cover them. Matlock would then purchase money orders or cashier's checks to pay rent, utilities, and other routine office expenses. His annual salary soared, jumping from $14,500 in July 1975 to $35,000 in September 1975. In October 1975, James A. Stinson quietly purchased the House of Diggs, leaving Diggs responsible for its debts.

In late April or early May 1976, Stultz told Diggs she was "agitated and frustrated" with several of her colleagues and uncomfortable with the inflated salary arrangement, which substantially increased her tax liabilities. "I just wanted to be free of it," Stultz said later, and she handed Diggs a resignation letter.[27] Days later over lunch Diggs offered her a part-time schedule and proposed moving her out of the "office manager" role and continuing as his personal secretary. Stultz agreed to stay through the August 1976 primary elections.

DESPITE HIS MONEY TROUBLES Diggs's congressional activities kept expanding, and he remained effective. He continued to monitor Henry Kissinger's "shuttle diplomacy" in Africa, lobbied for repeal of the Byrd Amendment, and kept pushing for a new Black-led American organization devoted to Africa.

Anticipating Stultz's eventual resignation, and the clerk-hire funds it would free up, Diggs made a fateful move. He hired Randall Robinson as his administrative assistant, the equivalent to chief of staff today. In addition, and more importantly, Robinson was also responsible for organizing TransAfrica.[28]

Robinson's office was in the same suite that Jean Stultz once occupied and where Diggs's payroll and personnel files remained just as she left them.

Robinson had administrative responsibilities and soon undertook what he later described as a "full evaluation of staff operations"; and he went through the files.[29] Robinson likely saw that Diggs had hired George Johnson, and he probably recognized Ofield Dukes's name in the personnel files. What stood out to Robinson most, however, were the salaries for Stultz ($37,355) and Matlock ($39,000), which were substantially higher than his own salary of $27,500. That was highly unusual. The chief of staff is typically the highest paid employee in a member's office.

Robinson, who died on March 24, 2023, never publicly revealed precisely what he found in Diggs's office files. However, he did tell his friend Willard Johnson "he was alarmed at what was going on in Diggs's office," including "no show people on the payroll."[30] Robinson had good reason to be alarmed. A string of legislators found themselves ensnared in a web of investigations. In most cases, current or former staff members reported suspicious activity, often regarding alleged improper use of Congress's clerk-hire allowance, to journalists or the Justice Department. Eventually nearly a half dozen members of Congress were under investigation.[31]

The most prominent and sensational scandal involved Wayne Hays, the powerful Democratic committee chair, who paid his mistress a congressional salary. Although Hays avoided indictment, he resigned as committee chair. And a month after Robinson joined Diggs's staff, former Republican representative James F. Hastings was indicted for a payroll scheme involving his congressional staff, and a few months later, he was convicted and sentenced to prison.[32]

Robinson told Willard Johnson that he was so alarmed that he "confronted Diggs," likely in early December 1976, after they returned from the Lesotho conference in Africa.[33] While the specifics of the conversation between the two men are unknown, Robinson later testified that they discussed Matlock's salary.[34] Robinson probably questioned why Matlock's salary was higher than his own. Diggs likely shared that he authorized Matlock's salary increase to pay the office expenses for the Detroit field office. And Robinson probably reminded Diggs about what was happening to former Representative Hastings. Robinson recommended that Matlock's salary be lowered to $20,000 and that Matlock should no longer pay the district office's expenses from his salary. According to Robinson, Diggs put up no resistance and "complied."[35]

It is not clear what else Robinson told Diggs he discovered in the personnel files.

DESPITE HIS FINANCIAL CHALLENGES, Diggs looked forward to the new year. On December 2, 1976, he celebrated his fifty-fourth birthday, and his daughter Cindy was born on Inauguration Day. Diggs was hopeful that President Jimmy

Carter would bring real change to US-Africa policy. In March 1977, President Carter invited Diggs and other House and Senate members to the White House for a bill signing ceremony to repeal the Byrd Amendment.[36] While Diggs was celebrating, his life was about to change dramatically.

On March 10, 1977, the assistant US attorney for the District of Columbia, wrote a two-page memo to the chief of the Fraud Division of the US Justice Department detailing information he received via a telephone call from a member of Diggs's congressional staff.[37] The informant reported the congressman was using the clerk-hire allowance in a payroll kickback scheme. In the memo, the assistance US attorney general identified the caller and stressed the informant "would like this information to be kept strictly confidential."[38] Justice Department officials now knew that Diggs's clerk-hire salary scheme had violated the law.

Coincidently, that spring Black leaders publicly criticized law enforcement for what they viewed as a pattern of disproportionate investigation directed at them for what they called a conscious conspiracy to harass Black elected officials out of office. Black journalist Carl Rowan had written a lengthy article in *Ebony* entitled "Is There a Conspiracy against Black Leaders," detailing over a dozen investigations, including those targeting Representatives William Clay and Shirley Chisholm.[39] Black Americans, already distrustful of American governing institutions, embraced the harassment conspiracy.[40]

Diggs was perhaps the most respected Black person in Congress. Given the highly charged racial political context of harassment, racial double-standards, and conspiracies, the new US attorney general Griffin Bell, a judicial conservative and civil rights moderate who won Senate confirmation over the opposition of the CBC and other Black groups, deliberated with Justice Department officials about how to proceed with the information about Diggs. After nearly two months of internal discussion, the US Justice Department decided to "vigorously" pursue an investigation to determine whether Diggs committed fraud against the US government.[41] On Wednesday, April 27, 1977, the assistant US attorney for Washington, DC, informed the FBI Office of Public Corruption of the allegations. Special Agent James Milton Reed, a veteran agent with background and training in public accounting, was assigned to the case.

Prosecutors and FBI agents knew the identity of the informant, described by the FBI as "a source of unknown reliability."[42] On Monday May 2, Agent Reed "attempted to" arrange a meeting with the informant. The person refused. The next day, members of the US Attorney's Office and FBI agents met and concluded the informant "should be interviewed by the FBI after appropriate background investigation is completed."[43]

To date, the US government has not revealed the identity of the confidential informant. However, Diggs's FBI file, obtained through the Freedom of

Information Act, shows that the FBI's background investigation identified a Black male with ties to Harvard University and Roxbury, Massachusetts. The investigation found "no indication" that he was involved in "some violence advocating groups" like the "Black Panther Party, Malcolm X University, Republic of New Africa [or] Congress of African People." However, the report noted that the informant had been active in "the Boston African Liberation Committee," the "African Liberation Support Committee," and had helped in "planning to bring thousands of Black people" to Washington, DC, for African Liberation Day in May 1972.[44] Although the name of the person is redacted, that background parallels the biography and activities of Randall Robinson, as later described in his own memoir published in 1998.[45]

ON MAY 5, 1977, Agent Reed updated FBI director Clarence M. Kelly on the investigation. Reed told his boss that the informant "refused to be interviewed."[46] Reed, however, provided Kelly with the starting and ending salaries of a female member or former female member of Diggs's staff—likely that of Jean Stultz.[47] A short time later Reed subpoenaed Stultz's bank records. Bank officials immediately notified her and Stultz learned about the investigation for the first time. She hired an attorney, met with Assistant US Attorney Eric Marcy, and told Marcy about the kickback scheme and how it personally benefited Diggs.

Meanwhile, on June 1, 1977, FBI agents interviewed Felix Matlock, George Johnson, and Jeralee Richmond. All three were issued subpoenas to appear before a federal grand jury. Distraught, Richmond, who had known the Diggs's family since 1950, quickly telephoned the congressman. Diggs tried to calm her down. "There is nothing for you to do but to tell the truth," Diggs told her.[48]

On Wednesday June 8, 1977, Stultz, the prosecution's key witness, testified before the grand jury in Washington, DC. A few days later Matlock, Johnson, Richmond, and Dukes testified as well. Prosecutors also subpoenaed the payroll records of others listed on Diggs's congressional payroll, including Maria Reynolds, the sister of Diggs's ex-wife Juanita. Prosecutors later alleged that Diggs hired his sister-in-law for a "no-show" job to funnel alimony to Juanita.[49]

On June 15, 1977, the *Washington Post* broke the story about the investigation. Word spread quickly on Capitol Hill. Congressman Louis Stokes, a CBC member, recalled that when "we heard that about Charley, it was sort of disbelief. You just couldn't figure Charley doing something wrong."[50]

Diggs released a statement saying, "I am aware that certain preliminary explorations are underway concerning my activities.... I have received no official communication from investigating authorities concerning these explorations.

I will have no comment until such time as I do receive such notification. I have not retained counsel, since there are at this time no identified problems for which counsel is necessary."[51]

After the *Washington Post* broke the story, the *Detroit Free Press* and the *Detroit News* soon reported the details of Diggs's financial woes, citing sources indicating that Diggs's personal indebtedness totaled over $100,000 and that the funeral home had left him with massive debt. The articles also detailed Diggs's three divorces, alimony, and child support payments. A *Free Press* headline blared, "Women, Failing Business, Put Rep. Diggs in Debt."[52]

The *Washington Post* quoted acquaintances who claimed Diggs was a heavy gambler at the suburban Maryland racetracks.[53] The *Washington Star* carried a detailed report covering "a history of deep sustained indebtedness going back about 20 years," revealing that at one point Diggs was threatened with arrest in Detroit for failing to pay a Boston-based casket company a court-ordered judgment.[54]

Diggs told reporters he did not know the extent of his debt. When asked why he was so far in arrears, Diggs said, "I don't have any unconventional response to why I accumulate any indebtedness. Why does anybody? It's a matter of assuming certain obligations.... Most people have these types of problems at some time.... Deficit financing is as American as apple pie."[55]

Black leaders in Detroit quickly came to Diggs's defense. Horace Sheffield, the president of the Coalition of Black Trade Unionists and a friend and political ally, announced that the coalition would organize a legal defense fund to "assure" that Diggs "gets adequate legal counsel in the event it is needed," setting a goal of $50,000.[56]

The CBC also rallied behind Diggs with a fundraiser. Charles Rangel told the crowd of about 200 that "Charlie has been on a list. I'm giving to myself, not Charlie Diggs, because we all don't know when we will need counsel to prove we just want to serve our country."[57] Louis Stokes reminded the crowd that Adam Clayton Powell "went through the trials and tribulations now facing Charlie." Asked about the conspiracy theory, Diggs reportedly said, "Others have said that. There are coincidences that are difficult to explain—let's put it that way."[58]

Diggs soon retained the services of the law firm Williams and Connolly, headed by Edward Bennett Williams, one of the premier legal defense firms in the country. Williams, a courtroom legend, had won an acquittal for Teamsters leader Jimmy Hoffa and successfully represented former Congressman Adam Clayton Powell on a tax evasion case.

Meanwhile, Diggs somehow remained focused on his congressional work, which did not suffer during the investigation, attending the inaugural fundraiser for TransAfrica held at the Washington, DC, home of Randall Robinson's brother, news anchor Max Robinson.[59] Yet what should have been a crowning achievement was likely an awkward experience.

On November 1, 1977, responding to a grand jury subpoena, Robinson and other staff members delivered eight cardboard boxes containing Diggs's personnel and payroll records from 1971 through 1977 to the federal courthouse in Washington, DC. Included were 102 separate files of check stubs, canceled checks, receipts from money orders and cashier's checks, and Jean Stultz's ledgers for the "special account."[60]

In December Diggs turned fifty-five years old and the government completed its investigation. Attorney Vincent Fuller of Williams and Connolly held a series of sessions with Justice Department attorneys arguing that Diggs's alleged crimes were actually common practice, that members of Congress had wide discretion in the use of clerk-hire allowances, and that Diggs was being prosecuted because of his race. At times, according to news reports, the meetings were akin to "'tentative plea bargaining sessions'" as Diggs's lawyers "attempted to see if the government would agree, in return for a guilty plea, to limit its charges in a manner that would enable Diggs to keep his House chairmanship and voting rights in Congress."[61]

The *Washington Post* reported that defense lawyers convinced Attorney General Bell to review the Diggs matter. Eventually, the Justice Department decided to drop some of the charges so they would not exceed the number included in the case against recently convicted former congressman Hastings.[62]

That's where negotiations ended. Diggs would not avoid prosecution.

In February 1978, Diggs told several close friends that "he would be indicted within a few days."[63] Although his lawyers warned him an indictment was likely pending, on Monday, March 20, 1978, Diggs flew to Africa for a nine-nation visit. On Thursday, March 23, 1978, the federal grand jury indicted Diggs on thirty-five counts, including fourteen counts of mail fraud and twenty-one counts of making false statements. The indictment alleged that Diggs defrauded Congress of $101,000 by padding his payroll and taking kickbacks from staff members to pay for his congressional expenses and personal debts.

The next day, newspapers nationwide carried an Associated Press report, which often appeared with a photo of Diggs, under a variety of headlines, most a variation of "Rep. Diggs Indicted on Kickback Scheme." The Associated Press included a statement Diggs released from Mozambique: "I am innocent of the charges being leveled against me. I do not believe that I have violated any federal law, House rule or precedent. Allegations in an indictment do not prove guilt and I am confident that due process of law will vindicate me."[64] Charles Diggs would soon have his day in court.

Chapter 22

THE TRIAL

ON FRIDAY, APRIL 7, 1978, Congressman Charles Diggs Jr. made his way through the gaggle of reporters and photographers and into the E. Barrett Prettyman Federal Courthouse in downtown Washington, DC. Reporters noted that upon entering, "He talked quietly and laughed with a few friends and aides in the court room."[1] Diggs likely felt fortunate that US District Court judge Joseph C. Waddy, a Black jurist, had been randomly assigned his trial. When asked his plea to the charges Diggs said, "Not guilty," in "barely audible tones."[2] Waddy suggested that Diggs's attorney and prosecutors discuss possible "disposition of the case," perhaps a plea bargain.[3] A trial date was set for June 26, 1978.

Released on a personal bond, Diggs read a prepared statement to the press, affirming his innocence and saying, "[I am] deeply distressed by the charges leveled against me. . . . I do not believe that I have violated any federal law or any House rule or precedent." Diggs also announced that he would continue all his duties as a member of Congress and seek reelection.[4]

Although many of Diggs's supporters believed he was the victim of selective prosecution, his staff knew a conviction was likely. As Herschelle Challenor recalled, "His lawyers basically told us we should start looking for new jobs," and soon after the indictment, many staff members departed.[5] On May 9, Judge Waddy denied motions from Diggs's attorney to dismiss the charges and hold a hearing to determine whether the Justice Department's prosecution was racially motivated.[6] He did agree to postpone the trial and set a new date for September 26. But before the trial began, Waddy became ill and passed away. US District Court judge Oliver Gasch took over. Diggs would later claim that what set Waddy and Gasch "apart was that the black judge was a liberal and Gasch was a conservative."[7]

Although Diggs had often run unopposed for renomination, three opponents emerged. The most visible and vocal challenger was twenty-nine-year-old community activist Ray Rickman.[8] For the first time since 1954, Diggs had to actively campaign for reelection. Diggs tried to frame the indictment as racially motivated and as part of a conspiracy to harass Black officials, saying, "The devils are out to get me."⁹ On August 8, 1978, Diggs won the Democratic primary, garnering 62 percent of the votes.

ON TUESDAY, SEPTEMBER 26, in courtroom 21 in the DC federal courthouse, Judge Gasch presided over jury selection, eventually seating eight Black women, three Black men and one white man.¹⁰ Diggs and his lawyers likely felt the nearly entirely Black jury would benefit the congressman. After a series of pretrial negotiations, prosecutors agreed to lower the number of charges in their indictment from thirty-five to twenty-nine counts—eleven of mail fraud and eighteen of making false official statements. Due to the extensive media coverage, the jury was sequestered. Judge Gasch endeavored to complete the trial as expeditiously as possible.

Forty-year-old prosecutor John Kotelly had cut his teeth trying hundreds of murders, robbery, and other criminal cases in Washington, DC. His strength, noted a flattering profile, was "his meticulous trial preparation, a keen memory, and most of all, his calm, courteous style that defies the image of a conviction-hungry prosecutor."¹¹ He had an unbroken streak of convictions dating back to 1975, including the prosecution of the former congressman Hastings in a similar payroll kickback scheme. Kotelly would be assisted by Assistant US Attorney Eric Marcy.

Diggs's lead trial lawyer was David Povich, a forty-three-year-old partner with Williams and Connolly. Povich had faced Kotelly before; Povich had represented Hastings in his corruption trial.

At 9:35 a.m., on Wednesday, September 27, Judge Gasch ordered the government to present its opening statement. Kotelly read each of the twenty-nine counts against Diggs. Pacing before the jury, Kotelly told jurors that Diggs knowingly devised a scheme to defraud the United States for his own benefit. Kotelly told the jury of the staff members who would testify that they earned a salary but did little or no congressional work and that the evidence would show that Diggs raised his secretary's salary and used the funds to pay his personal bills. The trial, he emphasized, was not about Diggs's effectiveness in Congress, his leadership during the civil rights movement, or anything else: Diggs had defrauded the government. It was wrong.¹²

In his opening statement, David Povich acknowledged that Diggs had used portions of his staff members' salaries to pay office and some personal expenses but argued that the alleged kickbacks were legitimate payments used to cover Diggs's congressional expenses. Povich noted that Congress had recently relaxed its rules and that members could use unused clerk-hire funds to pay for reimbursable office expenses. The prosecution, he said, was seeking to criminalize common legislative behavior. Jean Stultz, he claimed, had voluntarily used her salary to pay Diggs's personal expenses.

Povich then began to highlight Diggs's distinguished record, but when Povich began to recount how Diggs raised money for the 1955 Montgomery bus boycott, Kotelly jumped to his feet. "Objection!" he roared, saying that Diggs's supporting the bus boycott was not relevant.[13] Judge Gasch agreed and admonished Povich to move on. Before taking his seat, Povich pointed to Diggs and told the jury that he was a man of high moral standards who would never intentionally defraud the government.

OVER FOUR DAYS OF TESTIMONY, the prosecution called eighteen witnesses, nearly all of them "fact" witnesses with knowledge about the facts of the case. John Lawler, the chief of the House Finance Office, explained the financial ins and outs of congressional office operations, the use of "payroll authorization forms," and how staff members are reimbursed for expenses related to their jobs. He also identified canceled payroll checks and travel reimbursement vouchers for members of Diggs's staff, including Jeralee Richmond and George Johnson; and he testified that clerk-hire funds were used by members of Congress to pay "employees in the discharge of their official duties."[14] When cross-examined by Povich, Lawler admitted that clerk-hire regulations, which had been changed in January of 1977, were vague and didn't define "official duties."[15]

When the trial resumed the next day Kotelly called Jean Stultz to the stand. Described by the *Detroit Free Press* as "precise and poised," Stultz recounted the origins of the payroll kickback scheme, noting her initial objection to a salary increase to pay for Diggs's $2,500 "chairman's portrait."[16] After Kotelly showed Stultz a list of checks and money orders, Stultz explained that she used the funds to pay Diggs's mortgage, insurance premiums, and other personal expenses. As Diggs watched unemotionally from the defense table, Stultz told the jury, "These payments were always made at the direction of Congressman Diggs."[17] She also testified that George Johnson and Jeralee Richmond were added to the staff's payroll on Diggs's direction, but that neither did any congressional work and that Felix Matlock, whom she described as Diggs's "most loyal" staffer, paid the Detroit office expenses out of his salary. "The actual instructions to Mr. Matlock came from me, but I got those instructions from the congressman," she testified.[18]

The next day, Friday, September 29, the courtroom was packed with Diggs's supporters, many in town for the annual CBC legislative weekend. Upon his arrival, Diggs shook hands with his old friends, and then sat impassively as Stultz took the stand again.[19] She insisted that the kickback scheme was Diggs's idea. "I felt I didn't have too much choice if I wanted to retain my position," she testified.[20] She also provided the jury with a bleak picture of Diggs's personal finances, noting that in 1975 she took out a personal loan to loan Diggs money to avert foreclosure on his home. When defense attorney Povich asked her why she took out the loan, Stultz said she was sympathetic to Diggs's plight, maintaining, "I would be sympathetic with you or anybody else ... if they had bills over their head."[21] Povich then tried, and failed, to get Stultz to say she volunteered to pay Diggs's bills. She insisted she felt pressured to do so and that whenever she asked to end the arrangement, she "got the usual response from the Congressman, which was a wave of the hand," she said.[22]

Later that evening, Diggs acted as if nothing was amiss and attended several CBC functions. Several hundred supporters attended a fundraiser at the Washington Hilton Hotel to help with his legal fees, and the *Washington Post* reported that Diggs appeared "relaxed, outgoing and spirited."[23]

The following morning, Povich requested a bench conference. He claimed that a "very important witness" in California could not appear due to a prior commitment, and he wanted attorneys to fly to the West Coast to take a deposition.[24] Kotelly "strenuously" objected and demanded to know the witness's identity. Povich, blurted out, "The character witness is President Gerald Ford." Judge Gasch, however, was not impressed, and said, "Let Mr. Ford come here. Tell him I said so."[25]

Felix Matlock, Diggs's longtime Detroit field representative, then attested that Diggs and Stultz had instructed him to use part of his congressional salary to pay expenses for the Detroit office. Ofield Dukes testified that he voluntarily accepted an inflated salary to pay expenses related to his political work and stressed that he thought nothing was illegal about the arrangement. House of Diggs CPA George Johnson told the jury that although Diggs never told him he was hiring him to repay him, he nevertheless did no congressional work but still received a congressional salary. Jeralee Richmond testified that only about 20 percent of her time was devoted to congressional duties; the rest was devoted to the House of Diggs. Randall Robinson then testified he had told Diggs that Matlock's salary was out of scale and unjustified by his duties, and that his pay should be reduced. Robinson testified that Diggs did not resist any of the salary changes he recommended. FBI Special Agent James Reed, using payroll and personnel records, explained how he was able to trace the money used to pay Diggs's congressional and personal expenses. Reed testified that over one-half of the funds from Stultz's inflated salary covered Diggs's personal expenses. The evidence was devastating. The prosecution rested.

UNABLE TO REFUTE the financial evidence, the defense focused on character witnesses, hoping that the vagueness of the clerk-hire regulations and Diggs's exalted reputation would be enough to sway the jury. They planned to call four of America's most prominent Black leaders—Coretta Scott King, Jesse Jackson, Andrew Young, and Detroit mayor Coleman A. Young. However, Judge Gasch, at a bench conference, reminded Diggs's attorneys that the testimony had to be relevant to the defendant's "truthfulness, integrity, and honesty."[26] He also warned he would not allow the witnesses to bring in racial matters that were immaterial to the case. The defense did what they could with the little they had.

Walter Fauntroy testified that he had known Diggs since the early 1960s when he began working for Dr. King's SCLC, but each time he started to discuss Diggs's work with Dr. King, Judge Gasch interrupted. On cross-examination Fauntroy admitted that he had no personal knowledge of Diggs's financial condition.

The same pattern continued the following day, Wednesday, October 4, when Coretta Scott King, Jesse Jackson, US ambassador Andrew Young, and Detroit mayor Coleman Young all told how they came to know and work with Diggs. "It was one of those rare moments for the predominantly black jury to be close to people who were newsmakers. There was a strong feeling that they would sway the jury," recalled Diggs's former press secretary Carolyn DuBose.[27]

When King told the jury that she had known Diggs since the 1955 Montgomery bus boycott, Gasch told Mrs. King to limit her answer to the question of Diggs's honesty and integrity. And on cross-examination Kotelly asked her if she had any knowledge of Diggs's financial condition, of how he paid his congressional staff and office expenses, or the financial status of the House of Diggs? Each time Mrs. King answered "No."[28] The pattern continued as Jackson, ambassador Andrew Young, and mayor Coleman Young testified. Each man admitted he had no "personal knowledge" of Diggs's finances, how he paid his employees and office expenses, or how he managed the finances at the House of Diggs.

The defense called only two fact witnesses. Diggs's defense was in trouble. The defense then made a last-ditch, last-minute decision to call Diggs to the stand. Kotelly complained that the government had not been informed that Diggs would testify. But after a lunch recess, Gasch allowed Diggs to be sworn in.

The courtroom buzzed as Congressman Diggs took center stage. Nattily dressed, Diggs "sat with palms down on the witness table."[29] For ninety minutes, "in a deep, steady voice," he tried to explain his actions and intentions.[30] After walking the jury through Diggs's basic background, things got heated when Povich asked Diggs to describe the issues he addressed when he arrived in Congress in 1955. Kotelly objected and in conference argued that Diggs's involvement in "the civil rights movement or in Africa have absolutely nothing to do with the issues in this case."[31] Gasch interrupted, saying that because of the composition of the jury, race was already a "sensitive issue," and then admonished Diggs's lawyers, saying, "Let's not play upon that section of the scale."[32]

Povich asked Diggs to describe his congressional activities from 1955 to 1971 "briefly and succinctly."[33] When Diggs began to mention his fundraising for the Montgomery bus boycott, Kotelly again objected. Gasch ruled Diggs's testimony "inappropriate" and asked him to focus on his congressional activities.[34]

When the questioning turned to the charges in the indictment, Diggs acknowledged he had used his staff member's inflated salaries to pay his personal and business bills and expenses related to his congressional office. For example, Diggs recounted that he hired Jeralee Richmond because "I needed her over at the funeral home as a bookkeeper to take care of the books and to do in addition to that what has been traditionally done by her in the past: handle constituent services."[35] But Diggs took issue with the testimony of CPA George Johnson, claiming Johnson was a "consultant" on Black economic development issues and that he was not aware that Johnson credited his congressional salary to the House of Diggs's account. Diggs claimed that "not at any time at all" did he tell Johnson to do so.[36]

Povich turned next to the damaging testimony of Jean Stultz. Diggs testified that Dorothy Quarker recommended that Stultz's salary be increased to cover the cost of the "chairman's portrait." Diggs, sounding somber, told the jury that he "was in very dire financial straits" and that he asked Stultz, "Can you help me out?"[37] Diggs claimed that Stultz put up no resistance and appeared willing to do it.

As Povich ended his questioning, he queried Diggs about each of the violations stipulated in the government's indictment, asking if he intended to violate any laws of the United States. Each time Diggs responded, "No sir." Povich then asked if Diggs intended to violate the law regarding the salary arrangement with Jean Stultz. Once again Diggs answered, "No sir. I felt that she had every right to do what she wished to do with her salary."[38] With that, Povich announced, "I have no further questions, Your Honor."

AFTER NEARLY NINETY MINUTES of testimony, Diggs faced two hours of cross-examination. Although Diggs had remained composed thus far, he now turned combative, testy, and defensive, adding, as one reporter noted, "a touch of personal drama to a trial that has been concerned mostly with details of money orders, salary schedules and congressional rules and regulations."[39] Kotelly began by questioning Diggs's about campaign fundraising, something Diggs had testified he seldom did. In response, Kotelly presented evidence of a January 1973 "Salute to Congressman Diggs" reception that raised nearly $10,000 and a December 1975 fundraiser at a Washington, DC, hotel. When Kotelly asked Diggs what happened with those funds, Diggs testified that he could not remember. Asked why he didn't use them to pay for the "chairman's portrait," Diggs said, "I have already testified that that was paid for by Jean Stultz."[40]

Kotelly then shifted gears, questioning Diggs about the testimony by Jean Stultz. Diggs reluctantly confirmed that he and Stultz used the term the "special account" to refer to the monies from her inflated salary. At 5 p.m. Judge Gasch called a recess. The last day of trial would begin the next morning.

On Thursday morning October 5, Kotelly resumed questioning Diggs about the "special account," the tension rising with each inquiry. Kotelly pressed Diggs on why he made Stultz pay his personal bills. "I did not tell her to pay it. I asked her to pay it. I asked her if she would help out," said a defiant Diggs.[41] Asked if he thought there "was anything improper" for one of his employees to be paying his bills, Diggs acknowledged, "There is no question" that Stultz "voluntarily" paid his personal bills.[42] Kotelly probed whether Diggs thought it was "unusual" for Stultz to pay for the "chairman's portrait." "It was an unusual gesture and without question her willingness to do it I considered unique," Diggs said.[43] When asked if he had requested Dorothy Quarker to pay for the portrait, Diggs responded, "No"; and he maintained that he also did not try to raise funds for the payment. Kotelly finished by asking Diggs if he thought it "unusual" for Stultz to pay his personal bills when he earned significantly more than she and the average American. Diggs insisted she was willing to do it. After nearly six hours of testimony over two days, Diggs's left the stand.

The next morning, during closing arguments, Kotelly attacked Diggs's testimony as "preposterous," "ludicrous," "ridiculous," "unbelievable," and "incredible."[44] In a powerful summation, Kotelly told the jury that it made no sense for Stultz voluntarily to pay Diggs's personal bills and expenses. Diggs's testimony, Kotelly argued, "doesn't square with life, doesn't square with the facts and doesn't square with reality." Kotelly told the jury to decide the case on the facts. Diggs's contribution to civil rights and as a congressman, Kotelly said, "had absolutely nothing to do with this case."[45] The evidence, he argued, was "so overwhelming" that they must find him guilty.[46]

David Povich then gave an impassioned hour-long closing argument that sought to convince the jury that Diggs never intended to violate the law. He did not dispute most of the facts of the case; the question was one of intent. Povich maintained that the rules governing staff payroll were so vague that finding Diggs guilty would be akin to convicting him for "violating an unwritten law," inferring that the prosecution was going after Diggs for what were common practices on Capitol Hill. "The government is not seeking to prosecute this case. They are seeking to punish. This is a gut fight," he exclaimed.[47]

Povich attacked Jean Stultz, questioning her immunity agreement, hoping to call her integrity into doubt. "There really is something unholy in all this," Povich said.[48] Last, Povich asked the jury to take the "full measure" of Diggs into account, referring to Coretta Scott King and other character witnesses. "We have brought you people who can help you decide that question," Povich said.[49]

As Povich concluded, he became more dramatic, pacing the floor before the jurors who had been sequestered for over a week. Povich told them they would soon be able to walk out of the courtroom. Then, turning to look at Diggs, Povich raised his voice. "The lawyers will go out the door, the court personnel will go out the door. We would like Congressman Charles Diggs to come with us."[50] As Povich walked to take his seat next to his client, Diggs began to sob. He removed his thick-lensed glasses and wiped his eyes with a handkerchief.

The prosecution's rebuttal to the Povich's summation was brief, powerful, and effective. Kotelly told the jury Stultz had been offered immunity because Diggs had put her in legal jeopardy. The star character witnesses, he said, were all "fine people" but had no knowledge of the facts of the case.[51] The civil rights leaders were the "last people" Diggs would want to know about his scheme, Kotelly emphasized. "If this were a testimonial dinner, we could all applaud Congressman Diggs," he added. "But this is not a testimonial dinner."[52] Responding to Povich's description of Diggs as a man of integrity, Kotelly asked, "What kind of integrity does a man have who's living off his employee's salary?"[53]

With that, deliberations began.

AS DIGGS AWAITED THE VERDICT, his former press secretary recalled that he appeared "extremely tired . . . behind his tinted glasses, his eyes were so puffy they were nearly squeezed shut."[54] After deliberating for less than twenty-four hours, at about 2:40 p.m. on Saturday, October 7, word came that a verdict had been reached. About ten minutes later Diggs was back at the defense table.

"All rise," the bailiff announced as Judge Gasch took his place at the bench. The twelve jurors who held Diggs's fate filed in and took their place in high back leather chairs. Diggs looked at the jurors' faces. They all were expressionless. The judge asked the jury foreman, a young Black man, to stand. "Have you reached a verdict?" Gasch asked. The foreman answered, "Yes, Your Honor." Judge Gasch then asked Diggs to stand. Wearing a green corduroy suit, Diggs stood with his hands folded in front of him.

The courtroom clerk read off each count to the jury foreman. "Count one," the clerk read. "Guilty," the jury foreman replied. "Count two," said the clerk. "Guilty," the jury foreman replied. The clerk continued through all the twenty-nine counts, and each time the foreman responded "Guilty." Povich asked the judge to poll the jury and one after the other each confirmed the verdict.[55] Clearly, the jury of largely working-class Black women did not believe that a mid-level staffer would voluntarily pay her boss's bills.

Carolyn DuBose recalled, "The unanimous verdict was stunning. Many people wept openly in the courtroom. It seemed that nearly everyone was sobbing except Diggs, who was sitting quietly and dispassionately with his hands folded on the tabletop" and "look[ing] hard at the jury" as they sat impassively.[56] Judge Gasch released Diggs on his own recognizance and told him not to leave the country without informing the court. No date for sentencing was set. Diggs turned away and made his way out of the courtroom. He and his wife "huddled together in the hallway," but reporters and others could not hear what was said.[57]

Diggs emerged from the courthouse before dozens of assembled reporters and photographers. "I'm just generally disappointed," he said, before adding that he would remain the Democratic nominee in the November election and expected to win. "I will continue to represent my people as I always have," he told the reporters, adding that he looked forward to an appeal.[58]

Diggs then left the reporters and went back near the courthouse to talk to his wife. "They were so deep in conversation it was if they had not spoken to each other before," recalled DuBose.[59] Diggs got into the back seat of a waiting car alone, and Janet watched as "the driver quickly made a U-turn and sped toward Capitol Hill. Diggs never looked back. His wife waited at the curb until his car disappeared from sight."[60]

Reaction to the verdict in the press was, in general, surprisingly sympathetic. *Washington Post* columnist William Raspberry wrote that he found himself "thinking of Diggs not as a sleezy [sic] fat cat leaning on his underlings but as a pretty decent fellow who couldn't bring himself to admit that he wasn't the wealthy man everybody took him for."[61] Decades later, a similar sentiment was expressed by Congressman John Dingell Jr. of Michigan, who had served with Diggs since the 1950s. "There wasn't a crooked bone in Charley Diggs," he said. "He was desperate," Dingell added emphatically.[62] The editors of the *Michigan Chronicle* suggested that Diggs was blind to the political reality of racial politics. Black elected officials, especially in the era of Watergate, must take "more than usual care ... and personal responsibility in both fiscal and interpersonal affairs," they opined.[63] But not everyone was so understanding. Although many still admired the man and appreciated his efforts during his time in Congress, in a story that asked Diggs's constituents how they felt about the verdict, one middle-aged Black man responded, "Politics is a dirty game, so if you play it, you should be prepared to pay the price if you make a mistake." Another was more matter of fact, "They caught him plain and simple," he said. "What can you say?"[64]

Chapter 23

DIGGS MEETS NEWT

ON SUNDAY, OCTOBER 8, 1978, the day after the verdict, Charles Diggs Jr. flew to Detroit reportedly "in relatively good spirits," and the congressman's home office was "flooded with telephone calls pledging support."[1] Many continued to believe he was the victim of selective prosecution, a conspiracy to silence and punish Black leaders.

At a press conference Diggs declared that if reelected, he would not vacate his congressional seat. "The rules don't require that. This is a matter left to an individual's constituency," he said.[2] House rules stipulated that a member convicted of a crime with a sentence of two or more years was allowed to participate on committees and cast votes if the conviction was overturned on appeal or if the member was reelected after the conviction.

As expected, on November 7, 1978, one month after his conviction, Diggs was reelected with 80 percent of the votes. Democrats retained control of the House of Representatives, 277 to 157. Republicans gained fifteen new House members. Georgian Newt Gingrich, a brash thirty-five-year-old former history professor, in his third try, was among them. In two previous unsuccessful campaigns against conservative Democrat John Flynt Jr. in 1974 and 1976, Gingrich had made corruption and congressional ethics an issue. After Flynt retired, Gingrich fully embraced the anti-tax and anti-government posture that would soon catapult Ronald Reagan into the White House and, using negative campaign ads, wrongly imply that his Democratic challenger was morally and ethically corrupt. Gingrich believed the same strategy could be used by the GOP to help bring down the Democratic majority in the House.[3]

Gingrich eyed Congressman Diggs as an obvious target.

ON MONDAY, NOVEMBER 20, 1978, Diggs, dressed in a dark suit, "stood with his hands clasped behind his back, his head erect," before Judge Gasch for sentencing. Diggs told the judge the conviction was a "devastating experience" and had "shaken the faith" of his many supporters. Diggs asked Gasch to spare him prison time in favor of probation and public service.[4] Diggs's lawyers argued that he had suffered enough, that the sums he defrauded went toward congressional-related expenses, and that the sale of his Capitol Hill home would help pay restitution. Prosecutors, by contrast, urged "a moderate prison term" to reflect "the seriousness of the fraud and abuse of public trust."[5]

Gasch sentenced Diggs to a maximum of three years in prison with no minimum limit, his ultimate sentence to be determined by the presidentially appointed US Parole Commission. Court observers speculated that Diggs would likely serve no more than eighteen months. He would remain free until he exhausted his appeals.

The following day, Diggs informed Speaker Thomas P. "Tip" O'Neill Jr. that consistent with precedent, he was stepping aside as chair of the House Committee on the District of Columbia until final resolution of his appeals. Diggs, however, insisted on remaining chair of the Subcommittee on Africa and told O'Neill that he planned to exercise his "full legislative responsibilities."[6]

On December 2, 1978, Diggs turned fifty-six years old. Observers wondered, as one Black journalist put it, how he "managed to maintain a calm exterior" while facing the likelihood of prison.[7] Although Diggs seldom showed his emotions, a close associate confided, "Inwardly this thing is beating the hell out of him. It has almost consumed him."[8]

The pressure and the political fallout from his conviction, however, was about to become more intense. O'Neill and other Democratic leaders were increasingly concerned about the potential political repercussions from Diggs's troubles. The question of race created a quandary for leadership. The House's senior Black member was now a convicted felon yet had just been reelected overwhelmingly in a predominantly Black district. Many Democratic members, some of whom remembered the racially inspired controversy after the House voted to exclude Adam Clayton Powell in 1967, worried about the racial fallout, and many newer Democratic members elected after Watergate were sensitive about the optics. They believed scandals like Diggs's could erode the Democrat's moral advantage following Watergate and encouraged O'Neill to take further action. He did.

On Wednesday, December 6, Democratic members voted on an amendment to the rules that would require the full caucus to vote on appointments of any nominee convicted of a felony or censured during the preceding Congress to a subcommittee chair, a rule that would apply only to Diggs.[9] Diggs didn't have enough support to stop it, telling CBC members "they ought not to try to fight an anticipated losing battle."[10] The new rule passed the Democratic caucus overwhelmingly. Diggs was stripped of his leadership roles in the next Congress.

THE DEMOCRATS' ACTIONS emboldened congressman-elect Gingrich, who thirsted for attention and looked to score partisan points. He planned to use Diggs to embarrass House Democrats. In Atlanta, Gingrich told reporters, "The citizens of Detroit have the right to the representation they want to elect, but the Congress at the same time clearly has the right to not have convicted felons who have not served their time voting on the laws of the country."[11] Gingrich reached out to newly elected Republicans and convinced them to support a plan to use Article I, Section 5, of the US Constitution and, by a two-thirds vote, expel Diggs during the first week of the new session of Congress.

Expulsion was the most severe punishment the House could render against a member at the time. Only three members had ever been expelled from the House—all for treason during the Civil War. Republican leaders supported Gingrich's effort but realized the racial overtones that would develop by targeting a prominent Black member. Nevertheless, House Republicans leaders announced plans to file a complaint against Diggs with the House Ethics Committee.[12]

That wasn't enough for the grandstanding Gingrich. On January 11, 1979, he wrote Illinois congressman John Anderson (R-IL), chair of the House Republican Conference, that he was "morally repulsed" serving with a convicted felon. Gingrich urged them to request that Diggs not vote on any "substantive matter" until the Ethics Committee released its findings. Gingrich warned Anderson that if Diggs voted, he would move to expel him.[13]

On January 17, Gingrich and other freshman Republicans adopted a resolution calling upon any member convicted of a felony to refrain from voting on the floor and in committee, to expeditiously pursue their appeals, to relinquish leadership of any subcommittees, and to resign if an appellate court affirmed any of the charges against them.[14]

Gingrich's strategy gained traction as reporters and editorialists dug into Diggs's saga. Even Garry Trudeau's popular *Doonesbury* comic strip chronicled the ethical and political implications of Diggs's reelection.[15]

Ultimately, pressure from Gingrich, the GOP, and some concerned Democrats forced O'Neill to press Diggs to step aside as chair of the Subcommittee on Africa. On January 23, 1979, Diggs reluctantly agreed, describing his twenty years on the Foreign Affairs Committee as among his "most cherished congressional experiences."[16] Diggs, however, made clear his intent to carry out his full responsibilities as a member as far as House rules allowed.

Gingrich kept pushing. A few weeks later, he and a group of Republicans filed a formal request with the Ethics Committee to investigate Diggs's conduct "as expeditiously as possible."[17] Gingrich then played the race card and openly identified and directly criticized the twenty-seven House Democrats who in 1976 had supported investigating Congressman Robert Sikes (D-FL), a conservative Southerner, but who now opposed investigating Diggs, calling it a racial "double standard," and saying, "We should have one standard of justice for all Americans—and for all Congressmen—for white conservative Southerners and for black Northern liberals," he wrote for *Human Events*.[18]

Then Gingrich got even more aggressive. In a *Washington Post* op-ed, he argued that convicted felons "should refrain from voting" on legislation.[19] The next day Gingrich gave Diggs a tersely written letter threatening expulsion should he vote on any substantive matter. House Democrats received a similar letter asking them to convince Diggs to refrain from voting and threatening his expulsion.[20] Diggs was livid. He wrote a one-sentence letter—addressed to "Newton Leroy Gingrich"—saying he would "exercise all" his rights under House rules.[21]

A showdown loomed.

ON WEDNESDAY, FEBRUARY 28, as members prepared for a late vote on a resolution to increase the federal debt limit, the first major vote of the Ninety-Sixth Congress, Gingrich made an emotional speech appealing to Diggs "one last time to consider the honor and dignity of the House" and refrain from voting. "If he persists in voting we have no alternative but to introduce a motion of expulsion," Gingrich threatened.[22] Shortly after Diggs voted to raise the debt limit, Gingrich filed the expulsion motion.

Even some Republicans were taken aback by Gingrich's audacity. Traditionally, each party disciplined its own members and Democrats had already done so by stripping Diggs of his committee chairmanships. Most Democratic members believed preventing Diggs from voting disenfranchised his district. After Gingrich's motion the Democrats met and voted overwhelmingly not to tell Diggs to refrain from voting.[23]

On Thursday, March 1, Speaker O'Neill presided over the expulsion debate. Diggs "sat in a prominent position behind the speakers' table throughout the sometimes-dramatic debate" but did not speak, and his colleagues rarely consulted him.[24] Every member knew there was not a two-thirds majority to expel Diggs. Although Gingrich claimed the "honor and dignity" of the House was at stake, the fledgling gadfly just wanted to force Democratic members to record a vote in support of a convicted felon. It was scandal politics 101.

Democratic Majority Leader Jim Wright (D-TX) was designated to defend Diggs. Tempers flared when Parren Mitchell (D-MD) of the CBC tried unsuccessfully to block a Republican from reading incriminating portions of Diggs's own testimony at his trial. In an "impassioned" speech, Wright argued that

Diggs had not yet exhausted his appeals, nor had the Ethics Committee investigated the charges. Diggs, Wright said, deserved due process, and voters in Diggs's district had a right to be represented "by a person of their choice."²⁵ He made a motion to send the matter to the Ethics Committee, which the House approved by a vote of 322 to 77.

In early April 1979, the Ethics Committee formally charged Diggs with eighteen rules violations regarding the payroll kickback scheme. Over the next two months, his lawyers filed unsuccessful motions with the Ethics Committee to delay or stop its investigation. Meanwhile, news reports regularly rehashed Diggs's personal finances and his role in the payroll scheme. On June 7, the Ethics Committee voted to begin public hearings on the charges and began issuing subpoenas.

On June 29, just as the committee members were preparing to hold the hearings, Diggs and his lawyers reached an agreement with the Ethics Committee. Diggs admitted misusing clerk-hire funds for his personal use but denied that the violations were intentional. Diggs, however, did not admit to the charges related to the inflated salaries that went toward the payment of congressional office expenses, because those charges were part of his appeal. The Ethics Committee agreed to drop those charges. Diggs also agreed to repay the government $40,000, apologized for bringing "discredit" to the House, and said he would accept censure. Short of expulsion, censure is the most severe punishment available to Congress.²⁶

DIGGS WAS CENSURED JULY 31, 1979, by a vote 414 to 0, with four members, including Diggs, voting present. CBC members Augustus Hawkins (D-CA) and Parren Mitchell voted present as "a show of compassion for the senior member of Congress who had ushered in the era of civil rights on Capitol Hill," observed *Jet* magazine. Robert Garcia (D-NY) also voted present.²⁷

In Detroit, the reaction to the censure was mixed. A Black woman told the *Michigan Chronicle* that before Diggs confessed, she "thought there was some sort of conspiracy against Blacks in politics. . . . But when someone confesses to something, what can you say"?²⁸ But the dominant opinion among Diggs's constituents was that white politicians had done more and not been severely reprimanded. Diggs brushed aside calls for him to resign.

In his appeal, Diggs's lawyers argued that the prosecution failed to distinguish between his use of the inflated salaries for his personal bills and his congressional office expenses, depriving the jury of the chance to fairly determine Diggs's guilt or innocence, maintaining that it was not clear if the jury based its convictions on the diversion of payroll funds for office expenses or for personal use. On November 4, in a 2–1 decision, a three-judge federal appeals court panel upheld Diggs's conviction. The majority ruled that an "obvious reading" of the House payroll authorization forms indicated that an employee's pay is intended for the employee and not for paying office expenses.[29] The dissenting judge agreed with Diggs's lawyers but noted that even he would have vacated only thirteen of the twenty-nine felony counts. Diggs filed another appeal.

On December 2, 1979, Diggs reaffirmed his intention to seek reelection in 1980 and publicly stated he believed his conviction would be reversed. In Detroit, Democratic politicians openly discussed running against Diggs. "It seems difficult to imagine Congressman Diggs being in the race again," Reverend Nicholas Hood III told reporters, adding he was exploring becoming a candidate.[30]

The new year did not bring good news. On January 30, 1979, the full US Court of Appeals for the District of Columbia refused to consider Diggs's conviction. He announced that he would appeal to the US Supreme Court, but observers noted the high court was unlikely to intervene. A flood of high-profile Black Detroit politicians soon announced plans to run for Diggs's congressional seat.

As late as April 1980, Diggs still maintained he would remain a candidate. But on Tuesday, May 14, 1980, Diggs held a news conference in his Capitol Hill office. Sitting behind his desk, with a trove of books and memorabilia from his many trips to Africa in the background, Diggs read "calmly and without visible emotion" from a statement. He said he was confident he would have been reelected and remained hopeful that the Supreme Court would overturn his conviction but that he had decided to retire at the end of his term and would withdraw from the primary to give potential candidates enough time to campaign. He noted that he had spent thirty years, more than half his life, in elected public office, saying, "I leave Congress with a clear conscience and with deep appreciation for the historic role I have been privileged to play for the past 26 years on behalf of the disadvantaged, both here and abroad." Diggs added that he hoped his "accomplishments . . . will not be forgotten."[31]

A few weeks later, on Saturday evening, May 31, Diggs was among the more than 1,000 largely Black attendees who crowded into a ballroom of the Washington Hilton Hotel for the third annual fundraising dinner for TransAfrica. At an emotional point during the program, Diggs was acknowledged. Wearing a dark suit, with a red, black, and green Pan-African pin in its lapel, Diggs stood to be recognized. The audience gave Diggs a standing ovation, paying homage to "Mr. Africa." Diggs stood for a few moments, smiled, and waved to the many familiar faces.[32]

It was the last official public appearance of Charles Diggs as a member of Congress.

ON MONDAY, JUNE 2, 1980, the US Supreme Court announced its refusal to hear Diggs's appeal. The next day, in a two-sentence letter to Speaker O'Neill, Diggs resigned "effective immediately."[33] Diggs told the *Michigan Chronicle*, "The past two years have been a difficult period," but he pledged "to continue to use my knowledge and experience to fight for the causes of peace, justice, and equal opportunities, both here and abroad."[34] Diggs endorsed seventy-year-old George Crockett Jr., a recently retired Detroit judge, who would go on to an easy victory.

With incarceration looming, Diggs focused on his immediate future. Diggs had been caring for his mother but now arranged for her to live with a cousin in Tennessee until he was released from prison. She would return to Washington, DC, after Diggs's release.

On Monday, July 14, Diggs appeared before Judge Gasch to plead for a reduced sentence. A despondent Diggs spent most of the thirty-minute hearing "gazing at the floor" and told the judge "I have acknowledged my guilt and wrongdoing.... I'm here to further acknowledge my misconduct."[35]

Gasch refused to reduce the sentence, but added he did not believe a long sentence would serve the public interest. Since there was no minimum sentence, Diggs could appeal to the parole commission almost immediately. The judge granted Diggs's request to serve his sentence at Maxwell Air Force Base, a minimum-security facility outside Montgomery, Alabama, and ordered him to report "sometime after July 23."[36]

ON JULY 20, Diggs attended his daughter Denise's wedding in Detroit. The occasion was happy and sad. Dozens of family members, including all of Diggs's six children, were there. Among the more than 300 guests were Dr. Alvin Loving, Diggs's high school debate coach; and Lillian Hatcher, the labor leader and state Democratic Party heavyweight who had played a key role in Diggs's first campaign for Congress.[37]

Diggs went about the wedding and reception characteristically, as if nothing were wrong. "He was there socializing. He was smiling and talking to people. It didn't faze him that day.... He didn't show it if it was," recalled Denise.[38] After the big affair, however, when he was alone with family, it all sunk in. "I remember him being over at the house crying and everything. He was ten sheets to the wind," recalled Diggs's son.[39] Decades later, Weston Diggs Jr. broke into tears as he remembered thinking to himself at the time, "I'm glad Uncle Charles (Papa Diggs) is not here because he would have ... he might have killed himself."[40]

July 24, 1980, was a sad day. Nearly forty years after reporting for duty as an officer in the segregated army, Diggs returned to Alabama to report to prison. He spent his last night of freedom at the home of a physician friend, Dr. Moses Jones, who had served with him at TAAF. The two men "stayed up half the night talking about old times," and Diggs's friends told reporters afterward that he was in "high spirits."[41] Another friend drove Diggs to the prison. Wearing a light blue suit with a sport shirt and no tie, Diggs got out of the car and greeted the waiting news reporters. Diggs carried a folder, while his friend "carried a piece of single luggage for him."[42] A *Detroit Free Press* reporter noted that Diggs "began his prison term at 8:50 a.m. Detroit time."[43]

Diggs became inmate number 07142-016E.[44]

MAXWELL AIR FORCE BASE was considered sort of a country club for felons. Diggs worked in the library, tutoring inmates in English and government and assisting a lawyer who helped other inmates; and he became editor of the prison newspaper, aptly named *Hard Times*.[45] Diggs also wrote letters to federal agencies on behalf of fellow inmates. He spent a lot of time chatting and answering questions about politics and government. "I feel like a professor of political science, given all my new colleagues' questions," Diggs wrote from prison.[46]

Diggs received a constant stream of letters and visitors (weekends and holidays only) from family and friends who kept him abreast of what was happening in Detroit and Washington, DC. He joked about constantly hearing officers announcing over the speaker system: "Diggs, come to control for your legal mail" every time a parcel arrived for him.[47] His three-year old daughter Cindy and wife, Janet, visited, and Diggs had to dissuade Detroiters from chartering a bus as so many visitors would violate the maximum number allowed.[48]

For the first time in decades, Diggs's pace slowed down. His daily routine included breakfast at 6 a.m. and taking in a couple of morning national news shows before reporting to the library from 7:30 a.m. to 3 p.m. He walked "two or three miles daily" and his blood pressure dropped.[49] Diggs also regularly attended and participated in Sunday church services held at the prison.[50]

Diggs had ample time to consider what happened to him. In early August 1980, utilizing the Freedom of Information Act, Diggs requested his FBI file.[51] Ten years later, Diggs confirmed to author Robert Massie that he had received a copy of the FBI file. Yet Diggs, as far as it can be determined, never told others what he learned from his file nor what he knew or suspected about the confidential informant who reported his payroll violations to the Justice Department.[52]

Diggs was not looking back but ahead to freedom. In September 1980, in Washington, DC, the CBC held its annual legislative weekend, and Janet Diggs accepted the CBC's "Chair Award" on behalf of her husband.[53] Congressman Crockett told the crowd he was lobbying the US Parole Commission to reduce Diggs's sentence, and in October, the commission cut Diggs's sentence to fourteen months, making him eligible for parole in September 1981.

On September 9, 1980, Wiley A. Branton, dean of Howard University Law School, who had known Diggs since 1955 when he had introduced the new congressman to the large crowd in Mound Bayou, Mississippi, wrote his friend and saluted his contributions, writing, "So many of us owe you a debt of gratitude for your many legislative and civil rights battles on behalf of so many people, not only here in America, but in Africa as well."[54] Branton also thanked Diggs for donating his congressional papers to Howard University and enclosed a check for Diggs's "commissary account."

Diggs wrote back that he was "very touched" by Branton's letter and gesture.[55] He told Branton, "The ambition to be a lawyer still prevails" and asked his advice. If he could not go directly into a law school, Diggs said he would still "want to go back to college" to earn his undergraduate degree hopefully "in the shortest period of time and with as little classroom attendance as possible."[56]

On December 12, ten days after his fifty-eighth birthday, the US Parole Commission reduced Diggs's sentence further, allowing his release on February 24, 1981, after serving seven months.[57]

He left prison to little fanfare, flying to Washington, DC, where he immediately checked into a halfway house. Diggs was expected either to go to work each day or to actively be seeking work. The *Washington Post* reported that Diggs "dodged reporters" and did not address questions.[58]

According to the *Washington Post*, "News of his homecoming drew warm responses from Washington's black political leaders . . . and several said they would help close ranks around the man they respected for his legislative ability despite his trouble in the kickback scheme."[59] Randall Robinson told a reporter he hoped Diggs was "successful in finding a job to match his expertise," adding, "If Charlie Diggs made any mistakes, he has certainly paid for those mistakes. As far as I am concerned, he is home and very much welcomed home."[60]

But home was no longer the place where he had lived so much of his public life, in the House of Representatives.

Conclusion

AFTER CONGRESS

CHARLES DIGGS JR. had no trouble finding a job while completing his time at the halfway house. As a courtesy and sign of support, the CBC hired him as a consultant for ninety days.[1] Diggs continued to maintain that he was wrongly prosecuted. "I will go to my grave continuing to profess my innocence. I considered myself a political prisoner during my incarceration," he stated.[2] Yet when asked by the *Michigan Chronicle* if he was bitter, Diggs said, "No, I'm not bitter."[3] According to family members, "He was never bitter. Perhaps frustrated and hurt but never bitter or angry. . . . He was motivated to do good things, to lead and help," writes Carla Diggs Smith.[4]

The embrace by the CBC was the kind of welcome Diggs hoped would continue, and he was immediately seen in public and proceeded as if nothing ever happened. Many expected Diggs to leverage his considerable experience and cash in by representing African interests in the United States. However, no African nation hired Diggs. In his book, *Just Permanent Interests*, Congressman William Clay blasted the leaders of African nations for turning their backs on Diggs, adding, "It is too bad that the 'prophet' of the continent could not himself 'profit' from the tens of millions of dollars he was responsible for delivering to African governments and to firms doing business in African nations."[5]

Diggs's annual pension was not affected by his conviction. Shortly after leaving the halfway house, he relocated to Prince George's County, Maryland, which would quickly become a majority-Black DC suburb. Apart from a couple of arrests for drunk driving, Diggs focused on moving forward.[6]

Diggs tried to return to the funeral profession, but in 1981, the Maryland State Board of Morticians denied his application for a funeral director's license, maintaining that Diggs's conviction violated the "good character" standard as required by state statute. Diggs then launched a two-year legal battle to reverse the decision. After a circuit court judge ruled in his favor, Diggs's application was approved.[7]

In May 1982, Janet Diggs was awarded an uncontested divorce along with custody of their five-year old daughter, Cindy. On Good Friday, April 1983, the sixty-year-old Diggs married for the fourth time, wedding Darlene Exposé, who was twenty-one years younger than he and the former companion of Congressman Adam Clayton Powell Jr.[8] People remember her as looking almost "like a movie star" and "very polished."[9] She had worked on Capitol Hill before becoming Powell's secretary shortly before Powell left Congress. She later moved to the Bahamas with Powell and was with him the last three years of his life. "The gossips can't say that I married Charlie for money," she told *Jet* magazine, adding that she "tried to show Adam that what he had done had made a difference. I intend to show Charlie that he, too, can find peace and happiness."[10] Walter Fauntroy married the couple in a small ceremony in Diggs's two-bedroom apartment, and a reception was held in a nearby community room in the same building. Simeon Booker served as Diggs's best man.

Shortly after earning his freedom, Diggs enrolled in Howard University's University without Walls program, which combined self-directed study with traditional classroom learning and allowed students to earn college credits for relevant work experience. A faculty adviser, political scientist Russell Adams, worked closely with Diggs on a draft of a seventy-page final paper on Africa.[11] Before submitting the paper, Diggs promised Adams he would make changes before turning it in. But the next time Adams saw Diggs was in a *Washington Post* photograph with a caption noting he was graduating from Howard. Decades later, Adams explained that Diggs went to James E. Cheeks, the president of Howard University, and told him, "He's done."[12] Diggs never made the corrections and changes to his final paper. On May 14, 1983, at age sixty, Diggs finally received his degree in political science.

Diggs and Darlene purchased a townhome in Hill Crest Heights in Prince George's County, adjacent to heavily Black Southeast Washington, DC, in a neighborhood composed of professionals, government workers, and low-income service workers. Diggs soon became the vice president of Hill Crest Heights Community Association and "laid the groundwork" for the nearly dormant group's revitalization.[13] Jesse Jackson's 1984 run for the Democratic nomination for president galvanized Diggs and many other Black leaders in the county to focus on Black voter registration and political mobilization.[14]

In May 1985, Mayme Diggs, Charley's eighty-seven-year-old mother, died in Washington, DC. Diggs traveled back to Detroit to bury her. Mayor Coleman Young and Damon Keith, by then a judge of the US Sixth Circuit Court of Appeals, spoke at the funeral. Years later Keith remembered, "The death of Charley's mother was devastating to him. I can just see Charley going up to that casket and crying," says Keith.[15]

After some encouragement from Mayor Coleman Young, Diggs decided to throw his hat in the ring for an open seat on the Wayne County Board of Commissioners. In summer 1987, he returned to Detroit to campaign for the vacant position representing Detroit's East Side. On Election Day, Diggs lost his first election since 1953.[16] For a time, Diggs turned his back on Detroit and would not return for several years.

IN 1986, DIGGS JOINED the Ebenezer African Methodist Episcopal Church, a fast growing, Black middle class, activist church in Prince George's County. The church's pastor, Reverend Grainger Browning, was a close friend and ally of Jesse Jackson. "We became one of the churches that people look to for community activism and leadership," said Pastor Browning.[17]

For the most part, Diggs's religious life had been intertwined with the funeral home business. However, after he left Congress, family members noticed that Diggs "became more of a spiritual person."[18] He attended Sunday service regularly, recalled Reverend Browning. Although Diggs seldom displayed his emotions, Reverend Browning sensed that Diggs's life work in politics "was anchored in faith," adding, "He could not have done what he did without having a strong faith in God."[19]

Joining Ebenezer, however, did not help Diggs in the mortuary business. With no capital and no partners, Diggs was unable to build a viable business in Prince George's County. While Diggs obtained a Maryland funeral director's license, it is not clear that he ever received a license to be a mortician, to handle a body in preparation for a funeral.

Meanwhile, Diggs's activism in Prince George's County politics continued. He became "intimately involved" in the county's branch of the NAACP, serving on the local board of directors and spending time "telephoning friends" encouraging them to join.[20] In 1990 he ran unsuccessfully for a seat in the Maryland House of Delegates.[21]

DIGGS INCREASINGLY BEGAN to view himself as an elder statesman. After Albert Wynn, a Black Democrat, won election to the US House from Prince George's County in 1994, Diggs encouraged him to lobby Democratic leaders for an assignment on the Armed Services Committee, writing Wynn "a very detailed letter" explaining the value of such an assignment.[22] Ronald Dellums, the leading anti-apartheid voice in Congress after Diggs's resignation, often heard from Diggs. In 1993, when Dellums became chair of the Armed Services Committee, Diggs called to congratulate him. "He was super proud of me," Dellums recalled.[23]

Diggs followed the House of Representatives on C-SPAN, continued to pay attention to what was happening in the country and around the world, and communicated with members of Congress, especially CBC members. But things were different now; he was no longer part of the club. "The tragic reality is way too often... people forget very quickly. When you're off the stage you're out of mind. Charley Diggs was off the stage," Dellums explained.[24] "One of the hardest things for people who've been in Congress to accept is that the moment you leave Congress, no matter what the circumstance, you lose all that juice," Wynn offered.[25]

Diggs remained most interested in what was happening with US policy in South Africa. By 1990, TransAfrica, led by a determined and ambitious Randall Robinson, had become the most influential American organization on Africa policy. Beginning in the fall of 1984, Robinson had organized a series of high-profile demonstrations and civil disobedience actions at the South African embassy. Every day a big-city mayor, a member of Congress, or someone else newsworthy would get arrested at the South African embassy. The protests soon spread to Los Angeles, Boston, New York City, and other parts of the country. Thousands were arrested. In 1986, the Free South Africa Movement, as it became known, eventually led Congress to pass comprehensive sanctions against South Africa. Other nations joined in, soon bringing an end to apartheid.

On February 11, 1990, came the moment for which Diggs had long helped fight for. After twenty-seven years of imprisonment, Nelson Mandela walked out of the prison on Robben Island. Four months later, Mandela toured the United States to thank the nation and raise funds for the freedom struggle. On June 26, 1990, Diggs was on the floor of the US House of Representatives to hear Mandela's historic address to a joint session of Congress. When Mandela completed his speech, Diggs positioned himself at the rear of the chamber. As Mandela drew near, Diggs stretched out his right hand. A photographer captured the two leaders shaking hands.

In a private meeting with members of the CBC (a meeting Diggs likely attended), Mandela reportedly attributed his release from prison and the tremendous economic pressure on South Africa to the "dedication and steadfastness" of the CBC.[26] Four years later, in April 1994, millions of Black South Africans cast their votes for the first time in a national election. Apartheid was dead. Nelson Mandela was elected President of South Africa. Diggs, now recovered from a mild stroke he had suffered two years earlier and that for a time had left him unable to speak, had to feel a sense of personal accomplishment.

TransAfrica and Randall Robinson were receiving a measure of media attention as well, not only for the role they played in South Africa but also because in April 1994, Robinson went on what became a twenty-seven-day hunger strike to protest the Clinton administration's policy toward Haiti, an act covered extensively by national newspapers. Diggs "maintained periodic contact" with "Randy," as Diggs called him, because of their shared interest in Africa.[27] During the hunger strike, Diggs had even gone to TransAfrica's headquarters "to wish him well."[28] There remained a significant measure of personal and professional respect between the two men. Years later, in his memoir, Robinson would correctly write about Diggs that he "cared about people—too much and too many."[29]

The November 1994 elections marked a seismic shift in American politics. Republicans won a majority in the House of Representatives for the first time since 1954, and they controlled the Senate. In January 1995, Newt Gingrich, the Georgia Republican who had targeted Diggs in 1979 and who in 1989 destroyed the career of Speaker Jim Wright, was elected Speaker of the House.

When Diggs learned that the Republicans planned to abolish the House District of Columbia Committee, Diggs placed his "chairman's portrait," the same one at the heart of the origin of the payroll violation, in the custody of the Washington, DC, government.[30] On July 11, 1995, the DC City Council held a ceremony to unveil the portrait. Mayor Marion Barry joined several current and former DC council members in acknowledging Diggs's role in restoring home rule to the District. Diggs said he hoped his portrait would serve as a reminder that "home-rule did not just fall out of the sky."[31]

A few months later, on September 11, 1995, Diggs was among the several founding members of the CBC honored at a luncheon in Washington at the CBC's twenty-fifth annual legislative weekend. "People all over the world owe you for what you did and the vision you had some 25 years ago," Louisiana Congressman William Jefferson told Diggs.[32]

On September 27, 1995, the University of the District Columbia celebrated its First Annual Opening Convocation, and Diggs was honored as the "Father of UDC." Diggs viewed his role as the author of the 1974 legislation that established the university with great pride. He considered it one of his most important legislative contributions. Diggs, dressed in a cap and gown and "spoke with eloquence and emotion."[33] "What are you going to do to emulate those of us who made accomplishments in the twentieth century?" he asked. As Diggs concluded his remarks, "The entire student body and faculty rose in an ovation that sent chills down everyone's spine. The applause was sustained and heartwarming."[34]

The stroke a few years earlier had slowed Diggs down. His hair was thin and gray, as were his trademark sideburns. Yet Diggs appeared content. Carolyn DuBose, who stayed in touch with Diggs, recalled that Diggs "lived in a climate of solitude." If he now "missed the comings and goings on Capitol Hill," she wrote, "he did not mention it."[35] As Diggs once told a reporter, "When I drive by [the Capitol Building] or see it on TV it's almost like an old dream. It's part of my experience, but I don't sit around crying about it."[36]

In the summer of 1996, Diggs returned to Detroit to help his son, thirty-two-year-old Douglass, run for Congress in the Democratic primary. He was one of six candidates vying against embattled Congresswoman Barbara-Rose Collins. But the power of the Diggs's name had waned. Carolyn Cheeks Kilpatrick, a popular state legislator, won the primary and general election.

On June 27, 1997, Diggs spoke at the retirement party of Johnson Publishing Company photographer Maurice Sorrell, a pioneering Black photojournalist. The event drew a crowd of over 150 politicians and leaders, including President Bill Clinton, Vice President Al Gore, Mayor Marion Barry, and several other civil rights leaders.[37] Although Diggs had been out of office for more than seventeen years, he was greeted like a celebrity. It was a full-circle moment for Diggs. Among the other guests were *Jet* magazine reporter Simeon Booker and photographer Ernest C. Withers. Diggs had met both men more than forty years earlier in Mound Bayou, Mississippi, and at the trial of the two white men who murdered Emmett Till.

Diggs was now at a different stage in life. He looked forward to spending more time with his thirteen grandchildren, as he did one weekend in August 1998 when Denise and her young children came to visit. The former congressman turned grandfather was in a great mood and visited a nearby amusement park with his grandchildren. On Monday, August 24, 1998, after breakfast, Denise and the family headed back to Michigan. Diggs drove his car ahead of Denise to direct her to the freeway entrance, and as she turned off, he blew the horn and waved goodbye.[38]

Once back home, Diggs and Darlene talked about the weekend. Darlene retreated to the kitchen to prepare dinner. Suddenly, she heard a loud sound from the bathroom. Darlene ran to the bathroom and found Diggs lying on the floor. He had suffered another stroke. Hours later, he died at Greater Southeast Community Hospital in Washington, DC.

Charles C. Diggs Jr. was seventy-five years old.

DIGGS'S DEATH NOTICE appeared in newspapers around the country. Although the headline for Diggs's obituary in the *New York Times* read, "Charles Diggs, 75, Congressman Censured over Kickbacks," the newspaper also emphasized Diggs's political legacy and recounted his efforts to address racial discrimination and his leadership in US-Africa policy.[39] The Associated Press, by contrast, characterized Diggs as a once powerful Black official who was forced to resign because of a payroll kickback scheme, making his other accomplishments seem like an afterthought.[40]

On Tuesday, September 1, 1998, more than 600 people, including several members of the CBC, turned out to the Ebenezer AME Church to pay tribute to Congressman Diggs.[41] During the service, more than a dozen former colleagues and acquaintances honored his memory.[42] Congressman Louis Stokes spoke on behalf of the CBC. Marion Barry told the church that Diggs "spent a lot of time trying to free D.C." Professor Ronald Walters described Diggs's leadership in Africa and in the formation of TransAfrica. Dorothy Height, the president of the National Council of Negro Women, recounted how Diggs hired and promoted Black women into positions of authority. Andrew Young told the mourners that Diggs's role was "to affect change for poor people within the system" by challenging the status quo. William Broadwater, a past president of the East Coast Chapter of Tuskegee Airmen, Inc., reminded the audience that Diggs was part of the "greatest generation" in America's segregated military.[43]

Reverend Grainger Browning delivered the eulogy titled "Can You Digg It?" drawn from Genesis 26, the story of how Isaac discovered the wells that had been dug by his father, Abraham.[44] Reverend Browning connected Diggs's work in Washington and Africa with the "wells dug," or the legacy built, by his pioneering father, Papa Diggs. Browning proclaimed that Diggs's contributions were such that his "body should have been laid in state at the US Capitol. Governments should have shut down when this man died."[45]

On Thursday, September 3, Detroiters celebrated the life of one of the city's most consequential native sons. Clergy, politicians, neighbors, former staff members from Diggs's congressional office and the former House of Diggs crowded into Hartford Memorial Baptist Church.[46] Diggs's casket was covered with the American flag. Before the service started, Wayne County sheriff deputies stood at attention at each end of the casket until everyone was seated before marching out of the church in silence.[47] The service was one that Diggs would have approved of.

Darlene and all three of Diggs's ex-wives entered the church together. According to Diggs's close friend, Damon Keith, Douglass Diggs, the child whose professional life and career most paralleled his father's, "was just torn apart" over his father's death.[48] Damon Keith spoke about his long friendship with Diggs and his family and told the crowd he would not be a federal judge had it not been for the persistent lobbying and advocacy of his friend. Congressman John Conyers noted that Diggs had arrived in Washington ten years before he had, and he described how Diggs had shown him how to negotiate the politics on Capitol Hill. "Congressman Diggs was not afraid to speak the truth," said Conyers. "His was a resounding voice for millions of African Americans whose words were muted and whose dreams were bruised by cruel forces of discrimination and intimidation."[49]

At the end of the service, a soloist sang "When We All Get to Heaven." Then Charles C. Diggs Jr. took the same journey he and his family had helped so many make before him and was buried next to his father, Papa Diggs, and his mother Mayme, in Detroit Memorial Park, the same cemetery his father founded so many years before to protest racial discrimination.

His life and work had taken him from Detroit to Washington DC, Issaquena, and Mound Bayou, to Africa, the halls of Congress, and to the penitentiary. He had been born into a world where Black people in America and in Africa had been oppressed, and he had spent much of his life fighting for freedom.

Now, at last and forevermore, he was free, and back home. His gravestone reads,

CHARLES COLES
DIGGS JR.
12-2-22—8-24-98
SON   HUSBAND
FATHER   GRANDFATHER
MORTICIAN
STATE SENATOR
CONGRESSMAN
NATIONAL
AND
INTERNATIONAL LEADER

Epilogue

UP UNTIL THE mid-twentieth century, most Black Americans lacked the right to vote, attend schools of their choice, or exercise basic civil liberties. Then, the civil rights movement transformed America. The rise of strong Black leaders who displayed great courage in confronting injustice and righting past wrongs was a major reason for the movement's success. The civil rights–era leaders—Martin Luther King Jr., A. Phillip Randolph, Fannie Lou Hamer, Malcom X, Stokely Carmichael, Whitney Young, Bayard Rustin, Medgar Evers, Ella Baker, Roy Wilkins, and Jesse Jackson—have been the focus of scholarly attention and their contributions never forgotten.

As detailed in this book, Charles Coles Diggs Jr. played a consequential and often overlooked role in America's civil rights movement from the early 1950s until he resigned from Congress in 1980. Most people familiar with Congress during this period think of Adam Clayton Powell as the leading Black congressman. Diggs was overshadowed by Powell, but Diggs accomplished far more.

Beginning in 1955, when Diggs risked his life traveling to Mississippi to "observe" the five-day trial of the two white men who murdered Emmett Till, Diggs was an out-front participant in the American civil rights movement. Diggs's roots reached back to evangelical ancestral service in Africa, religious and educational leadership in Mississippi, and to his father, who was himself a civil rights and Black political and business pioneer in Detroit.

Diggs was the personification of the shift in Black politics from protest to elections. He employed a politics of strategic moderation and sought to recruit supporters across the political spectrum with the goal of helping Black Americans achieve inclusive political incorporation into the Democratic Party. He worked within the system, and through his savvy manipulation of the congressional committee system and the seniority system, he endeavored to make the system work—sometimes slowly and often awkwardly—to advance the cause of civil rights.

Diggs's efforts manifested themselves in an astonishing number of ways, starting with his savvy advocacy for equality in air transportation, in the military, in voting rights, and in home rule for the District of Columbia. Then there was his shrewd use of the authority of his office to forge alliances within the civil rights community and to empower his colleagues through the formation of the Congressional Black Caucus and TransAfrica; and he inspired others to elected office through his role as a core leader of the 1972 National Black Political Convention. Diggs also spearheaded American support of various African liberation movements and in the fight against apartheid.

Throughout his congressional career, Diggs felt a responsibility not only to represent his Detroit district but to also represent Black Americans across the country, and to tie the civil rights movement in America to the larger battle for civil rights and social justice for all people, everywhere. As Representative Ronald Dellums explained, "What Charles Diggs was really saying was we're not only citizens of the United States. We're citizens of the world . . . and he went out there and showed the way."[1]

Diggs was, at his core, a coalition builder. He got along with others. "All over the Hill I have a network of friends in the system," Diggs told an interviewer in 1972.[2] Congressman William Clay remembered that Diggs "was well respected across the board, whites and Blacks."[3] According to Congressman Louis Stokes, it was Diggs's "demeanor, his manner. . . . Over the years he was there he had built a lot of respect. I mean in his own quiet way. . . . They respected him highly," Stokes emphasized.[4]

Diggs was also a serious and policy-oriented legislator and a stunningly effective warrior for social justice for Black people everywhere and for freedom. "When he took a position, it was a strong position. He didn't waver. . . . And he wasn't a guy that was very noisy. He was very quiet in his leadership role," remembered Stokes.[5] "By virtue of his longevity in Congress, he was the most influential and [he] used it," John Conyers offered.[6] Sharon Pratt Kelly, who in 1990 became the first Black woman elected mayor of Washington, DC, remembered Diggs as a "sophisticated man" who "understood power in the truest sense of the word. It's one thing to talk about it, or even be a great orator about it, [however it] is important to be able to really know what levers are there and how to manipulate those levers to the advantage of a community," she explained.[7] Goler Teal Butcher, who worked closely with Diggs on Africa policy, said of Diggs, "The man was a prince among men with respect to principles of carrying out his job."[8] Congressman Stokes concluded that Diggs was "probably one of the most effective legislators that served."[9]

Diggs's political career ended sadly when he resigned from office in 1980. Perhaps, if not for the personal failures and political circumstances that resulted in his resignation, the name of Charles Diggs Jr. would also be far better known today. But his errors of judgment and mistakes primarily impacted his personal legacy. They do not diminish his larger contributions to history.

Diggs's story is that of a man who loved his country and who wanted it to live up to its creed of equality; he was an imperfect man who nevertheless responded to a higher calling to serve and enabled genuine and lasting changes on American life. When Diggs's work in the civil rights movement is considered alongside his pioneering accomplishments in Congress, few other Black civil rights leaders of his time, and perhaps no other Black member of Congress, can match either the scope of his achievements or the lasting, tangible impact of his life's work upon the American people.

Acknowledgments

WRITING MY FIRST BIOGRAPHY about an unsung Black civil rights hero and pioneering congressman was a fascinating journey, especially for a political scientist who writes about politics and public policy in US cities. After working on this book for nearly a decade, I am grateful to many people.

My wife, Ramona L. Burton, deserves special acknowledgment. Ramona is a natural encourager. When I was pondering whether to write a biography of Charles C. Diggs Jr., Ramona's encouragement helped solidify my decision to plunge ahead. She assured me that I had the skills to write a political biography and supported me throughout the process. Ramona is also a superbly trained political scientist. She read the manuscript closely, identified sections requiring clarity, and provided feedback. Ramona was patient when I spent too much time in my basement study working on the book. She jokingly told friends, "Congressman Diggs lives in our basement!" Whenever I got stressed, Ramona was always there to ease my anxiety and to reassure me.

I thank the Diggs family. All of Diggs's six children participated in this study. They granted me interviews, took my telephone calls, answered text messages, and responded to email queries about their father. Charles C. Diggs III, Denise Diggs-Taylor, Alexis Diggs-Robinson, and Carla Diggs-Smith shared letters, telegrams, and photographs from their personal papers. Weston Diggs Jr. and Weston Diggs III were generous with their time and shared family photographs, documents, and valuable insights about their famous cousin. Mrs. Juanita R. Diggs, Diggs's first wife, was a source of valuable information. In addition to a formal oral history interview, we had several conversations over the telephone. A few times she called to remind me that she was over ninety years old and wondered when the book would be published. I am also appreciative of Meghan Wilson, a former Brown University PhD student and Detroit native, who introduced me to the Diggs family.

The book benefited from chapter-by-chapter critiques, suggestions, and feedback from three retired political scientists, all of whom have substantive knowledge of Black politics. Russell Adams, a former chair of Howard University's Afro-American Studies Department, was also Diggs's faculty adviser when he earned his undergraduate degree after resigning from Congress.

Russ was exceedingly generous in providing copious comments based on his broad knowledge of Black studies and his personal interactions with Diggs. Wilbur C. Rich, a longtime friend and mentor of mine, who wrote a pioneering biography of Detroit's mayor Coleman A. Young, provided helpful comments and editorial suggestions on each chapter. Robert C. Smith, another friend and mentor, was one of the nation's leading authorities on Black politics until his death in 2023. Given his well-known, encyclopedic knowledge of Black politics, I was always encouraged after Robert read a chapter and commented that what he read was revelatory. Russ, Wilbur, and Robert challenged and supported me. I appreciate them for giving so much of their time.

Several colleagues read and provided feedback on individual chapters, including Andrew James Deroche, Michael K. Fauntroy, Minion K. C. Morrison, Elsie Scott, Ron Stodghill, Clarence N. Stone, Kathleen Stone and Ronald Williams.

Among my colleagues at Brown University, Katherine Tate, an expert on Black Americans in Congress, read the manuscript and provided suggestions and ideas for improving it. Wendy Schiller pointed me to recent books and articles on Congress and legislative behavior. Richard Arenberg, who came to Brown University after decades as a senior staff member in the US Senate, helped me make sense of the rules and norms of Congress. James Morone and Melvin Rogers offered advice and insight along the way. Karen Ball provided critical administrative and institutional support for this book.

Darrell M. West, a former Brown University colleague, now at the Brookings Institution, provided helpful suggestions. Gretchen Bauer at the University of Delaware directed me to important studies on US-Africa policy. Robert Kinloch Massie shared transcripts of the oral history interviews he conducted (including one with Diggs) more than thirty years ago.

Paul Butler, Karra McCray Gibson, Christopher Meyers, and Michelle Togbe, Brown University students, helped compile and analyze election returns, tracked down newspaper articles, and assisted in other ways.

I benefited from the assistance of Karen A. Bouchard, Carina Cournoyer, Bart Hollingsworth, Daniel O'Mahony, Kimberly Silva, and Holly Snyder, all librarians at the John D. Rockefeller Library at Brown University.

I also relied on many archivists. I especially appreciate JoEllen El-Bashir, Richard Jenkins, Ida Jones, and Sonja Woods at the Moorland Spingarn Research Center at Howard University who helped me access the Diggs Papers. Christopher Anglim, at the University of the District of Columbia, pointed me to documents related to home rule for Washington, DC. Archivists at the Eisenhower, Kennedy, Johnson, Nixon, Ford, and Carter presidential libraries, the University of Oklahoma, the University of West Georgia, George Washington University, the Bentley Historical Library at the University Michigan, the

Michigan State Archives, and the Burton Historical Collection at the Detroit Public Library also assisted in the completion of this book.

I appreciate the people I interviewed for this book. Almost everyone I contacted was happy to participate. I will always remember Congressman Charles Rangel remarking, "I am glad you are doing this. Charley deserves it." I am grateful to Bonnie Gallagher, a member of Diggs's congressional staff. Bonnie provided an informative oral history, answered my follow-up calls and emails, and shared her personal papers, including letters Diggs wrote to her from prison.

My work on this book would not have been possible without the generous financial support for research and travel from Brown University, my institutional home for the last twenty-five years. I am grateful to former university president Ruth J. Simmons for appointing me the inaugural Frederick Lippitt Professor of Public Policy and to the Lippitt family for their generous gift to the university.

Leah Spiro, my literary agent, immediately saw value and inspiration in Diggs's story and worked to place my book with the right publisher. Leah used her wide journalistic skills and network in numerous ways to improve my book. At a critical juncture she read the manuscript and provided important editorial advice. Leah is a consummate professional and a joy to work with. Leah connected me with Glenn Stout, a leading author, editor, and editorial consultant. Glenn's keen eye and skillful writing techniques helped shape a lengthy first draft into a publishable manuscript and, along the way, taught me a lot about writing. I thoroughly enjoyed working with Glenn.

I thank Brandon Proia for acquiring the book for the University of North Carolina Press. Brandon's positive reaction to my book proposal convinced me that my book found the right home. I appreciate Dawn Durante and the staff at UNC Press for guiding the manuscript to publication. I acknowledge the helpful comments and suggestions of the anonymous evaluators who reviewed the manuscript.

I am grateful to Dorothy Cochrane and Robert van der Linden for inviting me to participate in the Smithsonian Institution Air and Space Museum's Aviation Adventures Lecture Series. Andra Gillespie, the director of Emory University's James Weldon Johnson Institute on Race and Difference, and John Aldrich of Duke University's Department of Political Science were wonderful hosts and gave me a chance to discuss my research.

This book has deep intellectual roots that reach back to my undergraduate training at Savannah State College (now university), where Hanes Walton Jr. introduced me to political science and Black politics. Professor Walton spent twenty-five years at Savannah State, from 1967 to 1992, before he moved to the University of Michigan. He published his pioneering, first-in-the-field textbook, *Black Politics: A Theoretical and Structural Analysis*, and his groundbreaking critique of the behavioral approach in political science, *Invisible Politics*, while at Savannah State. We were fortunate to have Walton at our small Black college. He was arguably one of the greatest political scientists of his generation. I had a close mentor-protégé relationship with him. He remained my mentor and friend until his untimely death in 2013. I was humbled and honored when the American Political Science Association awarded me the 2019 Hanes Walton Jr. Career Award. Much of what I have accomplished as a political scientist I owe to Hanes Walton Jr.

At Savannah State, Annette Brock, Thomas Byers, Marilyn Stewart-Gaulden, Otis S. Johnson, Isaiah McIver, Luetta C. Milledge, John Simpson, and Steven R. Smith were also early professional role models. Nothing in my career has been more rewarding than when I delivered the commencement address to the 2018 graduating class of Savannah State. It was a full-circle moment. I will always appreciate Savannah State and what it did to shape my life.

In graduate school at Atlanta University (now Clark Atlanta), Mack H. Jones introduced me to the epistemological foundations of political science, and William H. Boone and Robert A. Holmes taught me a lot about legislative politics. At the University of Maryland, I benefitted from seminars on the US Congress taught by Roger H. Davidson and Eric M. Uslaner. I owe a large debt to Clarence N. Stone, who guided me through Maryland's PhD program. Clarence also provided helpful comments and sage advice on this book.

I acknowledge support from the Biographers International Organization's (BIO) and thank its leadership for awarding me its 2022 Frances "Frank" Rollin Fellowship. I benefited from the camaraderie of BIO members. I am grateful to Kate Clifford Larson, Kerri K. Greenidge, James "Jamie" McGrath Morris, Steve Paul, Tamara Payne, Kathleen Stone, Elizabeth Taylor, Eric K. Washington, Sonja Willams, and other BIO members for welcoming me into the art and craft of biography.

I am thankful for family and friends who listened to my stories about Diggs and who showed a keen interest in the book, among them David Blanding, Wendell Burns, Eleanor Burton, Howard Burton, Dudley and Linda Bynoe, Jonathan Collins, Joseph and Barbara Faw, Curtis "Koolie" Feggins, Jerald Andrew Jeffrey, Valerie C. Johnson, Joseph McIntosh, Domingo Morel, Ravi Perry, Doug Powell, Tony Riley, Jeffrey Rose, Hilary Silver, Donald Williams, Michael Williams, and Barry Wright.

I thank all our friends at Ebenezer Baptist Church, especially Reverend Carl H. Balark Jr. and the teachers and "scholars" in the "Adult A" Sunday School class for showing interest in my work: Mary Blackwell, Carol Brown, Joanne Buckmire, Brenda Carr, Henry and Shelia Coleman, Irene Colin, Judith Covington, Vertie Gay, Ava Gist, Mable Howard, Freda Hughes, Elaine Isom,

Yvonne Jarrett, Gibson Karngar, Eugene Lundsford, Barbara Montague-Davis, Benjamin and Josie McClary, Cassandra Parson, Aldwyn Reid, Dottie Silva, Diane Straker, Lynn Strodder, Gladys Thomas, Conway Toliver, Rhea Turner, and Ethel Williams.

As I completed this book, my family experienced deep loss. My brother, Robert, died in July 2023. Robert enjoyed calling me "Doctor." Perhaps heartbroken, my mother, Delores B. Orr, passed away unexpectedly in December 2023. "Mama" was a caring and loving mother. She shaped and influenced me in many positive ways. I miss them both. My father, Robert Lee Orr, would have been proud to know I authored a biography of a consequential Black leader. My sister, Rhonda Gale Orr, told me several times she could not wait to read about Diggs. I appreciate her love and support.

Ramona was not the only person at home who endured the long slog it took me to complete this book. Our daughter, Willia, was in middle school when I started my research for this book. I always looked forward to putting Diggs aside to watch Willia play basketball or softball and display her talents in dance and other performances. Now in college, Willia has a better understanding and appreciation for why "Pop" spent so much time in the basement. I could not have completed this biography without the love and support of Ramona and Willia. For all this and more, it is to them that I dedicate this book.

Notes

NOTE ON SOURCES

In writing this biography, I have relied on numerous primary and secondary sources. The Charles C. Diggs Jr. Papers and the Charles C. Diggs Jr. South Africa Papers, archived at Howard University's Moorland-Spingarn Research Center, are the largest repositories of information about Diggs. The collection comprises more than 750 boxes (approximately 781 cubic feet of materials) and includes correspondence, speeches, constituent inquiries, personal, family and business papers for the House of Diggs Funeral Home and Diggs Enterprises.

Diggs was a prolific writer of letters, telegrams, and memoranda to US presidents, cabinet secretaries, and agency heads. I gathered documents from the presidential libraries of every president who served over the years when Diggs was a member of Congress—Eisenhower, Kennedy, Johnson, Nixon, Ford, and Carter. I also accessed documents of multiple politicians and national leaders, including the papers of Speaker Carl Albert at the University of Oklahoma and Speaker Newt Gingrich at the University of West Georgia (Gingrich's papers are now at Tulane University). The Martin Luther King Jr. Papers, published by the University of California Press, provide a revealing view of the relationship between Diggs and Dr. King. Additional materials on Diggs's congressional career are in the National Association for the Advancement of Colored People (NAACP) Papers (available through ProQuest). The National Archives in College Park, Maryland, contain numerous documents about Diggs's effort to address racial discrimination in the US military. Several archives in Michigan, including the Bentley Historical Library at the University of Michigan, the Michigan State Archives, and the Detroit Public Library contain valuable documents pertaining to Diggs's life and work in Detroit. In addition, this book is informed by letters and other correspondences from the personal papers of Diggs's family members.

The book draws on more than thirty oral history interviews I conducted with Diggs's family members, friends, and professional acquaintances as well as with former members of Congress and staffers who worked with Diggs on Capitol Hill. These interviews were complemented by oral histories conducted by others, including interviews with Congressman Diggs.

The biography benefited from a wealth of information from US government documents. I was able to reconstruct passage of the home-rule legislation for Washington, DC, in part from background information, members' letters, and correspondence published as a report of the US House District of Columbia Committee. Also, especially useful were several reports of committee hearings and study missions of the US House Foreign Affairs Committee and its Subcommittee on Africa. The reconstruction of the events surrounding Diggs's indictment and conviction relied in part on the 1,200-page transcript of his 1978 federal trial that was published as a report of the US House Committee on Standards of Official Conduct.

Through the Freedom of Information of Act, I obtained Diggs's FBI file (no. 1407075-001), which dates from 1954 through 1980. There are six components to the file: (1) an early probe into whether Diggs had a relationship with the Communist Party; (2) newspaper clippings and correspondence from citizens about Diggs's speeches and activities in the South; (3) death threats; (4) an extortion attempt; (5) someone impersonating Diggs; and (6) Diggs's indictment and conviction. The FBI file about the US Justice Department's investigation into Diggs's payroll violations is the most substantial.

Diggs was widely covered in the national press. Contemporary accounts from local and national newspapers illuminate Diggs's career in Detroit and on Capitol Hill. Such accounts were gleaned literally from hundreds of different newspapers, many accessed through Newspapers.com and ProQuest. Finally, Diggs's remarkable contributions are scattered in the pages of dozens of books and other secondary sources covering twentieth-century Black American politics and history and US-Africa policy. These sources are listed below.

ABBREVIATIONS

BAA	*Baltimore Afro-American*
BGP	Bonnie Gallagher Papers, personal papers (in the author's possession)
CCDP	Charles C. Diggs Jr. Papers, Moorland-Spingarn Research Center, Howard University, Washington, DC
CCDSAP	Charles C. Diggs Jr. South African Papers, Moorland-Spingarn Research Center, Howard University, Washington, DC
CD	*Chicago Defender*
CR	*Congressional Record*
DDTP	Denise Diggs-Taylor Papers, personal papers (in the author's possession)
DFP	*Detroit (MI) Free Press*
DN	*Detroit (MI) News*
LBJL	Lyndon B. Johnson Presidential Library, Austin, TX
MC	*Michigan Chronicle*
NAACP Papers	NAACP Papers, Library of Congress, Washington, DC (ProQuest)
NACPM	National Archives, College Park, MD
NYT	*New York Times*
PC	*Pittsburgh Courier*
RMNL	Richard M. Nixon Presidential Library, Yorba Linda, CA
WHCF	White House Central File (located in various presidential libraries)
WP	*Washington Post*

PROLOGUE

1. Diggs spelled "Charley" with an "-ey" instead of the more common "-ie."
2. Mary Russell, "House Votes to Censure Rep. Diggs," *WP*, August 1, 1979.

3. *CR*, July 31, 1979, 21592.
4. William J. Mitchell, "Diggs Quietly Accepts Censure," *DFP*, August 1, 1979.
5. Quoted in James H. Cleaver, "Diggs Faces His Biggest Obstacle," *Los Angeles Sentinel*, July 5, 1979.
6. Mary Russell, "House Votes to Censure Rep. Diggs," *WP*, August 1, 1979.
7. *CR*, July 31, 1979, 21592.
8. On Walton's contribution to American political science, see Orr, "Hanes Walton, Jr."; and R. C. Smith, *Hanes Walton*. In 2012, the American Political Science Association (APSA) established the "Hanes Walton, Jr. Career Award," which is given to a political scientist "whose lifetime of distinguished scholarship has made significant contributions to our understanding of racial and ethnic politics and illuminates the conditions under which diversity and intergroup tolerance thrive in democratic societies." APSA, "Hanes Walton, Jr. Career Award," accessed December 9, 2024, https://apsanet.org/programs/apsa-awards/hanes-walton-jr-award.

INTRODUCTION

1. "Mr. Diggs Goes to Congress," *Ebony* 10 (April 1955): 104–9.
2. Wilson, *Negro Politics*; Walton, *Invisible Politics*, 231–68.
3. Browning, Marshall, and Tabb, *Protest Is Not Enough*; Haynie, *African American Legislators*; Orr, "Black Political Incorporation"; R. C. Smith, *We Have No Leaders*; Tate, *Concordance*.
4. Aldrich, *Why Parties?*
5. Aldrich, *Why Parties?*, 3–61.
6. Manning, *William L. Dawson*.
7. Walton, *Black Politics*, 209–11.
8. Manning, *William L. Dawson*, 120.
9. Manning, *William L. Dawson*, 140–59.
10. Pinderhughes, *Race and Ethnicity in Chicago*; Grimshaw, *Bitter Fruit*; Cohen and Taylor, *American Pharaoh*.
11. Manning, *William L. Dawson*, 136–37, 151–53.
12. Manning, *William L. Dawson*, 138.
13. Manning, *William L. Dawson*, 125.
14. Manning, *William L. Dawson*, 163.
15. Hamilton, *Adam Clayton Powell*; Haygood, *King of the Cats*.
16. Quoted in Haygood, *King of the Cats*, 269.
17. Hamilton, *Adam Clayton Powell*, 182.
18. Hamilton, *Adam Clayton Powell*, 483.
19. Hamilton, *Adam Clayton Powell*, 360.
20. Stone, *Black Political Power in America*, 190.
21. Hamilton, *Adam Clayton Powell*, 173.
22. Haygood, *King of the Cats*, 134. Powell's amendment eventually became Title VI of the Civil Rights Act of 1964, which prohibits discrimination based on race, color, or national origin in programs that receive federal funding.
23. Quoted in DuBose, *Untold Story*, 35.
24. Quoted in Fenno, *Congressmen in Committees*, 131.
25. Hamilton, *Adam Clayton Powell*, 357.

26. Quoted in Wilson, "Flamboyant Mr. Powell," 32.
27. Hamilton, *Adam Clayton Powell*, 483.
28. Hamilton, *Adam Clayton Powell*, 380–83.
29. Hamilton, *Adam Clayton Powell*, 480.
30. Wilson, "Two Negro Politicians."
31. Fenno, *Home Style*; Bernhard and Sulkin, *Legislative Style*; Volden and Wiseman, *Legislative Effectiveness in the United States*.
32. Thomas, *Life for Us*, 265–70.
33. Dillard, *Faith in the City*, 71–72.
34. Meier and Rudwick, *Black Detroit and the Rise of the UAW*.
35. Poinsett, *Walking with Presidents*, 11–36.
36. Meier and Rudwick, *Black Detroit and the Rise of the UAW*, 206.
37. Noer, *Soapy*, 63.
38. Noer, *Soapy*, 83–126.
39. Noer, *Soapy*, 147.
40. Thompson, *Whose Detroit?*, 48–70; Dillard, *Faith in the City*, 210–20.
41. Jack Casey, "'Elect 3' Seeks Congress Seats for Negro Trio," *DFP*, July 10, 1960.
42. Charles C. Diggs Jr. to Charles C. Diggs Sr., June 29, 1960, box 49, CCDP (emphasis in the original).
43. Diggs Jr. to Diggs Sr., June 29, 1960.
44. Nadine Brown, "Fight against Diggs Drive for 3 Negroes in U.S. Congress Fails," *PC*, July 30, 1960.
45. Joseph, *Waiting 'Til the Midnight Hour*, 54–63; Dillard, *Faith in the City*, 237–85. In 1967, Cleage changed the name of his Central Congregational Church to Shrine of the Black Madonna.
46. Drake and Cayton, *Black Metropolis*, 393.
47. "We Can Elect Three Negroes to Congress," *Illustrated News*, May 28, 1962, box 51, CCDP (emphasis added).
48. Quoted in DuBose, *Untold Story*, 33.
49. Charles C. Diggs Jr. to Christine Davis, November 14, 1958, box 12, CCDP.
50. Charles C. Diggs Jr. to Honorable John W. McCormack, September 11, 1956, box 46, CCDP.
51. Charles C. Diggs Jr., oral history interview, January 28, 1970.
52. Charles C. Diggs Jr. to James Connell, February 5, 1960, box 4, CCDP.
53. Quoted in DuBose, *Untold Story*, 33.
54. Reverend Richard A. Lowe to Charles C. Diggs Jr., December 6, 1956, box 48, CCDP.
55. "Diggs Blasts Powell Bolt to Republicans," *Los Angeles Sentinel*, October 18, 1956.
56. Telegram, Charles C. Diggs Jr. to Adam Clayton Powell, October 27, 1956, box 48, CCDP.
57. Clayton, *Negro Politician*, 89–90; Charles C. Diggs Jr. to Adlai Stevenson, February 9, 1956, box 48, CCDP.
58. Manning, *William L. Dawson*, 212.
59. A. Phillip Randolph to Charles C. Diggs Jr., September 8, 1958; Charles C. Diggs, Jr. to A. Phillip Randolph, September 23, 1958, box 13, CCDP.
60. Charles Rangel, interview by author, February 6, 2015, New York.
61. Masters, "Committee Assignments in the House of Representatives," 352.

62. Bardolph, *Negro Vanguard*, 258.
63. Ethel L. Payne, "Diggs Gives New Leadership in Congress: Hard Worker in 8th Term," *CD*, April 9, 1969.
64. Editors, "Diggs and Black Caucus," *CD*, July 22, 1974.
65. Rangel, interview by author, February 6, 2015.
66. Booker, *Shocking the Conscience*, 302.
67. DuBose, *Untold Story*, 144.
68. Ralph Matthews, "Youngest Congressman Fills Odd Role: Charlie Diggs Is 'Mr. In-Between,'" *BAA*, March 16, 1957.
69. Matthews, "Youngest Congressman Fills Odd Role."
70. Louis Martin, "Dope and Data," *MC*, December 18, 1954.
71. John Conyers, interview by author, August 15, 2014, Detroit, MI.
72. Ronald Dellums, interview by author, July 24, 2014, Washington, DC.
73. Ethel L. Payne, "Diggs Establishes 'Combat' Record," *PC*, February 19, 1972.
74. Lenore Cooley, "Charles C. Diggs, Jr.: Democratic Representative from Michigan," *Ralph Nader Congress Project: Citizens Look at Congress* (Washington, DC: Grossman Publishers, 1972), 12, box 58, CCDP.

CHAPTER 1

1. "The Spectator," *MC*, May 13, 1950.
2. Photographs of Woodland Baptist Church and its cornerstone, Charles C. Diggs III Papers, personal papers (in the author's possession).
3. Halfmann, *Midnight Teacher*; Behrend, *Reconstructing Democracy*, 60–61.
4. James Diggs is listed in the 1870 US Federal Census as a "Justice of the Peace" in Issaquena County.
5. Dansby, *Brief History of Jackson College*, 23.
6. L. G. Jordan, *Up the Ladder in Foreign Missions*, 98.
7. Reverend James J. Diggs fathered a son during his mission in Liberia. See Massie, *Loosing the Bonds*, 264; Weston Diggs Jr., telephone interview by author, April 28, 2014.
8. Coles, *Africa in Brief*.
9. Key, *Southern Politics*; Cobb, *Most Southern Place*; McMillen, *Dark Journey*.
10. Franklin and Moss, *From Slavery to Freedom*, 238.
11. Wilkerson, *Warmth of Other Suns*.
12. "The Man Who Wanted to Be Senator," *BAA*, February 20, 1937.
13. "Man Who Wanted to Be Senator."
14. Mayme Jones Diggs, "The Family Tree of Mayme Ethel Jones," n.d., DDTP.
15. *Detroit City Directory*, 1917, 397, Burton Historical Collection, Detroit Public Library.
16. Conot, *American Odyssey*.
17. Thomas, *Life for Us*; Miller, *Managing Inequality*.
18. Thomas, *Life for Us*, 31.
19. S. E. Smith, *To Serve the Living*; Holloway, *Passed On*.
20. "Death Is Big Business," *Ebony* (May 1953): 20–23.
21. Mayme Jones Diggs, "Family Tree of Mayme Ethel Jones."

22. Gomez-Jefferson, *In Darkness with God*, 74–75.
23. Turner and Moses, *Colored Detroit*, 29.
24. Levine, *Internal Combustion*, 81. Green was a member of the board of directors of the Detroit Urban League.
25. DuBose, *Untold Story*, 6.
26. Turner and Moses, *Colored Detroit*, 29.
27. "A Dinner Dance in Honor of Chas. C. Diggs," n.d., Charles C. Diggs Sr. file, Burton Historical Collection, Detroit Public Library.
28. Hill, *Marcus Garvey and Universal Negro*.
29. Wright, *Detroit Memorial Park*, 5.
30. Quoted in Wright, *Detroit Memorial Park*, 5–6.
31. Wright, *Detroit Memorial Park*.
32. Widick, *Detroit*, 43.
33. Conot, *American Odyssey*, 277.
34. Widick, *Detroit*, 44.
35. "Osmond Diggs Ends Life by Gas in Detroit," *CD*, July 19, 1930.
36. Moon, "Charles C. Diggs, Jr.," 52.

CHAPTER 2

1. Dunbar, *Michigan*, 181–92.
2. "Three Angry Men Led Bloodless Revolution," *MC*, February 25, 1956.
3. "Funeral Directors to Meet in Detroit," *CD*, June 11, 1932.
4. Stovall, "Before Coleman Young," 28–49.
5. Stovall, "Before Coleman Young," 73.
6. Thomas, *Life for Us*, 267.
7. "The Man Who Wanted to Be Senator," *BAA*, February 20, 1937.
8. "Man Who Wanted to Be Senator."
9. Poinsett, *Walking with Presidents*, 17–23.
10. Fine, *"Expanding the Frontiers."*
11. Moon, "Charles C. Diggs, Jr.," 53.
12. Quoted in Greenstone, *Report of the Politics of Detroit*, sect. V, p. 27.
13. Thomas, *Life for Us*, 267. Funeral home employees referred to Diggs, Sr. as "Senior" and Diggs, Jr. as "Junior." After his election to Congress, employees referred to Diggs Jr. as "the Congressman."
14. Weston Diggs Jr., interview by author, August 6, 2015, Novi, MI.
15. Quoted in DuBose, *Untold Story*, 4.
16. Moon, "Charles C. Diggs, Jr.," 52.
17. Moon "Charles C. Diggs, Jr.," 52.
18. Moon, "Helen Nuttall Brown," 38.
19. Clegg, *An Original Man*, 14–37.
20. Rich, *Coleman Young*, 47.
21. C. Young and Wheeler, *Hardstuff*, 18.
22. Charles C. Diggs III, interview by author, August 4, 2015, Ypsilanti, MI; "Seek More Aid for Family Hit by Fire," *MC*, November 30, 1957.
23. Damon Keith, interview by author, November 25, 2014, Detroit, MI.
24. Roberta Hughes Wright, interview by author, September 9, 2014, Detroit, MI.

25. Boyd, *Black Detroit*; Coleman, *Million Dollars' Worth of Nerve*.
26. DuBose, *Untold Story*, 5.
27. Charles C. Diggs III, interview by author, August 4, 2015.
28. Quoted in DuBose, *Untold Story*, 5.
29. Charles C. Diggs Jr., interview by Elaine Latzman Moon, unabridged transcript, December 6, 1991, 6, Alexis Diggs-Robinson Papers, personal papers (in the author's possession).
30. Mirel, *Rise and Fall*.
31. Mirel, *Rise and Fall*, 189.
32. Mirel, *Rise and Fall*, 189.
33. DuBose, *Untold Story*, 11.
34. Peckham, *Making of the University of Michigan*, 58.
35. "Charles Diggs's Lecture," Black History Panel Part 1 (audiocassette), February 13, 1978, box 28, Center for Afro-American and African Studies Records, Bentley Historical Library, University of Michigan, Ann Arbor.
36. Diggs Jr., interview by Moon, 6.
37. Diggs Jr., interview by Moon, 6.
38. Bordin, *Women at Michigan*, 50.
39. "Charles Diggs's Lecture."
40. "Charles Diggs's Lecture."
41. Diggs Jr., interview by Moon, 8. The US Census shows Miller was born in 1922 in Illinois. Her father was a Black man, and her mother was German. Miller never graduated from Michigan.
42. Diggs Jr., interview by Moon, 8.
43. Diggs Jr., interview by Moon, 8.
44. Diggs Jr., interview by Moon, 8.
45. Quoted in *United States vs. Charles C. Diggs, Jr.* (D.C. Circuit 78-142, 1978), 1058.
46. Out of nineteen courses, Diggs earned 4 Bs, 5 Cs, 4 Ds, 4 Fs, 1 W, and 1 P. See "Official Transcript for Charles Coles Diggs, Jr.," University of Michigan, August 25, 2015, Charles C. Diggs III Papers, personal papers (in the author's possession).
47. Motley, *Equal Justice Under the Law*, 42.
48. Charles C. Diggs Jr. to Senator and Mrs. Chas. C. Diggs, November 30, 1942, DDTP.
49. Charles C. Diggs Jr. to Senator and Mrs. Chas. C. Diggs, November 30, 1942.

CHAPTER 3

1. Sandler, *Segregated Skies*, 29–30.
2. Francis, *Tuskegee Airmen*, 238.
3. Francis, *Tuskegee Airmen*, 238.
4. Delmont, *Half American*.
5. DuBose, *Untold Story*, 12.
6. Moon, "Charles C. Diggs, Jr.," 55.
7. Moon, "Charles C. Diggs, Jr.," 55.
8. Charles C. Diggs Jr., interview by Elaine Moon, unabridged transcript, December 6, 1991, Alexis Diggs-Robinson Papers, personal papers (in the author's possession).

9. Diggs Jr., interview by Moon, 9.
10. Diggs Jr., interview by Moon, 9.
11. Diggs Jr., interview by Moon, 8–9.
12. Formed in 1907, the Air Force was initially a part of the United States Army. It became a separate military branch in 1947.
13. City of Detroit, *Final Report: Proposed Arden Park-East Boston Historic District*, accessed December 10, 2024, https://detroitmi.gov/document/arden-park-east-boston.
14. Osur, *Blacks in the Army Air Forces*, ii.
15. Diggs Jr., interview by Moon, 9.
16. Osur, *Blacks in the Army Air Forces*, 37.
17. Diggs Jr., interview by Moon, 9.
18. Diggs Jr., interview by Moon, 9.
19. Charles C. Diggs Jr. to Senator and Mrs. Charles C. Diggs Sr., April 18, 1944, DDTP.
20. Charles C. Diggs Jr. to Senator and Mrs. Charles C. Diggs Sr., March 14, 1944, DDTP.
21. Gropman, *Air Force Integrates*, 167.
22. Charles C. Diggs Jr. to Senator and Mrs. Charles C. Diggs Sr., April 18, 1944, DDTP.
23. Rubenstein and Ziewacz, *Payoffs in the Cloakroom*. Two of the indictments against Senator Diggs were eventually dropped.
24. "Senator Diggs to Run Again," *CD*, March 25, 1944.
25. Weiss, *Farewell to the Party*, 267–95.
26. Moye, *Freedom Flyers*.
27. Moye, *Freedom Flyers*, 41–42.
28. "Aviation: Perpetuating Segregation," *PC*, March 29, 1941.
29. Moye, *Freedom Flyers*, 31.
30. Moye, *Freedom Flyers*, 53–58.
31. "Interview with Charles Coles Diggs Jr.," November 6, 1986, in Hampton, *Eyes of the Prize*.
32. DuBose, *Untold Story*, 14.
33. Norrell, *Reaping the Whirlwind*, 48.
34. Sandler, *Segregated Skies*, 29.
35. Litwack, *How Free Is Free?*
36. Teola Hunter, interview by author, October 1, 2014, Detroit, MI. Hunter served in the Michigan House of Representatives from 1981 to 1992.
37. "Eloise Burial Is Monopoly," *DN*, November 7, 1941.
38. Diggs Jr., interview by Moon, 4.
39. S. E. Smith, *To Serve the Living*, 88.
40. Diggs Jr., interview by Moon, 4.
41. "Diggs Beaten in High Court: Curb on Undertakers and Insurance Upheld," *DN*, September 6, 1951.
42. Holloway, *Passed On*, 26.
43. Charles C. Diggs III, interview by author, August 4, 2015, Ypsilanti, MI.
44. Charles C. Diggs III, interview by author, August 4, 2015.
45. Holloway, *Passed On*, 47–48.
46. Denise Diggs-Taylor, interview by author, August 4, 2015, Ypsilanti, MI.

47. Weston Diggs Jr., interview by author, August 6, 2015, Novi, MI.
48. Quoted in *USA v. Charles C. Diggs Jr.*, 613 F.2d (D.C. Cir.1978), 1067.

CHAPTER 4

1. Weston Diggs Jr., interview by author, August 6, 2015, Novi, MI.
2. Weston Diggs Jr., interview by author, August 6, 2015.
3. "House of Diggs Radio Script," boxes 46, 49, and 51, CCDP.
4. Denise Diggs-Taylor, interview by author, August 4, 2015, Ypsilanti, MI.
5. Juanita R. Diggs, interview by author, September 12, 2014, Ypsilanti, MI.
6. Quoted in "Young Diggs to Join Business with Father," *MC*, June 9, 1945.
7. Damon Keith, interview by author, November 25, 2014, Detroit, MI.
8. Stephens, *Idlewild*, 130–31.
9. Keith, interview by author, November 25, 2014.
10. Quoted in Gary F. Schuster, "The Rise and Decline of Charles C. Diggs," *DN*, July 22, 1979.
11. Charles C. Diggs III, interview by author, August 4, 2015, Ypsilanti, MI.
12. Charles C. Diggs III, interview by author, August 4, 2015.
13. Charles C. Diggs Jr. to Senator and Mrs. Charles C. Diggs Sr., August 12, 1944, DDTP.
14. DuBose, *Untold Story*, 227.
15. DuBose, *Untold Story*, 227.
16. Juanita R. Diggs, interview by author, September 12, 2014.
17. Juanita R. Diggs, interview by author, September 12, 2014.
18. Juanita R. Diggs, interview by author, September 12, 2014.
19. Juanita R. Diggs, telephone interview by author, January 22, 2015.
20. "3 Duos Splash Matrimonial Sea," *MC*, August 9, 1947.
21. "Nacirema Week, Diggs Wedding Highlight," *MC*, August 16, 1947.
22. Juanita R. Diggs, telephone interview by author, October 15, 2014. Mrs. Diggs is mistaken. James "Jimmy" Diggs didn't arrive in Detroit until about 1955.
23. "Bribe Taker Loses Plea to Escape Jail," *DFP*, December 7, 1948.
24. Quoted in DuBose, *Untold Story*, 16.
25. Rich, *Coleman Young*, 56.
26. "Ex-Legislators Complete Prison Terms," *DFP*, March 18, 1950.
27. "The Week's News in Tabloid," *BAA*, April 1, 1950.
28. "Scan Prison Bill for Diggs: May Have to Pay for Care Behind Bars," *DN*, November 24, 1950.
29. "Diggs Seeks Re-election as Senator," *DFP*, June 24, 1950.
30. "Find Charles M. Diggs Dead in Hotel Room," *MC*, November 14, 1959.
31. DuBose, *Untold Story*, 17.
32. "Michigan Senate Denies Diggs Seat," *BAA*, January 20, 1951.
33. "Michigan Senate Denies Diggs Seat."
34. "Veterans Bow Out, 'Frosh' Takes Over," *DFP*, January 14, 1951.
35. "Democratic Posts Vacant Till Spring," *DFP*, January 12, 1951.
36. Weston Diggs Jr., interview by author, August 6, 2015, Novi, MI.
37. Juanita R. Diggs, interview by author, September 12, 2014.
38. Diggs-Taylor, interview by author, August 4, 2015.

39. Weston Diggs Jr., interview by author, August 6, 2015.
40. "Son to Seek Ousted Senator's Seat," *CD*, January 27, 1951.
41. "Son to Seek Ousted Senator's Seat."
42. DuBose, *Untold Story*, 18.

CHAPTER 5

1. "Waitress Accused in Diggs Case," *DFP*, October 5, 1951.
2. "Shot at Closed Doors," *DFP*, April 6, 1952.
3. Noer, *Soapy*.
4. Fine, *"Expanding the Frontiers."*
5. Noer, *Soapy*, 93.
6. The Michigan legislature was malapportioned until after the US Supreme Court's ruling in *Baker v. Carr, 369, U.S. 186* (1962).
7. Staebler, *Out of the Smoke-Filled Room*, 67. Staebler was chair of the Michigan Democratic Party from 1950 to 1961.
8. "Civil Rights Measure Defeated," *DFP*, March 8, 1952.
9. "Shot at Closed Doors."
10. Juanita R. Diggs, interview by author, September 12, 2014, Ypsilanti, MI.
11. Juanita R. Diggs, interview by author, September 12, 2014.
12. Charles C. Diggs Jr., interview by Elaine Moon, December 6, 1991, unabridged transcript, Alexis Diggs-Robinson Papers, personal papers (in the author's possession).
13. Orr, "Black Political Incorporation," 104–27; Fragnoli, *Transformation of Reform*.
14. Dillard, *Faith in the City*, 158–68.
15. Sugrue, *Origins of the Urban Crisis*.
16. Capeci, *Race Relations in Wartime Detroit*.
17. Sugrue, *Origins of the Urban Crisis*, 209–29.
18. Sugrue, *Origins of the Urban Crisis*, 209–29.
19. "Renters Group Plead to Continue Controls," *DFP*, September 9, 1952.
20. DuBose, *Untold Story*, 20.
21. "Candidates Near Campaign Close," *MC*, October 31, 1953.
22. "Detroit Can Do It Too!" *DFP*, September 13, 1953.
23. "Detroit Can Do It Too!"
24. "CIO Seeks Coalition," *DFP*, August 14, 1953.
25. Stovall, "Before Coleman Young," 99.
26. "Diggs Sets Precedent in Primary," *MC*, September 26, 1953.
27. Horace White, "Facts in the News: The Coming Councilmanic Elections," *MC*, October 10, 1953; "Tough Electioneering ahead for Old Hands," *DFP*, September 20, 1953.
28. Stovall, "Before Coleman Young," 99.
29. "Ex-Councilwoman Blanche P. Wise Is Dead at age 65," *DFP*, April 13, 1973.
30. Paid advertisement in *DFP*, November 1, 1953.
31. "Candidates near Campaign Close," *MC*, October 31, 1953.
32. Stovall, "Before Coleman Young," 100.
33. "Diggs Bid Fails: Senator Finishes Tenth," *MC*, November 7, 1953.

34. Juanita R. Diggs, telephone interview by author, February 13, 2017.
35. "Election Recount Now Certain, says Diggs Committee," *MC*, November 14, 1953.
36. Juanita R. Diggs interview by author, February 13, 2017.
37. Stovall, "Before Coleman Young," 100.
38. "Election Recount Now Certain."
39. "Diggs Halts Recounts, Cites Need for Voting Machines," *MC*, November 28, 1953.

CHAPTER 6

1. DuBose, *Untold Story*, 20.
2. Capeci, *Race Relations in Wartime Detroit*, 79.
3. William J. Coughlin, "Know Your Congressman and District: Populous Thirteenth Attract Candidates," *DFP*, June 14, 1942; G. Mennen Williams to Charles C. Diggs Jr., December 28, 1954, box 30, CCDP.
4. Grant, *Great Migration*.
5. Bunche, *Political Status of the Negro*, 584–91.
6. "Diggs Announces Candidacy for Congress in 13th," *MC*, January 23, 1954.
7. Juanita R. Diggs, interview by author, September 12, 2014, Ypsilanti, MI.
8. "Diggs Announces Candidacy."
9. "Diggs Announces Candidacy."
10. "Asa Canadia, 48, buried in Detroit," *BAA*, February 25, 1961.
11. "Neighbors, Friends, VIPs Call Reuthers 'Magnificent,'" *DFP*, May 11, 1970.
12. See "Diggs Campaign Based on Sound Approach to Modern Problems," n.d.; and "The Diggs Platform," n.d., both in box 44, CCDP.
13. "Kick Off Dinner: Diggs for Congress Program," October 8, 1954, box 44, CCDP.
14. "Diggs Sure to Win if Voters Turn Out," *MC*, July 24, 1954.
15. "Leading Churches in the 13th District"; Charles C. Diggs to Dear Reverend [blank], n.d., box 44, CCDP.
16. Salvatore, *Singing in a Strange Land*, 147.
17. "Diggs Reminds Voters of Registration Deadline," *MC*, July 17, 1954.
18. Memorandum, "Organizational Structure: Diggs for Congress Campaign," n.d., box 44, CCDP.
19. Memorandum, "Organizational Structure," n.d.
20. Memorandum, "Organizational Structure," n.d.
21. Memorandum, "Organizational Structure," n.d.
22. "UAW Mum in Fight of Democrats in 13th," *DFP*, July 29, 1954.
23. "3 Big Issues Face Congress in Drive to End This Week," *NYT*, August 16, 1954.
24. "Diggs Sure to Win if Voters Turn Out."
25. DuBose, *Untold Story*, 20.
26. "Diggs Reminds Voters, 'It's in Your Hands,'" *MC*, July 24, 1954.
27. Collins George, "Diggs Upset O'Brien in Key 13th District," *DFP*, August 5, 1954.
28. Charles J. Wartman, "The Spectator," *MC*, August 14, 1954.
29. Greenstone, *Report on the Politics of Detroit*, sect. V, p. 29.
30. Wartman, "Spectator."
31. "Primary Voters Reflect True Michigan Democracy," *MC*, August 14, 1954.
32. "Letter to the Editor," *MC*, August 14, 1954.

33. "Undertaker May Become 3rd Congressman," *BAA*, August 14, 1954; "Diggs of Detroit May be Third Negro in Congress," *CD*, August 21, 1954.
34. "Diggs Calm, Eyes Big Job Ahead," *MC*, August 14, 1954.
35. "Diggs to Kickoff Campaign on Oct. 8," *MC*, September 25, 1954.

CHAPTER 7

1. "Bi-partisan Crowd Attends Diggs Campaign 'Kickoff,'" *MC*, October 16, 1954.
2. Charles C. Diggs Sr. to *MC*, n.d., box 44, CCDP; "Knight's Campaign Tactics Are Unfair," *MC*, October 30, 1954.
3. Charles C. Diggs Jr., "Speech Rendered by State Senator Charles C. Diggs, Jr., Kickoff Banquet, Detroit Leland Hotel," October 8, 1954, box 44, CCDP.
4. Diggs Jr., "Speech Rendered by State Senator."
5. Whited, *Knight*, 21–22, 24–25.
6. Whited, *Knight*, 163.
7. Hub M. George, "Landon Knight Backs Ike's Ideals," *DFP*, August 6, 1954.
8. See Knight's campaign flyer, "House of Diggs Anti-labor, National Labor Relations Board Cases," box 44, CCDP.
9. Geoffrey Howes, "Diggs Rally Slated: Knight Hits Democrats," *DFP*, October 25, 1954.
10. Knight advertisement in *DFP*, October 31, 1954.
11. Diggs Jr. developed several policy papers. See, for example, "Diggs Campaign Based on Sound Approach to Modern Problems," n.d., and "The Diggs Platform," n.d., box 44, CCDP.
12. Diggs Jr., "Speech Rendered by State Senator."
13. "Diggs's Platform," n.d.
14. Fauntroy, *Republicans and the Black Vote*, 17.
15. Thurber, *Republicans and Race*, 58–64.
16. James M. Haswell, "13th District Sure to Elect New Name," *DFP*, August 26, 1954.
17. Diggs Jr., "Speech Rendered by State Senator."
18. Diggs Jr., "Speech Rendered by State Senator."
19. Hub M. George, "Landon Knight Backs Ike's Ideals," *DFP*, August 6, 1954.
20. Quoted in Howes, "Diggs Rally Slated."
21. Jack E. Strohm, "Knight, Diggs Clash on U.S. Economy," *DFP*, October 15, 1954.
22. Strohm, "Knight, Diggs Clash."
23. Joe Strickland, "Diggs-Knight Clash in Debate," *MC*, October 23, 1954.
24. Strickland, "Diggs-Knight Clash in Debate."
25. Asa T. Canadia, "Treasury Report," November 9, 1954, box 44, CCDP.
26. "Elks to Present Dawson and Diggs," *MC*, October 30, 1954.
27. Quoted in Haygood, *King of the Cats*, 195.
28. Hub M. George, "Wilson Predicts 'Balancing Out' of Employment," *DFP*, October 12, 1954.
29. Memorandum, John Murray to Charles C. Diggs Jr., October 21, 1954, box 44, CCDP.
30. Pousant Norigian, et al., to Dear Friends, October 29, 1954, box 44, in CCDP.
31. "Knight Denies He OK'd Attack on Foe," *DFP*, October 31, 1954.

32. "Campaign Leaflet Condemned," *DFP*, November 3, 1954.
33. Howes, "Diggs Rally Slated."
34. Charles J. Wartman, "Williams, Diggs Build Leads in Big Democratic Surge," *MC*, November 6, 1954.
35. Hub M. George, "Jobs without War, Ike Promises State," *DFP*, October 30, 1954.
36. George, "Jobs without War."
37. Chester Higgins, "'Pioneer' Has Tremendous Responsibilities—Diggs," *PC*, November 13, 1954.
38. John Griffith, "Diggs Is Serious on Big Day," *DFP*, November 4, 1954.
39. Griffith, "Diggs Is Serious on Big Day."
40. Richard B. Henry, "Congressman Diggs," *MC*, November 13, 1954.
41. Esther Van Wagoner, "Supporters will see Diggs Take his Oath of Office," *Holland (MI) Evening Sentinel*, November 22, 1954.
42. Higgins, "'Pioneer' Has Tremendous Responsibilities."
43. Griffith, "Diggs Is Serious on Big Day."

CHAPTER 8

1. Quoted in DuBose, *Untold Story*, 22.
2. "Diggs Boosters Plan to See Swearing-In," *BAA*, January 8, 1955; Ethel Payne, "Young Diggs Seated as 400 Followers Cheer," *CD*, January 15, 1955.
3. Charles C. Diggs Sr. to Dear Citizen and Friend, n.d.; "The Trip of Your Lifetime Brochure"; and "Diggs, Jr. Congressional Special Streamliner," box 44, CCDP.
4. Quoted in DuBose, *Untold Story*, 22.
5. Louis Martin, "Dope and Data," *MC*, December 18, 1954.
6. Quoted in Carl Muller, "Diggs' Well-Wishers Fill Train to Capital," *DN*, January 5, 1955.
7. "400 Ride Diggs' Special to Capital," *PC*, January 15, 1955.
8. "400 Ride Diggs' Special."
9. "400 Ride Diggs' Special."
10. DuBose, *Untold Story*, 22.
11. Quoted in DuBose, *Untold Story*, 22.
12. "'Electrifying Experience,' says Rep. Charles C. Diggs," *BAA*, January 15, 1955.
13. "'Electrifying Experience.'"
14. Collins George, "Friends Pay Tribute at Diggs Swearing," *DFP*, January 6, 1955.
15. "'Electrifying Experience.'"
16. "Diggs' Well-Wishers Fill Train."
17. "'Electrifying Experience.'"
18. George, "Friends Pay Tribute."
19. DuBose, *Untold Story*, 24.
20. Morris, *Eye on the Struggle*.
21. Payne, "Young Diggs Seated as 400 Followers Cheer."
22. "Office Assistants Named by Congressman Diggs," *MC*, December 25, 1954.
23. Ethel L. Payne, "Staff Careerists on Capitol Hill Lead Interesting, Varied Lives," *CD*, August 24, 1957.
24. Payne, "Young Diggs Seated as 400 Followers Cheer."

25. Ethel L. Payne, "Youngest Congressman Impresses D.C. Politicians," *MC*, January 15, 1955.
26. "400 Ride Diggs' Special."
27. Payne, "Young Diggs Seated as 400 Followers Cheer."
28. "National Council Entertains for Dawson, Powell, Diggs," *BAA*, January 15, 1955; "D.C. Welcomes Charles Diggs, New Congress," *Atlanta Daily World*, January 14, 1955.
29. "D.C. Welcomes Charles Diggs."
30. "D.C. Welcomes Charles Diggs."
31. "National Council Entertains for Dawson, Powell, Diggs."
32. "D.C. Welcomes Charles Diggs."
33. Carl Muller, "Gala Dance Climax Trip to Capital by Diggs Friends," *DN*, January 6, 1955.
34. "400 Ride Diggs' Special."
35. Payne, "Young Diggs Seated as 400 Followers Cheer."
36. "400 Ride Diggs' Special."

CHAPTER 9

1. Booker, *Black Man's America*, 161; "13,000 Hear Diggs Hit Bias in Miss. Speech," *Jet*, May 12, 1955; "Rep. Diggs Rouses Mississippi Rally," *CD*, May 14, 1955.
2. Beito and Beito, *Black Maverick*, 45.
3. Hamlin, *Crossroads at Clarksdale*, 9–34; Dittmer, *Local People*, 32–33; Payne, *I've Got the Light of Freedom*, 31–34.
4. Evers and Peters, *For Us the Living*, 89.
5. Evers and Peters, *For Us the Living*, 75–76.
6. M. V. Williams, *Medgar Evers*, 110.
7. Dittmer, *Local People*, 34.
8. C. M. Payne, *I've Got the Light*, 32.
9. Dittmer, *Local People*, 34.
10. Quoted in Dittmer, *Local People*, 37.
11. McMillen, *Citizens' Council*, 94.
12. Tyson, *Blood of Emmett Till*, 98.
13. C. M. Payne, *I've Got the Light*, 37.
14. Quoted in Tyson, *Blood of Emmett Till*, 105.
15. *CR*, March 31, 1955, 4149.
16. Cross Reference Sheet, Charles C. Diggs Jr. to Dwight D. Eisenhower, March 31, 1955, General File, box 124, Dwight David Eisenhower Library, Abilene, KS.
17. Booker, *Shocking the Conscience*, 17.
18. Booker, *Shocking the Conscience*, 17.
19. "Program of the Fourth Annual Meeting of the Mississippi Regional Council of Negro Leadership," April 29, 1955, Mound Bayou, Mississippi, NAACP Papers.
20. "13,000 Hear Diggs."
21. "13,000 Hear Diggs."
22. "Program of the Fourth Annual Meeting."
23. Tyson, *Blood Emmett Till*, 111.

24. Booker, *Black Man's America*, 161.
25. M. V. Williams, *Medgar Evers*, 119.
26. Booker, *Black Man's America*, 162.
27. Booker, *Black Man's America*, 162.
28. "Program of the Fourth Annual Meeting."
29. Raymond F. Tisby, "'Victory Will Be Ours,' Diggs Tells Miss. Group," *Atlanta Daily World*, May 3, 1955.
30. Charles C. Diggs Jr., interview, November 6, 1986, in Hampton, *Eyes on the Prize*; Charles C. Diggs Jr., interview by Elaine Moon, unabridged transcript, December 6, 1991, 11, Alexis Diggs-Robinson Papers, personal papers (in the author's possession).
31. Tisby, "'Victory Will Be Ours.'"
32. Booker, *Shocking the Conscience*, 17.
33. "Rep. Diggs Rouses Mississippi Rally."
34. Booker, *Shocking the Conscience*, 17.
35. "Full Fight Promised by Diggs," *PC*, May 7, 1955.
36. Tisby, "'Victory Will Be Ours.'"
37. "Rep. Diggs Rouses Mississippi Rally."
38. "Rep. Diggs Rouses Mississippi Rally."
39. "Rep. Diggs Rouses Mississippi Rally."
40. Tisby, "'Victory Will Be Ours.'"
41. "13,000 Hear Diggs."
42. Charles C. Diggs Jr., interview, November 6, 1986, in Hampton, *Eyes on the Prize*.
43. Charles C. Diggs Jr. to Dwight D. Eisenhower, May 3, 1955, Records of the Department of Justice, Class 144 (Civil Rights) Litigation Case Files, 1936–1997, box 1887, case file 144-012-17, NACPM.
44. Diggs to Eisenhower, May 3, 1955.
45. Dittmer, *Local People*, 53–54.
46. Quoted in Mendelsohn, *Martyrs*, 7.
47. Beito and Beito, *Black Maverick*, 109.
48. William Rogers to Charles C. Diggs Jr., May 26, 1955; and William Rogers to Warren Olney III, May 16, 1955 (note), Records of the Department of Justice, Class 144 (Civil Rights) Litigation Case Files, 1936–1997, box 1887, case file 144-012-17, NACPM.
49. "Diggs Speaks at Hampton Commencement," *Detroit (MI) Tribune*, June 11, 1955; "Diggs to be Wilberforce commencement speaker," *BAA*, May 28, 1955.
50. "Diggs Suffers Severe Stroke; Condition Improved," *MC*, July 2, 1955.
51. Juanita R. Diggs, interview by author, September 12, 2014, Ypsilanti, MI.
52. Juanita R. Diggs, interview by author, September 12, 2014.

CHAPTER 10

1. Anderson, *Emmett Till*, 45–47; Tyson, *Blood of Emmett Till*, 62–63.
2. J. Williams, *Eyes on the Prize*, 43.
3. Anderson, *Emmett Till*, 133–37.
4. Tyson, *Blood of Emmett Till*, 53.

5. Tyson, *Blood of Emmett Till*, 54.
6. Tyson, *Blood of Emmett Till*, 54.
7. Anderson, *Emmett Till*, 36.
8. Anderson, *Emmett Till*, 37.
9. Anderson, *Emmett Till*, 49.
10. Tyson, *Blood of Emmett Till*, 106.
11. Till-Mobley and Benson, *Death of Innocence*, 142.
12. Houck and Grindy, *Emmett Till and the Mississippi Press*, 31.
13. "Lynched Boy Lived Here," *MC*, September 10, 1955.
14. "Lynched Boy Lived Here."
15. Charles C. Diggs Jr., interview, November 6, 1986, in Hampton, *Eyes on the Prize*.
16. Charles C. Diggs Jr., interview, November 6, 1986, in Hampton, *Eyes on the Prize*.
17. "Rep. Diggs on Scene of Till Trial," *MC*, September 24, 1955.
18. "Rep. Diggs on Scene."
19. "Rep. Diggs on Scene."
20. Charles C. Diggs Jr., "Emmett Till Trial Over But Negroes Should Never Forget Its Meaning," *PC*, October 8, 1955.
21. Diggs, "Emmett Till Trial."
22. Diggs, "Emmett Till Trial."
23. All uncited quotations are from Booker, *Shocking the Conscience*, 69–70.
24. Terry, *Missing Places*, 139.
25. Halberstam, *Fifties*, 439.
26. Halberstam, *Fifties*, 439.
27. Anderson, *Emmett Till*, 88.
28. Tyson, *Blood of Emmett Till*, 137.
29. Tyson, *Blood of Emmett Till*, 137.
30. Anderson, *Emmett Till*, 105–6.
31. Diggs, "Emmett Till Trial."
32. Diggs, "Emmett Till Trial."
33. "Prosecution Wins Race Trial Delay," *DFP*, September 21, 1955.
34. Terry, *Missing Pages*, 140–42.
35. Terry, *Missing Pages*, 140.
36. Terry, *Missing Pages*, 140.
37. Terry, *Missing Pages*, 141–42.
38. D. L. Jordan with R. L. Jenkins, *David L. Jordan*, 56–57.
39. Charles C. Diggs Jr., interview, November 6, 1986, in Hampton, *Eyes on the Prize*.
40. Diggs, "Emmett Till Trial."
41. Booker, *Shocking the Conscience*, 73.
42. Booker, *Shocking the Conscience*, 71.
43. Tyson, *Blood of Emmett Till*, 137.
44. Tyson, *Blood of Emmett Till*, 132.
45. Jay Milner, "Jittery News Men at Sumner Kept in a Dither by Rumors," *Jackson (MS) Clarion-Ledger*, September 22, 1955.
46. "The Lynching of Emmett Till, Roman Circus," *Jackson (MS) Daily News*, September 22, 1955.

47. DuBose, *Untold Story*, 53.
48. Charles C. Diggs Jr., interview, November 6, 1986, in Hampton, *Eyes on the Prize*.
49. Anderson, *Emmett Till*, 114–17.
50. Till-Mobley and Benson, *Death of Innocence*, 176.
51. Till-Mobley and Benson, *Death of Innocence*, 182.
52. Anderson, *Emmett Till*, 132.
53. Tyson, *Blood of Emmett Till*, 161.
54. Diggs, "Emmett Till Trial."
55. Anderson, *Emmett Till*, 135.
56. Booker, *Shocking the Conscience*, 78–79.
57. Anderson, *Emmett Till*, 143.
58. Anderson, *Emmett Till*, 144–47.
59. James Hicks, "Called Lynch-Murder, 'Morally, Legally,' Wrong," *Cleveland Call and Post*, October 1, 1955.
60. Anderson, *Emmett Till*, 148.
61. Tyson, *Blood of Emmett Till*, 170.
62. Anderson, *Emmett Till*, 148.
63. Anderson, *Emmett Till*, 149.
64. Till-Mobley and Benson, *Death of Innocence*, 189.
65. Tyson, *Blood of Emmett Till*, 170.
66. Till-Mobley and Benson, *Death of Innocence*, 188.
67. Tyson, *Blood of Emmett Till*, 173.
68. Tyson, *Blood of Emmett Till*, 173–74.
69. Anderson, *Emmett Till*, 153.
70. Anderson, *Emmett Till*, 153.
71. Tyson, *Blood of Emmett Till*, 175.
72. Tyson, *Blood of Emmett Till*, 175.
73. Anderson, *Emmett Till*, 153.
74. Till-Mobley and Benson, *Death of Innocence*, 189.
75. Till-Mobley and Benson, *Death of Innocence*, 189.
76. Till-Mobley and Benson, *Death of Innocence*, 189.
77. Charles C. Diggs Jr., interview, November 6, 1986, in Hampton, *Eyes on the Prize*.
78. "Mother of Till Expected Verdict," *Jackson (MS) Clarion-Ledger*, September 24, 1955.
79. Anderson, *Emmett Till*, 158. In 1956, Milam and Bryant confessed to a *Look* magazine reporter how they abducted, tortured, and murdered Till. Diggs read into the *CR* the entire magazine article. See, *CR*, January 12, 1956, appendix, A247–49. Milam and Bryant likely gave a false confession, lying to the *Look* reporter about where it happened and who was involved. See Thompson, *Barn*.
80. Anderson, *Emmett Till*, 158–59.
81. "Mother of Till Expected Verdict."
82. Charles C. Diggs Jr., interview, November 6, 1986, in Hampton, *Eyes on the Prize*. Around 1959, Reed began working as an orderly in a Chicago hospital and retired in 2006. Reed died in 2013.
83. "The Verdict at Sumner," *Jackson (MS) Daily News*, September 25, 1955.

284   Notes to Chapter 11

84. Diggs, "Emmett Till Trial."
85. Charles C. Diggs Jr., interview, November 6, 1986, in Hampton, *Eyes on the Prize*.
86. Quoted in DuBose, *Untold Story*, 50.
87. Diggs, "Emmett Till Trial."

CHAPTER 11

1. Bay, *Traveling Black*, 192–229.
2. Ortlepp, *Jim Crow Terminals*, 18.
3. Ortlepp, *Jim Crow Terminals*, 14.
4. "Congress Asked to Bar Segregation at Airport," *NYT*, November 18, 1947.
5. Ortlepp, *Jim Crow Terminals*, 65.
6. Bay, *Traveling Black*, 221–22.
7. Roy Wilkins to Ross Byers (manager, Braniff Airlines), July 17, 1950, in Legal Department Files, NAACP Papers.
8. Bay, *Traveling Black*, 223.
9. Quoted in Ortlepp, *Jim Crow Terminals*, 39.
10. Ortlepp, *Jim Crow Terminals*, 39.
11. Charles C. Diggs Jr. to Robert F. Six, May 12, 1955, box 42, CCDP. The same letter was sent to the other airlines.
12. Diggs to Six, May 12, 1955.
13. S. G. Tipton to Charles C. Diggs Jr., August 2, 1955, box 42, CCDP.
14. G. T. [George Theodore] Baker to Charles C. Diggs Jr., May 20, 1955, box 42, CCDP.
15. Ortlepp, *Jim Crow Terminals*, 92.
16. Charles C. Diggs Jr. to Sinclair Weeks, July 7, 1955, box 42, CCDP.
17. Telegram, Philip A. Ray to Charles C. Diggs, July 12, 1955, box 42, CCDP.
18. Alice A. Dunnigan, "Diggs Urges End to Discrimination at Airports," *PC*, July 30, 1955.
19. Dunnigan, "Diggs Urges End to Discrimination."
20. J. Francis Pohlhaus to Charles C. Diggs Jr., July 28, 1955, box 42, CCDP.
21. Memorandum, J. Francis Pohlhaus to Robert Carter, "Segregation and Racial Discrimination in the Operation of Airport Terminal Facilities," May 10, 1955, box 42, CCDP.
22. "U.S. Apologizes for Race Mistake," *Baltimore Sun*, August 23, 1955.
23. "Houston Color Line Is Studied by C.A.A.," *NYT*, August 28, 1955.
24. Benjamin E. Mays, "My View: Apologizes but Damage Remains," *PC*, September 24, 1955.
25. Editorial, "So Sorry, Thought You Were Negroes," *PC*, September 3, 1955.
26. Charles C. Diggs Jr. to Sinclair Weeks, September 16, 1955, box 42, CCDP.
27. Press release, "Diggs Seeks to Withhold Financial Funds from Segregated Airports," n.d., box 42, CCDP.
28. J. S. Stewart to Charles C. Diggs Jr., October 20, 1955, box 42, CCDP.
29. Charles C. Diggs Jr. to J. S. Stewart, December 1, 1955, box 42, CCDP.
30. Memorandum, "Telegrams to Be Sent," September 28, 1955, box 42, CCDP.
31. Memorandum, "Telegrams to Be Sent," September 28, 1955.
32. Memorandum, "Telegrams to Be Sent," September 28, 1955.

33. "Airmen Buck Slight," *BAA*, October 1, 1955.
34. Telegram, Sinclair Weeks to Charles C. Diggs Jr., October 5, 1955, box 42, CCDP.
35. "Diggs Protest on Airport Segregation Gets Results," *PC*, October 22, 1955.
36. "Segregated Airport to Lose Aid," *Baltimore Sun*, May 5, 1956.
37. Charles C. Diggs to Charles C. Lowen, May 8, 1956, box 4, CCDP (emphasis in the original).
38. Diggs to Lowen, May 8, 1956.
39. F. B. Lee to Charles C. Diggs Jr., August 10, 1955, box 42, CCDP.
40. Ortlepp, *Jim Crow Terminals*, 95.
41. Ortlepp, *Jim Crow Terminals*, 97.
42. Ortlepp, *Jim Crow Terminals*, 69–75.
43. Barry, *Femininity in Flight*, 11–35.
44. Barry, *Femininity in Flight*, 12.
45. Vantoch, *Jet Sex*, 60.
46. Vantoch, *Jet Sex*, 60.
47. "Report on Airline Employment Practices with Respect to the Non-employment of Negroes in Flight Service Positions," n.d., box 47, Detroit Urban League Papers, Bentley Historical Library, University of Michigan, Ann Arbor.
48. Vantoch, *Jet Sex*, 58–90.
49. Charles C. Diggs Jr. to C. E. Woolman, June 4, 1956, and others are in box 42, CCDP.
50. "An Editorial: Jim-Crow Wings," *PC*, May 12, 1956 (emphasis in the original).
51. Diggs to Woolman, June 4, 1956.
52. Diggs to Woolman, June 4, 1956.
53. J. J. Feeney to Charles C. Diggs Jr., June 18, 1956, box 42, CCDP.
54. C. E. Woolman to Charles C. Diggs Jr., June 15, 1956, box 42, CCDP.
55. Charles C. Diggs Jr. to Richard Nixon, July 17, 1956, box 42, CCDP.
56. Vantoch, *Jet Sex*, 58–90.
57. Vantoch, *Jet Sex*, 61–85.
58. Charles C. Diggs Jr. to Lyndon Johnson, March 26, 1962, box 267, Vice Presidential Papers, 1962 Congressional File, LBJL.
59. Lyndon Johnson to Charles C. Diggs Jr., March 30, 1962, box 42, CCDP.
60. Lyndon Johnson to Charles C. Diggs Jr., April 16, 1962, box 42, CCDP.
61. John G. Field to The Vice President, April 10, 1962, box 139, Vice Presidential Papers, LBJL.
62. Sterling Tucker to Charles C. Diggs Jr., May 17, 1962, box 42, CCDP.

CHAPTER 12

1. Clay, *Just Permanent Interests*, 86–87.
2. William L. Clay Sr., interview by author, December 11, 2014, Silver Spring, MD.
3. In 1968, Clay was elected Missouri's first Black member of the US House.
4. Clay, interview by author, December 11, 2014.
5. "Diggs Asks Probe of Bias at WAC Center," *MC*, February 19, 1955.
6. Charles C. Diggs Jr. to Robert S. McNamara, February 12, 1962, in Records Relating to History and Organization Group 341-P-.5, NACPM.

7. Mary Thomas to Charles C. Diggs Jr., August 3, 1960, box 6, CCDP.
8. Herbert Jones to Charles C. Diggs Jr., March 8, 1960, box 5, CCDP.
9. Jones to Diggs, March 8, 1960.
10. William F. Hart Jr. to Charles C. Diggs Jr., June 17, 1960, box 5, CCDP.
11. MacGregor, *Integration of the Armed Forces*, 522.
12. Nalty, *Strength for the Fight*, 277.
13. Gropman, *Air Force Integrates*, 115–16.
14. *CR*, HR 6390, April 14, 1959, 58230.
15. Mershon and Schlossman, *Foxholes and Color Lines*, 277.
16. "U.S. Bias Follows GIs To France," *PC*, August 14, 1954.
17. Hart to Diggs, June 17, 1960.
18. Hart to Diggs, June 17, 1960.
19. Charles C. Diggs Jr. to Stephen S. Jackson, March 6, 1962, Records Relating to History and Organization Group 341-P-.5, NACPM.
20. "Diggs Calls Discharge of GI Unjust," *MC*, April 23, 1955.
21. "Diggs Calls Discharge of GI Unjust."
22. "Diggs Wins Round for Ousted GI," *MC*, May 7, 1955.
23. Charles C. Diggs to Wilbur Brucker, September 27, 1957, box 11, CCDP.
24. "Diggs Raps AF on Race Report," *CD*, March 2, 1960.
25. "Diggs Raps AF."
26. "Diggs Raps AF."
27. "Diggs to Tour Overseas Bases," *BAA*, April 9, 1960.
28. All uncited quotations in this section are from Diggs, "The Diggs Report."
29. Quoted in Schneller, *Blue and Gold and Black*, 41.
30. John Mintz, "Clinton Nominates First Black Admiral," *WP*, May 14, 1996.
31. Bonnie Gallagher, interview by author, December 8, 2014, Washington, DC.
32. Robert L. Carter to De Witt Paul Garth Jr., March 27, 1962; and Maria L. Marcus to W. B. Ellison, October 21, 1963, both in NAACP Papers. There are numerous correspondences from the NAACP lawyers to Black servicemen directing them to Diggs.
33. Carlisle P. Runge to Charles C. Diggs Jr., March 15, 1961, in Records Relating to History and Organization Group 341-P-.5, NACPM.
34. MacGregor, *Integration of the Armed Forces*, 504–29.
35. Charles C. Diggs Jr. to Robert S. McNamara, August 24, 1961, Records Relating to History and Organization Group 341-P-.5, NACPM.
36. Diggs to McNamara, August 24, 1961.
37. Carlisle Runge to Charles C. Diggs Jr., September 5, 1961, Records Relating to History and Organization Group 341-P-.5, NACPM.
38. Charles C. Diggs Jr. to Robert S. McNamara, September 11, 1961, Records Relating to History and Organization Group 341-P-.5, NACPM.
39. Adam Yarmolinsky to Harris L. Wofford Jr., September 20, 1961, Harris Wofford Papers, box 2, John F. Kennedy Library, Boston, MA.
40. Charles C. Diggs Jr. to Robert S. McNamara, February 12, 1962, Records Relating to History and Organization Group 341-P-.5, NACPM.
41. Diggs to McNamara, February 12, 1962.
42. Diggs to McNamara, February 12, 1962.

43. Diggs to McNamara, February 12, 1962.
44. Memorandum, John L. Fallon to Adm. Clancy, February 16, 1962, Records Relating to History and Organization Group 341-P-.5, NACPM.
45. Robert S. McNamara, oral history interview, January 8, 1975, Lyndon B. Johnson Oral Histories, LBJL.
46. Stephen S. Jackson to Charles C. Diggs Jr., March 6, 1962, Records Relating to History and Organization Group 341-P-.5, NACPM.
47. Jackson to Diggs, March 6, 1962.
48. MacGregor incorrectly claims that Yarmolinsky "conceived" the citizen's committee; see MacGregor, *Integration of the Armed Forces*, 536.
49. Charles C. Diggs to John F. Kennedy, June 27, 1962, Gesell Papers, box 1, John F. Kennedy Library, Boston, MA; "Diggs' Requests Starts Probe of military bias," *Detroit (MI) Tribune*, March 24, 1962.
50. Diggs to Kennedy, June 27, 1962.
51. MacGregor, *Integration of the Armed Forces*, 548.
52. MacGregor, *Integration of the Armed Forces*, 621.
53. MacGregor, *Integration of the Armed Forces*, 621.
54. McNamara, *Essence of Security*, 122–27; MacGregor, *Integration of the Armed Forces*, 606.

CHAPTER 13

1. Eig, *King*, 139–94; Garrow, *Bearing the Cross*, 11–82.
2. Charles C. Diggs Jr., interview, November 6, 1986, in Hampton, *Eyes on the Prize*.
3. Telegram, Charles C. Diggs Jr. to Martin Luther King Jr., April 20, 1956, Carson, *Papers of Martin Luther King*, 3: 218; "Diggs to Lend Aid to 'Bama Bus Boycotters,'" *CD*, March 17, 1956.
4. Martin Luther King Jr. to Charles C. Diggs Jr., April 26, 1956, Carson, *Papers of Martin Luther King*, 3: 218.
5. Charles C. Diggs Jr., interview, November 6, 1986, in Hampton, *Eyes on the Prize*.
6. Charles C. Diggs Jr. to Dwight D. Eisenhower, November 9, 1956, box 20, CCDP; "Diggs Raps Johnson's Stand on Filibuster," *Atlanta Daily World*, December 5, 1956.
7. Thurber, *Republicans and Race*, 99–108.
8. Carson, *Papers of Martin Luther King*, 4:389.
9. Eig, *King*, 183.
10. "Remarks of Congressman Charles C. Diggs, Jr.," May 17, 1957, NAACP Papers.
11. Caro, *Years of Lyndon Johnson*, 863–70.
12. Martin Luther King Jr. to Charles C. Diggs Jr., June 11, 1959, box 2, CCDP.
13. Ransby, *Ella Baker*, 179.
14. Telegram, Charles C. Diggs Jr. to Martin Luther King Jr., March 13, 1958, box 15, CCDP.
15. Martin Luther King Jr. to Charles C. Diggs Jr., March 25, 1958; Carson, *Papers of Martin Luther King*, 4: 389.
16. King to Diggs, March 25, 1958.
17. Charles C. Diggs Jr. to Martin Luther King Jr., November 6, 1961, Carson, *Papers of*

Martin Luther King, 7: 323–24. The FBI described Diggs as "a rather close associate" of Dr. King. See internal note attached to J. Edgar Hoover to Charles C. Diggs, November 21, 1967, Diggs FBI file, no. 1407075-001 (in the author's possession).
18. C. M. Payne, *I've Got the Light*, 132–79.
19. "Rep. Diggs Asks Protection for Mississippians," *Alabama Tribune* (Montgomery), February 22, 1963.
20. Hamlin, *Crossroads at Clarksdale*, 109.
21. Henry with Curry, *Aaron Henry*, 141.
22. Henry with Curry, *Aaron Henry*, 222.
23. Henry with Curry, *Aaron Henry*, 142.
24. Henry with Curry, *Aaron Henry*, 142.
25. Henry with Curry, *Aaron Henry*, 142.
26. "Negro Congressman Is Unhurt in Clarksdale, Miss. Bombing," *NYT*, April 13, 1963.
27. Quoted in "Arson Charged," *Greenwood (MS) Commonwealth*, April 13, 1963.
28. Quoted in "Negro Lawmaker Here Describes Fire Bombing," *Los Angeles Times*, April 13, 1963.
29. "27 Are Arrested in Jackson Riots after Evers Rite," *NYT*, June 16, 1963.
30. Salvatore, *Singing in a Strange Land*, 246.
31. Martin Luther King Jr., "'Great March to Freedom Rally' Speech, Detroit, Michigan, June 23, 1963," posted September 25, 2025, by nicholasflyer, YouTube, 33 min., 58 sec., www.youtube.com/watch?v=0aO7mXbx2lo.
32. Memorandum, Charles A. Horsky, Meeting with Congressman Diggs, May 9, 1963, Lawrence O'Brien Papers, box 4, John F. Kennedy Library, Boston.
33. L. Payne and T. Payne, *Dead Are Arising*.
34. Memorandum, Charles A. Horsky, Meeting with Congressman Diggs, May 9, 1963.
35. Charles C. Diggs Jr. to Martin Luther King Jr., June 27, 1963, NAACP Papers. Diggs's letter to King came after House Democratic leaders had warned Diggs of rumors that plans for the demonstration included a "sit-in" protest in the halls of Congress. See Whalen and Whalen, *Longest Debate*, 19–20.
36. Diggs to King, June 27, 1963.
37. Abernathy, *And the Walls Came Tumbling*, 275.
38. Charles Diggs, oral history transcript, March 13, 1969, NAID 24617781, LBJL.
39. Diggs, oral history transcript, March 13, 1969.
40. Morrison, *Aaron Henry of Mississippi*, 113–36; McLemore, "Mississippi Freedom Democratic Party."
41. Henry with Curry, *Aaron Henry*, 181.
42. Larson, *Walk with Me*; Lee, *For Freedom's Sake*; Blain, *Until I am Free*.
43. Dittmer, *Local People*, 289, 293.
44. Quoted in Lee, *For Freedom's Sake*, 92. Diggs assured Bob Moses and Courtland Cox he supported seating MFDP and persuaded them to share the names of MFDP's supporters on the Credentials Committee. Johnson applied direct pressure, including specific threats, on each of them to withdraw their support. See Forman, *Making of Black Revolutionaries*, 388; Dittmer, *Local People*, 289–90.
45. O'Reilly, *Nixon's Piano*, 248–49.
46. Forman, *Making of Black Revolutionaries*, 389.

47. Henry with Curry, *Aaron Henry*, 194.
48. Quoted in Lawson, *Black Ballots*, 305.
49. Telegram, Andrew Young to Charles C. Diggs Jr., September 15, 1964, box 8, folder 22, MLK Papers, King Library and Archives, Atlanta, GA.
50. Dallek, *Flawed Giant*, 212.
51. Lawson, *Black Ballots*, 278.
52. A. Young, *Easy Burden*, 338; Rice, *Hosea Williams*, 113.
53. Garrow, *Bearing the Cross*, 359.
54. A. Young, *Easy Burden*, 349–50.
55. Dallek, *Flawed Giant*, 213–14.
56. Peter J. Kumpa, "Postmaster Voter-Listing Urged," *Baltimore Sun*, February 5, 1965.
57. "State Congressmen to Visit Selma, Watch Work of 'Rump' Delegation," *Montgomery (AL) Advertiser*, February 5, 1965.
58. James Robinson, "Conyers, Diggs to visit Selma," *DFP*, February 5, 1965.
59. James Robinson, "King Seeks LBJ Aid in Ala. Vote crusade," *DFP*, February 6, 1965.
60. Paul Good, "King to Ask Johnson to act on Alabama," *WP*, February 6, 1965.
61. A. Young, *Easy Burden*, 349–50; Lewis, *Walking with the Wind*, 314.
62. *CR*, February 9, 1965, 2424.
63. Quoted in Good, "King to Ask Johnson to Act on Alabama."
64. *CR*, February 9, 1965, 2424.
65. *CR*, February 9, 1965, 2424.
66. *CR*, February 9, 1965, 2424.
67. "15 Solons Urge New Voting Laws," *CD*, February 11, 1965.
68. "Humphrey Meets Vote Bill Backers," *NYT*, February 26, 1965.
69. Quoted in "Humphrey Meets Vote Bill Backers."
70. Lawrence O'Brien to Charles C. Diggs Jr., March 13, 1965, Name File Charles Diggs, box D 183, WHCF, LBJL.
71. Diggs donated the money raised from the dinner to the SCLC. "King to Speak at Testimonial for Diggs," *MC*, October 2, 1965.
72. "Diggs Appreciation Dinner Head Table List," in Records of the SCLC, 1954–1970, Charles C. Diggs Dinner—1965, NAACP Papers.
73. "Workers Need $2 Minimum Wage, Not Welfare, King," *Jet*, December 9, 1965, 16.
74. Fine, *Violence in the Model City*, 17–37.
75. Charles C. Diggs Jr., oral history interview, January 28, 1970.
76. Jerry M. Flint, "Detroit Leaders Were Optimistic," *NYT*, July 25, 1967.
77. Hammer and Coleman, *Crusader for Justice*, 92.
78. Fine, *Violence in the Model City*, 212.
79. Quoted in Hammer and Coleman, *Crusader for Justice*, 93.
80. Fine, *Violence in the Model City*, 207.
81. Charles C. Diggs Jr, interview by Paige Mulhollan, March 13, 1969, oral history transcript, NAID 24617781, LBJL.
82. Memorandum, Barefoot Sanders to Marvin Watson, July 26, 1967, Charles C. Diggs, box D 183, WHCF, LBJL.
83. Quoted in William C. Selover and Lyn Shepard, "Opposition to Great Society Hardens," *Christian Science Monitor*, August 5, 1967.

84. "Diggs Lauds ICBIF Program," *MC*, May 24, 1969.
85. Alex Coffin, "200,000 Pay Tribute to King," *Atlanta Journal Constitution*, April 10, 1968.
86. Abernathy, *And the Walls Came Tumbling*, 461.
87. Juanita R. Diggs, interview by author, September 12, 2014, Yisplanti, MI.
88. "Funeral of Dr. Martin L. King 1968," posted May 10, 2011, by historycomestolife, YouTube, 3 min., 14 sec., www.youtube.com/watch?v=mU1634eB6uk; Coffin, "200,000 Pay Tribute to King."

CHAPTER 14

1. Joseph, *Waiting 'Til the Midnight*; Bloom and Martin, *Black Against Empire*.
2. Burk, *Eisenhower Administration*, 89–108.
3. Charles C. Diggs Jr. "The Urban Crisis Revisited," November 4, 1975, box 209, CCDP.
4. John H. Johnson to Charles C. Diggs Jr., January 23, 1957, box 28, CCDP.
5. Johnson to Diggs, January 23, 1957. Johnson's letter is the first known written proposal for creating what would become the Congressional Black Caucus.
6. Adam Clayton Powell to John H. Johnson, February 8, 1957, box 28, CCDP.
7. Charles C. Diggs Jr. to John H. Johnson, January 30, 1957, box 28, in CCDP.
8. Diggs to Johnson, January 30, 1957.
9. "Philadelphia's Robert Nix," *Jet*, June 5, 1958, 10; "4th Negro in Congress Is Sworn In," *WP*, June 5, 1958.
10. Clay, *Just Permanent Interests*, 90.
11. Adair, "Black Legislative Influence," 25.
12. DuBose, *Untold Story*, 81.
13. Adair, "Black Legislative Influence in Federal Policy Decisions," 25.
14. William L. Clay Sr., interview by author, December 11, 2014, Silver Spring, MD; Jack Anderson and Les Whitten, "Witnesses Say Rep. Nix Drinks," *WP*, December 17, 1976.
15. Marguerite Ross Barnett, "Congressional Black Caucus," 31.
16. Quoted in Paul R. Hathaway, "The Black Caucus," *Essence*, October 1971, 39–40.
17. Charles C. Diggs Jr., "A Transcript of Tape-Recorded Interview," The Civil Rights Documentation Project, January 28, 1970, Moorland-Spingarn Research Center, Howard University, Washington, DC.
18. Hathaway, "Black Caucus."
19. R. C. Smith, *We Have No Leaders*, 111.
20. Charles C. Diggs Jr. to Fred Harris, May 8, 1969, Michigan Democratic Party Papers, box 22, Bentley Historical Library, University of Michigan, Ann Arbor.
21. Clay, interview by author, December 11, 2014.
22. Tim Poor, "Tailoring his Legacy: Portraits of St. Louis Bill Clay," *St. Louis-Post Dispatch*, January 25, 1998.
23. Quoted in Stokes, *Gentleman from Ohio*, 139.
24. Louis Stokes, interview by author, December 11, 2014, Silver Spring, MD.
25. Quoted in Timothy Bleck, "Black Caucus Becoming a Vital Force," *St. Louis (MO) Post-Dispatch*, March 1, 1970.

26. Charles C. Diggs Jr. to The President, February 18, 1970, box 130, WHCF, RMNL.
27. William E. Timmons to Charles C. Diggs Jr., February 20, 1970, box 130, WHCF, RMNL.
28. Kruse, *White Flight*, 220–29.
29. Saul Friedman, "Diggs, Maddox Clash over 'Slur' in Dining Room," *DFP*, February 25, 1970; "Ax 'Drumsticks' Get Maddox in Capitol Stew," *Atlanta Journal Constitution*, February 25, 1970.
30. Quoted in "Diggs, Maddox Clash over 'Slur' in Dining Room."
31. "Ax 'Drumsticks.'"
32. Vanderbilt News Archives, "Maddox/Diggs Shouting Match," *CBS Evening News*, February 24, 1970.
33. O'Reilly, *Nixon's Piano*, 317–18.
34. William Raspberry, "Negro Congressmen View Nixon," *WP*, January 30, 1971.
35. "Negro Congressmen View Nixon."
36. Memorandum, Leonard Garment to Hugh Sloan, February 24, 1970, box 130, WHCF, RMNL.
37. Peter Kihss, "'Benign Neglect' on Race Is Proposed by Moynihan," *NYT*, March 1, 1970.
38. Memorandum, Hugh Sloan to John Ehrlichman, March 2, 1970; Memorandum, Hugh Sloan to Richard Nixon, March 3, 1970, box 130, WHCF, RMNL.
39. Memorandum, William Timmons to Dwight Chapin, April 13, 1970, box 130, WHCF, RMNL.
40. Hugh Sloan to Charles C. Diggs Jr., April 20, 1970, box 130, WHCF, RMNL.
41. O'Reilly, *Nixon's Piano*, 277–329.
42. Clay, *Just Permanent Interests*, 140; memorandum, Charles C. Diggs Jr. to "Shadow Cabinet" Members, December 4, 1970, Hobart Taylor Papers, box 5, Bentley Historical Library, University of Michigan, Ann Arbor.
43. Clay, *Just Permanent Interests*, 117.
44. Clay, interview by author, December 11, 2014.
45. Clay, *Just Permanent Interests*, 197.
46. R. C. Smith, *We Have No Leaders*, 111.
47. Clay, telephone interview by author, December 2, 2016.
48. Clay, interview by author, December 11, 2014.
49. Clay, *Just Permanent Interests*, 257.
50. Stokes, *Gentleman from Ohio*, 146.
51. Clay, interview by author, December 11, 2014.
52. Clay, interview by author, December 11, 2014.
53. Shirley Chisholm et al. to Mr. President, January 21, 1971, box 155, WHCF, RMNL. On March 23, 1971, Walter Fauntroy (D-DC), a Black minister and civil rights leader, was sworn in as the delegate representing the District of Columbia in the US House. Fauntroy became the thirteenth member of the CBC.
54. Clay, *Just Permanent Interests*, 143.
55. Clay, *Just Permanent Interests*, 144.
56. Charles C. Diggs et al. to The President, February 16, 1971, box 155, WHCF, RMNL.
57. Paul Delaney, "President Agrees to a Meeting with 12 Black House Members," *NYT*, February 19, 1971.

58. Memorandum, Clark MacGregor to The President, March 19, 1971, box 5, WHCF, RMNL.
59. Memorandum, William Timmons to Dwight Chapin, February 25, 1971, box 88, WHCF, RMNL.
60. Clay, interview by author, December 11, 2014.
61. DuBose, *Untold Story*, 100.
62. DuBose, *Untold Story*, 101.
63. Clay, *Just Permanent Interests*, 146.
64. Quoted in Stokes, *Gentleman from Ohio*, 148.
65. Paul Delaney, "Blacks in House Get Nixon Pledge," *NYT*, March 26, 1971.
66. Barnett, "Historical Look," 3.
67. Saul Friedman, "Blacks Give Nixon Action Deadline," *DFP*, March 27, 1971.
68. Charles C. Diggs Jr. to Richard Nixon, April 5, 1971, box 155, WHCF, RMNL.
69. Richard Nixon to Charles C. Diggs Jr., May 18, 1971, box 5, WHCF, RMNL.
70. Memorandum, Clark MacGregor to Dwight Chapin, May 11, 1971, box 5, WHCF, RMNL.
71. Clay, *Just Permanent Interests*, 151.
72. "Black Caucus Presses for Corporate Support," *CD*, June 17, 1917.
73. Clay, *Just Permanent Interests*, 160.
74. Hathaway, "Black Caucus."
75. DuBose, *Untold Story*, 113–16.
76. Hathaway, "Black Caucus."
77. Ethel L. Payne, "Black Caucus Moves into New Headquarters," *PC*, September 25, 1971.

CHAPTER 15

1. DuBose, *Untold Story*, 121; Clay, *Just Permanent Interests*, 192.
2. F. C. Harris, *Price of the Ticket*, 3–34.
3. Rustin, "From Protest to Politics."
4. Carmichael and Hamilton, *Black Power*.
5. Woodard, *Nation within a Nation*; 162–72; Johnson, *Revolutionaries to Race Leaders*, 74–82.
6. Moore, *Defeat of Black Power*, 40
7. Curwood, *Shirley Chisholm*, 216–29.
8. Baraka, "Gary and Miami," 78.
9. Baraka, "Gary and Miami," 60.
10. Moore, *Defeat of Black Power*, 49–62.
11. Clay, *Just Permanent Interests*, 195.
12. Lawrence Taylor, "... While Blacks Stay at Arm's Length," *St. Louis (MO) Post Dispatch*, November 21, 1971.
13. Baraka, "From Gary to Miami," 62.
14. Baraka, "From Gary to Miami," 60.
15. Baraka, "From Gary to Miami," 63.
16. Moore, *Defeat of Black Power*, 60.
17. Clay, *Just Permanent Interests*, 197.

18. Quoted in Moore, *Defeat of Black Power*, 61.
19. DuBose, *Untold Story*, 153.
20. "Has Time Come for Blacks to Build Political Party," *Cincinnati Inquirer*, November 25, 1971.
21. Clay, *Just Permanent Interests*, 205.
22. DuBose, *Untold Story*, 153.
23. DuBose, *Untold Story*, 135.
24. Paul Delaney, "Rep. Stokes Heads the Black Caucus," *NYT*, February 9, 1972.
25. Ethel L. Payne, "Why Rep. Diggs Quit Caucus: Inside Story," *CD*, February 14, 1972.
26. "Louis Stokes takes Caucus Reins as Diggs Steps Down," *Jet*, February 24, 1972.
27. Quoted in DuBose, *Untold Story*, 153.
28. DuBose, *Untold Story*, 153.
29. "Political Platform Drafted by Blacks," *Chicago Tribune*, March 6, 1972.
30. Moore, *Defeat of Black Power*, 94.
31. Quoted in "Black Convention to Open," *Baltimore Sun*, March 9, 1972.
32. Quoted in Moore, *Defeat of Black Power*, 64.
33. Woodard, *Nation within a Nation*, 204.
34. Quoted in DuBose, *Untold Story*, 162.
35. Thomas A. Johnson, "Blacks Convene National Session," *NYT*, March 11, 1972.
36. Angela Parker, "NAACP Opposition to Militant Issue Threatens Parley Split," *Chicago Tribune*, March 11, 1972.
37. Moore, *Defeat of Black Power*, 90.
38. Ethel L. Payne, "Post-Convention Patchwork for Unity," *CD*, April 1, 1972.
39. Moore, *Defeat of Black Power*, 160.
40. Memorandum, John A. Morsell to NAACP Representatives at the Black Political Convention, March 9, 1972, National Black Political Convention, NAACP Papers.
41. "Statement of Congressman Diggs," March 11, 1972, box 305, CCDP.
42. DuBose, *Untold Story*, 161.
43. Quoted in, "Gary Convention: A History Maker," *News Journal* (Wilmington, DE), March 13, 1972.
44. Moore, *Defeat of Black Power*, 105.
45. Woodard, *Nation within a Nation*, 209.
46. Simeon Booker, "Black Political Convention Is Successful Despite Splits and Tactical Differences," *Jet*, March 30, 1972, 15.
47. Moore, *Defeat of Black Power*, 110.
48. Quoted in Moore, *Defeat of Black Power*, 110.
49. DuBose, *Untold Story*, 169.
50. Booker, "Black Political Convention Is Successful."
51. DuBose, *Untold Story*, 169.
52. Moore, *Defeat of Black Power*, 110–12.
53. Booker, "Black Political Convention Is Successful."
54. Moore, *Defeat of Black Power*, 130–32.
55. Moore, *Defeat of Black Power*, 133.
56. Moore, *Defeat of Black Power*, 135.
57. Clay, *Just Permanent Interests*, 210–11.
58. C. Young and Wheeler, *Hard Stuff*, 189–90.

59. C. Young and Wheeler, *Hard Stuff*, 190.
60. C. Young and Wheeler, *Hard Stuff*, 190.
61. C. Young and Wheeler, *Hard Stuff*, 190–91.
62. Quoted in "Impact of Black Convention Awaited," *San Francisco Examiner*, March 13, 1972.
63. "Black Leaders Agree: Can't Take Mrs. Chisholm Lightly," *The Republic* (Columbus, IN), March 13, 1972. Diggs endorsed Chisholm in the Michigan Democratic primary on the House of Diggs's radio program. See DuBose, *Untold Story*, 173.
64. Quoted in DuBose, *Untold Story*, 175.
65. Quoted in DuBose, *Untold Story*, 175.
66. "Black Caucus Hits Anti-Israeli Views," *NYT*, March 23, 1972.
67. Clay, *Just Permanent Interests*, 205.
68. Roy Wilkins to Charles C. Diggs, May 3, 1972, National Black Political Convention, NAACP Papers.
69. Paul Delaney, "Black Convention Eases Busing and Israeli Stands," *NYT*, May 20, 1972.
70. Paul Delaney, "House Caucus Lists 'Black Bill of Rights,'" *NYT*, June 2, 1972.
71. Walters, *Black Presidential Politics*, 91–92.
72. Paul Delaney, "House Caucus Lists 'Black Bill of Rights,'" *NYT*, June 2, 1972.
73. Quoted in Walters, *Black Presidential Politics*, 92.
74. R. W. Apple Jr., "Black Bloc Pledges Votes to McGovern," *NYT*, June 27, 1972.
75. Amiri Baraka, "A Post Convention Strategy for Black People," n.d, National Tenants Organization Papers, National Black Political Convention, Moorland-Spingarn Research Center, Howard University, Washington, DC.
76. Baraka, "Post Convention Strategy."
77. Quoted in DuBose, *Untold Story*, 81.

CHAPTER 16

1. US House, *Unveiling of a Portrait*.
2. US House, *Unveiling of a Portrait*, vii.
3. US House, *Unveiling of a Portrait*, 7.
4. Fauntroy, *Home Rule or House Rule?*, 28–37; C. W. Harris, *Congress and the Governance*, 49.
5. Asch and Musgrove, *Chocolate City*; Masur, *An Example for All*.
6. Asch and Musgrove, *Chocolate City*, 195–96.
7. Asch and Musgrove, *Chocolate City*, 152–84.
8. Fauntroy, *Home Rule or House Rule?*, 46–49.
9. McMillan served as chair of the committee during the 79th (1945–47), 81st (1949–51), 82nd (1951–53), and the 84th through the 92nd Congresses (1955–73).
10. Martin Weil, "John McMillan Dies, Opposed Home Rule as Congressman," *WP*, September 4, 1979.
11. Stone, *Black Political Power in America*, 211.
12. Pearlman, *Democracy's Capital*.
13. Pearlman, *Democracy's Capital*, 72–74.
14. Pearlman, *Democracy's Capital*, 45–50.

15. Charles Rangel, interview by author, February 6, 2015, New York.
16. Quoted in Chuck Stone, "Rep. Diggs: Navigating Between Racism and Thick-Headedness," *WS*, September 12, 1976.
17. "Five Negro Lawmakers Given 8 Jobs," *PC*, February 9, 1963.
18. Charles C. Diggs Jr. to John McMillan, April 3, 1969, box 128, folder 23A, Carl Albert Papers, University of Oklahoma, Norman.
19. In 1970, a Black physician forced McMillan into an unsuccessful Democratic primary runoff election. Diggs, Fauntroy, and other Black leaders traveled to South Carolina to support the Black candidate. "Diggs comes to McMillan District, Urges his defeat in Primary Vote," *WP*, June 22, 1970.
20. Martha M. Hamilton, "Diggs fires aides of D.C. Committee," *WP*, January 20, 1973.
21. Carl Albert to Charles C. Diggs Jr., January 6, 1973; Charles C. Diggs Jr. to Carl Albert, January 8, 1973, box 180, folder 47, Carl Albert Papers, University of Oklahoma, Norman.
22. Ronald Dellums, interview by author, July 24, 2014, Washington, DC.
23. Dellums, interview by author, July 24, 2014.
24. Pearlman, *Democracy's Capital*, 200.
25. Charles C. Diggs Jr. to Brock Adams, May 2, 1973, "Home Rule for the District of Columbia 1973–1974: Background and Legislative History," 93rd Cong., 2nd sess. (Washington, DC: Government Printing Office, 1974), 13.
26. Martha M. Hamilton, "House Unit Votes Home Rule," *WP*, August 1, 1973.
27. Toni Jones, "Quiet, persuasive Charlie Diggs," *DFP*, May 16, 1976.
28. Quoted in DuBose, *Untold Story*, 187.
29. Charles C. Diggs Jr. to Gerald R. Ford, September 21, 1973, in "Home Rule for the District of Columbia," 1747.
30. Quoted in Martha M. Hamilton, "3 Men—Diggs, Nelsen, Nixon—Hold Key to Home Rule," *WP*, September 16, 1973.
31. Quoted in DuBose, *Untold Story*, 187.
32. Charles C. Diggs Jr. to William Natcher, September 21, 1973; William Natcher to Charles C. Diggs Jr, September 22, 1973, in "Home Rule for the District of Columbia," 1741–42.
33. Charles C. Diggs Jr. to Dear Colleague, October 3, 1973, in "Home Rule for the District of Columbia," 1742–43.
34. The layover requirement of thirty "legislative" days makes for long delays in passing bills adopted by the city council.
35. Cathe Wolhowe, "Diggs Is Accused of 'Power Ploy,'" *WP*, October 8, 1973.
36. Quoted in Wolhowe, "Diggs Is Accused."
37. C. W. Harris, *Congress and the Governance*, 9.
38. Quoted in Martha M. Hamilton, "Home Rule Bill Is Amended: Concessions Seen Improving Chances," *WP*, October 9, 1973.
39. Hamilton, "Home Rule Bill Is Amended."
40. Dellums, interview by author, July 24, 2014.
41. Martha M. Hamilton, "Natcher Agrees to Back D.C. Suffrage," *WP*, October 10, 1973.
42. *CR*, October 9, 1973, 33354.

43. *CR*, October 10, 1973, 33634.
44. *CR*, October 10, 1973, 33611.
45. Albert Swanson, "Home Rule for D.C. Due House Test," *BAA*, October 13, 1973.
46. *CR*, October 9, 1973, 33384.
47. *CR*, October 9, 1973, 33384.
48. *CR*, October 9. 1973, 33358.
49. *CR*, October 10, 1973, 33646.
50. The federal enclave amendment was adopted in final passage. It is known as National Capital Service Area (NCSA). The act has not been implemented. See C. W. Harris, *Congress and the Governance*, 15–42.
51. Richard Nixon to Charles C. Diggs Jr., January 14, 1974, box 202, WHCF, RMNL.
52. US House, *Unveiling of a Portrait*, 12–13.

CHAPTER 17

1. Mayhew, *Congress*.
2. Schraeder, *United States Foreign Policy*.
3. Von Eschen, *Race Against Empire*, 8; Plummer, *Rising Wind*, 100; Dudziak, *Cold War Civil Rights*. But see also Anderson, *Bourgeois Radicals*.
4. Lynch, *Black American Radicals*.
5. Collins, *Ubuntu*.
6. Diggs, "Role of the American Negro," 448–52. This essay is a reprint of an address Diggs gave at the Second Annual Conference of the American Society of Africa Culture, June 26–29, 1959, New York City.
7. Massie, *Loosing the Bonds*; Horne, *White Supremacy Confronted*.
8. Representative Francis Bolton to Dwight D. Eisenhower, January 15, 1957, WHCF, box 763, Dwight David Eisenhower Library, Abilene, KS. Bolton was a former chair and the senior Republican on the Africa Subcommittee.
9. John F. Dulles to Dwight D. Eisenhower, February 26, 1957, WHCF, box 763, Dwight David Eisenhower Library, Abilene, KS. Adam Clayton Powell's request to be a part of the delegation was blocked by Speaker Sam Rayburn because of Powell's endorsement of Eisenhower's reelection.
10. Morrow, *Black Man in the White House*; Morris, *Eye on the Struggle*, 196–99.
11. Quoted in Morrow, *Black Man in the White House*, 134.
12. Quoted in DuBose, *Untold Story*, 64.
13. Charles C. Diggs Jr. to Wilbur D. Mills, October 4, 1958, box 16, CCDP.
14. Plummer, *Rising Wind*, 278–79.
15. "Diggs Urges NAACP Go International," *New York Amsterdam News*, January 3, 1959.
16. "Diggs Wants Negroes to Talk for US in Africa," *DFP*, January 11, 1959.
17. Fenno, *Congressmen in Committees*.
18. Charles C. Diggs Jr. to Doubleday Book Store, July 1, 1959; November 20, 1959; and August 3, 1959, box 1, CCDP. Doubleday Book Store was in Detroit.
19. Charles C. Diggs Jr. to Christian A. Herter, September 15, 1960, box 30, CCDP.
20. "South Africa on Trial," *NYT*, May 30, 1960.
21. Press Release, "NAACP Urges U.S. to Cut Off Relations with South Africa,"

March 24, 1960, NAACP Papers; Walter Reuther to Dwight D. Eisenhower, March 25, 1960, NAACP Papers.
22. Schraeder, *United States Foreign Policy*, 199.
23. Thurber, *Republicans and Race*, 119–52.
24. Noer, *Soapy*, 209.
25. Meriwether, "'Worth a Lot of Negro Votes.'"
26. Meriwether, "'Worth a Lot of Negro Votes.'"
27. Rusk and Williams disagreed on US Africa policy. Rusk, *As I Saw It*, 274; Noer, *Soapy*, 235–41.
28. Noer, *Soapy*, 268.
29. Plummer, *In Search of Power*, 122–28.
30. Noer, *Cold War and Black Liberation*, 186.
31. Noer, *Cold War and Black Liberation*, 185–237.
32. US House, Committee on Foreign Affairs, *Report of Study Mission to Africa*, 3.
33. US House, Committee on Foreign Affairs, *United States–South African Relations*.
34. "South African Paper Assails Hearing in U.S. on Apartheid," *NYT*, March 4, 1966.
35. William Roundtree to Dean Rusk, June 22, 1966, William M. Roundtree Papers, box 2, Dwight David Eisenhower Library, Abilene, KS. This letter was marked "Secret."
36. "U.S. Protests Snubbing of Diggs," *DFP*, June 6, 1966.
37. Charles C. Diggs Jr. to A. Phillip Randolph, July 5, 1966, box 300, folder 13, CCDSAP.
38. Massie, *Loosing the Bonds*, 219.
39. DeRoche, *Black, White, and Chrome*; Lake, *"Tar Baby" Option*.
40. Lake, *"Tar Baby" Option*, 101–3.
41. Massie, *Loosing the Bonds*, 234–35; Plummer, *In Search of Power*, 317; Coker, *United States and South Africa*, 20.
42. Lake, *"Tar Baby" Option*, 123–57.
43. Newsom, *Witness to a Changing World*, 214.

CHAPTER 18

1. Goler Teal Butcher, interview by Robert Kinloch Massie, May 24, 1990.
2. Charles C. Diggs Jr. to Barrett O'Hara, December 30, 1968, box 306, CCDSAP.
3. As subcommittee chair, Diggs significantly increased his "oversight" of US Africa policy. See Minta, *Oversight*.
4. Charles C. Diggs Jr. to Clarence Mitchell, February 12, 1969, box 306, CCDSAP.
5. Press Release, "Africa Is the Continent of the Future," n.d., box 310, CCDSAP.
6. Diggs to Mitchell, February 12, 1969.
7. Diggs's letters requesting this information from cabinet officials and agency heads are in box 310, CCDSAP.
8. Telegram, Charles C. Diggs to Richard Nixon, February 7, 1969, box 306, CCDSAP.
9. *CR*, March 26, 1969, 7790.
10. US House, Committee on Foreign Affairs, *South Africa and United States*, 33.
11. "South Africa Trip Assailed," *Baltimore Sun*, April 24, 1969; *CR*, June 11, 1969,

15465. In the 1970 Democratic primary, Friedel was defeated by Parren Mitchell, a Black civil rights activist.
12. Grisinger, "'South Africa Is the Mississippi of the World.'"
13. US House, Committee on Foreign Affairs, *South Africa and United States*, 71.
14. US House, Committee on Foreign Affairs, *South Africa and United States*, 59.
15. US House, Committee on Foreign Affairs, *South Africa and United States*, 67.
16. "House Votes Extension of Sugar Act," *WP*, June 11, 1971.
17. "Vorster: Critical Guest Not Welcome," Associated Press, August 10, 1969.
18. US House, Committee on Foreign Affairs, *Report of Special Study Mission*.
19. "Diggs Says U.S. Is Headed for New Vietnam in Africa," *DFP*, September 15, 1969.
20. US House, Committee on Foreign Affairs, *Report of Special Study Mission*, 34–35.
21. Simeon Booker, "Ticker Tape," *Jet*, July 21, 1969.
22. US House, Committee on Foreign Affairs, *Foreign Policy Implications of Racial Exclusion*.
23. US House, Committee on Foreign Affairs, *Report of the Portuguese Guinea*.
24. US House, Committee on Foreign Affairs, *Policy toward Africa*, 2.
25. Charles C. Diggs Jr., "Some Observations on Contemporary Africa," September 8, 1970, box 306, CCDSAP.
26. J. C. Smith, "United States Foreign Policy."
27. "Woman Lawyer Provides advice to Diggs on Africa," *Jet*, January 6, 1972.
28. Charles C. Diggs Jr., interview by Robert Kinloch Massie, May 24, 1990.
29. US House, Committee on Foreign Affairs, *U.S. Business Involvement*.
30. US House, Committee on Foreign Affairs, *U.S. Business Involvement*, 70.
31. US House, Committee on Foreign Affairs, *U.S. Business Involvement*, 182.
32. Charles C. Diggs Jr. to Rep. John Brademas, July 17, 1973, box 226, CCDSAP.
33. "Comments on Planning the Itinerary of CODEL Diggs in South Africa and Namibia," n.d., box 340, CCDSAP.
34. "Comments on Planning the Itinerary."
35. The description of Diggs's CODEL to South Africa is based, in part, on the extraordinary typewritten notes (likely written by Goler Butcher) of each meeting. Uncited quotations are from the CODEL. See "CODEL Report," box 224, CCDSAP.
36. Diggs Jr., interview by Massie.
37. "CODEL Report," 62.
38. Quoted in "CODEL Report," 65; Paul Dold, "Congressman Jolts Along on African Visit," *Christian Science Monitor*, August 14, 1971; Massie, *Loosing the Bonds*, 298.
39. Horne, *White Supremacy Confronted*, 504.
40. "CODEL Report," 67.
41. "South Africa's Travel Restrictions Irk Diggs," Associated Press, August 13, 1971.
42. "South Africa's Travel Restrictions Irk Diggs."
43. DuBose, *Untold Story*, 127.
44. US House, Committee on Foreign Affairs, *Faces of Africa*, 83.
45. US House, Committee on Foreign Affairs, *Faces of Africa*, 159.
46. US House, Committee on Foreign Affairs, *Faces of Africa*, 159.
47. US House, Committee on Foreign Affairs, *Faces of Africa*, 163.
48. Massie, *Loosing the Bonds*, 253–59. Biko died in South African police detention from a traumatic brain injury on September 12, 1977.

49. Massie, *Loosing the Bonds*, 299–301.
50. Diggs Jr., interview by Massie.
51. Quoted in Massie, *Loosing the Bonds*, 763. When he returned to the United States, Diggs met with James Roche, the CEO and chair of General Motors, and demanded GM improve its record of hiring, training and compensating Black Africans. See Massie, *Loosing the Bonds*, 305.
52. "Rep. Diggs So. African Race Conditions Appalling," *PC*, August 28, 1971.
53. "Rep. Diggs So. African Race Conditions."
54. Press Release, "Diggs Meets Press at End of South Africa Tour," box 345, CCDSAP.
55. "Diggs Meets Press."
56. Diggs Jr., "Remarks of the Honorable Charles C. Diggs, Jr."
57. Press Briefing, "Congressman Charles C. Diggs, Jr.," September 20, 1971, box 340, CCDSAP.

CHAPTER 19

1. *CR*, January 18, 1972, 113; Terrence Smith, "Rep. Diggs Resigns as a UN Delegate," *NYT*, December 18, 1971.
2. *CR*, January 18, 1972, 114.
3. DuBose, *Untold Story*, 148.
4. Richard M. Nixon to Prime Minister John Vorster, June 30, 1972, box CO 66, RMNL.
5. Charles C. Diggs to Richard M. Nixon, October 23, 1971, box 340, CCDSAP.
6. Charles C. Diggs Jr., "Recommendations for United States Policy as a Result of my Trip to South Africa, Guinea-Bissau, and Cape Verde," box 252, RMNL.
7. Memorandum, Marshall Wright to Henry Kissinger, December 4, 1971, NSC 35403, RMNL.
8. Tillery, *Between Homeland and Motherland*, 125–48; Talton, *In This Land of Plenty*, 109–47; Dellums and Halterman, *Lying Down with the Lions*, 123.
9. Clay, *Just Permanent Interests*, 247–52.
10. Robinson, *Defending the Spirit*, 21–22, 15.
11. Robinson, *Defending the Spirit*, 89–93.
12. Randall Robinson to Charles C. Diggs Jr., February 6, 1971, box 306, CCDSAP.
13. Clay, *Just Permanent Interests*, 247–48.
14. Charles C. Diggs Jr., interview by Robert Kinloch Massie, May 24, 1990.
15. Charles C. Diggs Jr., "Keynote Address: African American National Conference on Africa," May 25–26, 1972, box 226, CCDSAP.
16. Richard E. Prince, "12,000 Blacks March to Support Africa," *WP*, May 28, 1972.
17. Editorial, "African Togetherness," *BAA* May 27, 1972.
18. Quoted in Prince, "12,000 Blacks March to Support Africa."
19. R. C. Williams, "Adversarial Diplomacy and African American Politics," 123–27.
20. Robinson, *Defending the Spirit*, 95.
21. "U.S. Vetoes Move on S. Africa," *NYT*, May 23, 1973.
22. John Lewis Jr., "South Africa Now Free to Flood U.S. with Sugar," *BAA*, June 15, 1974.
23. Charles C. Diggs Jr., "Statement before the Democratic Platform Committee," June 22, 1972, box 226, CCDSAP.

24. Butcher, "Southern African Issues in United States."
25. See, for example, *Diggs v. Shultz*, 470 F.2d 461 (D.C. Cir. 1972), https://casetext.com/case/diggs-v-shultz.
26. "Caucus Meets with Ford over Jobs, Inflation," *BAA*, August 24, 1974.
27. "Full Employment a Must, Caucus Tells Ford," *BAA*, August 31, 1974.
28. Memorandum of Conversation, August 21, 1974, box 5, National Security Adviser Collection, Gerald R. Ford Library, Ann Arbor, MI.
29. Memorandum of Conversation, August 21, 1974.
30. Massie, *Loosing the Bonds*, 373–85.
31. "Statement of Charles C. Diggs, Jr. at Press Conference in Africa," February 25, 1975, box 345, CCDSAP.
32. DeRoche, *Andrew Young*, 41–69.
33. Kissinger, *Years of Renewal*, 922.
34. Memorandum, Herschelle S. Challenor to Charles C. Diggs Jr., "Report on Black Caucus Meeting with Secretary of State Kissinger," August 19, 1975, box 209, CCDSAP.
35. "Report on Black Caucus Meeting."
36. Herschelle Sullivan Challenor, interview by author, March 18, 2015, Atlanta, GA.
37. Memorandum, Herschelle Challenor to Charles C. Diggs Jr., October 9, 1975, box 209, CCDSAP.
38. "Founding Member Invitees, Black Forum on Foreign Policy," November 19, 1975, box 209, CCDSAP.
39. Willard Johnson, interview by Robert Kinloch Massie, December 19, 1989.
40. "Press Statement on Angola by Congressman Charles C. Diggs, Jr.," January 11, 1976, box 224, CCDSAP.
41. "Press Statement on Angola."
42. Memorandum of Conversation, January 8, 1976, box 17, National Security Adviser Collection, Gerald R. Ford Library, Ann Arbor, MI.
43. Memorandum of Conversation, January 8, 1976.
44. DeRoche, *Black, White, and Chrome*, 195–241.
45. Memorandum, Yvonne Burke and Charles C. Diggs Jr. to Henry Kissinger, April 14, 1976, box 345, CCDSAP.
46. Walton, Stevenson, and Rosser, *African Foreign Policy*, 121–30.
47. Editorial, ". . . a Forward Policy," *NYT*, April 28, 1976.
48. Charles C. Diggs Jr., "The United States and Rhodesia: Where Do We Stand?," May 12, 1976, box 340, CCDSAP.
49. Massie, *Loosing the Bonds*, 397–401.
50. Mitchell, *Jimmy Carter in Africa*, 18–64.
51. "Black Caucus Weekend Brings Out Stars, Goodwill, Big Plans," *Jet*, October 14, 1976, 28–29; "U.S. Group Formed to Press for Black Rule in Africa," *NYT*, September 26, 1976.
52. "The African-American Manifesto on Southern Africa," *Black Scholar*, 8 (January–February 1977), 27–32.
53. Diggs Jr., interview by Massie.
54. Clay, *Just Permanent Interests*, 89.

55. "Black Leadership Meeting with Secretary of State Henry Kissinger—Talking Points," October 5, 1976, box 345, CCDSAP.
56. "Diggs says he will report to Carter," Associated Press, November 7, 1976.
57. Charles C. Diggs to Cyrus R. Vance, January 5, 1976 [sic; 1977], box 340, CCDSAP; Cyrus R. Vance to Charles C. Diggs, April 24, 1977, box 340, CCDSAP.
58. R. C. Williams, "Adversarial Diplomacy and African American Politics," 168.
59. "The African-American Participants in the African-American Conference, Maseru, Lesotho," n.d., box 410, CCDSAP.
60. Quoted in Robinson, *Defending the Spirit*, 103.
61. Quoted in Robinson, *Defending the Spirit*, 103.
62. Challenor, interview by author, March 18, 2015.
63. Smith, *We Have No Leaders*, 147–53.

CHAPTER 20

1. "Prospectus of Diggs Enterprises, Inc.," *DFP*, August 6, 1955.
2. "Diggs Donates Home to Workers," *DFP*, July 13, 1957.
3. "Undertakers Meet in Capital to Wage Fight," *DN*, May 10, 1949; "Wolverine Assn. Charges Diggs Double Cross," *Detroit (MI) Tribune*, June 28, 1947.
4. "O.K. Is Given to Burial Bill," *DN*, May 13, 1949. The WFDA was angry at Diggs for reneging on what they claimed was his promise ten years earlier to support legislation banning all burial insurance. For background on the dispute, see "Funeral Directors Still Bar Diggs," *PC*, August 20, 1955.
5. "O.K. Is Given to Burial Bill."
6. Thomas A. Cleveland to Harry S. Tressel, June 6, 1959, box 34, CCDP; Charles C. Diggs Jr. to E. E. Fort, November 30, 1960, box 4, CCDP.
7. Quoted in Gary Schuster, "The Rise and Decline of Charles C. Diggs," *DN*, July 22, 1979.
8. "Women, Failing Business Put Rep. Diggs in Debt," *DFP*, June 26, 1977.
9. Frederick C. Brown to Charles C. Diggs Jr., January 3, 1961, box 34, CCDP. Diggs received other complaints, see Lillie Mason to Charles C. Diggs Jr., April 28, 1960; Thelma Farrar to Charles C. Diggs Jr., April 20, 1960, box 34, CCDP.
10. Charles C. Diggs Jr. to Charles C. Diggs Sr., August 14, 1961, box 34, CCDP.
11. Memorandum, Charles C. Diggs Jr. to Ernest Davenport, September 13, 1961, box 34, CCDP.
12. Ernest Davenport to House of Diggs, Inc., April 3, 1959, box 34, CCDP.
13. Charles C. Diggs III, interview by author, August 4, 2015, Ypsilanti, MI.
14. Weston Diggs Jr., interview by author, August 6, 2015, Novi, MI.
15. Weston Diggs Jr., interview by author, August 6, 2015.
16. Ernest Davenport to House of Diggs, Inc., April 3, 1959, box 34, CCDP.
17. Ernest Davenport to House of Diggs, Inc., July 18, 1959, box 34, CCDP.
18. Richard Austin to Charles C. Diggs Jr., June 18, 1960, box 32, CCDP.
19. Ernest Davenport to House of Diggs, Inc., April 3, 1959, box 34, CCDP.
20. Sugrue, *Origins of the Urban Crisis*, 125–26.
21. Richard Austin to House of Diggs, Inc., July 18, 1959, box 34, CCDP.

22. Quoted in *USA v. Charles C. Diggs, Jr.*, 613 F.2d (D.C. Cir.1978), 1134–35.
23. Quoted in *USA v. Charles C. Diggs, Jr.*, 1134–35; Schuster, "Rise and Decline."
24. Charles C. Diggs Jr. to John C. Mackie, March 3, 1958, box 34, CCDP.
25. Richard Austin to House of Diggs Board of Directors, November 30, 1959, box 34, CCDP.
26. Charles C. Diggs Jr. to Representative Robert Nix, January 11, 1961, box 34, CCDP.
27. "Detroit Firm Will Merge into Mammoth Life," *Courier-Journal* (Louisville, KY), June 22, 1961.
28. Maraniss, *Once a Great City*, 96–97.
29. House members earned $22,500 in 1955; $30,000 in 1965; and $42,000 in 1969.
30. Memorandum, Charles C. Diggs Jr. to Charles T. Coles Jr., March 28, 1960; Memorandum, Charles C. Diggs Jr. to Ted Riley, March 17, 1960, box 34, CCDP.
31. Memorandum, Charles C. Diggs Jr. to Richard Austin and Clarence Carter, December 6, 1960, box 34, CCDP.
32. Weston Diggs Jr., interview by author, August 6, 2015.
33. Charles C. Diggs Sr. to Charles T. Cole, April 21, 1959, box 34, CCDP.
34. Damon Keith, interview by author, November 25, 2014, Detroit, MI.
35. Keith, interview by author, November 25, 2014.
36. Keith, interview by author, November 25, 2014.
37. Laura A. Kiernan, "The Image: Lifestyle Belies Financial Burden," *WP*, March 24, 1978.
38. Booker, *Shocking the Conscience*, 302.
39. "'But I Still Love Him': Explains Rep. Diggs' Wife," *BAA*, August 1, 1959.
40. "'But I Still Love Him.'"
41. "'But I Still Love Him.'"
42. Juanita R. Diggs, interview by author, September 12, 2014, Ypsilanti, MI.
43. Denise Diggs-Taylor, interview by author, August 4, 2015, Ypsilanti, MI; Charles C. Diggs III, interview by author, August 4, 2015, Ypsilanti, MI.
44. "Paternity Suit Names Diggs," *DFP*, August 22, 1959.
45. "Paternity Case Test Supports Diggs, Jr.," *CD*, November 30, 1959.
46. Keith, interview by author, November 25, 2014.
47. Keith, interview by author, November 25, 2014.
48. "Diggs Says He's Running in the Red," *DFP*, August 8, 1959; "Diggs Must Pay $1,350 Monthly," *BAA*, February 6, 1960.
49. Quoted in "'I Need Your Prayers . . .' Diggs Appeals to Voters back Home," *BAA*, August 22, 1959.
50. "Rep. Diggs Weds Lawyer," *Detroit (MI) Tribune*, April 2, 1960.
51. "Cong. Diggs Takes Lawyer as Bride," *BAA*, April 2, 1960.
52. In 1979, President Jimmy Carter nominated, and the Senate approved, Anna Diggs to a judgeship on the US District Court in Detroit.
53. "What's Behind Suicide of Charles Diggs, Sr.," *Jet*, May 11, 1967, 14.
54. "Hundreds Mourn at Rites for Charles C. Diggs, Sr.," *MC*, May 6, 1967.
55. "Hundreds Mourn at Rites."
56. "Hundreds Pay Last Tribute at Charles Diggs' Funeral," *DFP*, April 29, 1967.
57. Quoted in "Hundreds Mourn at Rites."
58. "Hundreds Mourn at Rites."

59. "Detroit Spot Lite," *Detroit (MI) Tribune*, July 9, 1960.
60. Charles C. Diggs, Jr. to Janet Hall, June 4, 1970, box 307, CCDP.
61. Jack Cloherty and Bob Owens, "Courting on the Taxpayers," *Washington Star*, February 3, 1977.
62. Cloherty and Owens, "Courting on the Taxpayers."
63. "Former Rep. Diggs Gets Divorce in D.C. Court," *Jet*, May 31, 1982, 18.
64. Cloherty and Owens, "Courting on the Taxpayers."
65. "Congressman Still Has Wife; But He'll Wed," Associated Press, November 1, 1971.
66. Ethel L. Payne, "Hall-Diggs Nuptials Are Impressive at St. Moritz," *MC*, November 20, 1971.
67. Charles Rangel, interview by author, February 6, 2015, New York.
68. Juanita R. Diggs, interview by author, September 12, 2014.
69. Weston Diggs Jr., interview by author, August 6, 2015.
70. "Failing Business, Ex-Wives. Help Put Diggs Deep in Debt," *DFP*, June 26, 1977.
71. "Failing Business, Ex-Wives."
72. "Diggs Is Deep in Debt, Business Associates Say," *DN*, June 18, 1977.
73. "Failing Business, Ex-Wives."
74. "Diggs Is Deep in Debt."

CHAPTER 21

1. *USA v. Charles C. Diggs, Jr.*, 613 F.2d (D.C. Cir.1978), 317.
2. Rebecca Leet, "Overburdening Debts Put Diggs in Unenviable Hole," *Washington Star*, June 29, 1977.
3. *USA v. Charles C. Diggs, Jr*, 378.
4. *USA v. Charles C. Diggs, Jr*, 96.
5. Charles C. Diggs III, interview by author, August 4, 2015, Ypsilanti, MI.
6. Quoted in Gary Schuster, "The Rise and Decline of Charles C. Diggs," *DN*, July 22, 1979.
7. Weston Diggs Jr., interview by author, August 6, 2015, Novi, MI.
8. Parker, *Homeward Bound*.
9. Frederick H. Pauls and Paul E. Dwyer, *Clerk Hire Authorizations for Senators and Representatives: 1884–1993* (Washington, DC: Congressional Research Service, Library of Congress, 1993).
10. Stultz was born Jean Audrey Gillette in Washington, DC, on November 30, 1930. After working for Diggs, she married and changed her name to Jean Gillette Hicks. See Legacy.com and *WP*, June 29–July 1, 2008.
11. Parker, *Homeward Bound*, 3.
12. Parker, *Homeward Bound*, 95.
13. *USA v. Charles C. Diggs, Jr.*, 1047.
14. *USA v. Charles C. Diggs, Jr.*, 1117.
15. Lenore Cooley, *Charles C. Diggs, Jr. of Michigan*, Ralph Nader Congress Project (Washington, DC: Grossman Publishers, 1972), box 58, CCDP.
16. Jack Anderson, "US Rep. Whalley Accused of Taking Staff Kickbacks," *Boston Globe*, September 27, 1971.
17. "Ex-Rep. Whalley Put on Probation," *NYT*, October 16, 1973.

18. *USA v. Charles C. Diggs, Jr.*, 1092.
19. *USA v. Charles C. Diggs, Jr.*, 158.
20. *USA v. Charles C. Diggs, Jr.*, 158.
21. *USA v. Charles C. Diggs, Jr.*, 1092.
22. *USA v. Charles C. Diggs, Jr.*, 159.
23. *USA v. Charles C. Diggs, Jr.*, 159.
24. *USA v. Charles C. Diggs, Jr.*, 163.
25. *USA v. Charles C. Diggs, Jr.*, 160.
26. *USA v. Charles C. Diggs, Jr.*, 687–89.
27. *USA v. Charles C. Diggs, Jr.*, 459.
28. Charles C. Diggs Jr., interview by Robert Kinloch Massie, May 24, 1990.
29. *USA v. Charles C. Diggs, Jr.*, 767.
30. Willard Johnson, interview by Robert Kinloch Massie, December 19, 1989. Robinson's obituary appeared in the *New York Times*. See Sam Roberts, "Randall Robinson, Anti-Apartheid Catalyst, Is Dead at 81," *NYT*, March 28, 2023, www.nytimes.com/2023/03/28/us/randall-robinson-dead.html.
31. Zelizer, *On Capitol Hill*, 181–85.
32. Zelizer, *On Capitol Hill*, 181–85.
33. Johnson, interview by Massie.
34. *USA v. Charles C. Diggs, Jr.*, 767–68.
35. *USA v. Charles C. Diggs, Jr.*, 767.
36. "Participants and Press Plan, Bill Signing—H.R. 1746," March 18, 1977, Diggs File, box 866, WHCF, Jimmy Carter Library, Atlanta, GA.
37. Memorandum, Assistant US Attorney [redacted] to Chief, Fraud Division [redacted] March 10, 1977, Diggs FBI file, no. 1407075-001 (in the author's possession).
38. Memorandum, Assistant US Attorney [redacted] to Chief, Fraud Division [redacted] March 10, 1977.
39. Carl T. Rowan, "Is There a Conspiracy against Black Leaders," *Ebony* (January 1976): 33–42.
40. Musgrove, *Rumor, Repression, and Racial Politics*; Crawford, *Marked Men*.
41. Memorandum, FBI Washington Field Office to FBI Director, June 9, 1977, Diggs FBI file, no. 1407075-001 (in the author's possession).
42. "Representative Charles Diggs, Jr., 13th Congressional District of Michigan . . . Fraud Against the Government," May 5, 1977, Diggs FBI file, no. 1407075-001 (in the author's possession).
43. "Representative Charles Diggs, Jr., 13th Congressional District of Michigan."
44. "Indices Search Slip, FBI Form FD-160," May 3, 1977, Diggs FBI file, no. 1407075-001 (in the author's possession).
45. See Robinson, *Defending the Spirit*. Robinson refused several of my requests to answer questions about his time working with Diggs. In a footnote, Robert Massie speculates that Robinson may have been the confidential informant. According to Massie, Robinson refused "to discuss what he discovered when he became Diggs's aide. . . . It is clear from the indictments that improprieties took place in the years before Robinson arrived; Robinson may have been the one who put an end to them." Massie, *Loosing the Bonds*, 784. An official note in Robinson's FBI file (no. 1590427-001), which I obtained through the Freedom of

Information of Act, likely relates to Diggs's indictment and conviction. The note refers to a request by President Jimmy Carter's White House counsel, Lloyd N Cutler, asking that information in Robinson's FBI file remain "classified to protect source who provided information in this matter who was [redacted]."

46. Memorandum, Special Agent in Charge (Washington Field Office) to Director, FBI, May 5, 1977, Diggs FBI file, no. 1407075-001 (in the author's possession).
47. Memorandum, Special Agent in Charge (Washington Field Office) to Director, FBI, May 5, 1977.
48. *USA v. Charles C. Diggs, Jr.*, 672.
49. "3 More Aides to Diggs Ordered to Turn over Records to Grand Jury," *Washington Star*, July 7, 1977; "Diggs Lawyers: Ethics Unit Evidence Gotten 'Illegally,'" *BAA*, May 26, 1979.
50. Louis Stokes, interview by author, December 11, 2014, Silver Spring, MD.
51. "Statement of Congressman Charles C. Diggs, Jr.," June 15, 1977, box 345, CCDSAP.
52. Remer Tyson, "Women, Failing Business Put Rep. Diggs in Debt," *DFP*, June 26, 1977.
53. Timothy S. Robinson, "Rep. Diggs Indicted for Alleged Illegal Payroll Fund Use," *WP*, March 24, 1988.
54. Leet, "Overburdening Debts."
55. Quoted in Leet, "Overburdening Debts."
56. "Defense Fund Being Raised in Community," *DN*, June 25, 1977.
57. "Diggs Fund-Raisers Pose Question of a Plot," *WS*, n.d., BGP.
58. Quoted in "Diggs Fund-Raisers Pose Question."
59. DuBose, *Untold Story*, 208.
60. *USA v. Charles C. Diggs, Jr.*, 810.
61. Robinson, "Rep. Diggs Indicted."
62. Among the charges dropped were two charges of payroll violations involving Maria Reynolds, the sister of Juanita R. Diggs.
63. Robinson, "Rep. Diggs Indicted."
64. Robinson, "Rep. Diggs Indicted."

CHAPTER 22

1. "Rep. Diggs Arraigned for Fraud," Associated Press, April 7, 1978.
2. "Rep. Diggs Arraigned."
3. Timothy S. Robinson, "Diggs Pleads Innocent in Fraud Case," *WP*, April 8, 1978.
4. "Statement of Congressman Charles Diggs," April 7, 1978, BGP.
5. Quoted in Ronald Cartell Williams, "Black Embassy" (unpublished book manuscript), chapter 2.
6. "Judge Rejects Rep. Diggs' Request to Dismiss Part of His Indictment," *WP*, May 10, 1978.
7. DuBose, *Untold Story*, 224.
8. Ray Rickman, interview by author, October 28, 2014, Providence, RI; Diane Brockett, "Fraud Charges, Serious Opposition Put Diggs on Rare Campaign Trail," *WS*, July 10, 1978; T. R. Reid, "Indictments Aid Congressman in Re-election Bid," *Arizona Republic* (Phoenix), September 4, 1978.
9. Quoted in Reid, "Indictments Aid Congressman."

10. During the trial, a Black male juror was replaced by a Black woman alternate. The final jury comprised nine Black women, two Black men, and one white male.
11. "Style a Key to U.S. Prosecutor's Success," *Los Angeles Times*, November 23, 1978.
12. Lawrence Meyer, "Defense Cites Public Service as Diggs' Fraud Trial Opens," *WP*, September 28, 1978.
13. Meyer, "Defense Cites Public Service."
14. *USA v. Charles C. Diggs, Jr.*, 613 F.2d (D.C. Cir.1978) 6.
15. *USA v. Charles C. Diggs, Jr.*, 108.
16. "Diggs' Ex-Aide Lists Salary Kickbacks," *DFP*, September 29, 1978.
17. *USA v. Charles C. Diggs, Jr.*, 224.
18. *USA v. Charles C. Diggs, Jr.*, 246.
19. Meyer, "Ex-Aide Says Diggs Sought Kickbacks," *WP*, September 30, 1978.
20. *USA v. Charles C. Diggs, Jr.*, 332.
21. *USA v. Charles C. Diggs, Jr.*, 379.
22. *USA v. Charles C. Diggs, Jr.*, 390.
23. Jacqueline Trescott, "The Black Caucus: Tense Politics and Changing Moods," *WP*, October 2, 1978.
24. *USA v. Charles C. Diggs, Jr.*, 516.
25. *USA v. Charles C. Diggs, Jr.*, 518.
26. *USA v. Charles C. Diggs, Jr.*, 1064.
27. DuBose, *Untold Story*, 200.
28. *USA v. Charles C. Diggs, Jr.*, 1005.
29. "I'm Innocent, Diggs Insists," *DFP*, October 5, 1978.
30. Lawrence Meyer, "Diggs Admits Using Staff for Bills," *WP*, October 5, 1978.
31. *USA v. Charles C. Diggs, Jr.*, 1063.
32. *USA v. Charles C. Diggs, Jr.*, 1064.
33. *USA v. Charles C. Diggs, Jr.*, 1066.
34. *USA v. Charles C. Diggs, Jr.*, 1066.
35. *USA v. Charles C. Diggs, Jr.*, 1072.
36. *USA v. Charles C. Diggs, Jr.*, 1082.
37. *USA v. Charles C. Diggs, Jr.*, 1096.
38. *USA v. Charles C. Diggs, Jr.*, 1120.
39. "I'm Innocent, Diggs Insists."
40. *USA v. Charles C. Diggs, Jr.*, 1128.
41. *USA v. Charles C. Diggs, Jr.*, 1194.
42. *USA v. Charles C. Diggs, Jr.*, 1199–200.
43. *USA v. Charles C. Diggs, Jr.*, 1192.
44. Lawrence Meyer, "Diggs Jury Meets 3 Hours Then Recesses," *WP*, October 7, 1978.
45. "Diggs Case Rests with D.C. Jury," *DFP*, October 7, 1978.
46. "Diggs Case Rests."
47. "Diggs Case Rests."
48. Meyer, "Diggs Jury Meets."
49. "Diggs Case Rests."
50. "Diggs Case Rests."
51. Meyer, "Diggs Jury Meets."
52. Meyer, "Diggs Jury Meets."

53. Meyer, "Diggs Jury Meets."
54. DuBose, *Untold Story*, 201.
55. Lawrence Meyer, "Congressman Convicted of Illegally Diverting Funds," *WP*, October 8, 1978.
56. DuBose, *Untold Story*, 202.
57. DuBose, *Untold Story*, 203.
58. William Mitchell, "Diggs Guilty on All Counts," *DFP*, October 8, 1978.
59. DuBose, *Untold Story*, 203.
60. DuBose, *Untold Story*, 203.
61. William Raspberry, "Charles Diggs: 'Weak, but Not Scurrilous,'" *WP*, October 11, 1978.
62. John Dingell, interview by author, August 12, 2014, Dearborn, MI.
63. Editors, "The Diggs Case: A Warning to Black Elected Officials," *MC*, October 28, 1978.
64. Ronald Fitten, "Detroiters' Reactions to Diggs' Conviction," *MC*, October 14, 1978.

CHAPTER 23

1. Nadine Brown, "Local Blacks Remain Loyal to Diggs," *MC*, October 14, 1978.
2. Quoted in Remer Tyson, "I'll Stay in Congress, Says Diggs," *DFP*, October 11, 1978; Charles C. Diggs Jr. to Thomas P. O'Neill, October 10, 1978, Diggs File, box 866, WHCF, Jimmy Carter Library, Atlanta, GA.
3. Zelizer, *Burning Down the House*.
4. Lawrence Meyers, "Diggs Sentenced To Three Years," *WP*, November 21, 1978.
5. "Lawyers Want Diggs to Lecture Teens," *Lansing (MI) State Journal*, November 17, 1978.
6. Charles C. Diggs Jr. to Thomas P. O'Neill Jr., November 21, 1978, BGP.
7. Chuck Stone, "House Vote Endangers Diggs' Chairmanships," December 7, 1978, BGP.
8. Stone, "House Vote Endangers Diggs's Chairmanships."
9. William Mitchell, "Diggs Loses Ley Battle in Dem. Caucus," *DFP*, December 7, 1978.
10. Stone, "House Vote Endangers Diggs's Chairmanships."
11. Quoted in "Freshman Congressman to Push for Public Vote on Diggs Seating," *Californian* (Salinas, CA), December 16, 1978.
12. Zelizer, *Burning Down the House*, 41.
13. Newt Gingrich to John Anderson, January 11, 1979, box 145, File: Diggs Stuff, Newt Gingrich Papers, University of West Georgia Special Collections, Carrollton, GA.
14. "Resolution Relating to Convicted Felons Serving in the U.S. House of Representatives," box 145, File: Diggs Stuff, Newt Gingrich Papers, University of West Georgia Special Collections, Carrollton, GA.
15. Garry Trudeau, "Doonesbury," Universal Press Syndicate, December 5–7, 1978, BGP.
16. Charles C. Diggs Jr. to Rep. Clement J. Zablocki, January 23, 1979, BGP.
17. Zelizer, *Burning Down the House*, 41.

18. Newt Gingrich, "Congressional Double Standard," February 22, 1978, box 145, File: Diggs Stuff, Newt Gingrich Papers, University of West Georgia Special Collections, Carrollton, GA.
19. Newt Gingrich, "A Precedent for Diggs," *WP*, February 21, 1979.
20. "Solon Vows Showdown," *Spokane (WA) Chronicle*, February 24, 1979.
21. Charles C. Diggs Jr. to Newton Leroy Gingrich, February 26, 1979, BGP.
22. Quoted in "Gingrich Plans Attempt to Have Diggs Expelled," *Atlanta Journal Constitution*, March 1, 1979.
23. Mary Russell, "Caucus Won't Tell Diggs to Refrain from Voting," *WP*, March 1, 1979.
24. Mary Russell, "House Strongly Rejects Move to Expel Rep. Diggs," *WP*, March 2, 1979.
25. Russell, "House Strongly Rejects."
26. Richard L. Lyons, "Rep. Diggs Admits Misuse of Funds, Accepts Censure," *WP*, June 30, 1979.
27. "House Censures Rep. Diggs, Defeats Expulsion Move," *Jet*, August 16, 1979, 5–6.
28. Emma Jordan, "Detroiters Defend, Decry Diggs," *MC*, August 11, 1979.
29. William J. Mitchell, "Conviction of Diggs Is Upheld on 1st Appeal," *DFP*, November 15, 1979.
30. Quoted in "Race Shaping Up for Diggs' Seat?," *MC*, December 22, 1979.
31. Quoted in Robert S. Boyd, "Diggs to Leave Congress Job, Cleared or Not," *DFP*, May 15, 1980.
32. DuBose, *Untold Story*, 208; *Jet*, June 19, 1980.
33. Marjorie Hunter, "Rep. Diggs Quits after 25 Years; Faces Jail Term," *WP*, June 4, 1980.
34. "Diggs Quits, Probation Last Hope," *MC*, June 7, 1980.
35. Quoted in Timothy S. Robinson, "Judge Turns Down Plea by Diggs, Orders Him to Serve 3-Year Term," *WP*, July 15, 1980.
36. Robinson, "Judge Turns Down Plea."
37. "Denise Marie Diggs Weds Raymond A. Taylor," *MC*, August 23, 1980.
38. Denise Diggs-Taylor, interview by author, August 4, 2015, Ypsilanti, MI.
39. Charles C. Diggs III, interview by author, August 4, 2015, Ypsilanti, MI.
40. Weston Diggs Jr., interview by author, August 6, 2015, Novi, MI.
41. William J. Mitchell, "Diggs Starts Sentence in State Where He's a Hero," *DFP*, July 25, 1980.
42. "Diggs Begins Sentence at Maxwell," *Montgomery (AL) Advertiser*, July 25, 1980.
43. Mitchell, "Diggs Starts Sentence."
44. Charles C. Diggs Jr. to Bonnie Gallagher, July 31, 1980, BGP.
45. DuBose, *Untold Story*, 225.
46. Diggs to Gallagher, July 31, 1980.
47. Charles C. Diggs Jr. to Bonnie Gallagher, November 17, 1980, BGP.
48. Diggs to Gallagher, November 17, 1980; D. Humphries Barker, "Diggs' Life as an Inmate," *MC*, August 30, 1980.
49. Barker, "Diggs' Life as an Inmate."
50. Charles C. Diggs Jr. to Bonnie Gallagher, September 15, 1980, BGP. A Sunday

service program attached to the letter lists Diggs as leading the "Responsive Reading."
51. Charles C. Diggs Jr. to Bonnie Gallagher, August 12, 1980, BGP.
52. Charles C. Diggs Jr., interview by Robert Kinloch Massie, May 24, 1990.
53. "Blacks to Unite Against 'Ultra-Right-Wing' Movement," *Jet*, October 16, 1980, 6.
54. Wiley A. Branton to Charles C. Diggs Jr. September 9, 1980, box 187-4, file 15, Wiley A. Branton Papers, Moorland-Spingarn Research Center, Howard University, Washington, DC.
55. Charles C. Diggs Jr. to Wiley A. Branton, September 15, 1980, box 187-4, file 15, Wiley A. Branton Papers, Moorland-Spingarn Research Center, Howard University, Washington, DC.
56. Diggs to Branton, September 15, 1980.
57. John Hyde, "Diggs Gets Time Off after Plea by Crockett," *DFP*, December 13, 1980.
58. Thomas Morgan, "Ex-Representative Diggs Enters NW Halfway House," *WP*, February 26, 1981.
59. Morgan, "Ex-Representative Diggs Enters."
60. Quoted in Morgan, "Ex-Representative Diggs Enters."

CONCLUSION

1. Michel McQueen, "Fauntroy to Hire Ex-Rep. Diggs," *WP*, March 6, 1981; Walter Fauntroy to General Eugene M. Poe, Jr., May 15, 1981, box 225, folder 41, WFP.
2. Quoted in "Diggs: Regrets, But a Clear Conscience," *DFP*, July 2, 1981.
3. Quoted in "Straight Talk . . . : Former Congressman Diggs," *MC*, May 30, 1981.
4. Carla Diggs Smith, text message to the author, March 4, 2021.
5. Clay, *Just Permanent Interests*, 89–90.
6. Keith Harriston, "Diggs Charged with Drunk Driving Again," *WP*, February 20, 1986.
7. "Judge Rules Diggs Should Be Granted Mortician's License," *WP*, July 30, 1983.
8. "Charles Diggs Takes Fourth Wife," *Jet*, April 25, 1983.
9. Reverend Grainger Browning, telephone interview by author, August 20, 2021; Powell described Exposé as "the most beautiful woman I've ever seen." See Powell, *Adam by Adam*, 235.
10. Quoted in "Charles Diggs Takes Fourth Wife."
11. Russell Adams, telephone interview by author, April 11, 2015.
12. Adams, telephone interview by author, April 11, 2015.
13. Beverly L. Perry, telephone interview by author, August 18, 2021. Perry served with Diggs as president of the Hill Crest Heights Community Association.
14. Johnson, *Black Power in the Suburbs*, 73.
15. Damon Keith, interview by author, November 25, 2014, Detroit, MI.
16. Darryl Fears, "Victor Over Diggs Pays Tribute," *DFP*, September 17, 1987.
17. Browning, telephone interview by author, August 20, 2021.
18. Charles C. Diggs III, interview by author, August 4, 2015, Ypsilanti, MI.
19. Browning, telephone interview by author, August 20, 2021.
20. DuBose, *Untold Story*, 219.

21. "House of Delegates," *WP*, September 12, 1990.
22. Albert R. Wynn, telephone interview by author, December 7, 2021.
23. Ronald Dellums, interview by author, July 24, 2014, Washington, DC.
24. Dellums, interview by author, July 24, 2014.
25. Wynn, telephone interview by author, December 7, 2021.
26. Frank Dexter Brown, "The Congressional Black Caucus: Thirty Years as the Conscience of the Congress," *BAA*, September 16, 2000.
27. DuBose, *Untold Story*, 235.
28. Carolyn DuBose, "The Man Who Started It All: Charles Diggs Was a Catalyst," *MC*, June 22, 1994.
29. Robinson, *Defending the Spirit*, 94.
30. As of this writing, Diggs's "chairman's portrait" is stored in a closet in the office of a District of Columbia government official. Joshua D. Gibson, email to author, August 24, 2024.
31. Quoted in Howard Schneider, "D.C. Council Agrees to Try District Building Renovation Plan," *WP*, July 12, 1995.
32. Quoted in DuBose, *Untold Story*, 239.
33. DuBose, *Untold Story*, 241.
34. DuBose, *Untold Story*, 241.
35. DuBose, *Untold Story*, 220.
36. Quoted in John Flesher, "Diggs Ask Voters for 2nd Chance," *Los Angeles Times*, May 6, 1990.
37. "Maurice Sorrell, Retired Johnson Publishing Photog, Honored in D.C.," *Jet*, July 28, 1997.
38. Denise Diggs-Taylor, interview by author, August 4, 2015, Ypsilanti, MI.
39. Irvin Molotsky, "Charles Diggs, 75, Congressman Censured over Kickbacks," *NYT*, August 26, 1998.
40. "Former Rep. Charles Diggs dies in Washington," Associated Press, August 25, 1998.
41. "Hundreds Pay Tribute to Late Rep. Charles Diggs' Civil Rights Records at Maryland Ceremony," *Jet*, September 21, 1998.
42. Funeral Program, "Celebration of the Home Going of Retired Congressman Charles C. Diggs, Jr.," September 1, 1998, Charles C. Diggs III Papers, personal papers (in the author's possession).
43. James Wright, "Hundreds Turn Out for Funeral of Rep. Charles Diggs," *BAA*, September 11, 1998.
44. Browning, telephone interview by author, August 20, 2021.
45. Quoted in Ronald Walters, "Goodbye to Congressman Charles C. Diggs, Jr.," *Washington Informer*, September 10, 1998; Wright, "Hundreds Turn Out."
46. Funeral Program, "Final Religious Rights for Charles C. Diggs, Jr." September 3, 1998, Charles C. Diggs III Papers, personal papers (in the author's possession).
47. Dalondo Moultrie, "Great Man respected, honored, laid to rest," *MC*, September 9, 1998.
48. Keith, interview by author, November 25, 2014.
49. *CR*, October 15, 1998, E2203.

EPILOGUE

1. Ronald Dellums, interview by author, July 24, 2014, Washington, DC.
2. Quoted in Lenore Cooley, "Charles C. Diggs, Jr.: Democratic Representative from Michigan," Ralph Nader Congress Project, 1972, box 58, CCDP.
3. William L. Clay Sr., interview by author, December 11, 2014, Silver Spring, MD.
4. Louis Stokes, interview by author, December 11, 2014, Silver Spring, MD.
5. Stokes, interview by author, December 11, 2014.
6. John Conyers, interview by author, August 15, 2014, Detroit, MI.
7. Sharon Pratt, telephone interview by author, August 19, 2021.
8. Goler Teal Butcher, interview by Robert Kinloch Massie, May 24, 1990.
9. Stokes, interview by author, December 11, 2014.

Bibliography

PRIMARY SOURCES

Manuscript and Archival Collections

Abilene, KS
   Dwight David Eisenhower Presidential Library
      General File
      William M. Roundtree Papers
      White House Central File
Ann Arbor, MI
   Bentley Historical Library, University of Michigan
      Center for Afro-American and African Studies Records
      Detroit Urban League Papers
      Michigan Democratic Party Papers
      Hobart Taylor Papers
   Gerald R. Ford Presidential Library
      National Security Adviser Collection
Atlanta, GA
   Jimmy Carter Presidential Library
      White House Central File
   King Library and Archives, King Center
      Martin Luther King Papers
Austin, TX
   Lyndon B. Johnson Presidential Library
      Vice Presidential Papers
      White House Central File
Boston, MA
   John F. Kennedy Presidential Library
      Gerhard A. Gesell Papers
      Lawrence O'Brien Papers
      Harris Wofford Papers
Carrollton, GA
   University of West Georgia Special Collections
      Newt Gingrich Papers

College Park, MD
   National Archives and Records Administration
      Records of the Department of Justice
      Records Relating to History and Organization Group

Detroit, MI
   Burton Historical Collection, Detroit Public Library
      Charles C. Diggs Sr. file

Norman, OK
   University of Oklahoma
      Carl Albert Papers

Washington, DC
   George Washington University
      Walter Fauntroy Papers
   Moorland-Spingarn Research Center, Howard University
      Wiley A. Branton Papers
      The Civil Rights Documentation Project
      Charles C. Diggs Jr. Papers
      Charles C. Diggs Jr. South African Papers
      National Black Political Convention
         National Tenants Organization Papers
   Library of Congress (ProQuest)
      NAACP Papers
         National Black Political Convention
      Records of the SCLC, 1954–1970

Yorba Linda, CA
   Richard M. Nixon Presidential Library
      White House Central File

Personal papers (in the author's possession)
   Charles C. Diggs III Papers
   Alexis Diggs-Robinson Papers
   Denise Diggs-Taylor Papers
   Bonnie Gallagher Papers

Newspapers and Periodicals

Alabama Tribune (Montgomery)
Arizona Republic (Phoenix)
Atlanta Daily World
Atlanta Journal-Constitution
Associated Press
Baltimore Afro-American
Baltimore Sun
Boston Globe
Californian (Salinas, CA)
Chicago Defender
Chicago Tribune
Christian Science Monitor
Cincinnati Inquirer
Congressional Record
Courier-Journal (Louisville, KY)
Detroit (MI) Free Press
Detroit (MI) News
Detroit (MI) Tribune
Greenwood (MS) Commonwealth
Holland (MI) Evening Sentinel

Jackson (MS) Clarion-Ledger
Jackson (MS) Daily News
Lansing (MI) State Journal
Los Angeles Sentinel
Los Angeles Times
Michigan Chronicle (Detroit)
Montgomery (AL) Advertiser
News Journal (Wilmington, DE)
New York Amsterdam News
New York Times
Pittsburgh Courier
The Republic (Columbus, IN)
San Francisco Examiner
Spokane (WA) Chronicle
St. Louis (MO) Post-Dispatch
Washington Informer
Washington Post
Washington Star

US House Hearings and US Government Documents

USA v. Charles C. Diggs, Jr., 613 F.2d (D.C. Cir.1978).

US House. Committee on Foreign Affairs. *The Faces of Africa: Diversity and Progress; Repression and Struggle*. 92nd Cong., 2nd sess., 1972. Washington, DC: US Government Printing Office, 1972.

US House. Committee on Foreign Affairs. *Foreign Policy Implications of Racial Exclusion in Granting Visas*. 91st Cong., 2nd sess., 1970. Washington, DC: Government Printing Office, 1970.

US House. Committee on Foreign Affairs. *Policy toward Africa for the Seventies*. 91st Cong., 2nd sess., 1970. Washington, DC: Government Printing Office, 1970.

US House. Committee on Foreign Affairs. *Report of Special Study Mission to Southern Africa*. 91st Cong., 1st sess., 1969. Washington, DC: Government Printing Office, 1969.

US House. Committee on Foreign Affairs. *Report of Study Mission to Africa*. 89th Cong., 2nd sess., 1965. Washington, DC: Government Printing Office, 1966.

US House. Committee on Foreign Affairs. *Report of the Portuguese Guinea and the Liberation Movement*. 91st Cong., 2nd sess., 1970. Washington, DC: Government Printing Office, 1970.

US House. Committee on Foreign Affairs. *South Africa and United States Foreign Policy*. 91st Cong., 1st sess., 1969. Washington, DC: Government Printing Office, 1969.

US House. Committee on Foreign Affairs. *United States–South African Relations Hearings Before the Subcommittee on Africa of the Committee on Foreign Affairs*. 89th Cong., 2nd sess., 1966. Washington, DC: Government Printing Office, 1966.

US House. Committee on Foreign Affairs. *U.S. Business Involvement in Southern Africa*. 92nd Cong., 1st sess., 1972. Washington, DC: Government Printing Office, 1972.

US House. Committee on Standards of Official Conduct. *In the Matter of Representative Charles C. Diggs, Jr.* 96th Cong. 2nd sess., 1979. Washington, DC: US Government Printing Office, 1979.

US House. Committee on the District of Columbia. *Home Rule for the District of Columbia 1973–1974: Background and Legislative History*. 93rd Cong., 2nd sess., 1974. Washington, DC: Government Printing Office, 1974.

US House. Committee on the District of Columbia. *Unveiling of a Portrait of the Honorable Charles C. Diggs, Jr.* 94th Cong., 1st sess., 1974. Washington, DC: Government Printing Office, 1974.

Interviews Conducted by Author

Former Members of Congress
William L. Clay Sr., December 11, 2014, Silver Spring, MD; December 2, 2016, telephone; December 16, 2021, telephone
John Conyers, August 15, 2014, Detroit, MI
Ronald Dellums, July 24, 2014, Washington, DC
John Dingell, August 12, 2014, Dearborn, MI
Charles Rangel, February 6, 2015, New York; April 6, 2021, telephone
Louis Stokes, December 11, 2014, Silver Spring, MD
Albert R. Wynn, December 7, 2021, telephone

Family Members
Charles C. Diggs III, August 4, 2015, Ypsilanti, MI
Cindy Carter Diggs, April 2014, Washington, DC
Douglass Diggs, August 14, 2014, Detroit, MI
Juanita R. Diggs, September 12, 2014, Ypsilanti, MI; October 15, 2014, telephone; January 22, 2015, telephone; February 13, 2017, telephone
Weston Diggs Jr., August 6, 2015, Novi, MI; April 28, 2014, telephone
Alexis Diggs Robinson, February 5, 2015, New York
Carla Diggs Smith, March 12, 2014, Chevy Chase, MD; March 4, 2021, text message
Denise Diggs-Taylor, August 4, 2015, Ypsilanti, MI
Denise Diggs-Taylor and Charles C. Diggs III, August 13, 2014, Ann Arbor, MI

Friends and Acquaintances
Russell Adams, April 11, 2015, telephone
Delores Bennett, September 9, 2014, Detroit, MI
Reverend Grainger Browning, August 19 and 20, 2021, telephone
Reverend Russell Campbell, April 15, 2015, Washington, DC
Herschelle Sullivan Challenor, March 18, 2015, Atlanta, GA
George Dalley, May 5, 2015, telephone
Bonnie Gallagher, December 8, 2014, Washington, DC
Teola Hunter, October 1, 2014, Detroit, MI
Damon Keith, November 25, 2014, Detroit, MI
Beverly L. Perry, August 18, 2021, telephone
Sharon Pratt, August 19, 2021, telephone
Ray Rickman, October 28, 2014, Providence, RI
O'Neil Swanson, October 2, 2014, Detroit, MI
Roberta Hughes Wright, September 9, 2014, Detroit, MI

Oral Histories Conducted by Others

Goler T. Butcher. Interview by Robert Kinloch Massie, May 24, 1990 (copy in the author's possession).
Charles C. Diggs, Jr. Interview by Robert Kinloch Massie, May 24, 1990 (copy in the author's possession).
Charles C. Diggs, Jr. Oral history interview, January 28, 1970. The Civil Rights

Documentation Project, Moorland-Spingarn Research Center, Howard University, Washington, DC.

Charles C. Diggs, Jr. Oral history interview, March 13, 1969. Lyndon B. Johnson Oral Histories, Lyndon B. Johnson Presidential Library, Austin, TX.

"Interview with Charles Coles Diggs Jr.," November 6, 1986. In *Eyes of the Prize: America's Civil Rights Years, 1954–1965* (documentary), produced by Henry Hampton. Blackside, 1987, 55 min. Henry Hampton Collection, Washington University Film and Media Archive, Washington University Libraries, St. Louis, MO.

Willard Johnson. Interview with Robert Kinloch Massie, November 21, 1989, and December 19, 1989 (copy in the author's possession).

Robert S. McNamara. Oral history interview, January 8, 1975. Lyndon B. Johnson Oral Histories, Lyndon B. Johnson Presidential Library, Austin, TX.

SECONDARY SOURCES

Books, Chapters, and Journal Articles

Abernathy, Ralph David. *And the Walls Came Tumbling Down: An Autobiography*. New York: Harper and Row, 1989.

Aldrich, John H. *Why Parties?: The Origin and Transformation of Political Parties in America*. Chicago: University of Chicago Press, 1995.

Anderson, Carol. *Bourgeois Radicals: The NAACP and the Struggle for Colonial Liberation, 1941–1960*. New York: Cambridge University Press, 2015.

Anderson, Devery S. *Emmett Till: The Murder That Shocked the World and Propelled the Civil Rights Movement*. Jackson: University Press of Mississippi, 2015.

Asch, Chris Myers, and George Derek Musgrove. *Chocolate City: A History of Race and Democracy in the Nation's Capital*. Chapel Hill: University of North Carolina Press, 2017.

Baraka, Amiri. "Gary and Miami—Before and After." *Black World* (October 1972): 54–78.

Bardolph, Richard. *The Negro Vanguard*. New York: Rinehart, 1959.

Barnett, Marguerite Ross. "The Congressional Black Caucus: The Illusion and Reality of Power." In *The New Black Politics: The Search for Political Power*, edited by Michael B. Preston, Lenneal J. Henderson Jr., and Paul Puryear, 28–54. New York: Longman Press, 1982.

Barnett, Marguerite Ross. "A Historical Look at the Congressional Black Caucus." *Focus* (August–September 1977): 3–28.

Barry, Kathleen M. *Femininity in Flight: A History of Flight Attendants*. Durham, NC: Duke University Press, 2007.

Bay, Mia. *Traveling Black: A Story of Race and Resistance*. Cambridge, MA: Harvard University Press, 2021.

Behrend, Justin. *Reconstructing Democracy: Grassroots Black Politics in the Deep South After the Civil War*. Athens: University of Georgia Press, 2015.

Beito, David T., and Linda Royster Beito. *Black Maverick: T. R. M. Howard's Fight for Civil Rights and Economic Power*. Urbana: University of Illinois Press, 2009.

Bernhard, William, and Tracy Sulkin. *Legislative Style*. Chicago: University of Chicago Press, 2018.

Blain, Keisha. *Until I Am Free: Fannie Lou Hamer's Enduring Message to America.* Boston: Beacon Press, 2021.
Bloom, Joshua, and Waldo E. Martin Jr. *Black against Empire: The History and Politics of the Black Panther Party.* Berkeley: University of California Press, 2013.
Booker, Simeon. *Black Man's America.* Englewood Cliffs, NJ: Prentice-Hall, 1964.
Booker, Simeon. *Shocking the Conscience: A Reporter's Account of the Civil Rights Movement.* Jackson: University Press of Mississippi, 2013.
Bordin, Ruth. *Women at Michigan: The "Dangerous Experiment," 1870s to the Present.* Ann Arbor: University of Michigan Press, 1999.
Boyd, Herb. *Black Detroit: A People's History of Self-Determination.* New York: Amistad, 2017.
Browning, Rufus P., Dale Rogers Marshall, and David H. Tabb. *Protest Is Not Enough: The Struggle of Blacks and Hispanics for Equality in Urban Politics.* Berkeley: University of California Press, 1984.
Bunche, Ralph J. *The Political Status of the Negro in the Age of FDR.* Chicago: University of Chicago Press, 1973.
Burk, Robert F. *The Eisenhower Administration and Black Civil Rights.* Knoxville: University of Tennessee Press, 1984.
Butcher, Goler Teal. "Southern African Issues in United States Courts." *Howard Law Journal* 26 (1983): 601–44.
Capeci, Dominic J., Jr. *Race Relations in Wartime Detroit: The Sojourner Truth Housing Controversy of 1942.* Philadelphia: Temple University Press, 1984.
Carmichael, Stokely and Charles V. Hamilton. *Black Power: The Politics of Liberation in America.* New York: Vintage Press, 1967.
Caro, Robert A. *The Years of Lyndon Johnson: Master of the Senate.* New York: Knopf, 2002.
Carson, Clayborne, ed. *The Papers of Martin Luther King, Jr.* Vol. 3, *Birth of a New Age, December 1955–December 1956*, edited by Stewart Burns, Susan Carson, Pete Holloran, and Dana L. H. Powell. Berkeley: University of California Press, 1997.
Carson, Clayborne, ed. *The Papers of Martin Luther King, Jr.* Vol. 4, *Symbol of the Movement January 1957–December 1958*, edited by Susan Carson, Adrienne Clay, Virginia Shadron, and Kieran Taylor. Berkeley: University of California Press, 2000.
Carson, Clayborne, ed. *The Papers of Martin Luther King, Jr.* Vol. 7, *To Save the Soul of America, January 1960–August 1962*, edited by Tenisha Armstrong. Berkeley: University of California Press, 2014.
Clay, William L. *Just Permanent Interests: Black Americans in Congress, 1870–1992.* New York: Amistad Press, 1992.
Clayton, Ed. *The Negro Politician: His Success and Failure.* Chicago: Johnson Publishing, 1964.
Clegg, Claude Andrew, III. *An Original Man: The Life and Times of Elijah Muhammad.* New York: St. Martin's Press, 1997.
Cobb, James C. *The Most Southern Place on Earth: The Mississippi Delta and the Roots of Regional Identity.* New York: Oxford University Press, 1992.
Cohen, Adam, and Elizabeth Taylor. *American Pharaoh: Mayor Richard J. Daley, His Battle for Chicago and the Nation.* Boston: Little, Brown, 2000.
Coker, Christopher. *The United States and South Africa, 1968–1985.* Durham, NC: Duke University Press, 1986.

Coleman, Ken. *Million Dollars' Worth of Nerve: Twenty-One People Who Helped to Power Black Bottom, Paradise Valley and Detroit's Lower East Side*. Detroit, MI: Coleman Communications, 2014.

Coles, John J. *Africa in Brief.* New York: Freeman Steam Printing Establishment, 1886.

Collins, Sheila D. *Ubuntu: George M. Houser and the Struggle for Peace and Freedom on Two Continents*. Columbus: Ohio University Press, 2020.

Conot, Robert. *American Odyssey: A History of a Great City*. Detroit, MI: Wayne State University Press, 1986.

Crawford, Nyron N. *Marked Men: Black Politicians and the Racialization of Scandal*. New York: New York University Press, 2024.

Curwood, Anastasia C. *Shirley Chisholm: Champion of Black Feminist Power Politics*. Chapel Hill: University of North Carolina Press, 2023.

Dallek, Robert. *Flawed Giant: Lyndon Johnson and His Times 1961–1973*. New York: Oxford University Press, 1998.

Dansby, D. B. Baldwin. *A Brief History of Jackson College: A Typical Story of Education among Negroes in the South*. Jackson, MS: Jackson College, 1953.

Dellums, Ronald V., and H. Lee Halterman. *Lying Down with the Lions: A Public Life from the Streets of Oakland to the Halls of Power*. Boston, MA: Beacon Press, 2000.

Delmont, Matthew F. *Half American: The Epic Story of African Americans Fighting World War II at Home and Abroad*. New York: Viking, 2022.

DeRoche, Andrew. *Andrew Young: Civil Rights Ambassador*. New York: Rowman and Littlefield, 2003.

DeRoche, Andrew. *Black, White, and Chrome: The United States and Zimbabwe, 1953–1998*. Trenton, NJ: Africa World Press, Inc., 2001.

DeRoche, Andrew. *Kenneth Kaunda, the United States and Southern Africa*. New York: Bloomsbury Academic 2016.

Diggs, Charles C., Jr. "The Diggs Report: Investigation of Alleged Discriminatory Practices in the Armed Forces." In *Blacks in the United States Armed Forces: Basic Documents*, Vol.12, edited by Morris J. MacGregor and Bernard C. Nalty, 318–38. Wilmington, DE: Scholarly Resources, 1977.

Diggs, Charles C., Jr. "Remarks of the Honorable Charles C. Diggs, Jr." *American Journal of International Law* 65 (September 1971): 299–302.

Diggs, Charles C., Jr. "The Role of the American Negro in American-African Relations." In *Apropos of Africa: Afro-American Leaders and the Romance of Africa*, edited by Martin Kilson and Adelaide Hill, 448–52. Garden City, NJ: Doubleday, 1971.

Dillard, Angela D. *Faith in the City: Preaching Radical Social Change in Detroit*. Ann Arbor: University of Michigan Press, 2007.

Dittmer, John. *Local People: The Struggle for Civil Rights in Mississippi*. Urbana: University of Illinois Press, 1994.

Drake, St. Clair, and Horace R. Cayton. *Black Metropolis: A Study of Negro Life in a Northern City*. Chicago: University of Chicago Press, 1945.

DuBose, Carolyn P. *The Untold Story of Charles Diggs: The Public Figure, the Private Man*. Arlington, VA: Barton Publishing House, 1998.

Dudziak, Mary L. *Cold War Civil Rights: Race and the Image of American Democracy*. Princeton, NJ: Princeton University Press, 2000.

Dunbar, Willis F. *Michigan: A History of the Wolverine State*. Grand Rapids, MI: William B. Eerdmans, 1995.

Eig, Jonathan. *King: A Life*. New York: Farrar, Straus and Giroux, 2023.
Evers, Myrlie B., and William Peters. *For Us the Living*. Garden City, NY: Doubleday, 1967.
Fauntroy, Michael K. *Home Rule or House Rule? Congress and the Erosion of Local Government in the District of Columbia*. Lanham, MD: University Press of America, 2003.
Fauntroy, Michael K. *Republicans and the Black Vote*. Boulder, CO: Lynne Rienner Publishers, 2005.
Fenno, Richard F. *Congressmen in Committees*. Boston: Little, Brown, 1973.
Fenno, Richard F. *Home Style: House Members in Their Districts*. Boston: Little, Brown, 1978.
Fine, Sidney A. *"Expanding the Frontiers of Civil Rights": Michigan, 1948–1968*. Detroit, MI: Wayne State University Press, 2017.
Fine, Sidney A. *Violence in the Model City: The Cavanagh Administration, Race Relations, and the Detroit Riot of 1967*. Ann Arbor: University of Michigan Press, 1989.
Forman, James. *The Making of Black Revolutionaries*. Seattle: University of Washington Press, 1997.
Fragnoli, Raymond R. *The Transformation of Reform: Progressivism in Detroit—and After, 1912–1933*. New York: Garland Press, 1982.
Francis, Charles E. *The Tuskegee Airmen: The Men Who Changed a Nation*. Boston: Branden Publishing, 1988.
Franklin, John Hope, and Alfred A. Moss. *From Slavery to Freedom: A History of Negro Americans*. New York: Knopf, 1988.
Garrow, David J. *Bearing the Cross: Martin Luther King, Jr., and the Southern Christian Leadership Conference*. New York: Vintage Books, 1986.
Gomez-Jefferson, Annetta Louise. *In Darkness with God: The Life of Joseph Gomez, a Bishop in the African Methodist Episcopal Church*. Kent, OH: Kent State University Press, 1998.
Grant, Keneshia N. *The Great Migration and the Democratic Party: Black Voters and the Realignment of American Politics in the 20th Century*. Philadelphia: Temple University Press, 2020.
Greenstone, David. *A Report on the Politics of Detroit*. Cambridge, MA: Joint Center for Urban Studies, MIT and Harvard University, 1961.
Grimshaw, William J. *Bitter Fruit: Black Politics and the Chicago Machine 1913–1991*. Chicago: University of Chicago Press, 1992.
Grisinger, Joanna L. "'South Africa Is the Mississippi of the World': Anti-Apartheid Activism through Domestic Civil Rights Law." *Law and History Review* 38 (November 2020): 843–81.
Gropman, Alan L. *The Air Force Integrates, 1945–1964*. Washington, DC: Smithsonian Institution Press, 1998.
Halberstam, David. *The Fifties*. New York: Villard Books, 1993.
Halfmann, Janet. *The Midnight Teacher: Lilly Ann Granderson and Her Secret School*. New York: Lew and Low Books, 2018.
Hamilton, Charles V. *Adam Clayton Powell, Jr.: The Political Biography of an American Dilemma*. New York: Cooper Square Press, 2002.
Hamlin, Francoise N. *Crossroads at Clarksdale: The Black Freedom Struggle in the Mississippi Delta after World War II*. Chapel Hill: University of North Carolina Press, 2012.

Hammer, Peter J., and Trevor W. Coleman. *Crusader for Justice: Federal Judge Damon J. Keith*. Detroit, MI: Wayne State University Press, 2014.
Harris, Charles Wesley. *Congress and the Governance of the Nation's Capital*. Washington, DC: Georgetown University Press, 1995.
Harris, Frederick C. *The Price of the Ticket: Barack Obama and the Rise and Decline of Black Politics*. New York: Oxford University Press, 2012.
Haygood, Wil. *King of the Cats: The Life and Times of Adam Clayton, Jr.* Boston: Houghton, Mifflin Company, 1993.
Haynie, Kerry L. *African American Legislators in the American States*. New York: Columbia University Press, 2001.
Henry, Aaron, with Constance Curry. *Aaron Henry: The Fire Ever Burning*. Jackson: University Press of Mississippi, 2018.
Hill, Robert A. *The Marcus Garvey and Universal Negro Improvement Association Papers*. Durham, NC: Duke University Press, 2011.
Holloway, Karla F. C. *Passed On: African American Mourning Stories*. Durham, NC: Duke University Press, 2002.
Horne, Gerald. *White Supremacy Confronted: U.S. Imperialism and Anti-Communism vs. the Liberation of Southern Africa, from Rhodes to Mandela*. New York: International Publishers, 2019.
Houck, Davis W., and Matthew A. Grindy. *Emmett Till and the Mississippi Press*. Jackson: University Press of Mississippi, 2008.
Johnson, Cedric. *Revolutionaries to Race Leaders: Black Power and the Making of African American Politics*. Minneapolis: University of Minnesota, 2007.
Johnson, Valerie C. *Black Power in the Suburbs: The Myth or Reality of African American Suburban Political Incorporation*. Albany: State University of New York Press, 2002.
Jordan, David L., with Robert L. Jenkins. *David L. Jordan: From the Mississippi Cotton Fields to the State Senate, a Memoir*. Jackson: University Press of Mississippi, 2014.
Jordan, Lewis Garnett. *Up the Ladder in Foreign Missions*. Nashville, TN: National Baptist Publishing Board, 1901.
Joseph, Peniel E. *Stokely: A Life*. New York: Basic Civitas, 2014.
Joseph, Peniel E. *Waiting 'Til the Midnight Hour: A Narrative History of Black Power in America*. New York: Henry Holt, 2006.
Katzman, David M. *Before the Ghetto: Black Detroit in the Nineteenth Century*. Urbana: University of Illinois Press, 1973.
Key, V. O., Jr. *Southern Politics in State and Nation*. New York: Alfred A. Knopf, 1949.
King, Coretta Scott. *My Life, Love, My Legacy*. New York: Henry Holt, 2017.
Kissinger, Henry A. *Years of Renewal*. New York: Simon and Schuster, 1999.
Kruse, Kevin M. *White Flight: Atlanta and the Making of Modern Conservatism*. Princeton, NJ: Princeton University Press, 2005.
Lake, Anthony. *The "Tar Baby" Option: American Policy toward Southern Rhodesia*. New York: Columbia University Press, 1976.
Larson, Kate Clifford. *Walk with Me: A Biography of Fannie Lou Hamer*. New York: Oxford University Press, 2021.
Lawson, Steven F. *Black Ballots: Voting Rights in the South, 1944–1969*. New York: Columbia University Press, 1976.

Lee, Chana Kai. *For Freedom's Sake: The Life of Fannie Lou Hamer*. Urbana: University of Illinois Press, 1999.

Levine, David Allen. *Internal Combustion: The Races in Detroit 1915–1926*. New York: Praeger Publishers, 1976.

Lewis, John. *Walking with the Wind: A Memoir of the Movement*. New York: Simon and Schuster, 1998.

Litwack, Leon F. *How Free Is Free? The Long Death of Jim Crow*. Cambridge, MA: Harvard University Press, 2009.

Lynch, Hollis R. *Black American Radicals and the Liberation of Africa: The Council on African Affairs, 1937–1955*. Ithaca, NY: Cornell University Africana Studies and Research Center, 1978.

MacGregor, Morris J., Jr. *Integration of the Armed Forces 1940–1965*. Washington, DC: Center of Military History, 1981.

Manning, Christopher. *William L. Dawson and the Limits of Black Electoral Leadership*. Dekalb: Northern Illinois University Press, 2009.

Maraniss, David. *Once a Great City: A Detroit Story*. New York: Simon and Schuster, 2015.

Massie, Robert Kinloch. *Loosing the Bonds: The United States and South Africa in the Apartheid Years*. New York: Doubleday Books, 1997.

Masters, Nicholas A. "Committee Assignments in the House of Representatives." *American Political Science Review* 55, no. 2 (June 1961): 345–57.

Masur, Kate. *An Example for All the Land: Emancipation and the Struggle over Equality in Washington, D.C.* Chapel Hill: University of North Carolina Press, 2010.

Mayhew, David R. *Congress: The Electoral Connection*. New Haven, CT: Yale University Press, 1974.

McMillen, Neil R. *The Citizens' Council: Organized Resistance to the Second Reconstruction, 1954–1964*. Urbana: University of Illinois Press, 1994.

McMillen, Neil R. *Dark Journey: Black Mississippians in the Age of Jim Crow*. Urbana: University of Illinois Press, 1989.

McNamara, Robert S. *The Essence of Security: Reflections in Office*. New York: Harper and Row, 1968.

Meier, August, and Elliott Rudwick. *Detroit and the Rise of the UAW*. Ann Arbor: University of Michigan Press, 1979.

Mendelsohn, Jack. *The Martyrs: Sixteen Who Gave Their Lives for Racial Justice*. New York: Harper and Row, 1966.

Meriwether, James H. "'Worth a Lot of Negro Votes': Black Voters, Africa, and the 1960 Presidential Election." *Journal of American History* 95 (December 2008): 737–63.

Mershon, Sherie, and Steven Schlossman. *Foxholes and Color Lines: Desegregating the U.S. Armed Forces*. Baltimore, MD: Johns Hopkins University Press, 1998.

Miller, Karen R. *Managing Inequality: Northern Racial Liberalism in Interwar Detroit*. New York: New York University Press, 2015.

Minta, Michael D. *Oversight: Representing the Interests of Latinos and Blacks in Congress*. Princeton, NJ: Princeton University Press, 2021.

Mirel, Jeffrey. *The Rise and Fall of an Urban School System: Detroit, 1907–1981*. Ann Arbor: University of Michigan Press, 1999.

Mitchell, Nancy. *Jimmy Carter in Africa: Race and the Cold War*. Stanford: Stanford University Press, 2016.

Moon, Elaine Latzman, ed. "Charles C. Diggs, Jr." In *Untold Tales, Unsung Heroes: An Oral History of Detroit's African American Community, 1918–1967*, 51–57. Detroit, MI: Wayne State University Press, 1994.

Moon, Elaine Latzman, ed. "Helen Nuttall Brown." In *Untold Tales, Unsung Heroes: An Oral History of Detroit's African American Community, 1918–1967*, 37–38. Detroit, MI: Wayne State University Press, 1994.

Moore, Leonard N. *The Defeat of Black Power: Civil Rights and the National Black Political Convention of 1972*. Baton Rouge: Louisiana State University Press, 2018.

Morris, James McGrath. *Eye on the Struggle: Ethel Payne, the First Lady of the Black Press*. New York: Amistad, 2015.

Morrison, Minion K. C. *Aaron Henry of Mississippi: Inside Agitator*. Fayetteville: University of Arkansas Press, 2015.

Morrow, E. Frederic. *Black Man in the White House: A Diary of the Eisenhower Years by the Administrative Officer for Special Projects, the White House, 1955–1961*. New York: Coward-McCann, 1963.

Motley, Constance Baker. *Equal Justice under the Law: An Autobiography*. New York: Farrar, Straus and Giroux, 1998.

Moye, J. Todd. *Freedom Flyers: The Tuskegee Airmen of World War II*. New York: Oxford University Press, 2010.

Musgrove, George Derek. *Rumor, Repression, and Racial Politics: How the Harassment of Black Elected Officials Shaped Post–Civil Rights America*. Athens: University of Georgia Press, 2012.

Nalty, Bernard C. *Strength for the Fight: A History of Black Americans in the Military*. New York: The Free Press, 1986.

Newsom, David D. *Witness to a Changing World*. Washington, DC: New Academia Publishing, 2008.

Noer, Thomas J. *Cold War and Black Liberation: The United States and White Rule in Africa, 1948–1968*. Columbia: University of Missouri Press, 1985.

Noer, Thomas J. *Soapy: A Biography of G. Mennen Williams*. Ann Arbor: University of Michigan Press, 2005.

Norrell, Robert J. *Reaping the Whirlwind: The Civil Rights Movement in Tuskegee*. New York: Alfred A. Knopf, 1985.

O'Reilly, Kenneth. *Nixon's Piano: Presidents and Racial Politics from Washington to Clinton*. New York: Free Press, 1995.

Orr, Marion. "Hanes Walton, Jr." In *American Political Scientists: A Dictionary*, edited by Glenn H. Utter and Charles Lockhard, 409–11. Westport, CT: Greenwood Publishing Group, 2003.

Ortlepp, Anke. *Jim Crow Terminals: The Desegregation of American Airports*. Athens: University of Georgia Press, 2017.

Osur, Alan M. *Blacks in the Army Air Forces during World War II: The Problem of Race Relations*. Washington, DC: US Air Force, 1986.

Parker, Glenn R. *Homeward Bound: Explaining Changes in Congressional Behavior*. Pittsburgh: University of Pittsburgh Press, 1986.

Payne, Charles M. *I've Got the Light of Freedom: The Organizing Tradition and the Mississippi Freedom Struggle*. Berkeley: University of California Press, 1995.

Payne, Les, and Tamara Payne. *The Dead Are Rising: The Life of Malcolm X*. New York: Liveright Publishing, 2020.

Pearlman, Lauren. *Democracy's Capital: Black Political Power in Washington, D.C., 1960s–1970s*. Chapel Hill: University of North Carolina Press, 2019.

Peckham, Howard H. *The Making of the University of Michigan, 1817–1967*. Ann Arbor: University of Michigan Press, 1967.

Pinderhughes, Dianne M. *Race and Ethnicity in Chicago Politics: A Reexamination of Pluralist Theory*. Urbana: University of Illinois Press, 1987.

Plummer, Brenda Gayle. *In Search of Power: African Americans in the Era of Decolonization, 1956–1974*. New York: Cambridge University Press, 2013.

Plummer, Brenda Gayle. *Rising Wind: Black Americans and U.S. Foreign Affairs, 1935–1960*. Chapel Hill: University of North Carolina Press, 1996.

Poinsett, Alex. *Walking with Presidents: Louis Martin and the Rise of Black Political Power*. Lanham, MD: Madison Books, 1997.

Powell, Adam Clayton Jr. *Adam by Adam: The Autobiography of Adam Clayton Powell, Jr.* New York: Kensington Publishing, 1971.

Ransby, Barbara. *Ella Baker and the Black Freedom Movement: A Radical Democratic Vision*. Chapel Hill: University of North Carolina Press, 2003.

Rice, Rolundus R. *Hosea Williams: A Lifetime of Defiance and Protest*. Columbia: University of South Carolina Press, 2021.

Rich, Wilbur C. *Coleman Young and Detroit Politics: From Social Activist to Power Broker*. Detroit, MI: Wayne State University Press, 1989.

Robinson, Randall. *Defending the Spirit: A Black Life in America*. New York: Dutton Company, 1998.

Rubenstein, Bruce A., and Lawrence E. Ziewacz. *Payoffs in the Cloakroom: The Greening of the Michigan Legislature, 1938–1946*. East Lansing: Michigan State University Press, 1995.

Rusk, Dean. *As I Saw It*. New York: W. W. Norton, 1990.

Rustin, Bayard. "From Protest to Politics: The Future of the Civil Rights Movement." *Commentary*, February 1965. www.commentary.org/articles/bayard-rustin-2/from-protest-to-politics-the-future-of-the-civil-rights-movement.

Salvatore, Nick. *Singing in a Strange Land: C. L. Franklin, the Black Church, and the Transformation of America*. Urbana: University of Illinois Press, 2006.

Sandler, Stanley. *Segregated Skies: All-Black Combat Squadrons of WWII*. Washington, DC: Smithsonian Institution, 1992.

Schneller, Robert J., Jr. *Blue and Gold and Black: Racial Integration of the U.S. Naval Academy*. College Station: Texas A&M University Press, 2008.

Schraeder, Peter J. *United States Foreign Policy toward Africa: Incrementalism, Crisis, and Change*. New York: Cambridge University Press, 1994.

Smith, J. Clay, "United States Foreign Policy and Goler Teal Butcher." *Howard Law Journal* 37 (1994): 138–211.

Smith, Robert C. *Hanes Walton, Jr.: Architect of the Black Science of Politics*. New York: Palgrave Pivot, 2018.

Smith, Robert C. *We Have No Leaders: African Americans in the Post–Civil Rights Era*. Albany: State University of New York Press, 1996.

Smith, Suzanne E. *To Serve the Living: Funeral Directors and the African American Way of Death*. Cambridge, MA: Harvard University Press, 2010.

Solberg, Carl. *Conquest of the Skies: A History of Commercial Aviation in America*. Boston: Little, Brown, 1979.

Staebler, Neil. *Out of the Smoke-Filled Room: A History of Michigan Politics*. Ann Arbor, MI: George Wahr Publishing, 1991.

Stephens, Ronald J. *Idlewild: The Rise, Decline, and Rebirth of a Unique African American Resort Town*. Ann Arbor: University of Michigan Press, 2013.

Stokes, Louis, with David Chanoff. *The Gentleman from Ohio*. Columbus: Ohio State University Press, 2016.

Stone, Chuck. *Black Political Power in America*. Indianapolis, IN: Bobbs-Merrill, 1968.

Sugrue, Thomas J. *The Origins of the Urban Crisis: Race and Inequality in Postwar Detroit*. Princeton, NJ: Princeton University Press, 1996.

Talton, Benjamin. *In this Land of Plenty: Mickey Leland and Africa in American Politics*. Philadelphia: University of Pennsylvania Press, 2019.

Tate, Katherine. *Concordance: Black Lawmaking in the U.S. Congress from Carter to Obama*. Ann Arbor: University of Michigan Press, 2020.

Terry, Wallace. *Missing Places: Black Journalists of Modern America; an Oral History*. New York: Carroll and Graf, 2007.

Thomas, Richard W. *Life for Us Is What We Make It: Building Black Community in Detroit, 1915–1945*. Bloomington: Indiana University Press, 1992.

Thompson, Heather Ann. *Whose Detroit?: Politics, Labor, and Race in a Modern American City*. Ithaca, NY: Cornell University Press, 2001.

Thompson, Wright. *The Barn: The Secret History of a Murder in Mississippi*. New York: Penguin, 2024.

Thurber, Timothy N. *Republicans and Race: The GOP's Frayed Relationship with African Americans, 1945–1974*. Lawrence: University Press of Kansas, 2013.

Tillery, Alvin B., Jr. *Between Homeland and Motherland: Africa, U.S. Foreign Policy, and Black Leadership in America*. Ithaca, NY: Cornell University Press, 2011.

Till-Mobley, Mamie, and Christopher Benson. *Death of Innocence: The Story of the Hate Crime That Changed America*. New York: Random House, 2003.

Turner, Arthur, and Earl R. Moses. *Colored Detroit: A Brief History*. Detroit, MI: Turner and Moses, 1924.

Tyson, Timothy B. *The Blood of Emmett Till*. New York: Simon and Schuster, 2017.

Vantoch, Victoria. *The Jet Sex: Airline Stewardesses and the Making of an American Icon*. Philadelphia: University of Pennsylvania Press, 2013.

Volden, Craig, and Alan E. Wiseman. *Legislative Effectiveness in the United States Congress: The Lawmakers*. Cambridge, MA: Cambridge University Press, 2014.

Von Eschen, Penny M. *Race against Empire: Black Americans and Anticolonialism, 1937–1957*. Ithaca, NY: Cornell University Press, 1997.

Walters, Ronald W. *Black Presidential Politics in America: A Strategic Approach*. Albany: State University of New York Press, 1988.

Walton, Hanes, Jr. *Black Politics: A Theoretical and Structural Analysis*. Philadelphia: J. B. Lippincott, 1972.

Walton, Hanes, Jr. *Invisible Politics: Black Political Behavior*. Albany: State University of New York Press, 1985.

Walton, Hanes, Jr., Robert Louis Stevenson, and James Bernard Rosser Sr., eds. *The African Foreign Policy of Secretary of State Henry Kissinger*. Lanham, MD: Lexington Books, 2007.

Weiss, Nancy J. *Farewell to the Party of Lincoln: Black Politics in the Age of FDR*. Princeton, NJ: Princeton University Press, 1983.

Whalen, Charles and Barbara Whalen. *The Longest Debate: A Legislative History of the 1964 Civil Rights Act*. Cabin John, MD: Seven Locks Press, 1985.
Whited, Charles. *Knight: A Publisher in the Tumultuous Century*. New York: E. P. Dutton, 1988.
Widick, B. J. *Detroit: City of Race and Class Violence*. Detroit, MI: Wayne State University Press, 1989.
Wilkerson, Isabel. *The Warmth of Other Suns: The Epic Story of America's Great Migration*. New York: Vintage Press, 2010.
Williams, Juan. *Eyes on the Prize: America's Civil Rights Years, 1954–1965*. New York: Viking Press, 1987.
Williams, Michael Vinson. *Medgar Evers: Mississippi Martyr*. Fayetteville: University of Arkansas Press, 2011.
Wilson, James Q. "The Flamboyant Mr. Powell." *Commentary* 41 (January 1966): 31–35.
Wilson, James Q. *Negro Politics: The Search for Leadership*. New York: Free Press, 1960.
Wilson, James Q. "Two Negro Politicians: An Interpretation." *Midwest Journal of Political Science* 4 (November 1960): 346–69.
Woodard, Komozi. *A Nation within a Nation: Amiri Baraka (LeRoi Jones) and Black Power Politics*. Chapel Hill: University of North Carolina Press, 1999.
Wright, Roberta Hughes. *Detroit Memorial Park Cemetery: The Evolution of an African American Corporation*. Southfield, MI: Charro Book Company, 1993.
Young, Andrew. *An Easy Burden: The Civil Rights Movement and the Transformation of America*. New York: Harper-Collins, 1996.
Young, Coleman, and Lonnie Wheeler. *Hardstuff: The Autobiography of Mayor Coleman Young*. New York: Viking Press, 1994.
Zelizer, Julian E. *Burning Down the House: Newt Gingrich, the Fall of a Speaker, and the Rise of the New Republican Party*. New York: Penguin Press, 2020.
Zelizer, Julian E. *On Capitol Hill: The Struggle to Reform Congress and Its Consequences, 1948–2000*. New York: Cambridge University Press, 2004.

Dissertations and Other Unpublished Works

Adair, Augustus Alven. "Black Legislative Influence in Federal Policy Decisions: The Congressional Black Caucus 1971–1975." PhD diss., Johns Hopkins University, 1976.
McLemore, Leslie Burl. "The Mississippi Freedom Democratic Party: A Case Study of Grassroots Politics." PhD diss., University of Massachusetts, 1971.
Orr, Marion E. "Black Political Incorporation, Phase II: The Cases of Baltimore and Detroit." PhD diss., University of Maryland, 1992.
Stovall, A. J. "Before Coleman Young: The Growth of the Detroit Black Elected Officialdom: 1870–1973." PhD diss., Union for Experimenting Colleges and Universities, 1983.
Williams, Ronald Cartell. "Adversarial Diplomacy and African American Politics." PhD diss. University of California, Berkeley 2011.
Williams, Ronald Cartell. "Black Embassy: TransAfrica and the Making of Adversarial Diplomacy." Unpublished book manuscript, 2023.

Index

Page numbers in italics refer to illustrations and captions.

Abernathy, Ralph, 116, 119, 123, 145–46, 154, 158
ACOA, 178, 184, 187
"Action Manifesto" (Diggs), 198
Adams, Brock, 172
Adams, Russell, 249
AFL, 48. *See also* AFL-CIO
AFL-CIO, 52, 181
Africa, 15, *136*, 177–208, 298n35. *See also names of specific African nations*
Africa Bureau, US State Department, 177, 195
African-American Manifesto on Southern Africa, The, 205–6
African American National Conference on Africa (1972), 200
African Liberation Day, 200
African liberation movements, 153, 158, 183, 189, 199–204, 206, 258. *See also names of specific African nations*
African Methodist Episcopal Zion Church, 16
African National Congress, 192
Africa Subcommittee, US Foreign Affairs Committee, *136*, 180, 183–84, 186–96, 203, 218, 240
Air and Space Museum, Smithsonian Institution, 91
air travel segregation, 93–100, 187. *See also* segregation and discrimination
Alabama, 29–34, 118–19
Albert, Carl, 144, 170, 171
Alcorn State Agricultural and Mechanical College, 16

All-African People's Conference (1958), 180
America by Air exhibit (2007), 91
American Airlines, 99
American Committee on Africa (ACOA), 178, 184, 187
American Federation of Labor (AFL), 48
American Federation of Labor–Congress of Industrial Organizations (AFL-CIO), 52, 181
American Negro Leadership Conference on Africa, 183
American Political Science Association (APSA), 269n8 (prol.)
Americans for Democratic Action, 48
American Society of International Law, 196
Anderson, John, 241
Andrews Air Force Base, 110
Angola, 178, 187, 188, 189, 197, 201, 202
anti-apartheid activism, 186, 190, 194, 198–99, 204, 209, 250
apartheid, 149, 178, 181, 183–85, 187, 190–91, 198, 204–8. *See also* Rhodesia; segregation and discrimination; South Africa
Asch, Chris Meyers, 168
Ashe, Arthur, *136*, 189–90
assassinations, 116, 119, 123–24, 150, 169
Austin, Richard, 211–14
Azores Islands, 178, 189

Baker, Constance Motley, 28
Baker, George T., 93

Baker v. Carr, 276n6
bankruptcy, 20, 21
Baraka, Amiri, *135*, 151, 153, 154, 156–61
Barry, Marion, 169, 252, 253, 254
Bell, Griffin, 226, 229
Bennett, Charles E., x
Bethel AME Church, 18
Bethune, Mary McLeod, 68
Biden, Joseph, 207
Biko, Stephen, 194, 298n48
Billingsley, Walter, *131*
Bingham, Jonathan B., 188
Black activism, 4, 10, 169, 198, 200. *See also* Black Power Movement
"Black Agenda" (1972 convention), *135*, 151–52, 154–66
"Black Bill of Rights" (1972), 164–65
Black Bottom, Detroit, 17, 22, 24, 44, 49, 52, 209, 212, 216, 217
Black Caucus. *See* Congressional Black Caucus (CBC)
Black Forum on Foreign Policy (BFFP), 203, 205
Black Leadership Conference on Southern Africa (1976), 205
Black National Newspaper Publishers Association, 81
Black Panther Party for Self-Defense, 115, 141, 144–45
Black Power (Carmichael and Hamilton), 153–54
Black Power Movement, 141, 152, 153–54. *See also names of specific organizations*
Bledsoe, Harold, 54
"Bloody Sunday," 120
Bolling Air Force Base, 102
Bolton, Francis, 296n8
Bond, Julian, 151, 154, 203
Booker, Simeon, 12, 75, 80, 84, 161, 189, 214, 249, 253
Bordin, Ruth, 26
Botswana, 188, 202
Bowles, Charles E., 19
Bradley, Amanda, 84, *131*
Brando, Marlon, 123

Branton, Wiley A., 74, 247
Breland, J. J., 79
bribery, 32, 40, 170, 209, 210
Briggs Manufacturing Company, 44
Broadwater, William, 254
Brooke, Edward, 123, *136*, 148
Brotherhood of Sleeping Car Porters, 68, 112
Brown, Basil, 80, 86
Brown, Frederick, 210–11
Brown, Helen Nuttall, 24
Brown, Robert, 150
Brown, Willie, 154
Brown II, 72
Browning, Grainger, 250, 254
Brown v. Board of Education, 59, 60, 71, 72
Broyhill, Joel, 175
Brucker, Wilbur, 104
Bryant, Carolyn, 78, 86
Bryant, Roy, 78–79, 87, 283n79
Bunche, Ralph, 59, 123, 179
Bureau of African Affairs, US State Department, 177, 195
burial insurance, 34–35, 40–41, 210
Burt, L. Juan, 217
busing, 141, 159, 161–62, 163, 164, 165
bus segregation, 112. *See also* segregation and discrimination
Butcher, Goler Teal, 190, 203, 258, 298n35
Byrd, Harry F., 197, 201
Byrd Amendment, *136*, 200–201, 204, 205, 224, 226

campaign finances, 221–22, 235–36
Canadia, Asa T., 53, *128*
Cape Verde, 178
Capital Airlines, 99
Carmichael, Stokely, 141, 153, 257; *Black Power*, 153–54
Carter, Jimmy, *136*, 171, 205, 206, 207, 208, 225–26, 304n45
Carthan, Adie, 79
Carthan, John, 79, *131*
Case, Clifford P., *136*
Cavanagh, Jerome, 115, 121

CBC. *See* Congressional Black Caucus (CBC)
censuring, of Diggs, x–xii, 137, 240–43, 253. *See also* Diggs, Charles Coles, Jr.
Centennial Baptist Church, 113–14
Central Congregation Church, 270n45
"chairman's portrait," 167, 176, 222, 223, 232, 235, 236, 310n30
Challenor, Herschelle, 200, 205, 207, 230
Chatham, Gerald, 87–88
Chavis, Benjamin, 160–61
Cheeks, James E., 249
Cherry, Gwendolyn, 155
Chicago, IL, 1–4
Chicago Defender, 12, 66, 79
Chisholm, Shirley, *134*, 143–44, 147, 148, 154–55, 156, 163, 226, 294n63
CIO, 7, 8. *See also* AFL-CIO; CIO-PAC; UAW-CIO
CIO-PAC, 48, 59
Citizens' Councils, 72, 73, 74, 75
Citizen Study Committee, 108
Civil Aeronautics Administration (CAA), 92, 94–95
Civil Rights Act (1957), 112–13, 118
Civil Rights Act (1960), 118
Civil Rights Act (1964), 97, 100, 109, 116, 118, 166, 198, 269n22
civil rights movement, 4, 107, 111–24, 178, 257. *See also* Black Power Movement; marches, civil rights; *and names of specific leaders and organizations*
Clark, Dick, *136*, 174, 206
Clark, James "Jim," 118
Clark, Mark, 144–45
Clay, William, *134*; CBC work of, 143–44, 147–50, 156, 198; on Diggs's career, 248, 258; *Just Permanent Interests*, 248; military service of, 101–2; political career of, 285n3
Cleage, Albert, Jr., 9, 270n45
clerk-hire allowances, 137, 221–26, 232, 235
Clinton, Bill, 251–52, 253
Clipper, Joseph Daniel, 222
Coalition of Black Trade Unionists, 228

Cobb, Charles, 205
CODEL, 183, 188–89, 191–93, 298n35
Coke, H. D., 97
Coke v. Atlanta, 97
Cole, Celeste, 40
Coles, Charles T., *126*, 210, 211
Coles, John, 15, *125*
Collins, Barbara-Rose, 253
Collins, George, 147
Committee on Conscience Against Apartheid, 184
Committee on Equal Employment Opportunity, 99
Committee on Equal Opportunity in the Armed Forces, 109. *See also* Gesell Committee
Committee on Standards of Official Conduct. *See* Ethics Committee
Congressional Black Caucus (CBC), 11, *134*, 141–57, 165, 205, 246–47, 248, 251
congressional delegation (CODEL). *See* CODEL
congressional run, of Diggs, 9–10, 51–56. *See also* Diggs, Charles Coles, Jr.
Congress of African Peoples, 154, 158
Congress of Industrial Organizations (CIO), 7, 8
Congress of Industrial Organizations–Political Action Committee (CIO-PAC), 48, 59
Congress of Racial Equality (CORE), 113, 154, 162
Conot, Robert, 20
Conyers, John, 12, 121–22, *134*, 143, 154, 217, 254, 258
CORE, 113, 154, 162
Corporations Committee, 45
corruption trial, of Diggs, 139, 230–38, 306n10. *See also* Diggs, Charles Coles, Jr.
Cosby, Bill, 123
Cotillion Club, 41, *127*
Council of African Affairs, 178
Council of Federated Organizations, 113
Counterintelligence Program (COINTELPRO), 162

Cox, Courtland, 288n44
Craigen, Joseph A., 21, 54
Crockett, George, Jr., 245, 247
"Crusade for Citizenship" (campaign), 113
Cuba, 202, 204
Cutler, Lloyd N., 304n45

Daley, Richard J., 2, 4, 147
Davenport, Ernest, 211–12
Davis, Jennifer, 191
Davis, Mamie, 92
Dawson, William L., 1, 2–4, 5, 6, 12, 10, 63, 67, 68, 89, *131*, 142, 143, 147, 169
DC Committee for Self-Determination, 174
Dellums, Ronald, 13, *134*, 147, 171, 174, 250–51
Delmont, Matthew F., 29
Del Rio, James, 54, 80
Delta. *See* Mississippi Delta
Delta Airlines, 99
Democratic National Committee, 3–4, 144, 201
Democratic National Convention (DNC), 116
Democratic Select Committee (DSC), 143–48
Department of Defense (DOD), 102, 107–10
Detroit, MI, 7–9, 16–28, 44–56, 121–22, *134*, 212
Detroit City Council, 46–50, 54
Detroit Memorial Park, 19, 217, 254–55
Detroit Metropolitan Mutual Assurance Company, 210, 213
Diggs, Alexis, 63, *127*, *128*
Diggs, Anna Johnston, *135*, 216, 217, 218, 302n52
Diggs, Carla, 216, 248
Diggs, Charles Coles, III, 35, 40, 63, *127*, *128*, *129*, 167, 215
Diggs, Charles Coles, Jr., 1–13, 209, 255, 257–59; "Action Manifesto," 198; Africa policy work of, 177–208, 298n35; CBC work by, *134*, 141–52, 248; censuring of, x–xii, 137, 240–43, 253; city council run of, 44–50; congressional runs of, 51–63, 230–31, 238, 239; corruption trial of, 139, 230–38, 306n10; death of, 253; desegregating air travel and, 93–100; Dr. King and, 111–24, *133*, 288n17, 288n35; early life in Black Detroit of, 18–20, 21–28, 38–39; early political career of, 37–43; at Emmett Till's murder trial, 78–90, *131*; family funeral business and, 34–36, 57, 210–20; financial and legal troubles of, 220–29, 304n45; first term as congressman of, 64–69; funeral of, 253–55; home rule and, 167–76; images of, *126*, *127*, *129–36*, *138–40*; imprisonment of, x, xii, 246–47; indictment of, 32, 229–30; military service of, 29–36; National Black Political Convention (1972) and, *135*, 153–66, 258; paternity suit of, 215; relationships and family of, 37–38, 39–40, 41, 63, 214–18, 248–49; return to Mississippi Delta of, 70–77; work after Congress, 248–55
Diggs, Charles Coles, Sr.: death and funeral of, *133*, 216–17; early life and family of, 14–16; health of, 76, 216; images of, *126*, *127*, *128*, *129*; legal troubles and imprisonment of, 40, 41–42, 210; mortuary businesses of, 17–18, 20, 31, 34–36, 209–19; political work of, ix–x, 7, 9, 14, 19–20, 23–25, 42–43
Diggs, Charles M., 42–43
Diggs, Cindy Carter, 218, 225, 248
Diggs, Darlene Exposé, 249, 253, 309n9
Diggs, Denise, 35–36, 41, 63, *127*, *128*, 215, 245, 253
Diggs, Douglass, 167, 216, 252–53, 254
Diggs, George, 20
Diggs, James J., Jr., 14, 15, 16, *125*, 177, 271n7
Diggs, James J., Sr., 15, 271n4
Diggs, James "Jimmy" (nephew of Charles C. Diggs Sr.), 40, *126*, 209, 218
Diggs, Janet Hall, 217–18, 220, 238, 246, 248–49

Diggs, Juanita Rosario, 37–38, 39–40, 50, *127*, *128*, 214–15, 218
Diggs, Lilly Granderson, 15, *125*
Diggs, Mayme Ethel Jones, 16, 18, 20, 21, 22, 37, 68, *127*, 249, *133*
Diggs, Oliver Roosevelt, 40, 42
Diggs, Osmond, 20
Diggs, Weston, Jr., 36, 37, 211, 214, 218, 245
Diggs, Weston, Sr., 16, 18, 20, 37, 40, 43, 216
Diggs Enterprises, 113, 209, 213
Diggs Funeral Home. *See* House of Diggs (formerly Diggs Funeral Home)
Diggs's Law, 23
Diggs-Stinson Funeral Home, 219. *See also* House of Diggs (formerly Diggs Funeral Home)
Diggs-Taylor, Denise. *See* Diggs, Denise
Diggs v. Schultz, 201
Dingell, John, Jr., 238
Dingell, John, Sr., 67
discrimination. *See* segregation and discrimination
District of Columbia, 149, 159, 162, 167–76
District of Columbia Home Rule Act (1973), 167
District of Columbia Self-Government and Governmental Reorganization Act (1973), 172, 175. *See also* District of Columbia Home Rule Act (1973); home rule
Dittmer, John, 72
Dixon, Julian, xi
DNC, 116
Dobbs House Restaurant, 93, 95, 97
DOD, 102, 107–10
Doonesbury (cartoon), 241
Douglass, Frederick, *132*, 170
DSC, 143–48
Du Bois, W. E. B., 33
DuBose, Carolyn, 30, 42, 43, 55, 234, 238, 252
Dukes, Ofield, 222, 225, 227, 233
Dulles, John Foster, 94
Dunbar Hospital, 19
Durham Committee on Negro Affairs, 95

Eagleton, Thomas, 167–68
Eastland, James O., 72
Ebenezer African Methodist Episcopal Church, 250, 253
Ebenezer Baptist Church (Detroit, MI), 61
Ebenezer Baptist Church (Atlanta, GA), 123
Ebony (publication), 1, 142, 156, 223, 226
Eckels College of Mortuary Science, 18
economic sanctions, 183–84, 207–8
Ehrlichman, John, 146
Eisenhower, Dwight, 58, 60, 73, 103, 104, 112
"Elect 3" campaign, 8–9
employment discrimination, 299n51
Equality of Treatment Executive Order, 108
Essence (publication), 151
Ethics Committee, x–xii, 222, 241–44. *See also* censuring, of Diggs
Evers, Medgar, 71, 73, 82, 84, 89, 114, 115, 124, 257
Executive Order 9981, 101
Executive Order 10925, 107
Exposé, Darlene, 249, 253, 309n9

FAAP, 93–97
Fair Employment Practices Bill (1972), 198, 208
Fair Housing Act (1968), 110
Farmer, James, 117
Farrakhan, Louis, 154
Fauntroy, Walter, *134*, 154, 157, 169–70, 234, 291n53, 295n19
Federal Airport Act Program (FAAP), 93–97
filibuster, 112, 120
Fisk University, 27, 30
Flynt, John, Jr., 239
Ford, Gerald R., *130*, 173, 176, 201, 202
Ford, Harold, 202
Ford Motor Company, 7–8, 25, 49, 107, 194
Foreign Affairs Committee, Subcommittee on Africa, *136*, 180, 183–84, 186–96, 203, 218, 240

Forman, James, 117
Fort, E. Earthmon, *126*
Fort McClellan, AL, 101–2
Francis, Charles E., 29; *The Tuskegee Airmen*, 29
Franklin, Aretha, 54, 123
Franklin, C. L., 54, 115
Franklin, John Hope, 15
Frederick Douglass National Historic Site, *132*, 170
Free DC Movement, 169
"Freedom Train," 64–65
Free South Africa Movement, 251
Friedel, Samuel A., 188, 297n11
Fuller, Vincent, 229

Gallagher, Bonnie, 106
gambling, 24, 214, 228
Gandhi, Mahatma, 194
Garcia, Robert, 243
Garment, Leonard, 146
Garvey, Marcus, 7, 19
Gasch, Oliver, 230, 231, 232, 234–36, 239–40
Gates, Thomas S., 105
General Motors, 7, 194, 222, 299n51
Germany, 107, 108
Gesell, Gerhard, 109. See also Gesell Committee
Gesell Committee, 109–10
Ghana, 112, 179–80
Gibbs, Angela, 215
Gibbs, Jacqueline Marion, 215
GI Bill, 41
Gibson, James, 156
Gibson, Kenneth, 154
Gingrich, Newt, x, *137*, 239, 241–47, 252
Gomez, Joseph, 18
Granderson, Lilly Ann (junior). *See* Diggs, Lilly Granderson
Granderson, Lilly Ann (senior), 14–15
Great Depression, 19–20, 21, 25
Great Migration, xii, 9, 15–16, 17, 18, 52
Great Society programs, 143
Green, Edith, 175
Green, George H., 18, 19, 21, 272n24

Griffiths, Martha, 121, 217
Guinea-Bissau, 178, 187, 197, 201

Hagans, Michele V., *140*
Haiti, 65, 251
Hall, Janet. *See* Diggs, Janet Hall
Hamer, Fannie Lou, 117, 257
Hamilton, Charles V., 5–6, 153; *Black Power*, 153–54
Hampton, Fred, 144
Hampton Institute, 76
Harrison, Antonio, 156
Hart, Philip A., 62, 121, *132*, 217
Hastings, James F., 225
Hatcher, Lillian, 53, 54, 245
Hatcher, Richard, *135*, 154, 156–58
Hawkins, Augustus, *134*, 143, 154, 156, 243
Hays, Wayne, 225
Height, Dorothy, 206–7, 254
Henry, Aaron, 72, 73, 113–14, 116, 117
Herter, Christian, 181
Hicks, James "Jimmy," 81, 82
Hicks, Jean Gillette, 303n10. *See also* Stultz, Jean
Hightower, Charles, 191
Hill, Charles A., 47
Hobson, Julius, 169–70
Holloway, Karla F. C., 35
home rule, 149, 162, 167–76
Home Rule Act (1973), 167
Hood, Nicholas, III, 244
House Committee on the District of Columbia, 221, 222–23, 224, 240
House of Diggs (formerly Diggs Funeral Home), 17–18, 20, 31, 34–36, 40–41, 57, 80, 209–20
House of Diggs gospel choir, 65
Houser, George, 178, 187
housing segregation, 3, 17, 25, 47, 49, 59, 103, 105, 109–10, 182
Howard, T. R. M., 71, 73, 74, 75, 76, 81, 82, 84, 85, 88, 89, *131*
Howard University, 66, 106, 157, 199, 200, 249
Hughes, Wilbur, *126*
Humphrey, Hubert H., 116, 123, *136*

Hurd, John, 193
Hurley, Ruby, 82

"I Have a Dream" (King), 115
immigrant communities, 52–53
imprisonment: of Diggs Jr., x, xii, 246–47; of Diggs Sr., 40, 41–42, 210. *See also* Diggs, Charles Coles, Jr.; Diggs, Charles Coles, Sr.
indictment, of Diggs Jr., 220–29, 304n45. *See also* Diggs, Charles Coles, Jr.
industrial labor union movement, 7–8
Inner-City Business Improvement Forum, 123
Innis, Roy, 154, 162
Interstate Commerce Act, 92, 94
Irene Morgan v. Virginia, 92
Irish immigrant community, 53

Jackson, David, 80–81
Jackson, Jesse, 123, *135*, 151, 154, 156, 160, 166, 206, 234, 249, 257
Jackson, Jimmie Lee, 120
Jackson, Mahalia, 123–24
Jackson, Maynard, 154
Jackson, Stephen S., 109
Jackson State University, 15, *125*
James, Daniel "Chappie," Jr., 105
James A. Stinson Funeral home, 219
Japan, 105
Jeffries, Edward, 47
Jenrette, John, 170
Jerusalem Baptist Church, 114
Jet (publication), 75, 79, 80, 142, 190, 214, 243, 249, 253
Johnson, George, 223–24, 225, 227, 233, 235
Johnson, John H., 142, 151, 290n5
Johnson, Lyndon: on African affairs, 183, 184, 187; on air travel discrimination, 99–100; on civil rights, 112–13, 116–18, 119–21; on Diggs Sr.'s death, 217; election of, 166; Great Society program of, 6; on home rule, 169
Johnson, Willard, 200, 225
Johnson Publishing Company, 151, 253

Johnston, Anna Katherine. *See* Diggs, Anna Johnston
Jones, Carter, *126*
Jones, J. Raymond, 6
Jones, Mayme Ethel. *See* Diggs, Mayme Ethel Jones
Jones, Moses, 246
Jones, Raymond, *129*
Jordan, Barbara, 154, 202
Jordan, Vernon, 154
Just Permanent Interests (Clay), 248

Kate Adams (steamboat), 16
Katz, Julius, 188
Kaunda, Kenneth D., 189
Keith, Damon, 24, 38, 121, 122, *127*, 214, 215, 249, 254
Kelly, Clarence M., 227
Kelly, Edward J., 2
Kelly, Sharon Pratt, 258
Kennedy, Edward, 188
Kennedy, John F., 6, 96, 107, 109, 114, 116, *132*, 141, 181–83
Kenya, 202
Khama, Seretse, 189
Kilpatrick, Carolyn Cheeks, 253
King, Coretta Scott, 112, 148, 151, 154, 182, 234, 237
King, Martin Luther, Jr., 93, 111–24, *133*, 169, 182, 288n17, 288n35; "I Have a Dream," 115
Kissinger, Henry, 185, 196, 198, 201, 202, 206, 224
Knight, John, 58
Knight, Landon, 56, 58, 60, 61
Kotelly, John, 231, 233, 235–36
Ku Klux Klan, 19, 72, 73. *See also* racial violence
Kunene, Daniel, 191

labor unions, 7–8
Lawler, John, 232
Leatherwood, Robert, *126*
Lee, George W., 71, 73, 80
LeMelle, Tilden J., *140*
Leroy Smith and His Orchestra, 40

Lesotho, 188, 206
Liberia, 15, 65, 177, 271n7
literacy, 14–15, 119–20
Look (magazine), 283n79
Loving, Alvin, 26, *130*, 171, 245
Lowen, Charles J., 96
Lucy, William, 203
lynch mobs, 15, 78–79. *See also* racial violence

MacGregor, Clark, 148, 150
Mack, Henry W., *132*
Maddox, Lester, 145
Mahoney, Charles A., 52
Malawi, 188
Malcolm X, 115, 119, 150, 151, 163, 257
Mammoth Life and Accident Insurance Company, 213
Mandela, Nelson, 206, 251
Mandela, Winnie, 192
Manning, Christopher, 4
marches, civil rights, 115–16, 118–19, 120, 123
March on Washington (1963), 115–16
Marcy, Eric, 227, 231
Marshall, Thurgood, 71, 123
Maryland State Board of Morticians, 248
Mason, Vivian Carter, 68
Massie, Robert, 246, 304n45
Master, Nicholas, 11–12
Matlock, Felix, *126*, 224, 225, 227, 232, 233
Matney, William T., Jr., *127*
Matthews, Ralph, 12
Maxwell Air Force Base, 103, 246
Mays, Benjamin, 95
McLeod, Clarence, 51, 58
McMillan, John, 169, 170, 250n19, 294n9
McNamara, Robert S., 107, 109
Meredith, James, 114
Metcalfe, Ralph, 147
Metropolitan Funeral System Association, 34–35, 40–41
Metropolitan Mutual Assurance Company, 210, 213
Metropolitan Washington Board of Trade, 168–69

MFDP, 116–17, 288n44
Michigan Chronicle, 12, 22, 50, 54, 56, 79
Michigan Civil Rights Commission, 121
Michigan Federated Democratic Club, 22
Milam, J. W., 78–79, 82, 85–86, 283n79
Milam, Leslie, 82, 85
military service, and discrimination, xii, 3, 27, 29–36, 101–10, 149, 286n32
Miller, Elsie Virginia, 27, 39, 273n41
missionary work, 15
Mississippi Delta, 14–16, 70–77, 78–79, 113–14
Mississippi Freedom Democratic Party (MFDP), 116–17, 288n44
Mitchell, Clarence, 94, 186
Mitchell, Parren, *134*, 147, 203, 242, 243, 297n11
Mitchell, Stephen A., 62
Molopo, Charles D., 206
Montgomery bus boycott, 111, 112, 119, 232, 234, 235
Moore, Amzie, 71, 73, 82
Morton, Azie Taylor, 171
mortuary businesses, 17–18, 20, 31, 34–36, 209–19
Moses, Robert "Bob," 116, 288n44
Mound Bayou, MS, 14, 70, 73, 74, 76, 81, 86, 88, 91, 247, 253, 255
Movement for the Popular Liberation of Angola, 201–2, 203
Moynihan, Daniel Patrick, 146
Mozambique, 178, 187, 188, 189, 201, 202
"Mr. Africa" (nickname), 198, 244. *See also* Diggs, Charles Coles, Jr.
Mugabe, Robert, 204, 208
murder, of Emmett Till, 4, 77, 78–79, 82, 283n79. *See also* racial violence; Till, Emmett
Murphy, Tom O., 188
Musgrove, George Derek, 168

NAACP: on African affairs, 178, 181; on Black servicemen, 31, 32, 104, 107, 286n32; branches of, 71, 73; civil rights bills and, 112, 153; Diggs's work with,

76, 250; Legal Defense and Education Fund, 71, 80, 97; on Till's murder, 79, 80, 81, 82, 111
Nalty, Bernard, 103
Namibia, 192, 206
NASA (National Aeronautics and Space Administration), 187, 193–94
Natcher, William, 173, 175
National Association for the Advancement of Colored People (NAACP). *See* NAACP
National Black Political Convention (1972), *135*, 153–66, 258
National Capital Service Area, 296n50
National Council of Negro Women, 68, 206–7, 254
National Front for the Liberation of Angola, 202
National Negro Funeral Directors Association, 21
National Security Study Memorandum (NSSM 39), 185
National Union for the Total Independence of Angola, 202, 203
National Union of South African Students, 194
National Urban League, 98, 100, 153, 154
Nation of Islam, 24, 115, 154
Naval Academy, 106
Naval Reserve Officers Training Corps (NROTC), 106
Nellum, Albert L., 151
Nelsen, Ancher, 167
New Bethel Baptist Church, 54
Newman, Paul, 123
Newsom, David, 185
Newsweek, 151
Newton, Huey, 141
New York State Commission Against Discrimination, 99
Nix, Robert, *134*, 143, 147
Nixon, Richard: Africa policy of, 196, 197; Diggs and Black politicians' work with, 99, *134*, 142, 143, 145–47, 148–50, 152; election of, 141; at Ghana's independence ceremony, 179; Home Rule Act and, 167; on home rule legislation, 175–76; at King's funeral, 123; resignation of, 201; Vietnam War policy of, 185
Nkomo, Joshua, 204, 208
Nkrumah, Kwame, 179, 180
"no-blast" pledges, 146, 148, 150
Northwest Airlines, 99
Nowak, Stanley, 7
Nowicki, Leo J., 22
Nteta, Christopher, 199
N-word, 102

O'Brien, George D., 51, 55–56
Officer Candidate School (OCS), 31
O'Hara, Barrett, 183–84
O'Neill, Thomas P. "Tip," Jr., xi, 240, 241, 242
Ortlepp, Anke, 91
Osnos, Max, 65
"Our Fighting Men Have Gone Soft" (*Saturday Evening Post*), 105

Palestine-Israel conflict, 162, 164
Pan-African Liberation Committee, 199, 200
Paradise Valley, Detroit, 17, 18, 22, 38, 49, 52
paternity suit, of Diggs, 215. *See also* Diggs, Charles Coles, Jr.
Patrick, William T., 54, 65, *127*
Patriotic Front, 204, 205
Payne, Ethel, 12, 13, 66, 67, 68
payroll kickback schemes, xii, xiii, 10, 137, 221–26, 231, 232, 235, 243, 247, 253
Peace Corps, 182
Perry, Beverly L., 309n13
Philippines, 105
Pohlhaus, J. Francis, 94
Poitier, Sidney, 92, 123
Polaroid Corporation, 191
police brutality, 122, 181, 298n48. *See also* racial violence
politics of strategic moderation, 2–3
poll taxes, 15
Portugal, 178, 189, 192, 197, 201, 202

Portuguese colonialism, 178, 180, 185, 189, 190, 192, 197, 198, 200
poverty, 121
Povich, David, 231–32, 234–35, 236–37
Powell, Adam Clayton, Jr., 1, 2, 5–7, 11, 61, 65, 68, 103, *130*, *131*, 142, 143, 144, 147, 228, 240, 249, 257, 269n22, 296n9, 309n9
Prayer Pilgrimage (1957), 112
Progressive Voters League, 71

Quarker, Dorothy, 66, 170–71, 221, 222–23, 224, 235, 236

racial "passing," 39
racial violence, 15, 76–79, 112–22, 181. *See also* murder, of Emmett Till; police brutality; segregation and discrimination
racism. *See* segregation and discrimination
Randolph, A. Philip, 68, 112, 178, 184, 257
Rangel, Charles, 7, 11, 12, *134*, 147, 157, 164, 170, 207, 218, 228
Raspberry, William, 238
Ray, Philip A., 94
Rayburn, Sam, 3, 66–67, *129*, 296n9
RCNL, 14, 70, 73
Reagan, Ronald, 239
Reason, Paul, 106
Reconstruction, 1, 15, 74, 112, 168, 202
Reed, Add, 84
Reed, James Milton, 226, 227, 233
Reed, Willie, 84, 85, 283n82
Regional Council of Negro Leadership (RCNL), 14, 70, 73
Reuther, Walter, 57, 115
Reynolds, Maria, 227
Rhodesia, *136*, 183–85, 189, 197, 200, 204–5, 206, 208
Richmond, Jeralee Williams, 224, 227, 233, 235
Rickman, Ray, 230
Robinson, Howard, 156
Robinson, Max, xii, 199, 229
Robinson, Randall, *137*, 199–200, 203, 205–6, 207, 224–25, 227, 233, 247, 251–52, 304n30, 304n45
Roche, James, 299n51
Rogers, William, 76
Romney, George, 121, 122
Roosevelt, Franklin, 47, 51
Rosario, Carmelita, *128*
Rosario, Clarine, *128*
Ross, Diana, 123
Roundtree, William, 184
Rowan, Carl, 226
Roxborough, Charles, 22, 38, 56
Roxborough, John, 41
Runge, Carlisle, 108
Rusk, Dean, 182
Rustin, Bayard, 148, 153, 178, 257

SAA, 187
SAG (South African government). *See* South Africa
Saulsberry, Guy O., 54
school segregation, 15, 59, 71–72. *See also* busing
Schuster, Roderick G., 54
SCLC, 112, 118, 145–46, 154, 234, 289n71
Scott, R. J., 194
Seale, Bobby, 141
segregation and discrimination: in air travel, 93–100, 187; against Black politicians, 226; on buses, 112; in Detroit, 17, 19–20, 23; Dr. King's work on, 111–24; in employment, 299n51; in funeral business, 19; in housing, 3, 17, 25, 47, 49, 59, 103, 105, 109–10, 182; in military, xii, 3, 27, 29–36, 101–10, 149, 286n32; in Mississippi, 14, 15–16; in schools, 15, 59, 71–72; in South Africa, *136*, 149, 178, 181, 183–85, 187–96, 198, 298n35; at University of Michigan, 26. *See also* racial violence
Selma, AL, 118, 119, 120
Senate Judiciary Committee, 144
Shabazz, Betty, 151, 154, 163
Sharp, Dudley C., 105
Sharpeville massacre (1960), 181
Sheffield, Horace, 228

Shrine of the Black Madonna, 270n45
Sidney D. Miller Junior High and High School, 25–26
Sigler, Kim, 32
Sikes, Robert, 242
Sloan, Hugh, 146
Slocum, William G., 194–95
slush funds, 221–22
Small Business Administration (SBA), 219, 224
Smith, Carla Diggs. *See* Diggs, Carla
Smith, George, 85
Smith, Ian, 183, 204–5, 206
Smith, John W., 19
Smith, Lamar, 76, 80
Smith, Robert, 87, 88
Smith, Robert S., 192
Smitherman, Joseph, 119
Smithsonian Institution, 91
SNCC, 113, 116, 117, 141
Somalia, 202
Sorrell, Maurice, 253
South Africa, *136*, 149, 178, 181, 183–85, 187–96, 197, 198, 200–208, 251, 298n35
South African Airways (SAA), 187
South African Open, *136*, 189–90
South African Relief Fund, 199
Southern Christian Leadership Conference (SCLC). *See* SCLC
Southern Regional Council, 113
South-West Africa (now Namibia), 192, 206
Southwest Chapel, 209, 218
Soviet Union, 202, 204
Soweto massacre (1976), 204
Staebler, Neil, 217, 276n7
Stevens, Robert T., 102
Stevenson, Adlai, 11, 48, 182
Stinson, James A., 219, 224
St. John CME Church, 24
Stokes, Carl, 198
Stokes, Louis, x, *134*, 143–44, 148, 156, 165, 227, 228, 254, 258
Stone, Chuck, 5
Strider, Henry Clarence "H. C.," 81

Student Nonviolent Coordinating Committee (SNCC), 113, 116, 117, 141
Stultz, Jean, 221, 223, 224, 225, 227, 232–33, 235–36, 303n10
Subcommittee on Africa, US Foreign Affairs Committee, *136*, 180, 183–84, 186–96, 203, 218, 240
suicide, 20, *133*, 216, 245
Sullivan, Leon, 191
surveillance, 162
Swango, Curtis, 82, 83
Swaziland, 188, 202
Sylvester, Edward, *127*
Symington, Stuart, 182

TAAF, 29, 32–33
Tanzania, 188, 199, 202
terrorism, 15. *See also* police brutality; racial violence
Thatcher, Margaret, 208
Thompson Avenue Baptist Church, 60
Till, Emmett: murder of, 4, 77, 78–79, 82, 115, 283n79; murder trial of, 80–90, 112, *131*
Till-Bradley, Mamie, 79, 83–84, 87–88, *131*
Till-Mobley, Mamie, 85. *See also* Till-Bradley, Mamie
Timmons, Willliam E., 146
trade embargo, 183, 184
Trade Union Leadership Council, 8
train travel segregation, 15. *See also* segregation and discrimination
TransAfrica, 137, 198, 205–6, 208, 209, 224, 228, 251–52, 254
Trudeau, Garry, 241
Truman, Harry S., 3, 59, 92, 101
Tucker, Sterling, 100, 174
Tuskegee Airmen, Inc., 254
Tuskegee Airmen, The (Francis), 29
Tuskegee Army Air Field (TAAF), 29, 32–33
TWA, 98, 99

UAW, 7–8, 25, 53, 55, 222
UAW-CIO, 53, 55, 56, 57, 60–61
unemployment, 20, 59, 60, 61, 121, 212

unionization, 7–8
United Auto Workers (UAW). *See* UAW
United Auto Workers–Congress of Industrial Organizations (UAW-CIO). *See* UAW-CIO
United Nations, 197, 207
Universal Negro Improvement Association, 7, 19
University of Michigan, 26, 273n46
University of the District of Columbia, 140, 252
University without Walls program, Howard University, 249
Urban Bantu Council, 192–93
US Air Force, 103, 104–5, 274n12
US Army, 274n12
US Army Air Force, 31–32
U.S. Business Involvement in South Africa (report), 191
US Department of Justice, 137, 208, 225
US Marines, 103
US Navy, 27, 103, 106
US Parole Commission, 240, 247
US State Department, 177, 195

Vance, Cyrus, 206, 207, 208
Verwoerd, Hendrik, 181, 188–89
Veterans Affairs Committee, 45
Vietnam War, 149, 185
Vorster, John, 188–89
voter registration campaign, 113
voting rights, 15, 17, 119–21, 145, 207, 251, 257
Voting Rights Act (1965), 120–21, 142, 153, 166, 170

Waddy, Joseph C., 230
Wallace, George, 141
Walters, Ronald, 157, 200, 254
Walton, Hanes, Jr., xii, 269n8 (prol.)
Wartman, Charles J., 49–50, 55, 62
Washington, Booker T., 17–18, 33
Washington, DC, 149, 162, 167–76
Washington, Robert B., Jr., 171

Washington, Walter, 169
Wayne State University, 34
Weeks, Sinclair, 93, 95, 96
West, Boyd, *126*
Whalley, J. Irving, 222
white supremacy, 15. *See also* Citizens' Councils; Ku Klux Klan
Whitten, John W., 88
Widick, B. J., 19
Wilberforce University, 76
Wilkins, Roy, 79, 116–17, 123, 148, 164, 257
Wilkowski, Anthony, 42–43
Williams, Edward Bennett, 228
Williams, G, Mennen, 8, 43, 45, 67, 68–69, 182
Williams, J. S., 210
Williams and Connolly (law firm), 228–29
Wilson, James Q., 7
Wilson, Sunnie, 54
Winston, James, 199
Wise, Blanche Parent, 49, 51
Withers, Ernest C., 253
Wolverine Funeral Directors Association, 210, 301n4
Woodland Baptist Church, 14
World News Tonight, 199
Wright, James "Jim," 175, 242–43, 252
Wright, Mose, 78–79, 85
Wright, Roberta Hughes, 25
Wyman, Thomas H., 191
Wynn, Albert, 250

Yarmolinsky, Adam, 108–9, 287n48
Young, Andrew, 118, 123, 154, 202, 203, 205, 234
Young, Coleman, 24, 38, 121, 162, 163, 217, 220, 234, 249
Young, Frank, 82
Young, Whitney, 154, 257

Zaire, 202
Zambia, 188, 189, 202
Zimbabwe, 208